Serves Me Right

ALSO BY SARAH MILES

A RIGHT ROYAL BASTARD

SARAH MILES

MACMILLAN

LONDON

First published 1994 by Macmillan London

an imprint of Macmillan General Books
Cavaye Place London SW10 9PG
and Basingstoke

Associated companies throughout the world

ISBN 0-333-60141-6

1 3 5 7 9 8 6 4 2

A CIP catalogue record for this book is available from
the British Library

Typeset by CentraCet Limited, Cambridge
Printed by Mackays of Chatham plc,
Chatham, Kent

Every effort has been made to trace all
copyright holders but if any have been
inadvertently overlooked, the author and
publishers will be pleased to make the
necessary arrangement at the first opportunity.

Death is not the end.
Life is not the beginning.
Birth to death is not a line,
But a circle of spirits spinning.

CHAPTER ONE

NEVER HAVE *all* your dreams come true, ticking them off as I did, one by one. My dreaming was potent and seductive in the anticipation, yet hardly ever in the fulfilment, and only those of you who have had all their dreams come true will know what I'm talking about.

But was I *lucky* – to be loved by those I dreamt of loving, to be a movie star? Was I lucky to live in Shangri-la? Ha! Ha! Ha! *Serves me right.*

Soon after my twenty-fifth birthday I made a film called *Ryan's Daughter*, on the west coast of Ireland. My character, Rosy Ryan, had recently married the elderly local schoolmaster, Mr Shaughnessy, played by Robert Mitchum. The local priest (a superb performance by Trevor Howard which slid by unnoticed) has reasons for concern when he sees Rosy mooning over the handsome young English major just arrived in the area. One day the priest bumps into Rosy hurrying mighty guiltily along the beach alone, so he decides to confront her and to point out the damage ahead if she forsakes her marriage vows. They have an argument, and because Rosy remains defiant, the priest warns her, 'Don't go nursin' your wishes, Rosy, or by God you'll get what you're wishin' for.' Rosy Ryan retaliates: the conflict spirals until the priest loses patience with her arrogance and slaps her across the face in the hopes of bringing her to her senses.

How devastating those words were for me at that time, for on the day we shot the scene, standing there on Inch beach, County Kerry, I realized that it was not only Rosy

Ryan who was heading for tragedy by having her dreams come true, but Sarah Miles as well. My dream list had been ticked off until it was finally complete. A cold shiver shot down my spine. A gang of goose-bumps poked up, warrior-like, through my thin pullover. I tried rubbing them away – most unglamorous for a movie star, I thought.

'Let's shoot the damn scene, for Christ's sake!' shouted Trevor Howard to David Lean, the director. 'The poor child is freezing to death.'

It might have been freezing, standing there with the grey Atlantic waves scudding, a Roedean-type howl to the wind and me dressed like an eternal spring day, but I hadn't noticed. My frozen limbs were merely surface stuff. A deeper freeze had set in.

'Right,' said David Lean. 'Rehearse the slap once more.'

Trevor gave me not so much a slap as a tickle. What I wanted was a slap. I wanted to be jolted out of the growing realization that I had no more dreams to dream – no more dreams to come true. Maybe if Trevor really hit me – and meant it – he could shake me free of the fast-approaching despair. I decided to speak up.

'Trevor, would you mind not slapping me gently, it feels silly. Really slap me, as if you mean business.'

'You mean, make contact?' asked an incredulous Trevor.

'Yes, send me reeling.'

He tossed me a disbelieving look, and shrugged.

'OK,' said David through his elegant silver and black cigarette holder, pretending that those pointed devil's ears of his hadn't heard a word we were saying. If he had connived in the slap plan, if he had admitted to hearing me say, 'Yes, send me reeling,' then he would have to tell Trevor not to listen to me, and that would have been inconvenient for David. He wanted Trevor to hit me hard, because it would be a hundred times better for the movie. And if anything happened to me – it was an accident. David's look escaped skyward.

'The seagulls look good – let's shoot.' (That's why there are so many seagull shots in *Ryan's Daughter* – it's David changing the subject.)

'Quick, take your first positions. Turn over!'

'Sound running!'

'Action!' shouted David, his keen eagle eye glistening next to the camera lens.

Playing the scene that cold afternoon on Inch beach was the first time I caught a glimpse of the chasm of nothingness that lay ahead of me. Yet there I was, still the same mass of yearning. Still the same insatiable creature in need of a lot more shallow dreams to fill the vacuum within.

'Don't go nursin' yer wishes, Rosy, or by God, you'll get what you're wishin' for.' Rosy failed to heed the priest's warnings, and so had Sarah. It was too late now. Where in God's name was I to go from here? Was it too late to destroy my dream list and start all over again? Why hadn't I been more aware of the quality of my dreams? Why couldn't I have made sure that it was a worthy list linked to a vocation or qualities that endure, rather than a materialistic one, linked to money, vanity, lust, fame and ego?

All these thoughts were streaming through my mind as Trevor and I played the scene. When it came to the slap, I saw his grey woolly mitten come up and shoot in towards me. I saw it plunging inwards to the side of my face. Christ! It was headed straight for my ear. I tried to turn away and stop the future. Too late – sweet, gentle Trevor had obeyed my wishes to the letter. He had decided to box my ears, just as any priest would do whose lamb had strayed from the flock. It was entirely in character and entirely my fault that I had neglected to warn him about the pain attached to my plastic-surgery, man-made ears. (They used to stick out like radar scanners.) Fortunately, so powerful was the impact that I went straight through the pain barrier – I was out for the count.

I returned to the land of the living in David Lean's

caravan, with his mouth in close-up blowing cigarette smoke from his holder into my face. I loathe the smell of Marlboro cigarettes, but David unintentionally had me cornered. 'Take it gently for five minutes, Sarah.'

'I'm fine now.'

He looked at me, blue eyes sparkling with challenge. 'Are you game enough to have another go?'

'Yes,' I said. 'As long as Trevor really hits me again.'

He looked at me, his fiery eyes challenging mine, as if checking that I meant it. He played cruel games with us actors, did David. Not respecting actors too much, finding their breaking point gave him a kick; so I was damned if he was going to find mine.

'Don't go nursin' yer wishes, Rosy, or by God, you'll get what you're wishin' for!'

We completed the scene without Trevor knocking me out a second time.

How I wish I'd had the wisdom in those days to see the quiet path, the more subtle way of true worth forking up ahead of me. But I didn't. I blundered onward down the wider path, hungrily seeking swift, easy progress. On I went, so blinded by desire for earthly things with which to stroke my vanity and ego that I failed to notice my path shrinking. Where it had once been wide and smooth it was slowly closing in on me, leading me into my first boggy gloom, where I became trapped, in those jagged cliffs above the void of despair only stumbled across when the *wrong* dreams come true.

Four years later when I'd still be down that same pathway to nothingness, tethered to those dreams, 'Something' would intervene, thank God for it. It would shake my blocked consciousness so violently that I'd have no choice but to go back up the path again. That mysterious 'Something' would have me retreating. I'd never done that before in my life.

*

I am now retreating to January 1961 and the tender age of eighteen, a time when I was totally oblivious of 'God', 'Somethings' or warnings of any kind. Bubbling over with excitement I kissed my boyfriend, Willy (James) Fox, goodbye as I boarded the Dublin plane to start shooting my first film, *Term of Trial*. How uncomplicated everything was then. My only preoccupation was that any moment now I would be making that first tick against my dream list. To be a movie star!

Mother had been thrilled to bits when I gave her the great news, for I had won the plum film role of the year. 'I'm so proud of you – and to think that Sir Laurence Olivier is your hero!'

Father grunted. 'Hmm. Where is it all going to lead, eh, Pusscat?' (My nickname.)

From the start he had never been too keen on 'this acting lark', or on Mother referring to Olivier as my hero, for till then Father had been my hero. Why can't a lass have more than one hero? Why can't a woman love more than one man?

I was to play a schoolgirl opposite Laurence Olivier's teacher, in a story of unrequited love. Shirley Taylor falls madly in love with her married English teacher, Mr Weir, who is always compassionate but never passionate. When Shirley yearns for more passion than compassion she tries to seduce him one night in a Paris hotel during a school trip. He attempts to calm her without damaging her already bruised pride, by gently explaining that if she returns to her bedroom, he will forget that the incident ever took place. Shirley is so insulted that she takes her revenge. Since hell hath no fury like a woman scorned, poor old Mr Weir finds himself in court, accused of indecent assault.

I'd fallen in love with Olivier at a Brighton cinema during one rainy Sunday-afternoon outing from Roedean School. I was eleven and my parents had taken me to see *Wuthering Heights*. The moment he stood at the window, looking out across the misty moor, searching for his soulmate and crying

'Cathy! Cathy! Cathy!' I was a goner. Olivier – or was it Heathcliff? – had awoken some seed within me. I kept his photograph under my pillow at Roedean, sometimes dreaming he would come galloping towards me on his white charger, scoop me up into his arms and carry me off. He had brought my first glimmer of sexual awakening and here I was about to star opposite him.

Term of Trial had a three-month schedule: ten weeks at Bray Studios outside Dublin and two weeks in Paris. Paris had been lucky for me once before when my agent, Robin Fox, had taken me over especially to see the woman who owned the sound that had haunted me all through my childhood – Edith Piaf. Yes, I was indeed lucky to *see* my childhood noise and to witness her art. Luckier still in her dressing room later, for meeting the woman herself was no let-down. She is what the word 'heroine' means to me. Was I heading for more good fortune when I got to Paris with my hero?

As the plane descended into Dublin and the pilot told us to fasten our seat belts, I was humming to myself. 'Once I had a secret love, that lived within the heart of me. All too soon that secret love became impatient to be free.' Would my love for Laurence Olivier always remain a secret? Of course it couldn't blossom unheeded. I was still with Willy Fox, and Laurence Olivier had a new wife – besides he was almost old enough to be my grandfather . . .

CHAPTER TWO

I WORKED HARD ON Shirley Taylor. Weekly rep had taught me a great deal about the process of developing a character, delving deep under the skin to find it. I always start with my hair: if I'm secure that I look right, then the digging begins and I'm off. I was wearing a blonde wig for Shirley Taylor. I practised my north-country accent at all hours, on and on into a tape recorder until I felt it was natural and unforced. Thora Hird was playing my mum, so I decided upon an accent as close as possible to hers.

The dining room at the hotel, outside Bray, where I sat most nights with Olivier, was large and usually empty. Against the candlelit wall a host of flickering penguins stood to attention. The hotel, partly Elizabethan, reminded me of another old school, Crofton Grange. To my uncouth taste it was immensely romantic – as everything was at that time of my life.

There were few guests apart from us, the film people. Terence Stamp, Simone Signoret, and Hugh Griffiths would come and go as the script required. I, like Olivier, was to stay in Bray for the whole ten-week stint.

Terence Stamp was a startling creature: dark brown glossy locks and piercing blue eyes, with a virgin complexion and rosebud lips. So striking were his features, within such a pale and sullen countenance, that any healthy young maiden would have been struck right between the eyes – before quickly being struck somewhere else. But not me. I had my Willy at home, and other fish to fry.

Simone Signoret displayed the dignified essence of true womanhood and she, like her bones, was completely straight. From Simone you'd get it exactly how it was with no frills.

Her legs were long and slender, branching out from narrow, well-oiled hips, which gave the impression of being even slimmer because of her unexpectedly ample breasts. Yet sometimes I thought I detected something out of step in her movements, nervousness perhaps in her laughter? I felt sure she was troubled.

Olivier, being fiftyish, was at that devilish mid-life crossroads, his career on the turn as a leading man. He had been Sir Laurence for quite a while, and had recently laid the foundation stone for Chichester Theatre; but the National Theatre wasn't even a speck on the horizon. I felt privileged observing him just as he had been forced to make the gritty gear change that had slapped him right into Osborne's *The Entertainer*. He had had the courage to identify with the new wave of working-class, kitchen-sink drama and join forces with one of its own, Joan Plowright. If you can't beat 'em, join 'em; and never consent to be stuck for too long in that ditch of type-casting. He had accepted to do *Term of Trial* because he had been offered nothing better, and he was nakedly aware of the possible pitfalls ahead. Also the part was a completely new challenge, being almost the only ordinary character this extraordinary actor would ever play; ironically Olivier yearned to put at least one everyday man on his list of accomplishments.

We would sometimes rehearse with Peter Glenville, the director, in Olivier's dressing room. The whole process of rehearsing and exchanging ideas with Olivier thrilled me. Seeing him in the flesh was an experience that way surpassed my Heathcliff on the screen. The smile, the wanton twinkle in his eyes, the friendly, springy gait, the determination in the set of his shoulder blades, the gentle stubbornness that continually won him his point on matters of detail – all this reminded me so much of my father.

Apparently I wasn't doing too badly with my accent and characterization. The hard work was paying off.

'Her accent's quite believable, isn't it, Larry?' asked Peter one morning.

'You'd never guess Shirley Taylor was a Roedean girl,' said Olivier, slightly teasing. He often sent me up, as if he felt threatened by behaving normally towards me, and needed to keep his distance. He called me 'Dame Sarah'.

'Why do you call me Dame Sarah?' I dared to ask one day.

'Because it tickles my fancy.'

One evening, when I was alone with Olivier in the dining room, he turned to me.

'Raise your wine glass.' He had no patience with my lack of enthusiasm for alcohol. I complied. Looking into my eyes, he said with genuine humility, the kind that's only found within the conviction of fact, 'I am going to be the first lord of the theatre.'

My mouth went dry as we shared an identical moment of doubtlessness; the same feeling that had gone shuddering through me when I was seven years old, on the day I knew that I was going to be a movie star. He would be a lord, as sure as eggs are eggs.

'I believe you.' We clinked glasses.

Another occasion sticks in my mind from that first month of shooting, during which I'd got to know a few of his tricks. We actors all have tricks, so why shouldn't Olivier have his share? There were some days, however, when I thought he had more than his fair share.

We were shooting a close-up on him. As I stood beside the camera feeding him lines off, I thought to myself, if I look up now and catch him raising that eyebrow of his – yet again signalling the fact that he was about to fly away from the script into his own invented gobbledegook – I'll burst out laughing. So, finding his eyebrow was indeed doing its usual dance, I did just that, and burst out laughing, unable to stop myself. An appalling silence fell over the set. I stopped then, all right.

Out of the silence, Peter Glenville said, 'Cut.' More silence. 'Perhaps, Sarah, you would be kind enough to share your sense of humour with us?' I couldn't speak. He tried again. 'What was so funny?'

'Come on, Dame Sarah, you were giggling at me, weren't you?' said Olivier, cocking his eyebrow even higher. I cleared my throat, ready for the truth I couldn't hide.

'Yes, sir.'

'Well, come on then, share it with us. You have no choice, for we all know now that it is I who am the fool.' I looked around to check out who was going to hear. Olivier added, 'Call a tea-break, Peter, I'm just going to my dressing room a moment.' As he was leaving he called to me over his shoulder, 'Follow me.'

Following him down the long corridors of Bray Studio reminded me of Roedean. The times I'd walked behind mistresses, waiting to hear their verdict. Once inside his dressing room, he pointed to a chair. 'What was it about me, Dame Sarah, that was so funny?'

I cleared my throat again and sat down. 'I had a bet with myself that if I looked up into your face during that close-up and found you raising your eyebrow yet again, sir, I'd burst out laughing.'

'Fair enough. But what was so funny about my raised eyebrow?'

'You always hoist it when there's danger ahead.'

'What danger is that?'

'A battalion of forgotten lines, sir,' I said, lowering my lashes.

When I lifted them again, Olivier was twitching his eyebrows in the mirror – well, wiggling them energetically. He caught my eye and beckoned. 'Come here and sit down.' He dragged a chair over so we could both look closely in the mirror. 'Right, let's go through the scene again.'

We did. Suddenly up ahead I knew those forgotten lines were lurking, because up went the brow—'There! Look, sir!'

He looked and indeed he saw. He pondered, and little by little something was dawning. Mumbling a few lines to himself, he fixed on keeping his eyebrows down, until there was not a single twitch to be seen. 'Right, I think I'm ready now. Let's go from the top once again.'

We went through the scene three more times, until he was word perfect.

It wasn't that he hadn't done his homework. There was something else on his mind. Something had been brewing nightly at the hotel. Simone had been with us on the set for a few days, clearly greatly upset; in the mornings her eyes looked as though they'd been weeping all night. Poor Simone, I thought, she needed to share her secret grief with someone, or else she might pop.

I was too young to be of any comfort, I thought, and just gave her space and quiet. But whatever tormented her was worrying Olivier. Enough to throw him off his lines. His eyes looked in need of sleep, too.

'Come, we'd better get back before they start playing hanky-panky with our absence.'

I mustered up as much innocence as I could and looked him full in the face. 'How do you play hanky-panky with someone's absence, sir?'

He wanted to quiz me, but instead hauled his eyes away. Was I having him on or not? He wasn't prepared to risk lingering, just in case. He returned to the mirror, exercising his eyebrows as he passed. 'Thank you for doing the director's job.' He pecked me formally on the cheek and looked me dead in the eye before once more weighing down his 'Dame Sarah' with mockery. 'Never rely on them doing it themselves, because more often than not, they don't. You'd think I had leprosy the way directors steer clear.' He checked his wig once more in the mirror. 'Awe isolates one so. They assume I know it all, so they never let me know when I stink.' He looked so sad and lonely that I wanted to hug him. 'Promise me that from now on you'll always tell me when I stink?'

'Only if you let me know when I do, sir. Oh, and, sir, how to play hanky-panky with an absence.'

'I'll tell you one day – bitch.'

One night over dinner Olivier was especially friendly, the kind of friendliness that overcame him whenever the call sheet showed the following morning off. He flirted quite outrageously, and insisted I acquire a taste for wine, first savouring it before swallowing.

'I just don't like the taste. Sorry, sir.'

He ordered me a crème de menthe frappée. 'You won't be able to taste the alcohol with this.' I couldn't. Anything too cold torments my gums; besides I dislike peppermint.

'It's known as the tart's drink.'

'Why's that, sir?' I asked.

'It's cheap and takes a long time to suck up.'

Why should one want to take a long time sucking it up? Not wanting to seem ignorant I thought it best to leave it at that. 'I wouldn't mind being a tart.' I was naïve enough to think that might shock him, but he came back, quick as a flash.

'I wouldn't, either.'

I wasn't sure how to take that. Was he wanting to be a tart or to have an easy lay? Hmph! Just let him try, I thought. I wasn't yet sure of his game. All I knew for certain was that, since the giggling episode, he had become much friendlier. Sometimes, too, he'd turn away quickly when I caught him looking at me.

'Why don't you call me Larry?' he said. 'You can't go on calling me sir for ever.'

I got the frappée to sparkle in my crème de menthe.

'Sir has a romantic ring to it.'

'And Larry doesn't?'

I shrugged. For some reason I wasn't madly keen on the name Larry.

'Then call me sir, and Lionel when we're alone.' He accompanied this line with such a queenly gesture that I wasn't at all sure what gender Lionel would turn out to be, on top of which I wasn't madly keen on the name Lionel either.

'Who's Lionel?'

'Lionel Kerr.'

I was none the wiser. 'Who's this Lionel Kerr?'

'Richard the Lionheart, and Kerr is my second name.'

We raised our glasses. 'To Lionel.'

I noticed a certain sadness as I sloshed and sucked up the remains of my drink.

'Hardly ladylike,' he said scornfully.

'I'm no lady,' I replied, for it was true.

'No . . .' he said thoughtfully, 'but you have potential.'

All good things come to an end, even crème de menthe frappées. Olivier – I mean Lionel – gave me his quizzing, droopy-eyed look while finishing off his whisky. I sat there, wallowing in the moment, knowing that any minute now we would trot off to our separate suites. I began humming, silently, to myself, 'Once I had a secret love—'

'Come to my room in ten minutes. Bring your script, help me to learn my lines. I want to practise my speech in the dock.' Off he went, with his head alert, looking just like Daddy.

I pinched myself to make sure I wasn't in the land of dreams. What a joke! A sophisticated chap like Olivier asking me to go up and hear his dock speech. I could still hear the invitation ringing in my ears. Cock an' bull speech more like! Does he expect me to believe that? It was pages long – probably the longest speech in film history (or so it seemed at the time). Lionel wanted to shoot it all in one take, with three cameras dotted about the courtroom, though Peter Glenville thought that might be a titsy bit too theatrical.

Ten minutes later, there was Lionel in his soft silk maroon and blue dressing gown, together with a whisky and the script.

'Come and sit down.' He indicated the other half of the sofa.

I couldn't resist asking, 'Where are your etchings?'

He didn't even raise an eyebrow. 'I'm afraid I only have my dock speech.' That threw me. 'Drink?'

'No, thank you.'

That threw him. He looked back. 'Not even a crème de menthe frappée?'

'No, thank you.'

'Right then. Page eighty-four.'

I turned to find the place and we worked and worked. We stopped once, while Lionel poured himself another whisky. 'A wee crème de menthe frappée before bedtime?'

'No, thank you.'

A knock on the door. I leapt out of my skin – or back into the room. I'd been playing out there on the clouds with silky Lionel.

'Good God, I wonder who that could be at this time of the night?' he said, checking his rather plain Rolex. He pulled himself together, stood up and retied his dressing gown before going to the door. 'Who's there?'

'It's me, Larry – Simone.'

He came back to me, whispering, 'Don't exit until I give you your cue. I'll retie my dressing gown into a bow.' He demonstrated with a great flurry of professionalism. 'Thus.' He repeated it. 'Get it?'

'Got it.'

'Good.'

I was to learn that Lionel relished playing games with life. I wasn't sure, at the age of eighteen, whether I was sufficiently sophisticated to keep up with this, but I was willing to have a jolly good try.

In came Simone, making a dressing-gown duet. Hers was dark green, tied in a bow which looked a bit droopy, like her at that moment. She jumped when she saw me. I wanted Lionel to retie his sash immediately – you could cut the tension with a knife.

14

'Oh, hello, Sarah.' She retied her dressing gown, making her appearance more formal. I was surely going to get muddled with all these sashes.

'Hello, Simone.' Olivier – I mean Lionel – attempted to clear some fishy air. 'Sarah here is kindly helping me with my dock speech.'

'Oh, yes.' Simone seemed relieved. 'It's very difficult speech, dat one. I'm glad it isn't for me,' she said, tripping over her laboured English. I didn't believe her; she would have loved it if her character had been given a speech like that. Her role of 'the wife' in *Term of Trial* was an insult to her talent, just as she deserved better than *Room at the Top*.

'Whisky, Simone?' Lionel washed his hands of guilt à la Pontius Pilate.

'Thank you, Larry.' She sat down in his dent, beside me on the sofa. More silence. Simone was left to break it.

'Have you told Sarah yet?'

'Of course I haven't.'

They were lovers! Why hadn't I twigged before? For some reason it had never crossed my mind. They didn't seem like lovers to me, but then it takes all sorts. 'Shall I leave?' I said, rising a little. Lionel gave me a desperate, yet reprimanding look from behind Simone, indicating his untouched dressing-gown tie.

I felt no twang of jealousy – none at all – and when the awkwardness wore off a little, I found myself growing more and more curious. It transpired that poor Simone's heart was broken, just as I had suspected. Her husband, Yves Montand, had made the film *Let's Make Love* the year previously with Marilyn Monroe. Though the movie was completed, their own personal 'let's make love' wasn't, lingering on painfully for all concerned, especially Simone. Now it seemed Yves was in America again at Marilyn's beck and call. It was the first time in their thirty-five years together that things had come to such a pass. Naturally Simone was haunted by Yves' gallivanting into such luscious pastures; Marilyn was no slouch, and capable of taking Yves from her for good and all. 'Dis time it is very serious. Yves' phone call tonight scared me, Larry. Marilyn always gets what she wants—'

Lionel stood up and impatiently paced about a bit. 'Of course, because that's all her narrow vision can encompass.'

Perhaps the reason Lionel proceeded to storm up and down, lost for words, was because he was of the same ilk. It takes one to know one. Finally – 'Spoilt, contaminated fat slug!' he spewed out. I'd never seen him so worked up. Apparently he'd lost all respect for Marilyn during the shooting of *The Prince and the Showgirl*, where she took him to the cleaners both professionally and financially. She'd shown up on set hours late, sometimes not at all. Olivier was producing, acting and directing, so he had a great deal riding on that film. When it finally came out, she buried him under her 'spell appeal'.

Lionel showed no sign of retying his dressing gown. Had he forgotten my cue? I indicated it every now and then, just to make sure I should still be there, but each time my attempted exit was brushed aside. I was sure Simone wanted to have Lionel all to herself. I felt awkward playing gooseberry: it wasn't a role I'd had much practice in. I went to the bathroom for a pee. When I returned, Simone was crying in Lionel's arms. I went to the door, but he looked up from her embrace, stopping me in my tracks with a look darker than thunder. Why was he so desperate for me to stay?

'What must I do, Larry? I am going mad,' said Simone, breathing against him, heavy with grief. Because Simone was such a classy, genuine woman, this outward show of floundering emotion was all the more uncomfortable to witness. I felt angry with myself for agreeing to wait for my exit cue. But if I left regardless, I would be letting Lionel down and perhaps he would never play games with me again.

'There, there, there.' Lionel was trying to extricate hmself from Simone's avid embrace.

'What can I do?' repeated Simone.

Lionel looked across in my direction. 'Ask Dame Sarah, she seems to know a thing or two.' Thank you, Lionel, for passing the buck.

Simone turned her tear-streaked face to me. 'OK, Sarah. What should I do? Hang on to de hope dat dis affair will blow over – or do I give him an ultimatum?'

I didn't know what on earth to say; besides, it wasn't my place to say anything.

'Come on, Dame Sarah, help. We have here a lady in distress.'

I was left no choice. 'I suggest you tread water gently, stay dignified – if you still love him, that is.'

Noticing her close proximity to Olivier, she pulled herself together, quickly unwrapping herself from his arms. 'I don't see any dignity,' she said, blowing her fine, swollen nose.

'She's right, Simone,' said Olivier. 'Men do stray from time to time. Just stand still and hold your head up, and Yves will come running home with his tail between his legs – you wait and see.'

As Simone made her exit he gave me a wicked little look, indicating Simone's spectacular bottom – no tail between her legs. At the door she turned and looked at Olivier. 'How long did you keep still, waiting for Vivien to return?'

Lionel hardly moved a muscle. 'Too long, much too long,' he reminisced, thoughtfully. 'We all should stand still for a few mishaps, a few infidelities, but not over and over again.'

I wasn't sure at that time what he meant. Had Vivien been promiscuous?

Simone came back and kissed him on the cheek, ruffling his sweet balding head. 'I will be brave, I promise. Thank you both.' She closed the door behind her.

'Why didn't you let me leave? She wanted to be with you alone.'

As Lionel handed me my script, his tone became business-like. 'Off you go. Well done, you saved me from the tiger's ravenous jaw.'

I found his sudden harshness most distasteful. He certainly was a man of changes.

'Simone needed you tonight.'

'Simone needs me every night, but I have to learn my lines sometime. Now off you go, it's well past your bedtime, young lady.'

'You used me.'

'I most certainly did. Just as Simone is using me, or trying to.'

'How do you mean?'

'She might get Yves back sooner if he thinks she's having hanky-panky with me.'

'What?' I said, keeping my eyes to the floor. 'Playing hanky-panky *in* his absence?'

Olivier laughed. 'Precisely. I'm being used, and in turn I'm using you. And I'll do the same tomorrow night, and the night after that.' He pushed my hair out of my eyes. 'And you, young lady, had better get used to it, because that's what everyone does. They use each other all the time.'

'I never will.'

'Oh, yes, you will. We all do. Now hop along, there's a good girl. It's you, not I, who have to look beautiful at six in the morning.' He smacked my bottom, rather like John Gielgud once had, on tour with *Dazzling Prospect*. A strange sort of a slap. I couldn't make it out, but out I went.

CHAPTER THREE

WE SPENT ALL the next day shooting what should have been a violent gang-rape scene, but which ended up as a polite simulation, late-fifties style. The schoolboy ringleader, Terence Stamp, leads his gang on to pin me down in the schoolyard while he, Terry, attempts to deflower me. It was cold and uncomfortable lying there in the unyielding schoolyard hour after hour, knowing none of it tasted of truth.

The Terence Stamp character fails to rape me, just as a would-be attacker had failed back in Austria four years previously. As I lay there on the cold ground I felt quite confident that I was well versed in the horrors of rape. I also wished fervently that it was Lionel who was attempting to rape me. Never mind: he had told me that I'd be back in his room that night, protecting him from the ardent embraces of Simone. Quite a life, this being a movie star! But why did he need protection from Simone Signoret? I pondered how it would feel if Simone Signoret knocked on my bedroom door. Would I get Lionel in to protect me? Certainly not. My curiosity would have bade me surrender to whatever it was that Simone required, whether it be love, sex, companionship or trouble sharing. Is that what tarts do? If so, then, yes – I was a tart.

Meanwhile I felt myself knotting up in that bleak school-yard. Although this was my first film, I realized, lying there with my skirt up, that *Term of Trial* wasn't going to turn out the winner that I felt it could have been. Later, with more experience, I would know within the first two days of the shoot whether or not a film was a success. *Term of Trial* was going to turn out worthy, but not great. Shame, that. Just like

Peter Glenville. Most films are an accumulation of all the director is capable of being. If he's second rate, you can bet your life the film will be too. Although Peter Glenville was a delightful, genuine, cultured man, far from second rate, he had something soft at his centre – it showed in the rape scene. He didn't know a damn thing about rape. I would happily have relived my rape terrors for real if it had been required of me. But whenever I raised my energy level to simulate the true terror of rape, Peter said, 'Cut. That's too much, Sarah – we'll have them fleeing the cinema scared to death.'

In the obligatory break I wanted to explain to Peter that rape was no tea party. Why was a nice polite rape scene more likely to penetrate an audience's awareness than giving them a slice of the real thing? But I knew my place; after all, I was only a naïve eighteen-year-old newcomer.

The strange thing about Lionel was that he deferred to me on set. 'What do you think, Dame Sarah?' he would say. He frequently came to find me and we'd sit and natter on the set, or often he'd ask me into his dressing room. I never went in without him coming to find me first – tart or not, I had my standards! I found it shocking to witness a woman doing the chasing. I still feel the same today.

Sometimes he'd come into my dressing room, nervously looking up and down the corridors in case someone was checking on him. I didn't understand that it was much better for him if I was caught in his dressing room – that way he could say I had instigated the whole thing. I felt sure, though, that his motives for inviting me in were not a quick game of hanky-panky. Maybe I'm fooling myself, but if he was primarily after that, how come he took so long getting there?

Next evening there I was on his sofa, with my knees up. He sat next to me and periodically peered over his specs trying to locate his whisky. 'Joanie arrives soon with our baby, Dicky.'

20

Although stunned at this news, I tried not to show it. He looked at me above his specs with sadness, but quickly cut the moment with a dismissive, ''Fraid so. We're trying to rent a house or cottage for a few weeks.'

Silence. This was sudden, I thought. Only yesterday he was saying that I'd be coming to his room night after night.

'Once we're safely ensconced you must come over with Simone for our house-warming dinner.'

Rather than look glum at this news, I kept smiling brightly. Thank God for dressing rooms. I still had his to look forward to in the daytime, along with the warm ache I felt waiting for his summons.

Through the silence he put his hand on my knee. 'Tell me about yourself.'

'My life's hardly begun, so there's nothing interesting to say.'

'Do you have a boyfriend?'

'Yes.'

'Is it serious?' He peered at me hard over his specs.

'If by serious you mean do we love each other, the answer is, yes.'

Lionel went on questioning me: about my family, my schools, how I lost my virginity; he could have been rehearsing me for *This Is Your Life*. He was certainly canny at bringing out stuff that I'd never spoken of with anyone – for instance, my passion throughout childhood for King George VI, a love that went on even after his death. Whatever possessed me to confess such a thing? I thought it best not to tell him about my picture of himself under my pillow at school. No, that must be kept secret, I thought – it might go to his head.

To my astonishment, before I could say Jack Robinson, he'd wheedled out of me most of my affair with Sylvia, the prostitute I lived with. I say most, because I thought it prudent to leave out my abortion, fearful that it might put him off for good. 'Would you say you were bisexual?'

In those days I wasn't sure what that meant, so I plumped

for a 'Yes', and hoped for the best. It certainly made him stare at me. His hazel, sometimes greeny-grey eyes were suddenly grateful, or was it relief? Whichever it was made him much more relaxed.

He put down the script. 'How about a crème de menthe frappée?'

'I'd like another orange juice, if I may.'

He went across to order room service with a new bounce in his step. I'd obviously said the right thing. Whatever bisexual meant, I could tell he really liked me for it.

'Do you prefer a man or woman for a lover?'

This was tricky, because I'd only had a couple of men and one woman. 'I don't know.'

'Come on, don't go all coy on me.'

'I like men, though occasionally I like to touch a female breast, if I were totally honest.'

He looked down at his chest, then shrugged rather sadly. He was a wicked fellow to get so many secrets out of me, knowing I hadn't the courage (or wasn't unladylike enough) to interrogate him in the same fashion. But that night it seemed my confessions bonded us closer. It was only with hindsight that I knew why: he also loved both men and women. And where's the harm in that? As long as nothing is achieved with force, against someone's will, why, then, all is well, surely? 'You should make a play for Simone – she has lovely breasts,' he said. From beneath those lush feminine lashes, his droopy eyelids were only feigning lack of interest in my response.

'Yes, I'll try her out after your house-warming party.'

CHAPTER FOUR

As I GOT dressed up for Lionel's house-warming, I couldn't help feeling sad. Joanie Plowright had been quick off the mark, giving him a baby boy so soon. Lucky her, being on the crest of the wave supporting the new kitchen-sink obsession. (I remember wondering how long a life this ghastly new fad would have!) I hoped she loved, revered and respected him as he deserved. Tonight I would find out.

Simone was waiting downstairs in the hall. She looked tired, even through her saucy, conspiratorial smile. Of course! I suddenly realized that she had decided Lionel and I were having an affair. She was bound to think that, after the other night. What other motive was there for me to remain in his room after she had departed? Oh, well. There was nothing I could do to put that right tonight.

In the chauffeur-driven car going to Lionel's new house, she said, 'I came to Larry's door last night, but I could hear you two laughing your heads off so I didn't knock. What was so funny?'

I was nowhere near sophisticated enough to respond immediately to Simone's lewd suspicions. Did I have to be sleeping with Olivier to enjoy a good giggle? I kept quiet.

'I didn't realize the situation, I'm sorry,' she said, wanting an answer.

'There is no situation.'

Simone looked out of the window, her hopelessness matching the Irish drizzle.

'Any news?' I asked, out of concern rather than needing gossip.

23

'Yves telephoned last night. He will be coming here next Thursday. We'll go back to Paris for a few days and talk it over, like grown-ups.'

While waiting for Joanie at Lionel's modest rented house, everyone had become a little tiddly – we were starving and it had been a long day. Finally Lady Olivier appeared, wobbling down the staircase in a heavily patterned blouse, plenty of jewellery, tight trousers and patent-leather high heels. I liked the quick darting eyes, the smirky smile, the low rich Marmite voice, warming up well with her drink. She seemed steeped in earthiness, though she had nowhere near the magnificence that illuminated Simone. In those first years of being Lady Olivier I suspect Joanie knew she was no lady, so she shrewdly shied away from any attempt at being compared with one.

Watching Lionel, I felt I didn't know this new person. I suppose that night was my first glimpse of one of the many different Lionels I was going to have to get used to. This Lionel didn't set my heart beating. His manner was staccato, crude, even a touch common. He was playing a new role in a play I wasn't familiar with, somewhere between Archie Rice and Mr de Winter. It was Simone who shone brightest. She only spoke when she had something interesting to share, and carried her pain throughout with quiet dignity. Lionel made strange unnecessary gibes at me, as if he needed to punish me in some way, yet I had no idea what I'd done wrong. Saying goodnight I felt full of prickly confusion.

My parents came over to watch the filming for a few days. They stayed in Dublin at the Shelbourne, not to be in the way, but one night Lionel asked them to join us for dinner. Joanie didn't come (Dicky was only two months old). I got a real kick watching Lionel flirting with Mummy. She was still a beautiful woman and had those same Vivien Leigh vixen eyes. Daddy and Lionel got on like a house on fire, equally aware of their resemblance to each other. Daddy was never

24

one to kow-tow, and I think Olivier appreciated this. It was a most memorable and happy occasion for me, knowing that the Mileses' unaffected behaviour had come as a relief to Lionel, who had been expecting an evening of stiff duty. That dinner was another miracle; the only problem was that I mustn't start getting used to them, for surely miracles come and go and there would soon be no more.

My parents' timing was good, for they had the opportunity to meet Yves Montand, who had arrived to collect Simone *en route* to Paris. His charm, as he sat between Mummy and Simone, talking about Hollywood, was almost irresistible. He seemed none the worse for wear from his nights between Marilyn's sheets. In fact quite the contrary, for his tail was not so much between his legs, as skyward and bushy. He shrugged as a finale to his Hollywood tales. "Ollywood ees 'Ollywood, but I'm so 'appy to be going 'ome.'

Father gave him a look. I could tell he hadn't taken to him at all, and when Daddy didn't take to people, that was that. Strange, it was, because I'd made no mention to my parents of Yves' infidelity with Marilyn Monroe, being too preoccupied elsewhere.

So I was amazed when Daddy piped up later, 'I wouldn't trust that chap Montand as far as I could throw him.'

Filming in Ireland was coming to an end. Olivier was back in the hotel, and I was doing lines in his bedroom for the last sequence of the film, the court scene. In the story, just at the moment when Mr Weir is about to be convicted of indecent assault, Shirley Taylor stands up and confesses that it was all her fault, that she lied, and now wants to repent. Strong stuff it was too.

When I saw the rushes of my confession, I didn't like them. I thought I lacked sufficient vulnerability for the climax of the story. My intention had been to underplay it, but Peter Glenville had wanted it tough and dramatic. The result was neither fish nor fowl. I plucked up the courage to go to Olivier with my fears. 'Come to my room and show me an alternative way of playing it, then.'

I did. He was impressed, and although he was meant to be leaving the next day to have a few days' break before we went on to Paris, he was prepared to stay an extra day to reshoot my scene, provided Peter Glenville was in favour. Simone was happy to do the same. So, with enormous trepidation, I knocked on Peter Glenville's door.

'Come in.'

I told him everything, and demonstrated how I should have pitched the scene.

'That's heartbreaking, Sarah, but I'm afraid it's too late.'

'But if I may say so, Peter, it was your idea to play it tough. I wanted to play it quietly.'

'I'm aware of that, but it's too late. The leading actors are on their way home, and the set is being struck at this very moment. I'm sorry.'

'Please! Please! Sir Laurence is happy to stay over for no money and so is Simone.'

That did it. The set was un-struck and rebuilt, and we played my whole scene quietly but with more passion. Peter Glenville was thrilled with the result and so was Olivier. I gave a sigh of relief.

'You've no idea how lucky you were,' said Olivier. 'It's unthinkable on a first film to get the whole set rebuilt. Cherish it, for it'll never happen again.'

CHAPTER FIVE

I F PARIS WAS cold, I hardly noticed. The sun meandered its way through a milky mist as I stood on my brother Chris's little studio balcony overlooking the rooftops of Montmartre. He was enjoying his two-year stint at IDHEC. Film-making was his life, and here he was in his favourite part of his favourite city, learning how to turn his favourite hobby into a profession. He joined me on the balcony, and we breathed in Montmartre's heartwarming smells of garlic, home-baked bread and coffee. A frisson of good luck shivered above us. There was something in that moment, as if we could simply reach up and touch it. The new decade of the sixties was upon us and we both stood poised in the excitement of dreams at last beginning to come true.

Our first piece of filming in Paris was a love scene (Shirley Taylor's attempt at one) in the Tuileries garden. It was meant to be spring, but snow was falling, pretty heavily. The art department did its best to camouflage this, by tying buds and spring leaves on the branches and sweeping up the areas in shot. This turned out quite a tiresome task because the snow was determined to do what it did best, which was to keep falling.

It wasn't as bad as all that, playing a love scene with two hot-water bottles each to help take our minds off the freezing cold. I was determined to forge on regardless like a true pro and not start whingeing just because I couldn't feel anything.

'Cut!'

I was incensed at Peter Glenville's shout, because, cold though it was, I thought I was doing a particularly good job of manifesting passionate warmth.

'It's your wigs, I'm afraid,' said Peter. 'There's no warmth

coming through from your heads, so the snow can't melt.' I
looked up at Lionel. So intent had I been on my love for him
that I had failed to notice. He sat there very serious, with a
heap of snow piled high on his head like a white fur hat. He
looked so utterly unromantic that I burst out laughing.

'You think *I* look funny. Here.' He handed me a mirror.
What a shock! I was looking even more idiotic.

'We'll have to call it a day, I'm afraid,' said Peter reluctantly. 'I'm so sorry, everyone. It's a wrap!'

That meant a whole afternoon off. What would I do with
it? He would be with Joanie, no doubt.

'What shall we do, play hookey?' Lionel was behind me
in a flash. I turned. His hooded eyelids drooped all over my
beating heart. Flecks of snow hung off the end of his girlish
lashes. Yet something told me to protect myself from his
flirtatiousness.

'I'm a lacrosse girl myself.'

After all the paraphernalia of getting our wigs removed,
he came into my dressing room. 'Come on, let's go.' It wasn't
a question, it was a statement. Outside he gave our drivers
the afternoon off and hailed a taxi. 'Have you ever been to
the left bank?' I told him I hadn't. This pleased him. 'In that
case I think we'll go there and have coffee.'

He chose a coffee shop which also sold bread and pâtisserie, and we watched the more bohemian Parisians going
about their daily tasks. The aroma in that pâtisserie lingers on
down the decades, still potent as yesterday. I don't think I
can recall a happier moment than smelling those sweet
smells, feeling those sweet feelings, and thinking of still
sweeter things perhaps to come. I could sense them in the
way he couldn't stop touching my hand. The smell of coffee,
I find, heralds a more exotic sensation than the taste itself. As
I breathed in those mingled scents I wondered whether my
senses were up the creek. Would all of them, like the taste of
coffee, let me down? He leaned across the table. 'What
thoughts are racing through that secret little mind of yours?'

'I'm not secretive.'

'You live in your own private world, so no one knows who you really are. Do they? Not even your father.'

'I've never thought about it before.'

'Well, think about it now, because from now on you and I are a secret. Our affair is our affair.'

'But we aren't having an affair,' I said, challenging him from the rim of my coffee cup.

'Let's have an Irish coffee to celebrate anyway, shall we?'

I didn't know what an Irish coffee was, but I was game for anything, in Paris.

After the snowstorm abated we walked for miles that first day. As dusk approached and windows were lighted, I noticed Lionel too was a part-time peeping Tom. We talked of the vulnerability of humans, and how by catching them off guard it became easier to penetrate through to their under-skin. We caught a man pulling off his trousers before walking out of shot. Lionel turned to me and said, 'Does that excite, eh? Do you want to wait and see if he comes back?'

'No, not particularly,' I said. 'You?'

'Not with you beside me, no.' But I wasn't wholly convinced.

'Come on, it's getting cold. I'll take you back to the hotel. You need a hot bath, and then – to the Ritz.'

Lying in my bath is where I do all my cogitating, and that evening I had quite a bit of cogitating to do. Was it my imagination, or were we about to embark on a secret affair? He'd kind of indicated that he wanted me to follow him into his suite, but I'd continued down the corridor. The truth was that I found myself more nervous than I'd ever imagined I could be.

I was guilty of being unfaithful to Willy in my heart, if not yet in deed. I still loved him, and I had no excuse for my behaviour. But I couldn't help feeling that if Willy had known about my secret love, he'd have wanted me to see it through. After all, nothing that we had between us was under any threat. I knew my place. A mistress is a mistress, a fiancée is a fiancée, a wife is a wife, a scrubber is a scrubber and a tart is a tart. At that time I was none of those. If Willy was my choir of angels, what was Laurence Olivier – apart from Lionel Kerr? I'd called him my 'No-man Allthings' back at Roedean, because he introduced me to my first sexy feelings, but little did I know then how apt that description would turn out to be. He was all things, all right. All the ordinary people he wanted to be and all the kings too.

The Ritz turned out much brighter than it had with Robin Fox, Willy's father. Perhaps that was because I was in love. Last time, too, I had butterflies in my stomach, thrilled with anticipation at seeing Edith Piaf. Tonight I had the same butterflies – how thrilling life could be!

'Good evening. Could we have one Scotch whisky, and a crème de menthe frappée—'

'I'll have a Bloody Mary, please.'

'And a Bloody Mary for my daughter.' We were at the bar, but fortunately the barman hadn't recognized Olivier – no one did, I noticed.

'James Mason is playing Humbert Humbert in the film of *Lolita*,' he said with heavy disappointment. Perhaps all this flirting with me was homework for a part he never got.

'Did you want it?'

'I suppose so, but I'd sooner live it.' He gave me a sleepy look. 'I never ever dreamt I'd be tempted by anyone so young.' Hearing his heart beating was hellish flattering.

'That's because within this shell there's a very old soul trying to get out.'

He laughed, stroking my wrist. 'Within that shell is my oyster nestling against you, my pearl.' He was such a devil. He knew how to deliver even the corniest line and make it sound perfect. 'Have you ever eaten oysters?'

'No, never.'

'Then that's what we'll do. We'll go to a little place I know where they have the best oysters you're ever likely to eat.'

I was far from keen to eat oysters, but he patiently taught me how to scoop them out of their shell then swallow them whole. The ritual seemed a terrible waste; fancy allowing money to slip down in a few repellent swallows. Though I gagged twice on the slimy taste, I was glad I didn't have to chew them up. 'Come. I'll take you to Montmartre and the Salon de Madame Arthure' (or something like that).

It was thrilling watching the women undress. I'd been to a few strip joints in Soho, but I'd seen nothing like these dishy dames, displaying their ripe abundance so stylishly. I was transfixed, aroused without a doubt by their artistic bravura. I tried to remain nonchalant; after all, I had seen it all before.

'Does this excite you?' he whispered, offering me another Bloody Mary.

Why not tell him the truth? No harm in that, surely?

'No more to drink, thank you. Yes, this does excite me, very much.' But not so much as his hand lying gently in my lap. I struggled to remain aloof.

'Look at this one coming on now – isn't she a peach?' 'Peach' hardly did her justice. Her long silky hair framed an equally long haughty body undulating with such feline flexibility that I had to restrain myself from flexing likewise to the soft, lilting music. She seemed so at ease with her sexuality. The whole experience was getting me devastatingly randy.

'She's perfect!' Just as I spoke, she turned to me and winked. Lionel laughed, pinching me just above my knee. 'What's so funny? I'm not used to women winking at me with no clothes on.' Most confusing, finding myself both enthralled and shocked at the same time.

'Imagine waking up one morning to that creature lying in bed beside you. Especially once you found out she was a fellah,' he said, again nipping my thigh.

'What?' He was having me on, surely?

'These aren't women. They're all men.'

'What utter rubbish!'

'I'll take you round afterwards if you like, and then you can see for yourself.'

Just as my heart had beaten loudly when Robin Fox took me round to meet Edith Piaf, so it did that night. Who could blame it? I hadn't known till then that men could have breasts. Once in her presence I was struck dumb, so it was fortunate her English wasn't too bad. My French was appalling anyway, and I knew Lionel's gift for language wasn't his strong point. He got by, but only just.

We stood there silently gazing at her while she recounted her *problème d'amour*. Her/his other half, the woman he lived with, whom he dearly loved, was insisting he/she gave up her night job. 'Why should I give up my art? Hmm? I'm proud of what I do, apart from being proud of them.' She uncovered those memorable breasts with as much innocence as a child showing you the bruise on her knee. 'You see? How could she want me without my breasts?' I became more and more confused. She was a man, who was in love with a woman.

'Can you still make babies?' I wanted to know everything, but this upset him.

'Of course I can. I am still a man, you know, and you are a very special young girl.' He came up and kissed me. The disorientation had me reeling, but I liked it. Yet when he went to kiss me again – Lionel didn't.

'Come on, it's time I got you home for your beauty sleep.'

I was silent in the taxi back to the hotel, feeling sick.

In the lift, he said, 'Care to come in for a nightcap?'

I froze. How I'd yearned for this moment – yet I froze. 'I want to go to my own bed tonight, I feel a little strange.'

'Please come in, for a while at least. I already know you're no crème de menthe frappée.'

'I think it must be the oysters. I'd rather be sick in my own room if you don't mind.'

'So be it.' He took my key, opened my door and led me in, so carefully. 'We must grab this time while we can, for life's gone before you can blink an eye.' He put on one small light by the window. As he turned back towards me, it gave him a soft becoming glow.

'Are you sure you wouldn't like a drink?' I do believe Heathcliff was nervous.

'No, thank you.' We both stood there, suspended within our separately woven dreams – mine, at any minute, about to crescendo into reality. He cleared his throat and loosened his Garrick Club tie. I'm very fond of those Garrick stripes; they particularly suited him. 'Will you lie with me?' he said, giving an erotic edge to that old-fashioned expression.

I was still feeling sick – was it oysters or guilt? 'I have a boyfriend at home and I love him.'

'I have a wife at home and I love her.' Unbearable silence. I had only my heartbeat to fan away my nausea and keep me company, because he was a long way away. He had to come to me; it wasn't correct that I should be the one to close the gap that lay between us. I willed him to come to me.

Lo and behold, the power of the will! He came over slowly and stood right before me, very still; in loosening his tie he had made it all asquiff. Through his slightly opened shirt I could see a few hairs escaping from that brave chest of his. Idiotic that a couple of stray hairs should thrill me to the very marrow; after all, I was no schoolgirl, and they were grey ones.

'My lovemaking's far from the cat's whiskers, I'm afraid,' he admitted ruefully, if like a cat whose whiskers showed every sign of stealing the cream.

'Look who's judging.' He was only my third lover, so what did I know? My hand automatically slid up to those straying chest hairs, but he misread my gesture and thought I intended to undo his remaining shirt buttons. Not wanting misunderstandings to ruin the moment, I began to unbutton, very slowly, mirroring the rate at which he was undressing me. As he finally removed my last stocking and stood there perusing his handiwork, I could have sworn my very being

33

burst out of the top of my head. Hells bells! I couldn't stand up. 'I feel dizzy. I'll have to stop. I'm sorry.'

He held my head in his hands, gently whispering, 'But we haven't yet begun.'

I had to get away! My aching for him was so powerful I thought I was going to faint. In a desperate effort to regain composure, I went and sat huddled up on the floor, against the wall.

'Do you want me to leave now, my pet?'

'I'm not a pet!' I barked. 'Never call me "pet" again!' Hearing my sudden temper, I burst into tears. This outburst of abominable childishness left me no option but to tell all. 'I have been in love with you since I was eleven years old. I kept your photo under my pillow for years and nobody knows to this day – except Matron and my parents.'

'Is this the bad news?' He touched the top of my head, which felt hot and sore.

'But don't you see? All this is too much for me.' His stroking the top of my head so caringly made me cry even more. Why couldn't I pull myself together? 'You'd better go before—'

'I've been selfish, I'm sorry.' Pulling me up, he yet kept separate, as if sensitive to my need for space. His fingertip slowly traced the shape of my breasts, without touching.

'Ah!' he quietly exclaimed. 'So sweet.' It was extraordinary, for his fingers had fire at their tips, heightening my euphoria. Yet we hadn't touched. He laid us down on the bed. Always, through all the years I knew him, even at the end when he was so unbearably frail with his fingertips seeping watery poison, the fire still remained. It will be his fingertips that I shall remember most, the way his heat flowed through them, scorching me without even touching.

I haven't a clue how long we lay there as our fingertips traced the burning etheric around our bodies, silent but for the steady heavings of anticipation. I tried to slow down my breathing, attempting to bluff it into a more mature calmness, because it was letting the cat out of the bag as to how much I was yearning for him. He became conscious of his own breathing. Trying in vain together to slow our passion, we started laughing – we laughed and laughed.

'Matron seeing a photo of me under your pillow.'

But I knew how to stop this image tickling him too greatly. 'She said, "You like Ronald Colman, don't you?"'

Although the laughter relaxed the tension for a moment, those slow, accurate, gentle, almost effeminate caresses of his began transforming the child into something else, forbidding me to remain either ladylike or childlike. In her place appeared a wanton, brazen hussy lusting with a new kind of hunger. He sensed the whore in me rising and slowly committed to the task of feeding the bonfire. Neither of us had anything to hide or prove any more, we had come home.

CHAPTER SIX

PETER GLENVILLE WAS getting rattled. We were way behind schedule, thanks to the snow we hadn't needed for our springtime shots. Olivier was wanted back home; his contract was up; and he was now on overtime. I wasn't, of course. But not only would I have done the film for free; I would have given all I had.

On the third evening we had just finished a gruelling day filming in the Louvre, and Lionel asked me if I wanted to meet Marlene Dietrich. He didn't wait for a reply. 'I'll meet you in the lobby at six.' He added that I'd have to disappear once I'd said hello, because the dinner party had been arranged months ago.

'I'd rather not come, I'd be too embarrassed.'

'Nonsense. You're not doing what I said.'

'Which was?'

'To grab life as it passes. Marlene is pretty much a recluse except for when she's performing, so you'll never get a chance again.' I wasn't sure I wanted to meet her that much. Waiting as if to see the lion at the zoo seemed not to be in the best of taste.

'Lionel—'

'Tell me tonight, in the lobby at six o'clock sharp.'

The room in which we awaited Marlene's entrance wasn't a drawing room, or a sitting room or a hall. It was the kind of room that I thought only existed in the theatre. Various doors led off, reminding me of a set for one of those Feydeau farces. Olivier said it was a typical French salon.

I felt most uncomfortable sitting there; so, I believe, did His Nibs. He looked left and right, then took my hand. 'I wish we could run off into the night and have an adventure.'

I got up to leave. '*We* can't, but *I* can.'

'Don't get all uppity with me, Dame Sarah, just because I can't invite you to dinner.'

'It's not *that* I object to. She's kept you waiting almost an hour. How could anyone behave so badly to my Lionel?'

He laughed, then kissed my hand.

I have to admit that Marlene's entrance, though rudely overdue, was worth it – if you're keen on grand entrances, that is. She was smaller than I expected, but her clothes were magnificent, pink and dove grey. Her make-up and hair – or was it a wig? – were of a spectacular subtle gold. She was the only person I'd ever come across a-shimmer in the same league as Mother.

'Larry, darling boy!' She kissed him like a long-lost lover – which he could easily have been, I suppose.

'Marlene my sweet, meet Dame Sarah.' He just couldn't resist playing his naughty games.

'Hello,' she said, without batting a perfectly made-up hooded eyelid. (Perhaps they were too heavily made up to bat.) Whatever her response, she wasn't prepared to look my way again. 'We must shoot off, darling boy, we're late.'

'I'm sorry about that, Marlene.' They batted heavy hooded eyelids at each other.

Outside, a dove-grey limousine awaited the pair of them. I watched them drive off, with a cold shiver of regret. I wished I had followed my own instinct and not gone to meet her. I hoped I'd never get myself into her position. Fancy being unable to bend the legend with sufficient grace to apologize for being late. But I need have no worries on that score.

Next morning the two of us were shooting a sequence on top of the Eiffel Tower. I'd never been there before, so I got a double whammy! Up the Eiffel Tower, just my love and me alone. (And the film crew, of course.)

Unfortunately there was a howling gale up there, which was conducive neither to romance nor to wearing our respective precarious wigs. During the long wait while they set up the shot, I asked Lionel if he'd had a good dinner. He pecked me on the cheek and said he'd been wanting to do more than that all evening long. My nose was still slightly out of joint, so I asked him why he'd made me go with him against my better judgement.

'You should meet her for posterity. Besides, it gave us more precious time together, for I knew she'd keep me waiting.' He kissed me on the end of my freezing nose. When he let in the charm there was nothing I could do but melt. 'What colour are your eyes?' He stared into them.

'I haven't a clue. They keep changing.'

He went fishing for a mirror. 'Guess what colour they are at this moment?' He hesitated before passing the mirror, urging me to take a guess. I shrugged. 'Their usual nothing colour probably. Why?'

'They've turned uncannily like my ex-wife's.' He handed me the mirror.

I was stunned. My eyes were vivid amber.

'My forever Amber.'

He meant it, I thought. 'But Vivien's were vivid green, not amber.'

'How do you know?'

I told him about my first professional engagement as a walk-on during *The Roman Spring of Mrs Stone*, when I'd had a set-to with Vivien over a dressing room. He laughed, but I was curious. 'What's her problem? She was in a real state.'

As he turned away to look across Paris, he murmured almost under his breath, 'She's a schizophrenic, manic-depressive nymphomaniac.'

I had no idea what he was talking about. 'I bet that happens to all your ex-loves.'

He glowered at me, then said, 'And like you, her green eyes sometimes turned amber.'

'Action!' shouted Peter Glenville from beside the camera.

During the playing of the scene, without any warning my

wig flew off. We all watched it bouncing down, bumping off each layer of the wedding-cake.

'Cut!' Peter Glenville wasn't at all pleased. 'I'm cursed by those wretched wigs of yours.'

Lionel became handless as he tucked his arm up his sleeve. 'Captain Hook, and the new bald look.'

I was astonished he still remembered me saying that at the audition. Lionel passed our one make-up mirror, which he liked having in his charge. God! I did look bald too with all my hair wrapped under a stocking top. 'Your eyes, without your wig, my love, have turned to the subtlest shade of shit.' He was right, the bastard.

Lionel took me to my one and only fashion show at Balmain, saying I could have any outfit I wanted. I was very excited; the show was like nothing I'd seen in my life, and just as magical in its way as the Salon de Madame Arthure.

'Come on, Dame Sarah; there must be something that tickles your fancy – hurry up and choose.'

'I'm not the type to dress up in smart clothes. They depress me, because I inevitably manage to spill something down them first time out. There's nothing suitable.'

'Everything we've seen is more suitable than these strange beatnik clothes of yours,' he said, pulling at my precious wooden beads.

'Do I embarrass you?'

'Hardly. Let's go.'

On our last evening in Paris, I was *très triste*. I couldn't bear the thought that my 'fling' (because that's all I thought it was going to be) was almost over. 'Cheer up,' he said as we arrived at Simone's enchanting home. 'I don't want Simone to see you miserable – after all, she believes we've been having an affair.'

We had a gay, easy last evening, as it turned out. Our hosts' estrangement had been patched up, and Yves spoke with great humour about his fling with Marilyn. Simone had already informed him that we knew, so he was free to keep us amused. Their genuine love for each other came shining through and neither seemed under strain. I was sure their marriage was secure again, which made me happy for Simone, because I thought she deserved the best.

Lionel was so pleased Marilyn hadn't broken them up that he told even more outrageous stories about her lack of professionalism on *The Prince and the Showgirl*. In one scene it had been essential that she cry, but on the day she said, 'I can't cry, Larry.'

'You don't have to, Marilyn. Just pretend.'

'I can't, Larry. I've never been able to cry to order.'

'You have to, Marilyn, it's in your contract.'

This went on for days, until Larry finally lost his temper. 'Cry, God damn you, woman!'

'OK, OK, Larry, I'll cry. Just let me hear a recording of "Danny Boy" and I'll cry.' (Lionel's Marilyn imitation had Yves laughing his socks off.)

He went to great lengths to find a particularly moving recording of 'Danny Boy' and put it on for her in her dressing room.

'It was lunchtime, as usual, before we could get to work.' While Marilyn's face was being made up Lionel played her 'Danny Boy'. 'Oddly enough,' he added, 'it's one of my favourites too.'

'She sat there like a big white lump of jelly, stubbornly refusing to cry.' Although Lionel disliked her intensely, his Marilyn imitation showed great compassion for her obvious frailty. '"I can't cry, Larry. I just can't cry!" Gradually her inability to cry made her unconsciously burst into tears. I carried her on to the set and shot the scene.'

As an afterthought Lionel added, 'Beware of actors who can cry to order.'

'Why?' I asked.

'Because very rarely can they act.' He went on to describe how Merle Oberon could control each tear. 'So phenomenal was her tear control that she could get them to sit wherever Wyler wanted. On her cheekbone, on her chin, up her bloody arse if need be.'

'Didn't you enjoy acting with her?'

'More than I did Marilyn,' he said unenthusiastically.

It was hard to believe anyone could behave as selfishly as Marilyn had. Perhaps she was mentally ill?

'Ill?' said Lionel, shaking his head. 'There's nothing innocent or ill about her, I can assure you.' The more he fulminated, the more Yves and Simone laughed.

I wasn't laughing later that night. When we'd left, Simone had kissed me warmly and made me promise to come and stay whenever I was in Paris. 'That goes for you too, Larry,' she'd said with a glint in her slanting almond eyes.

My sadness drew in on that last night together. If sexy goddess Marilyn hadn't managed to hang on to Yves, then I didn't stand a chance in hell. Simone Signoret and Yves Montand were together again, and tomorrow Sir Laurence would be with Lady Olivier, where he belonged, and from whom I had no right to have taken him – even though it was he who had taken me. I would never be a threat to Joanie, because it wasn't my aim to marry the man, just to love him whenever he needed me. I never pushed myself on to him, and he never pushed himself on to me.

As we lay there perfectly still, with his noble head using my bum cheeks for cushions, I thought I'd have a tease. 'Are you nothing more than a dirty old man?'

He turned me over with a look so deep I thought my eyeballs might bleed. 'You, Dame Sarah, for some profoundly mysterious reason, have allowed me to feel my best.' He returned to that favourite position of his, head on bum cheeks. 'Strange, that . . .' He paused, mid-sentence. Even stranger was the sensation of *feeling* him thinking. Is that what love did? He was still deep in thought, stroking me gently. 'I'd forgotten I even had a best.' He squelched some squashy bits. 'This knack of yours is most appealing – to a dirty old man, that is,' he quipped. 'What *is* the knack?'

How could he insult my love by flicking it off as a knack? Of course he felt his best. It was simple. My love for him was of the *better* kind. But that would have sounded pompous, so I settled for: 'All dirty old men like Shirley Taylor's bum cheeks.' He grabbed great clumps of both of them and sucked away like a schoolkid with Brighton rock.

Neither of us slept a wink that night. I lay there wishing it had all been a dream, that I would wake to find myself safe in Willy's arms with all the pain of parting safely behind me. He, being a disciplinarian, not only liked a plan or two but was determined they should be carried out to the letter; my father was in charge of his life in the same way. Olivier found great satisfaction in expanding his life, as if it, as well as his acting, was to be as near an art form as damn it. Thus he started to direct our future, as if he were directing *Romeo and Juliet*. 'Because I'm married I cannot expect you to wait for the phone to ring. However much I abhor the idea of you in someone else's arms, I'm going to have to put up with it.' He tossed and turned as he tried to find a way for us to meet in London without anyone knowing. He stroked my thigh. 'It won't be impossible if we're careful.'

I looked at him disbelievingly.

'Has anyone recognized me in Paris?' He was right about that. No one had indulged in second glances – no one. 'We'll make it, you'll see. I'll find a way.' He pulled me round to kiss me. I wish he hadn't for I was stuffed with misery and I didn't want him to see it.

He saw. 'O ye of little faith.' It was all going to be so hard. As I bade him farewell to go and pack, I knew realistically that we'd never be able to meet. My protective mechanism had come into play, and I began writing him off. I wasn't going to contact him, and I was sure my Lionel Kerr was never going to contact me. I'd given him my parents' home number, but I knew it was all over. Besides, I wasn't prepared to ruin Willy's life with my selfishness. It had been a location romance that would be forgotten in a few days. What was it they called it? Ah. Yes. 'Location fever'.

Having forced this cynical mood upon myself, I said goodbye to Paris. I'd need all the strength I could muster to keep those blissful ten days to myself. It was made easier if I reminded myself perpetually that I had no choice. A secret it would have to remain, whatever destiny had in store. And I was lucky, after all. Not many people have their romantic dreams fulfilled for five seconds, let alone days. I was the luckiest girl alive . . . or was I?

CHAPTER SEVEN

I WAS RELIEVED that in my absence Willy had got himself a job behind the honey counter in Fortnum and Mason. I was pushing him to become an actor, for I was convinced that he was much too beautiful and talented to be the officer he was still seriously considering. Why ignore the profession he had, after all, been trained for at the Central School? Besides, I had no intention of becoming a Coldstream Guards officer's wife – not on your nelly!

Mother had rented a flat in Judd Street near St Pancras for me, at Clare Court. A hideous modern block that had just been completed. I hadn't taken to that end of town one little bit. People seem to separate into north or south London folk, and I never felt at home in the north. Still, beggars can't be choosers, and I was lucky to have both parents' approval to live there with Willy. I think they thought I'd get up to less mischief, what with him being such a steady, gentle influence. Mother had taken him to her heart – mind you, most people did.

These thoughts were interrupted. 'Why do you keep turning away from me?'

I quickly turned back. I had just come home from Paris. Thinking I was safe in Willy's arms, my head, it's true, was turned away. It wasn't lack of love but shame at finding myself continually dwelling on Paris. I wanted to share it all with Willy. He deserved as much, but Lionel deserved secrecy. I was cornered in my deceitful triangle. Nothing could prevent my thoughts from sucking their way through the ceiling, up, up and away, searching for his spirit somewhere out there. Fortunately my body was more obedient, and therefore put up no opposition to being coiled in Willy's gentle strength.

44

Whether Willy had been unfaithful or not was of little importance. I had, and that was that. There's nothing like fidelity to give love that extra boost of dignity it deserves, and I was sad to find out that I was made of lesser stuff. I turned towards Willy and rejoiced at having him to love, and to be loved back. Lying there, profile towards me, he continually reminded me of some Greek god. Pity I never got further than the Stone Age at school, because I'd like to have known which god it was. I cuddled into him, his smell so irresistibly wholesome. He turned and looked into my eyes.

'I love you.' He meant it too.

Later in 1962, I returned to Worthing Rep to play Bernard Shaw's St Joan. It was a part I'd always longed to play, and I think it was one of my better efforts. It was the first time Daddy ever commented on my acting ability. 'By Jove, Pusscat, perhaps you can act, after all.' He was almost proud as he gave me a peck on the forehead. Eleven years later, at the Music Center in LA, I accepted to play St Joan again because I was dying to hear similar words from Father's lips just once more. I was sure that it would give him a kick too, seeing my improvement in the role. I arranged two return tickets to LA for my parents as a gift, but they never came. It broke my heart. Obviously I was going to have to make do with: 'By Jove, Pusscat, perhaps you can act, after all,' at Worthing Rep.

Over dinner that same night in 1962, Father told me he had recently been in the Ritz bar in Paris, and by chance had with him a copy of *Elle* or was it *Paris Match*? Whichever it was, my mug was plastered all over the cover. This apparently tickled Daddy's ego somewhat and after a few sips of whisky, he dared to brag to the barman.

'This is my daughter.'

'Are there two of you, sir?' replied the barman.

'What are you saying?' asked Daddy.

'This young lady was in here not so long ago with her other father.'

Daddy said he felt so profoundly snubbed that he couldn't find it in him to stay and finish his whisky. I just sat there, stunned.

'Who the hell was this chap pretending to be your father?'

'Some of the crew went to the Ritz for a farewell drink, and they were teasing me.'

'Laurence Olivier, probably,' said Mother, who never missed a trick. I didn't react.

I was furiously crossing off my list of dreams. I had to work fast, because you're only young once and, as Olivier said, 'must grab life while you can'. (He hadn't telephoned.) The reason for a Pyrenean mountain dog being on my dream list was because there was an enormous white one down the lane where I lived as a child. So magnificent was he that I called him God. I thought he *was* God – he was so aloof and majestic. I made a pact with myself that as soon as I became a movie star I'd buy one of my own. Off I went (even though *Term of Trial* wasn't out yet) to see a litter of Pyrenean puppies in Hampshire. There were seven in the litter, but only one was perfect. He had a complicated aristocratic name, but I just called him Addo.

One day I'd popped out to buy Addo's dinner – I had to be quick because he created havoc in the flat. When I returned fifteen minutes later, my two best pairs of Pinet shoes and Mother's ocelot coat, which I'd shrewdly left out of reach high up on the chest of drawers, had been mysteriously pulled off, chewed up and spat out all over the floor. I get quite hot when I think of the hundreds of pounds of money and red raw meat that vanished at such a fearsome rate down Addo's gullet. Although I never regretted buying him, and took him everywhere with me, he certainly was a bundle of trouble. Pyreneans don't bite their enemies – which consist of other big dogs, pin-striped suits, briefcases, window-cleaners, bowler hats, in fact hats of every kind and umbrellas – but squeeze them into submission with a devastating bear hug. With his upper lip snarling and his massive shoulders slowly looming up, Addo slowly throttled his opponent to the point of death. Why he pretended that my pulling his tail was in any way effective, only he and God knew. Walks in the park were fraught with danger, but never dull.

Addo found certain dry-cleaning fluids addictive, which could be tricky. When he smelt this aphrodisiac on some poor unsuspecting accountant's suit he'd start humping with no shame whatsoever. You can imagine my embarrassment when, scampering to pull his tail as usual, he completely ignored me. Nevertheless I committed myself to giving Addo the best I could offer, and I made an oath that come hell or high water when he was fully grown Addo would get at least one and a half hours' exercise every day. I ended up knowing every tree and shrub in Hyde Park, Holland Park, St James's Park and Hampstead Heath.

When Robin Fox rang one day and told me I had been offered a film in Spain with Laurence Harvey, I had no option but to accept, even though the thought of leaving Willy and Addo filled me with anguish. So there I was in December 1962 staying at a posh hotel in Madrid, doing *The Ceremony*, to start saving money for my dream list and Addo's gullet needs. Laurence Harvey was starring, directing and producing the film. Every day he arrived on set looking the epitome of a film director, even down to his cigarette-holder and sheepskin coat. How he revelled in playing captain of the ship.

I hated being away from home. I hadn't spoken to Lionel. I missed Willy and Addo so much that one afternoon I struck up a conversation with a camel in the park. This camel had the most seductive soft nose I had ever encountered. Never having had the privilege of being close to a camel before I became riveted to this exotic creature, which bore an uncanny resemblance to Sophia Loren. I hadn't a clue what sex it was so I crawled underneath, but that didn't enlighten me either. As it stood there, the thought of this magnificent beast humbling itself to serve mankind filled me with such awe that I brought down its head and kissed it reverently on its soft warm camel nose. The camel seemed to like it too.

A tap on my shoulder returned me to the here and now. It was my chauffeur.

'Dat no good. Com vid me.' He seemed in quite a state.

'Nonsense, I've been kissing animals on the nose since I was born,' I said boastfully.

'But camel no good for you.'

At that moment Larry Harvey's chauffeur, who spoke better English, appeared from nowhere. 'Miss Miles, you'd better come vid me to 'ospital.'

'Hospital?' I found this quite amusing. 'What on earth for?'

'Becau' di camel no good for you. Please – you come vid me.'

But I wasn't prepared to be driven off to hospital, just like that. 'Would you kindly take me to the production office instead?' I waved *au revoir* to my camel and off we went.

At the office Spanish panic began to fill the air. Within no time, Larry's chauffeur was rushing me off to hospital after all. Apparently, kissing camels is simply not done, because their saliva is almost as poisonous as a snake bite. Fearing I'd got rabies, they pumped me full of anti-tetanus vaccine and gave me various pills, insisting I stay in overnight, so they could keep an eye on me. It all seemed a fuss about nothing. They were probably just taking extra precautions for insurance reasons.

'I'll be at the Hilton Hotel, and if I feel ill, I'll ring you.' As I lay in my hotel I realized I was getting sicker by the minute, but not from the camel, no: home-sickness.

My camel-kissing came to nothing. I wondered whether camel saliva was as dangerous as I'd been led to believe, so a few weeks later when Omar Sharif entered the lobby of the hotel with an abundance of the charisma obvious in his famous entrance in *Lawrence of Arabia* – which had recently opened – I plucked up the courage to ask. After all, who better than an Arab to find out the real truth of camel saliva?

'It's very poisonous.' He advised me strongly to resist those wondrous Sophia Loren lips. 'Much safer to track down the lady herself.'

Omar escorted me round Madrid. He was splendid, a perfect gentleman. I felt quite at home with him, because each outing reminded me of Mummy's male admirers bumping into each other on our shopping sprees when I was young. It was delightful to witness women swooning as Omar made an entrance, for they were all identifying him with that other famous entrance, certainly the longest one in the history of cinema.

After one romantic night of continual flamenco serenading, Omar came to my bedroom door and, with his inky-black belladonna eyes, charmed his way in. Watching him undress I suddenly felt nauseous; it came in from left field freezing me to the spot. It had nothing to do with him personally. I'd never have allowed him in if I'd thought I couldn't go through with it. What was I going to do? I had to do something quickly, he was down to his underpants and one sock. So when Omar bent down to remove his other sock—

'Omar, I'm so awfully sorry, but I've suddenly become overloaded with guilt. You see I have my love at home, and—'

'Shush,' he said. 'Say no more. I understand exactly.' He gave me a compassionate, knowing look, then began putting on his socks again. What a gentleman to maintain such dignity in retreat: it's the kind of dignity you can only acquire through the confidence of knowing you are a genuine hot-blooded lover. At the door he turned and kissed my hand so charmingly, clicking his heels together, as if closing the main door to intimacy. He was one of the most generous, courteous men I have ever met, because he asked me out to dinner many times after that and never once put on any pressure at the evening's end.

Alas, all romance came to an end when the whole film circus went up to Toledo for night shooting. This ancient barbaric town gave me the creeps, probably because it was below zero, too cold to snow. Larry thought this a blessing because at least we could pretend it was springtime in Morocco. I found myself once again pretending to be hot when it was freezing, pretending it was day when it was night and trying to pretend that Larry was my other Larry as I ran up endless cobbled streets in a summer frock, night after night. But then that's filming.

'Smiles, but you look like a dragon belching fire through the lens,' said Larry, puffing at his cigarette-holder, all tightly cocooned in cuddly sheepskin. 'Give her ice to suck.'

We repeated the same sequence each night for a week. In the end I was lucky to get off with a tinge of frostbite on my left earlobe. I've always respected the word 'frostbite' since – it burns deeper than fire!

Back in Madrid, Mother telephoned to say that Addo was pining so much he'd begun to refuse his food. She was kindly looking after him for me at Barn Mead, our family's country home. 'If you don't come home soon, I won't be held responsible.'

What could I do? I'd asked Larry if I could go home for a few days on compassionate leave, but he refused. I was stuck in a city that made me sad. It wasn't the people but all the half-starved stray dogs mooching around the back-streets. Larry Harvey told me that the Spanish ate stray dog. He could have been teasing, knowing how I felt about them. I selfishly took a few back to the Hilton, where the manager finally asked me to leave with my 'pack'. I went to live in an apartment block called Torre de Madrid. After a few days I was told, 'No dogs allowed.' I tried to find homes for them but with so few contacts I only had one taker. The rest went back where I found them. That's what I mean by selfish – not having the wit to see where this misplaced sentimentality might lead. Although I gave them a few weeks of bingeing like billyo, my stray dogs certainly taught me a lesson.

The Ceremony was the last film I made abroad till Addo's death, nine years later: any possibility of an international film career was knocked on the head thanks to Addo's self-indulgent pining and the quarantine laws.

The Ceremony was behind schedule. This meant I had to tell Mother I wouldn't be back for Christmas. She was frantic.

'But I can't have this damn dog a moment longer. His pining's catching.'

'Well, I'm pining too. I hate it here, I want to come home.'

'Someone called Lionel Kerr telephoned. He asked when you were coming home and said he'd ring again on your birthday.'

I had to keep my voice casual and matter of fact while I almost dropped the phone with excitement. 'I doubt whether I'll be home then, even, by the looks of things.'

'Who is this Lionel Kerr, anyway?'

'Oh, just a photographer I met once.'

Silence. 'I see.'

I think she could, too. Mother could see down any telephone. Was I going to have to take her into my confidence? Barn Mead was the only place it was safe for Olivier to contact me. No. But at the flat Willy would ask questions. This game of intrigue could prove exhausting and I didn't think I was cut out for it. Still, love does indeed send you blind.

Larry Harvey stood firm. 'Sorry, Sarah, but there's nothing I can do.' He tried to cheer me up by taking me out one evening to meet a famous Andalusian fortune-teller. As the chauffeur escorted us to a room tucked away at the back of a shop that sold Spanish groceries, Larry dropped hints as to what a special treat it was, since she had now retired. As we entered through the clichéd dangling beads, my senses were blasted by flamenco music and exotic aromas. The fortune-teller was sitting all hunched up like a starved black beetle, and beside her was a small round table with a crystal on it.

Larry sat reverently while the chauffeur translated what she saw in his tea cup, palm and the cards. Undoubtedly pleased with the reading, Larry had gone quite pink. 'Go on, Smiles, your turn now.'

I sat in Larry's chair. The old lady took my left hand, opened my palm and looked into it for some time. Looking back at me for a moment, it seemed as if she was quizzing me from another time. I asked Larry's chauffeur Pedro what was wrong. They talked between themselves in Spanish, which made me nervous. I looked at Pedro for an explanation. 'Nada, Señorita, nada.'

Then the gnarled black beetle dropped my left palm, forgetting it was joined to my wrist, and shifted her considerable concentration into my right palm, pulling it this way and that. After another few minutes of scrutiny she looked into my eyes, shook her head slowly, closed my palm and passed my hand back as if she didn't want to leave it lying around. Larry asked what the hell was going on. She spoke to Pedro in Spanish. 'How much more money does she want?' said Larry.

'It's no money, sir. She no want to do it.' Larry felt she was prima donna-ing. He was a real fighter, was Larry, and I liked him for it, but on that occasion I just wanted to get out.

'But doesn't it alarm you?' he asked, disbelieving, as we got back into the car.

It's a good job I didn't take that hocus-pocus seriously at the time, or I'd have had a sleepless night. As it was I forgot about it – that night. But the memory of her gnarled old hand passing mine back to me, with such regret in her eyes, often seeps its way into my darker, more vulnerable moments, forcing me to wonder . . .

A few evenings later Larry asked me out again. I declined, but again he insisted that it was a treat not to be missed. A friend of his was giving a party and Antonio (the Spanish dancer of the day, some say of all time) had agreed to perform. It took place in a *palacio* filled with so many glamorous, sophisticated ladies, I felt out of place. There was strict security on the door. If Larry hadn't been recognized I doubt if we'd have got in. I'd never seen so many enormous rooms, all a bit forbidding, the dark paintwork and sombre marble floors. I could sense decadence in the air even though all the guests looked perfectly respectable.

Antonio danced magnificently. It was my first introduction to Spanish dancing, so naturally I wasn't able to appreciate the finer points, but any fool could see it was masterly. Hard to believe a pair of feet could caress the floor with such a show of speed and fury, tempered with easy, elegant style.

After the buffet dinner Larry came to check on me. I was relieved because I wanted to leave. I felt I didn't belong there, for I knew not a soul.

'I think I'll be off now, if that's all right?'

'Certainly it isn't. You can't miss the best part.' He led me up a steep staircase, along a high-ceilinged corridor and into an anteroom.

I looked through the half-opened door. A line of women with their backs to us were crouching on their haunches, leaning backwards on their elbows with their groins hoisted upwards and their dresses fanning out behind them *peeing*. About twenty men stood facing us at the far end of the room in front of the firelight, while more lined the side walls, all cheering and egging the women on.

'Come, let's have a closer look.'

He dragged me by the hand, but he didn't have to for long. Perhaps what tickled my curiosity was the contrast between their fully clothed upper halves and their naked white thighs and suspender belts. A couple wore corsets, black silk stockings and high-heeled shoes. The ritual would have been easier without the shoes, but I understood that it looked more sexy this way. It was a splendidly erotic sight. I asked Larry why none of them seemed to mind who was watching. He explained the tight security I'd noticed when we arrived. They knew who was here, and they knew they could trust everyone to be discreet. Such occasions were apparently commonplace in certain bullfighting circles and in parts of Spanish high society. He whispered, 'The men fight the bulls while the women fight to have balls.'

All of a sudden the women began collecting their underwear and got up to go. I started to leave also.

'Hold your horses, the next team will be in shortly.' As soon as the women had left, three men, looking rather like bellboys, began mopping up pee from the dark green diamond-patterned marble floor. Coloured ribbons were placed on chairs to mark the winners so far. Although I found the room austere, it was beautifully lit, with the fire still blazing behind the somewhat sizzled and certainly sozzled men.

'It's a great tradition here in Spain. The woman who can pee the furthest is held in high esteem.'

'Why?'

He gave me an old-fashioned look. 'Muscle control,' was all he said, leaving me to think it through for myself as eight more women came in, curtsied and got ready for the 'off'. A few other women were watching, like myself, and they, too, were clapping, while the men transformed into a mass of Antonios, all shouting, stamping and cheering. Larry joined in too. 'Come on, Smiles. Don't be a prude.' I was only nineteen and therefore not ashamed of being a little shocked, though I had to admit there was nothing remotely vulgar about any of it, probably due to the ethereal glow of the candlelight.

One elegant lady, magnificently got up in maroon velvet, was far superior to the rest. I began chuckling at the memory of when I was little at the London Zoo, and a lioness had turned her bum towards us and showered the whole family. But even the lioness wasn't in the same league as this queen bee. Perhaps she was cheating and had a secret pump fixed somewhere inside her. Whatever she had going for her, she won outright, shooting her pee at least a foot further than her nearest rival. Finally a handsome man of about fifty lifted her up on his shoulders, while she made her well-applauded lap of honour.

On the way home that night Larry said, 'Well, did you enjoy it?'

'I don't know about enjoy it, but it sort of thrilled me at the time.'

'Did you recognize the winner?'

The lighting in there had been so dim, I wouldn't have recognized my mother.

'I thought it might have been Ava Gardner,' he said. Joking, of course.

Over twenty years later Ava and I were making a film together in Seville a few years before she died. She had taken a liking to me because we were both Capricorns. A dangerous reason for liking someone, I would have thought, but Ava set great store by the stars.

After a few weeks I knew her well enough to mention the Spanish peeing occasion. 'The champion beat the other ladies by miles.' She didn't bat an eyelid – on the contrary, she smiled secretly to herself, almost like someone who was proud of their accomplishments. 'Yes, it was quite some ritual in those early days,' she said, pulling her yashmak back over that remarkably perfect mouth of hers because she was wanted on the set. We neither of us spoke of the incident again. Perhaps Larry Harvey hadn't been joking after all . . .

There is a footnote to my Ava story. We two Capricorns stayed friends until she died. She was a lonely woman towards the end, and I found there was a great deal for me to learn from this famous beauty, who had lived her life to the hilt. She held the same sentiments about dying as she did living, and was determined, even to the point of obsession, not to go gently into that good night. 'It suits my tempestuous lifestyle,' she said with a wry look. 'Tighten your seat belts, 'cos I'm planning on a stormy exit.'

I was in London on the morning of the great storm in '87. I heard on the news that it was dangerous to drive, but I had to get back to Robert Bolt because he was alone at our home in the country. It was an unforgettable ride, filling me with mourning for each tree I witnessed crashing down to the left and to the right of me, with my car lunging about all over the road. As I noticed the sky turning blackish indigo and swirling into feathered streaks of reddish grey, there came this announcement on the news: 'Ava Gardner died this morning.' She'd kept her word – and how!

CHAPTER EIGHT

I DID GET home for Christmas in the end. Larry Harvey felt compassion for his crew, all of whom had it in their contracts that they could go home then. It made no odds to him because he was staying in Madrid throughout the Christmas season anyway with his girlfriend, Joan Cohen. He offered them all (not me) enormously tempting overage but they didn't bite. That's something nice about the English (or was): they'd much rather be home with their loved ones than earn more money on overtime.

As I drove up to Barn Mead I felt excited: no one knew I would be back. I entered the drawing room quiet as a mouse to find Mother talking, as she bent down to put a log on the fire, about how sad it was that I wasn't coming home this Christmas.

'Boo!' I said. Mummy looked round, saw me, knocked herself badly on the mantelpiece and collapsed on to the floor. I felt sad at my surprise turning sour so soon. Fortunately she was only temporarily concussed.

'That's the first time I've seen those stars that everyone's always on about. Get me a gin and tonic, John,' she said, rubbing her dazed head.

'Really, Pusscat, you could have given her a heart attack barging in like that!' said Father.

Addo was over the moon to see me again, but Mummy could tell I was shocked at how thin he was. 'I've done my best, but I'll never do it again. Willy can play nanny from now on.'

We had a rare Christmas that year. Everything was so relaxed that Mother insisted we all went to church. Father, who hadn't been to church for quite some time, came too.

'Are you turning into a coward in your old age, Daddy?'

'Rubbish! We have an hilarious new vicar. Wait until he says, "And remember, you can't take your chequebook to heaven."'

The vicar imitated Daddy exactly. We laughed, and Mother gave us all a dirty look. Over Christmas lunch I gave Daddy a huge present which I'd wrapped up at the flat. He opened it with glee. In it were six bottles of champagne that Leslie Grade had given me. I'd seen nothing wrong in rewrapping them for Daddy. I'd put a card inside.

'Thank you, Pusscat, you must have been well paid on *The Ceremony*.' He bent forward to butt me with his forehead when his hand touched something else. He pulled out another card and read – 'To dearest Sarah. Happy Christmas! Love, Leslie Grade.'

Father never let that one go. I'm not sure why. He hadn't given me anything that Christmas; as usual, Mother had put his love on a card attached to some strange unwearable object. I could have saved the champagne for Willy – Lionel was pretty partial to it, too. It couldn't be that he thought I was mean since I'd bought so many gifts for everyone. Having pushed us all into becoming the achievers he wanted us to be, it must have been something more complicated than begrudging my success. 'It's your carelessness. You're so clumsy, in everything you do.'

Another episode blighted the peace of that Christmas. On Boxing Day I came downstairs early to put Addo out, and there, scattered and spat out all over the hall, was Ted. Ted was no more than the average family teddy, but perhaps with a more charming look on his face than most. Ted had been part of all our lives: he'd first belonged to Daddy, who passed him down to Jukes (Chris), who passed him down to Chuzzler (Martin), who in turn kindly passed him down to me. Ted was finally handed down to Pooker (Vanessa), who needed him because she was still away at boarding school. It hurt to see him there in pieces. I picked up what I could and tried to make the puzzle fit. My mouth suddenly tasted bitter; I rushed to the cloakroom, for I thought I might be sick.

It was quite a shock for me that Boxing Day to realize that however sophisticated I thought I had become I was still the same wretched clumsy little girl I always was. And as I stood there waiting for the vomit to rise I had my doubts that I would ever grow up properly like Mummy had. Or was she just the same little girl she always had been, under the façade of motherhood and housewife? Perhaps nothing of our fundamental nature ever changes. When I was a little girl I thought that when I grew up I wouldn't be able to spend my time on the floor with my animals any more. I remember mulling this over quite regularly and thinking, I'd better make hay while the sun shines, because I'll one day have to leave my beloved floor and sit in chairs with the grown-ups. But that day never came and I'm still all over the floors with my animals.

Daddy was downstairs first that morning and couldn't believe his water-brimmed eyes. 'Poor old Ted. I cannot envisage a world without Ted.' Obviously he, too, was still the same little boy he had always been. When Pooker appeared it was awful to watch her beautiful little face scrumple up into a flood of tears. The whole family took it to heart, and shoved Addo out in the cold of their hatred for the rest of the holidays. They never liked him anyway, and now they had a perfect reason for it.

Lionel rang on my birthday, the last night of the year, just as he had promised. 'Would you want to meet again?'

A damned stupid question deserved a stupid answer. 'It's a bit tricky right now.'

'For me too, but I'll phone again in a few days.'

I played it so cool, yet I wonder if he could hear my aching heart?

*

Willy and I had settled down to a rather simple life in Clare Court. He had surrendered, intelligently I may add, to the fact that the flat was now Addo's kennel. (On my list of dreams Addo's home was a conservatory, but Addo would have to make do with a flat until my country-house-conservatory dream had finally been ticked off.) Willy and I were closer than ever, except when he was threatening to become a full-time army officer. This panicked the living daylights out of me, and only when we were curled up in bed did I manage to exorcize this ghastly idea. My motive wasn't selfishly placed, I simply saw his destiny differently. Willy was now in advertising, dithering, perhaps, but nevertheless a step up the ladder from Fortnum and Mason.

'Nonsense. Eddie is the actor in the family,' he said.

'Why can't there be two Fox brothers on the stage?'

'Me on the stage? If pigs could fly!'

'How about films then?'

He'd change the subject, or usually Addo changed it for us. But, slowly, with all my hints and persuasion, he was contemplating becoming an actor. Once he had made the leap, I was convinced he'd never look back. I was as doubtless of Willy's success as a movie star as I was of Lionel becoming a lord.

Mother rang and, quick as a rattlesnake, guessed who Lionel Kerr was. 'He'll be ringing you at ten thirty tonight. I said you'd be there.' The silence that followed was deafening. 'Don't expect not to get badly damaged. It's inevitable.'

'I know.' I hardly gave her time to finish because I was too happy that he'd kept his word, yet again. He was a reliable chap, this Mr Lionel Kerr.

When he called I picked up the phone quietly and slowly, as only those who are deceiving their mates would appreciate. He planned our next rendezvous. 'Wear a plain old mac, no make-up, hair scraped back under a headscarf. I'll be looking like a failed travelling-salesman – in other words, like myself.' He gave a nervous laugh. He'd worked it all out, the devil.

A few days later we were ensconced in a seedy little hotel in Victoria. I'd arrived to see him waiting, bold as brass, in the dilapidated lobby. He greeted me in a travelling-salesman way. 'Hello, dear, I've already booked us in. Let's go to our room. I'm exhausted.'

Looking at the elderly man at the desk he unnecessarily added, 'Mother is arriving on the later train.'

Once in the rather smelly room I whispered. 'What was all that about?'

'You look like a child dressed like that.' His disdain was unfair considering it was he who'd orchestrated my wardrobe from top to toe. But I let it go and let go in his arms once again. 'Not the Ritz, but at least we have a bathroom *en suite.*'

He was wearing a moustache similar to Daddy's and a perfectly ghastly tartan trilby plopped too high on top of his head, with a feather as jaunty as his mood.

'I'm just going to have quick shower.' He went into the bathroom. 'Oh. It'll have to be a bath. Come in and join me.'

I burst out laughing because he looked like that wretched man who won't leave your front door until you've bought the blessed hoover. 'What's so funny?' said Archie Rice. He accompanied this with one of his camp gestures. In many ways, I suppose, he was the epitome of the actor. Yet he was as much *not* the actor as he *was* the actor, being far more complex than any of the actors I had met so far. He laughed while he dried his hands, changing parts yet again. Then hidden under a new role, a role I'd only see him play in bed with me, he undid my suspenders. Knowing full well this seedy joint wouldn't even give us a cuppa, he said, 'Shall we ring room service for crème de menthe frappée, Dame Sarah?'

His proximity was intoxicating, yet I was buggered if I would let him see the enormity of my yearning. But he cheated, and at once began to laugh in triumph, for he had laid his hand on my thumping heart. He hadn't been fooled for an instant. 'Come, my little cucumber, come and cool off in the bath.'

As we sat fooling around in the stained, tepid bath I was aware of some mysterious sameness, something mercurial, yet intangibly safe and fitting. I would spend decades of my life trying to fathom it, for underneath Lionel's ruthless ambition crouched a bundle of conflict, secured in a nest of profound sadness. It had always been there, the same sadness that had captured my heart at eleven years old.

'Neither of us are tip-top at fucking under water, are we?'

'Speak for yourself, sire.'

He carried me from the bath, flinging me none too gracefully on to the dippy bed, which dipped even more precariously as he joined me. Home again! We didn't speak or move for a moment or two. Out of nowhere he apologized for not contacting me; he claimed his pride had been hurt by the *Term of Trial* notices. The film had opened to worthy reviews but nothing better. On the other hand I got some unwarranted raves. Beginner's luck. Any thrill I might have felt from being the belle of the ball was eclipsed by the same critics' unanimous bleating about how I'd stolen the film from under Olivier's nose – and Signoret's come to that. I was no fool and I had seen the film too. They shot Olivier down because it was fashionable to do so – and here was he thinking he'd let me down.

'Nonsense. You've been too busy with Chichester.' It was somehow belittling to hear this great actor apologizing and looking so forlorn. 'I think your Mr Weir was different from anything you've ever done.'

He looked sheepish.

'The film's success rested on my shoulders.'

'I thought a film – or indeed a play come to that – was a team effort.'

He gave me a look and chose to let that one rest. 'The

critics were right, however. I gave a somewhat lazy performance.'

'You were playing a somewhat lazy schoolmaster.'

'None the less if I'd been on target the film would have taken off.'

'No, it wouldn't, couldn't – not directed in that tame, sweet Peter Glenville way.'

I didn't like the room at all. It smelt of depression. I crossed over to open the window, then turned round and looked at his naked body on the bed, a body that echoed his own inner conflict, for it was both finely masculine and beautifully feminine, as if he were an intertwined pair of twins. (I didn't know then about birth signs, or that he was a Gemini.)

'Come to me.' He gently repeated it, as if I hadn't heard the first time. I obeyed. He looked at me with a sudden seriousness. 'Being a chameleon will make your career extra tough.'

'How's that?'

'Though excellent for our illicit rendezvous, it's not so good for actors. Those who don't fit into a category, who aren't obvious type-casting, never immediately come to a casting director's mind. You'll do better over the long haul, but it'll always be tough for you.'

'Thanks. I like good news.' I looked into his droopy eyes, and he started tickling me. One thing about Lionel, he took direction well. Although my attempts at educating him on the finer points of tickling had only just begun, they were beginning to reap delicious rewards. He couldn't resist a little boyish roughness as he swept me towards childhood memories of being tickled to the last-death breath by my two elder brothers. I had to stop him because I had a serious question. I screamed.

'Shush, they'll think I'm murdering my daughter.'

'Let's hope Mother's train isn't too late.' He tweaked inner softnesses. 'Is it obligation only, us meeting like this?'

He was nonplussed by this and moved his head further away to get a clearer look in case I was having him on. 'I'm much too selfish and busy for that.'

I sighed with relief. I just couldn't have borne it if he was seeing me only because he thought he should.

'I feel an obligation to allow this thing to flourish in the place where I thought all hope had died.'

What utter bullshit, I thought. All hope was very much alive in his life and so was his love for Joanie and Dicky, I knew that, so I found it fascinating to try to pinpoint when he was acting and when he was simply being.

Later, quite a bit later.

'I'm trying to get hold of a room somewhere in Waterloo. Cheap but necessary.'

And so ended our first Victorian tryst.

CHAPTER NINE

I DIDN'T SEE Olivier for a while because I had to return to Spain to finish *The Ceremony*. I hadn't really bothered to look too deeply into the nature of Larry Harvey. He had struck me as a rather flippant playboy who was skimming along life's surface with a plethora of charm, balancing his many needs precariously with one arm round a rich dame and the other round his very rich mentor, Jimmy Wolfe. There's nothing so wrong with that, and who was I to judge? Except it isn't the great recipe for gaining respect. Jimmy Wolfe had given Larry the keys to the 'movie game' for a few months and in a happy-go-lucky way he was revelling in his new-found power. Joan Cohen was besotted with him but although he was fond of his heiress I believe he led her a merry dance. I thought he was similar to Peter Glenville, another from the Jimmy Wolfe stable, somehow weak at the centre.

Here again my impressions were proven wrong. Around the time of *The Ceremony* opening in London, Larry Harvey asked me to make up a foursome for dinner. He was staying at the Savoy and picked me up in a very flashy Rolls-Royce. He was looking most elegant, complete with black velvet slip-on shoes with his initials encrusted in pure gold, a plum velvet smoking jacket, like Daddy's, and his obligatory black cigarette-holder.

Sue Lloyd, the stunning model-turned-actress who was the spitting image of Kay Kendall, joined our table. After dinner we spun out in all our chauffeur-driven finery, dropping off Sue first. Lo and behold, there was a hole through her glass front door. Someone had broken in.

'I'll come in with you,' said Larry, beginning to get out of the Rolls.

Horrified, Sue stopped him. She clearly knew who was responsible. 'It was done as a dare, I promise you. I'll be fine.'

'I can't just leave you knowing someone has broken in.'

'I know exactly who it is, there's no cause for alarm. Please just drive off.'

'But—'

'Please! Tell him, Sarah, to drive away.'

She was adamant, I could tell. There was no doubt that she wanted us gone. Larry finally got the message too, took a puff from his dandy cigarette holder and said, 'I'll drive off once you go inside and I know that all's well.'

Sue didn't like this but shrugged. 'OK. If you insist.'

We waited for about a minute, and then, as Larry bent forward to tell the chauffeur to drive away, we heard an almighty racket coming from an upstairs room. Things were being smashed, a man was shouting, but it was nothing compared to Sue's piercing scream, which shortly followed.

'You wait here,' Larry ordered his chauffeur. 'Follow me, Smiles. I think we'd better investigate.'

In we went. The hallway faced a straight steep staircase. At the top we could see Sue Lloyd being thrown about the room by a man who looked the size of a heavyweight boxer. Larry, having caught my eye, sauntered towards the foot of the staircase. I stopped him. 'You don't stand a hope in hell. He's a monster.'

We could see a lot of blood coming from somewhere, and through the screams both Larry and I heard the monster say, 'How dare you go flaunting yourself up and down town with Jimmy Wolfe's ponce?'

This was too much for Larry. He called up the staircase, 'What did you say?'

The monster's gigantic frame loomed at us from the head of the stairs. 'Well, if it isn't Jimmy Wolfe's ponce himself!' He started rubbing his hands together. 'Right on cue.'

'Here,' said Larry, calmly taking off his beautiful velvet

smoking jacket. 'Hold this a moment, will you?' I obeyed. He climbed the stairs. I followed. At the top he gave over his cigarette holder too. 'This might get damaged in the fray.' In he went. I couldn't believe how cool he was. He must have been less than half the size of the monster, but he took him on like David with Goliath.

It looked just like one of those fifties B-movies – but for real. Although I'd never witnessed any real grown-up fighting before, I nevertheless didn't like the way Goliath was roaring blindly like an injured bull, having sliced his hand on some broken glass. The sight of his own blood spurred him into a new bloodthirsty madness. As he tossed both Sue Lloyd and Larry around the room before punching Larry ruthlessly in the stomach, I couldn't make up my mind what to do. Call the police? Or stay against the wall looking terrified while screaming and swooning? As I contemplated these alternatives Larry dragged himself up off the floor and promptly remanifested before my very eyes as a kind of James Bond. He swung his fear around, transforming it into an outraged, indignant fury. After about a minute he managed to get Goliath down. I was so proud! Larry was triumphing against all odds. I suppose most women must feel that, when they see their man winning in a brawl, and although Larry wasn't my man, I was profoundly impressed.

Just as we were counting our chickens, Goliath did some transforming of his own. He managed to twist his back so that Larry lost his grip around his neck. I had to do something while Goliath was still down. As I was searching around for a weapon, my eyes happen to fall upon my Pinet winkle-pickers. I dumped Larry's cigarette holder and plum smoking jacket in the corner and went into the fray, kicking and spiking any part of Goliath that was vulnerable. Winkle-pickers can come in dashed handy, I thought, as I hammered and poked away at the poor fellow. Soon it was all over, though I don't want to take a smidgin's-worth of credit for Larry's mission impossible.

Blood was everywhere. Sue Lloyd's nose was bleeding. Goliath was in a swoon. We tied a handkerchief around his wrist. 'That needs a doctor,' I found myself saying in a peremptory fashion.

Larry went to call the police, but Sue remained fiercely protective. She must have loved her Goliath, for she insisted that he apologize and that the two men shake hands.

As we drew up at the back entrance of the Savoy, I saw blood in Larry's tousled hair, and then much more all over his face. I took out his cream silk hanky. 'Here, spit into this.' A better way than Mother's passed-down habit of spitting in it herself. Larry obediently spat. I wiped off all the blood that I could see. 'There, you'll do till the policeman sees you. My mother always said that. God knows why.' We embraced warmly. I was at a loss for words, so I blurted out something silly: 'I would never have thought it of you.'

'No? We Lithuanians are lethal fighters and we always have a trick up our sleeve. On this occasion, a winklepicker.' With that he vacated the Rolls, brushed off any lingering memories, and entered the Savoy like the gentleman he was.

About eight years later, I met him in Malibu with his new wife, Pauline Stone. It was good seeing him again. Pauline kept in touch thereafter, and one day she rang to say Larry was dying. Apparently they had opened him up, taken one look, then promptly sewn him up again for his stomach cancer was too far gone and he only had six months to live. (Recollections of Goliath punching him in the stomach came streaming in.) It hardly needs saying that he lived those last six months to the hilt. When we met he was on tip-top form. Pauline assured me it wasn't bravura, but genuine acceptance.

That was backed up by a nurse, Jenny (later my son's nanny), who I met in hospital where I'd gone to have my appendix removed. She turned out to have been Larry's last nurse as he was dying in the London Clinic. Jenny laughed as she recalled one of his final moments. 'He was lying there, and I asked him whether he wanted to see one of his early movies on the telly. "If you insist," he said. He watched for a few moments, and then—"I wasn't much of an actor, was I?" Those were the last words I heard him utter,' said Jenny, tucking me up before bustling out of my room.

A little while after the episode of the fight, Sue Lloyd and I found ourselves on a train together on our way to Stratford-upon-Avon. Sue was up for the same film as I – probably the same part, I thought, as we hurtled our way through the beautiful countryside. Robin Fox had given me strict instructions to be nice to a producer who hadn't time this trip to meet me in London. 'Just escort him to a bit of culture. He's casting a big Hollywood film to be made here with an excellent part for you.'

I had never escorted a complete stranger before, but Robin assured me that the producer was powerful in Hollywood with an excellent reputation and no harm would come to me.

The producer was there to greet us. As the evening wore on I began to feel more and more uncomfortable as it transpired that the film for which we were both to audition hadn't got the green light yet. I began to wonder why Robin Fox had made it seem so urgent.

After dinner, which ended around midnight, he took me up to my room. I turned to bid him goodnight. 'Thank you for a delicious dinner.' I entered my room, and tried to close the door, to find he was already inside – quick as a skunk. I was dumbfounded. Who the hell did he think he was? More to the point, who the hell did he think *I* was? 'I'm sorry, there's some mistake.'

He was drooling, actually drooling. 'You're so cute.'

I tried to be sophisticated and lead him to the door politely, but it didn't work. He seemed quite excited by my rebuff and came at me a second time. I thought, Is this what we have to do to get Hollywood film roles? If so it was time I began searching for a new profession. Since he seemed to be deaf, blind and dumb, and all attempts at being polite had gone over his arrogant head, I decided to be totally straight with him.

'Get out of here at once.'

He couldn't believe that I'd said it.

'I mean it! Get out of my room. How dare you!'

He looked at me for quite a long beat, gave me the dirtiest look I'd ever had up till that moment, turned tail and departed. At the door he paused. 'You'll regret this.'

He was called Ray Stark, and he meant it. It didn't worry me. Had I been in one of his movies by opening my legs I would have been much more worried. I had no opportunity of asking Sue Lloyd whether she succumbed to him later, because I left town early. I take my hat off to her if she did: I bet she found it bloody tough going.

CHAPTER TEN

I WAS AT loggerheads with Binkie Beaumont, the impresario with whom I had a three-year contract. I wanted to go to Ireland to make a lovely Irish film, written by Edna O'Brien. *The Girl With Green Eyes* had been a terrific hit the year before and the new project was being made by the same team. Binkie, however, had different ideas, and sadly I was still under contract to him. Both he and Robin Fox were strongly recommending that I accept *The Rivals* at the Haymarket with Ralph Richardson; apparently it was an opportunity not to be missed. I knew they were right, but I also knew my mind was clear. I wanted to be in Ireland, filming by the sea. Besides, I could take Addo with me.

I'd recently bought my new home, 18 Hasker Street, Chelsea, but hadn't moved in yet. It was teatime and I was clearing up some of Addo's demolished objects when the doorbell rang in the Clare Court flat. Had Willy forgotten his key? I wasn't expecting anyone. Opening the door I was astonished to find Ralph Richardson standing there. I didn't know him, but felt I did because Olivier often spoke of him. 'Addo, get off!' Addo was obviously so bowled over by this charming stranger that he very nearly bowled him over. Standing on his hind legs, pinning Richardson to the far wall, he was roughly the same height. I ran to the fridge for a juicy bloody bone and tossed it under Addo's nose, whereupon he plopped down, happy to relinquish a new-found friend for more serious meat. 'There must be a smell on your jacket because he doesn't do that very often, I promise you.'

'I think I'm flattered, but I'm not entirely sure . . .'

Olivier had a lot of time for Ralphie: I had the impression he respected him more than any other actor – apart from

71

Wilfred Lawson, maybe. Ralphie was his greatest friend as well as his most dangerous rival. Add to that a soupçon of jealousy and you have a potent mixture. I think what bugged him was Ralphie's innocence, a quality you can't produce like a rabbit out of a hat. Some have it, others acquire it, but you can't act it. It won't come to order.

Watching Ralphie standing there nodding in my doorway, it was easy to see what Lionel was on about. But what was he doing on my doorstep? No doubt he'd come to persuade me to do *The Rivals*. Of course. Binkie had sent him!

'Hello,' I said, unable to think of what to do next.

'Well, aren't you going to ask the old fellah in?'

I was embarrassed because the place was a pigsty/dog kennel. 'If I'd known you were coming—'

'I know, Cocky, you'd have baked a cake.' He turned to look at me, nodding all the while. 'I hoped I might catch you unawares – it's so much more fun, eh?' Twinkling, he walked slowly round the sitting room, looking at my pictures, which weren't bad, but worthless.

'Well, aren't you going to ask if the fellah wants a cup of tea, Cocky?' I could feel him nodding over my shoulder while I was making it.

'Come clean with me, Sir Ralph. Binkie has sent you to woo me, has he not?' I asked, taking the tea tray into the sitting room.

'Binkie yes, but Larry, too.' He watched me closely with his head cocked to one side.

'Larry? Which Larry?' In having to pretend I didn't know Olivier that well, duplicity began wreaking its usual havoc. I had to play for time. I took a sip of Earl Grey.

'Which Larry? Come, come.' Was he fishing, mocking or teasing?

Holding on as best I could I asked, 'Harvey or Olivier?' It was a genuine query, after all. 'I've worked with both.'

He continued to look me hard in the eye before testing his

tea for heat. A peculiar silence fell over the flat, interrupted only by the slurping of hot tea and Addo's chewing.

Had Lionel shared our sacred secret? No, he wouldn't be so stupid . . . would he? But, then, if they were truly close perhaps he might, and this – surely – was against the rules. Fortunately Ralphie dropped the subject. 'Damn good play, *The Rivals*, and you can't fail with Lydia – she plays herself.' He had a fantastically eerie sparkle. 'We actors consider it an honour to perform at the Haymarket. It's the most beautiful theatre in the West End.' Although I hadn't worked there, I knew what he said was true. I longed to play at the Haymarket, but, 'I'm not ready to play at the Haymarket,' I said.

He looked at his watch. 'Good God! Have I left Isabella outside for all this time?' He stood up. 'Poor Isabella – how rude of me, she'll be so lonely.' He made for the door.

'Is she your wife?'

'Good God, how I wish she were!'

To forget someone he so obviously cared for seemed odd to me. 'Would you like to bring her in for a cup of tea?'

He advanced towards me with such a foxy look that I thought he was about to proposition me. 'How would you like to meet Isabella?' he whispered, dragging me by the arm. 'See if you can persuade her to come in. Eh, Cocky? Put on yer jacket, there's a nip in the air.' He took me out and proudly, nodding all the while, of course, introduced us. 'Isabella, meet Sarah – Sarah, this is Isabella!'

Standing there, dazzling in the early-evening sunshine, was the most space-age silver and black monster I'd ever clapped eyes on. There were motorbikes and motorbikes but this Harley Davidson, Isabella, was the mother of them all. Ralphie stood there, watching me. Slowly he advanced, whispering seductively, 'Would you care to go for a wee spin?' His eyes gleamed with daring. I wasn't too keen to go because I felt that incessant nod might get dodgy on the crowded rush-hour streets. Was he up to it, I wondered.

He dug me in the ribs. 'Come on, don't be a coward, Cocky!' That clinched it. I spread my legs and off we sped. Holy Moses! Was I terrified!

'That's right, hang on tight!' The last time I'd been on a motorbike I was on my first date. We crashed. But I love a bit of speed. Recently I'd swapped my beaten-up third-hand Mini Minor for a Mini Cooper S and spent a great deal of time trying to beat my own record – child's play compared to Ralph on the streets of London that day.

As we sped down St Martin's Lane something occurred to me, but I forgot what it was because Ralphie went through the traffic lights at the bottom of St Martin's Lane as they turned red. I closed my eyes and said a quick prayer. When I opened them again we were swirling round Trafalgar Square. Suddenly the thought I'd had at the lights returned. I kept my eyes on Ralphie to make sure I wasn't dreaming.

He wasn't nodding and hadn't nodded once throughout the journey. All the way home, not a single nod.

I'd never been so relieved to see Clare Court's ugliness as I was that day. Dismounting I noticed the almost immediate return of the nod. I thanked him for a truly exhilarating journey.

'You certainly know how to ride Isabella.'

He revved her a couple of times, chuffed at the compliment.

'Just one little question, Sir Ralph. You didn't nod once during the whole trip. How come?'

He revved her once more for luck, leaned forward and beckoned me closer. Then he whispered, 'When I'm on Isabella, Cocky, I can't afford to nod.' He winked, and off he went, a silver and black cloud of smoke.

I concluded later, after I had got to know Sir Ralph, that he had cultivated eccentricity to avoid the slings and arrows of showbiz. The nod gave him a hedge to hide behind, rather as some elderly people pretend to be deaf to protect themselves from others' incessant intrusive babbling. I noticed he never nodded when talking to Jose, his parrot, or Blossom, his hamster. Ralphie used his eccentricity more as his need for a private world grew.

I believe the true answer to my question should have been, 'When I'm on Isabella there is *no need* to nod.'

I was hurtling southwards on the stylish Brighton Belle for another few hours' bliss with Lionel. The last time I'd been puffing down that way had been to start term at Roedean. We were to meet under the clock at the station. My orders were to look really tarty.

'Hopefully the tart make-up will camouflage the lack of years,' he'd said dubiously.

In each film I'd made so far I'd worn a wig, or false pieces, so no one knew what I looked like in the flesh, which was handy. He saw me as he stood hunched up in a grey woolly scarf and old mac beside the magazine kiosk. He waved his stick at me, gesturing me to follow at a safe distance. I began to laugh to myself. There he was hobbling through Brighton station so unremarkably dressed as to go completely unde-tected, even in his home town. He was a master of disguise (as long as he didn't overdo it!) Yet even when he was dressed as Sir Laurence Olivier (whoever *he* was) few gave him a second glance. I had to brace myself against the knowledge that for him adopting a different disguise was probably the highlight of our lovers' tryst. Yet this was the day I had chosen to point out to him the dangers of meeting in tacky hotels and public places, which might lead to my own downfall. His need to live dangerously was becoming too much for me.

Once out of the station he hailed a taxi, which I thought pretty bold. Our hotel in Hove was horrendous, but impeccably suited to our appearance. We signed in as Mr Kerr and Miss Frappée, and climbed the stairs. Our room wasn't even facing the sea.

'Sorry, darling, but I had to pretend we couldn't afford a sea view. Anyway, I thought being a Roedean girl you'd be put off the sea for life.'

Even with my tarty gear on neither of us felt too lusty that afternoon, but it didn't matter. What we were after was respite from the world. Or was it something else? What I have failed to mention is my mysterious gift of massage. Lionel introduced me to it. I never learnt how to do it, I was simply able always to give a strong massage.

'Lionel—'

'Don't stop. Don't stop!' His pleadings were inevitably bolstered with endless flattery. 'You could earn a fortune this way, do you know that?'

I needed him to understand. Why was his finger always hovering on the self-destruct button?

'Lionel—'

'You're a natural healer, did you know that?' I gave up.

Later, we were looking out of the window at the brick wall while he was tickling me. Without any prompting, he reminded me of what it was I had wanted to say. 'I've rented a tiny room, our much-needed watering hole, in Waterloo.' I smothered him in kisses. So often it was the case that Lionel and I found ourselves cocooned in synchronicity.

'Steady, it's hardly the Taj Mahal.'

He loved to be kissed all over so I did just that, while telling him about Ralphie and the Harley Davidson. He laughed.

'Have you ever told him about us?'

'Why?'

'Because he brought you up, that's all.'

'Careful, he'll be inside yer knickers next!'

I found this hard to imagine, for I hadn't had the impression that Ralphie was flirting.

'Come to think, he did question me about you. He was most curious that my leading lady was such a young Lolita. I got a trifle teased.'

'I think he smells a rat.'

'Smelling rats is one thing, proof is another. Fancy him coming to check you out like that – sly old bugger!'

I watched him climbing into his clothes. Carefully he readjusted his appearance to suit a Royal Crescent homecoming, rather than a furtive afternoon in a sleazy Hove hotel.

'Do you want to get married to your Willy?' he asked.

'He hasn't asked me.'

'Will you when he does?'

Not if I couldn't keep the vows.

'Yes. There's no other reason for getting married.'

'Wait till you are,' he said sadly, donning his mac, and stuffing his trilby and woolly scarf in a briefcase. There was a silence as we stood there, either end of the room. 'Come here, Dame Sarah.'

I took a deep breath before going to him for a brave parting.

He left his stick behind, so I held it tight all the way back to London. Quite absurd how such a cheap, tacky stick could deliver such overwhelming comfort.

CHAPTER ELEVEN

TOGETHER ROBIN FOX and I finally won the battle of Willy becoming an actor. Robin put him up for a small but showy part in the last reel of Lindsay Anderson's movie, *The Loneliness of the Long Distance Runner*, starring, of all people, my old buddy and team-mate Tom Courtenay.

It was around this time, while I was still under contract to Binkie Beaumont, that Binkie rang, ordering me to pack my bags quickly and shoot up to Cambridge. His new play by the American Arthur Coppet, *Oh Dad, Poor Dad, Mamma's Hung You In The Closet And I'm Feeling So Sad*, was previewing there before coming into the West End.

'Darling, you must get us out of this hole – we're in terrible trouble. There's a disaster – not the play, sweet girl, but the leading lady.' She had been rushed off to hospital. Binkie purred his orders down the phone, instructing me to see the play that night, learn it during the night and take over the following night.

'How big is the part?'

'Big enough, darling, so best get a move on, don't you think?'

I couldn't very well argue. After all, I'd gone off to make two films while under contract to H. M. Tennant's to do theatre – but I still begrudged going.

The playwright, Arthur Coppet, took me under his wing. Andrew Ray, husband of the sick leading lady and who was himself playing the lead – the mixed-up retarded teenager with a terrible stammer – was superb. The stand-in playing 'my' part wasn't. No wonder Binkie was in a fix. The good news was that I thought the play, though not great, was a truly original black comedy. The even better news was that the part of the girl had sufficient comic possibilities for me to break free of my FO (Fuckable Object) image and return to making the audience laugh like I did at Worthing Rep. *Term of Trial* and *The Ceremony* had left the sex-symbol label all too neatly sewn on; I could only muster sufficient strength to rip it off altogether through making people laugh.

The FO get-rich-quick route was one I naturally found tempting. It continued to beckon, for I was being offered many such roles. Even Hollywood was showing interest, but I'd sworn that I'd never leave Addo for more than a week. I was offered a film in Africa called *Mr Moses* with Robert Mitchum and elephants, and although I'd always had an absolute pash for both, I couldn't get anyone to help me smuggle Addo across, however much money I offered. It was about this time that Terence Stamp gave a magazine interview in which he suggested that Sarah Miles wasn't interested in men, only her great white dog Addo and Terry's no fool. DOG = GOD – but perhaps Terry meant something else.

My coming Cambridge adventure would be too hectic to find time for walkies, so Willy kindly offered to look after Addo. Willy was now set for stardom and although his part had been small in Lindsay Anderson's film, he'd stood out just like I knew he would – a beacon of promise.

After seeing *Oh Dad* I didn't hang about longer than needs be to meet the cast, for I had to lock myself away and learn my lines. Arthur Coppet said he and Andrew would meet me on stage at ten thirty next morning to run through the difficult scenes. In one hard scene at the end my character tries all her skills of seduction to arouse the retarded young man and divert his attention from his stamp collection.

Not going to bed that night didn't worry me a jot. No, the only nightmare was the doubt. Anything entailing brain sweat (separate from emotional, physical or spiritual sweat) riddles me with such doubt that positive action plays second fiddle to all-time terror.

Next morning I entered the stage door like a sacrificial lamb. Andrew hadn't arrived so I sat on stage continuing to learn the lines. By lunchtime he still hadn't shown up, I assumed because of his wife. No one had told me why she had been taken to hospital and it didn't seem fit to ask. I looked at my watch. That night's full house was creeping dangerously close, only five more hours of learning to go.

Before curtain-up, the stage manager went on, to explain how I hadn't heard of the play until yesterday let alone seen it, so to have patience if and when words failed me. After a speech such as that how could I help but have the audience eating out of my hand? All went swimmingly until that bloody seduction scene. It was a stinker. Half-way through, when I was half undressed, I had to break off, and in my best imitation of Edith Evans, 'Script, please!' This is a request that has to be made with absolute authority, an apology would have been my death knell. My script was brought on stage – opened at the correct place, thank God – and on I went.

It was an interesting experience for me – and I'm sure for the audience, too – having to continue stripping myself, and caressing and kissing Andrew, with a script in my hand. I couldn't read from it, because it had gone all silver with my panic. But I knew that having it there somehow gave me a buffer, something solid to offset the fear; also it was excellent for drawing out the audience's sympathy. Andrew looked quite horrorstruck as I continued with no correct lines, just a general thrust of common sense.

To see a full house, with Binkie Beaumont (whom I'd really grown to respect), Mummy and Willy all sitting there proud as could be, was a mighty high. As the curtain call went on and on, I was able to experience a feeling of self-worth that I'd lost somewhere along the way. Binkie and Arthur Coppet told me I had lifted the play into a much higher gear, securing fresh hope for a long London run. No one thought I could be so off the wall in comedy. Binkie said he'd arrange for me to play Sally Bowles in *I Am a Camera*. I was finally where I wanted to be: part of a pre-West End run in a new funny play in a part that was a dream. In Cambridge the play was an undoubted hit. There would be quite a wait while a suitable West End theatre was found, but in the mean time I was content to revel in the security of knowing I'd be working in comedy again.

I was down at Barn Mead playing croquet with Daddy one weekend when Mummy called from the house, 'Sarah! Binkie Beaumont on the phone. Take it in the drawing room.'

In a moment or two she would regret saying that, because after I had rung off I went bananas. First I bashed my head against the wall over and over until I thought I saw a star or two, then I started smashing things (making sure they weren't precious.

Spears of injustice pierced me. I began frothing at the mouth and chewing at the rug. From time to time I'd give it a good gnaw, spitting out globules of froth and furry tufts. To an outsider it must have looked as if I was in the midst of an epileptic fit.

Enter Mother, who attempted to get a hold of me since I was in no condition to get hold of myself. Mother was always strong, especially when she needed to be. She held me down tight. I explained.

'Binkie said Andrew's wife had quickly recovered.'

'No doubt when she saw your reviews,' swooped in Mother.

'Too bad. She abandoned ship for an abortion.'

Why was I so lacking in curiosity that I'd never inquired why she was in hospital? 'I don't believe you!'

'It's true, Arthur Coppet told me.' She began to straighten the rug while I picked up the broken stuff. 'That part belongs to you. We must fight tooth and nail.'

'Binkie says she'll take him to court if her contract isn't honoured.'

I imitated Binkie's dulcet tones on the phone. 'Chin up, darling. How do you think I feel having to watch your character become a shadow of its former self?'

Mother became almost as mad as me. 'But I heard him say categorically that you would be taking the play into the West End. If I were you I'd sue Binkie Beaumont.'

'What for, breaking my heart?'

CHAPTER TWELVE

I T WAS THE BITTER WINTER OF 1963 when we started work on *The Servant*. Willy played the master and Dirk Bogarde was his servant. Wendy Craig played the fiancée and I was Vera, Dirk's girlfriend from up north. Because Robin Fox put the deal together he felt embarrassed pushing Willy forward too much but after I read the script I knew that only Willy could play it, and he needed no pushing from anyone. *The Long Distance Runner* was all the proof that was needed. Indeed, he was going to be as brilliant as Dirk Bogarde. Joe Losey was the director. The screenplay was by Harold Pinter from a novel by Robin Maugham. We shot most of it in Chelsea, off the King's Road.

'If that's how you see the part, Joe, then get another Vera.'

'Only you can play Vera, just play her straight, for God's sake!'

'I see her dippy and slightly kinky, so if you want her straight then get another Vera.'

I turned to leave the production office, but Joe called me back. 'OK, Sarah, you win, play the goddam part as you please. I wash my hands of it.'

England was bursting at the seams with FOs, and since Joe Losey had hired me I was going to make the part as amusing as truth permitted.

Joe was a spectacularly noble, almost Red-Indian-looking American. The reason I grew more and more fond of him over the years was because his integrity was gradually able to eclipse his stubbornness. Joe was a Capricorn, too, so we tended to butt horns during our friendship, which lasted till he died at the end of his swansong, *Steaming*, in which I starred with Vanessa Redgrave.

He told me he was dying before we even started shooting. Diana Dors knew she was too, likewise telling me in strictest confidence she hadn't long to live. It's unfortunate how, with some of us, the fear of death has such power over our virtues, for it made Joe's stubbornness blunder back in full cry. I suspect his wife, Patricia, managed to sprinkle some of her sweetness into his drink while his back was turned because he sweetened up considerably towards the end of shooting and his integrity returned. Acceptance, I suppose.

Diana's acceptance of death was remarkable. When we first met at Pinewood Studios it was as if we were rekindling some other experience. Even though I only believed then in one lifetime, her observation gave me the shivers. 'I think we met at the stake,' she said jovially. Our love blossomed like an orchid in a hothouse – inevitable, I suppose, with all that steam around. She was another blazing example of the hard-done-by FO. The media and show business regularly miss true worth, even when it's right at the end of their noses, because they're too lazy to look beneath the threatening shell of sex appeal. Women are just as bad; they never take kindly to other women who are sexy. Diana and I had great fun commiserating over the curse of being an FO (though I was never in her league).

'People either love us to death, or hate us,' she said laughingly. Diana Dors was a sensitive, wise and truly witty woman. Thank God we met, otherwise I'd never have known.

All Willy had to do was to stay strong and not feel that he had to become an alcoholic, or junkie even, just because the part called for it. Yet sadly while we were working together things became strained. After shooting all day, Willy would either go missing or arrive home wrapped so tightly in his character that I couldn't find him. I'd offer to help him unwrap the part and hang it up for the evening, but he'd get defensive and start clinging to it all night as well. And so it was that I gradually began losing him. I lost his name first. There was another actor called William Fox, so Equity said he had to change it. I lost my Willy to James, James both to his role in *The Servant* and to Dirk Bogarde. No doubt I was mainly to blame. Maybe I was losing my Willy because so many secrets had wormed their way in between our innocent and splendid first love.

If the relationship between servant and master was to reap dividends it was essential that Willy and Dirk were left alone. In their place I would have felt the same. We all put a great deal of hard work into that project, as well as risky soul-searching, but for their two characters the delving inward had to go even deeper, and it paid off a thousandfold in the finished film, the only place where it matters. I'm sure their exploration was never anything but professional, but even if it hadn't been I was in no position to get hot under the collar with my own infidelity looking me in the face. While Willy was away in Kenya and I was still at RADA rehearsing *Six Characters in Search of an Author*, I remembered only too well going home at night to research into prostitution with Sylvia, the whore I lived with in Half Moon Street. Why shouldn't they do the same? In *The Servant* Dirk Bogarde tries to control Willy's character by drawing him into lechery and decadence. Rehearsal was essential and since I was secretly seeing Lionel, on what grounds could I grumble?

I was still stinging from being let down by Binkie Beaumont. *Oh, Dad, Poor Dad, Mamma's Hung You In The Closet And I'm Feelin' So Sad* opened in London to pretty good reviews but not the raves I was expecting. It didn't run that long either.

'I told them all it would sink without Miles and I was right,' said Binkie later, when he was wooing me into doing something else. The experience had taught me a lesson: not to be such a spoilt brat; not to allow a little bit of rejection to send me up the Polly Tree. I had to learn that being duped is part of the actor's lot. But I so wanted to break this FO mould and do comedy.

So, determined to ease the pain, I found as many laughs as I could in my role as Vera. Joe was getting his knickers in a twist, for he knew this version of the truth wasn't what he saw on the page, and rightly challenged my interpretation. But the first set of rushes made him realize that perhaps what I was doing could work.

Dirk, being an absolute professional, was good fun to work with and I learnt a lot from him. His knife-sharp observation made him quick to grasp that I had a problem with gravity and he christened me 'Dainty' almost from day one. Alas, I'm still as dainty as ever.

CHAPTER THIRTEEN

I TURNED TWENTY-ONE with considerable absence of fuss. No party, because I didn't want one. It was round about then that Father and Mother went to see a preview of *The Servant*, and afterwards came to Hasker Street. As I opened the door I witnessed a most rare event. Both Mummy and Daddy up the Polly Tree together (an expression from my childhood meaning apoplectic rage). Neither stayed long enough for a cup of tea, but only to let me know that I had put myself beyond the pale and had finally succeeded in disgracing the family name.

'Don't you realize what a slamming that piece of sexually perverted tosh is going to receive from the critics? And quite right, too!' Daddy couldn't light Mother's cigarette – she was too upset, marching round the room. 'To associate yourself with a film of such debauched, unnecessary decadence! What's worse, all the servants will leave, or else stay and start taking over the household.' I felt very sad watching them furiously stumble into Father's latest charabanc without a backward glance. Addo barked them off handsomely, his tail in full plume as he cantered down the street beside them. I was unaware of the turn of fortune that was afoot.

The Servant was heralded as some kind of masterpiece. Some French critics claimed it was one of the greatest films of all time. Willy was instantly a star and Dirk was now wearing his well-earned crown. The reviewers peed themselves with superlatives and there was a long stretch of silence from Barn Mead.

I was asked to go to America to do some publicity. 'It's a great hit out there; you must go, it'll do you some good,' said Robin Fox.

'Is Willy coming too?'

'No. They want just you and Dirk.'

'But it's Willy's film, not mine.'

'That's the way it goes, I'm afraid.'

'But what about Addo?'

'Fuck Addo.'

It was my first trip to America, and I was more scared than excited. I was told that someone would meet me but I wasn't expecting to find Dirk and Joe waving from the barrier. Fancy them getting up at six o'clock in the morning in the middle of a gruesome publicity schedule to welcome me. I was deeply touched. Dirk handed me a big teddy bear, making me so warm with gratitude that the fear melted away.

It went swimmingly, with Joe, Dirk and the film being the toast of the town. Joe had been blacklisted years previously during the McCarthy era, so this was an emotional home-coming anyway; added to which he received an overwhelming critical response. A few days later, the buzz of adulation singing in that vibrant New York air, I lay in the splendour of my Plaza Hotel suite reminiscing over the last time I felt that same frenetic, yet empty showbiz energy.

It was the summer before, in 1963, when I went to Venice. *Term of Trial* was up for best film at the Venice film festival and I was up for best actress (in the event we all lost to *Lolita*). Early one morning, followed by a couple of paparazzi, I'd just laid my towel on the Lido sand, fumbling all the while, (hopeless at playing movie star), when floating up the beach towards me came more than a mere movie star. This delicious creature was surely a goddess. Through the flashing cameras I stood on tiptoe on my beach towel to see more of her, then followed discreetly in her wake. Why does it continue to enthrall me, that feeling of awe that wells up when a truly beautiful woman catches my eye?

Her name was Monica Vitti. I'd remembered seeing her in Antonioni's *La Notte* and *L'Avventura*. I'll never forget that walk of hers. The sun skipping over a full emerald bikini, from which long bronzed limbs tapered into a prowl, scuffing up the white sand of the Lido beach. 'Tall and tan and slender and lovely, the girl from Ipanema goes walking . . .'

That evening a party was given in *Term of Trial's* honour in a beautiful villa overlooking a bay. Monica was there. I prayed that I'd be seated near her, and although my prayers weren't answered I could see her. She was sitting two places away from Olivier, whom I hadn't expected to see at all, right up at the other end of the table. Lionel seemed to be directing most of his attention to the rather important Mafia-looking chap on his left. How could he, with Monica Vitti almost rubbing elbows with him? Sometimes he bewildered me. He did, however, often look down the table at me and send his love. His love sign was a fiddle with his breast-pocket handkerchief. I was so engrossed in watching the pair of them that I scooped up my peas the wrong way round and dropped a few down my dress. The elderly man sitting next to me, who looked rather like Binkie, hadn't introduced himself, yet had the audacity to ask me where I'd gone to school. 'A lady never scoops up her peas.'

I remembered Roedean and, laughing, spilt several more – over him, too.

'Why the hilarity?' he asked, checking his cravat for pea-droppings.

'Because where I went to school scooping peas was a serious crime, fit only for the kitchen.'

'I see they taught you well. What school was it?'

'Roedean.' He looked up. 'Where were you at school?' I asked him.

He ignored the question, but found a new line of attack. 'You young girls today wear your eyeliner too far inwards towards your nose. Eye beauty is all to do with giving them width, opening them up. Take the line outwards from the outer corner. Study Audrey Hepburn, she has the trick.'

'Yes. The trick is bone structure, sir.' I think he warmed towards me as the meal dragged on.

Afterwards I stole a few moments with Lionel, who wasn't a bit interested in my passion for Monica Vitti. All he wanted to know was what I talked about with Cecil Beaton.

'I thought he looked familiar.'

Olivier sighed with resignation. 'Only you would fail to recognize Cecil Beaton.'

Slightly unfair, I thought, considering I didn't move in high circles and, like eating peas the correct way up, had little interest in doing so.

'His place-name was staring you right in the face.' He looked as dejected as his hanky hanging from his pocket.

'You're all crumpled.' Fortunately I stopped myself in mid-gesture from rectifying its crinkles. I thought it would look too intimate.

Lionel saw this and smiled. 'Love you,' he said, looking at his hanky. It was obviously drooping worse than he'd realized. 'It's all those unrequited love signals.' With a camp gesture he floated the hanky through the air before stuffing it into his trouser pocket. Wistfully I watched it disappear.

We stood there looking at each other. Painfully beastly those public moments were, with no hope of embraces. He gave me his Heathcliff glance. Being aware of his instant ability to turn on that scrumptious pillow look didn't make the torment any easier.

We were interrupted by the publicist. 'Sir Laurence, your plane leaves in an hour, we'd better make a move.'

Now here I was again, briefly playing at movie star. New York was not Venice but this time there was no Olivier either. It was hot lying there in the suite at the Plaza and I couldn't work out how to put the air-conditioning on cool.

Having finished breakfast, I stopped day-dreaming, had a bath and got myself made up for the heavy schedule that lay ahead. Three radio interviews, one telly appearance and a magazine. Christ, the heat! I went to the window once more to see if I could open it, and this time my determination paid off. The bliss of breathing again! As nothing depresses me

Laurence Olivier as Graham Weir and Sarah Miles as Shirley Taylor in *Term of Trial*.
Cartoon by Ffolks.

Shirley Taylor plus blonde wig. I craved a shorter skirt, but Peter Glenville thought it improper, so I pulled it up whenever I got the opportunity.

With Lionel. Having yet to be seduced in real life I found the playing of this seduction scene most tricky.

Left: 'Wear no make-up and a head scarf,' demanded Lionel for our first tryst.
Shocked at my youthful demeanour he had to have a rethink. 'Next time
plaster it on like a tart.'
Right: Here I am as the tart, forever obedient.

With Willy (James) Fox
in *The Servant*.

Jimmy Wolfe gave Larry Harvey the
power to be actor/writer/director/
producer in *The Ceremony*, with me
playing the usual FO (Fuckable Object).

Right: I'll always be grateful to Ros Chatto, for without her and Robin Fox's forceful natures I'd never have met Robert Bolt. Daniel Chatto, the little frog (*far right*), grew up and turned into a prince.

Above: Father, Tomcat, Gulliver, Betty and me all looking a trifle glum. Sadly it was the only picture I could find of Father and me. None at all of Mother and me, hence the inset.

Right: Sister Nessie and brother Chuzzer at the local taverna on the island of Crete where he lived for many years.

Above: Me playing Bardot with Nicol Williamson in *The Six-Sided Triangle*, produced, written and directed by Christopher Miles.

The six parts I played: (*below, left*) unsexy English; (*below, right*) Japanese, which gave me trouble because of my piggy eyes; (*opposite, top left*) a kind of Claudia Cardinale; (*opposite, top right*) an Ingmar Bergman heroine; (*opposite, bottom left*) a version of Theda Bara; (*opposite, bottom right*) Brigitte Bardot.

My one-off Burlington Bertie,
Willy Donaldson.

Father
attempting to
angle himself
up with his
self-portrait
in bronze.

Brother Chris
beside his Rolls.
Chuzzer had
one too. I, on
the other hand,
was glad of
Chris's cast-off
Mini Minor.

Above: Having had a taste of Ralph Richardson's Harley Davidson, I go for a burn on mine in *Those Magnificent Men In Their Flying Machines.*

Right: I finally managed to inveigle my way up in one of those superb flying machines.

At the opening of *Flying Machines* my blasted frock split as I curtsied to the Duke of Edinburgh. The sound of ripping silk rippled down the whole line-up.

With the obligatory Addo in *Flying Machines*.

more than a half-eaten meal staring me in the face I wheeled my breakfast trolley out into the corridor and – *wham*! – the bedroom door slammed in my face.

I wasn't overly amused, standing in that unwelcoming corridor visualizing the future: 'Sarah Miles caught nude in Plaza corridor as a publicity gimmick for her steamily erotic film, *The Servant*.' No. 'Dainty' caught stark naked in public we needed like a hole in the head. Gossip was already bouncing around town after a live radio interview I'd done two days previously. I'd got a real idiot of an interviewer/disc jockey, the kind who asks a question and then answers it for you before you can draw breath. What should I do? Walk out or punch him in the mouth? Because the interview was going out live I was fearful of doing something I might regret. Yet I was unable to take the stream of regurgitated tripe a moment longer. I placed my mike on the carpet. 'Do you mind?' I asked politely. Not giving him time to reply I got on to my head.

A headstand for me is a quick route to heaven and although I couldn't see the interviewer's face too well, I could hear that he had stopped talking. I had triumphed. A moment or two went by while he pondered whether he had the wherewithal to describe a headstand on live radio and make it sufficiently interesting. He cleared his throat.

'Sarah Miles is now standing on her head.' Silence. 'Sarah Miles is still standing on her head.' Long silence. 'Sarah, tell me, do you go around London being interviewed on your head?'

'The opportunity has never arisen.'

He stopped talking for another glorious moment.

Feeling sorry for him I weakened. 'Go on, please talk to me. Ask me any question you like.' We finally got on with the interview. He was better from then on, thinking through his questions and listening to my answers, but, then, his whole world had been turned upside down.

Just as mine now was in that corridor. I looked left and

right. Next I listened. No one coming so far. I took the small napkin off my breakfast trolley. Small described it too damn well. I began to panic. I took courage and napkin in both hands and ran up the corridor trying to find a door that opened. Why were there no bathrooms, laundry rooms or lavatories? Not one bleedin' open door on the whole floor – and I couldn't very well go down in the lift. Strangely, not a soul appeared. The longer my luck lasted the sooner it would end.

I went back and nestled up to the trolley, defeated. It did allow me a degree of modesty, sitting there, knees inwards, flat on the floor with my feet sticking out and my napkin nearly stretching over half of each breast.

Unable to see it ending well I began to cry. I heard a noise. Someone was coming at last. My future was in her/his hands. Far from the bustle and rustle of a chambermaid, these footsteps were slow enough to signal an invalid. Around the corner came an old lady, bent over slightly. She was small, with white hair. As she made her way towards me I could tell she hadn't spotted me. I was so still beside my trolley that she passed by without seeing me. Half-way through my sigh of deliverance I realized – what the hell was I sighing with relief for? My only hope was slowly vanishing into a twentieth-floor Plaza sunset.

I bellowed. 'Excuse me!' No reaction. I tried a little louder. 'Excuse me!' Her steady step moved on regardless, so there was naught to do but jump up in all my lack of finery and scamper after her. She didn't bat an eyelid. 'Hey, honey, you look as if you could do with some help.' Her slow drawl matched her slow walk. 'Come. I'll sort you out,' closing us into the safety of her suite.

I told her my tale of woe. She was so sympathetic. Some rich ladies wear their rings with the stones on the inside of their palm, thus allowing their rings to glimmer with every point they wish to emphasize. My saviour liked emphasizing a lot.

'Let's call housekeeping.' Slow of step she might have been, but not of common sense. 'Wear this,' she purred, handing me her luxurious white Plaza dressing gown. 'Come over here and I'll teach you how to work the air-conditioning.'

I sent her a dozen red roses for saving my reputation – it was cheap at the price. Thanks to her, I can now work air-conditioning, but wherever I am in the world I never put it on. Hot or cold, I just can't breathe. It makes people's breath smell, I've noticed. I never go putting breakfast trays outside the door when naked, either.

CHAPTER FOURTEEN

IT WAS INEVITABLE. Willy asked to marry me, and I was truly tempted to accept. Though things hadn't gone too well while we were making *The Servant*, thereafter they had improved. Willy was the perfect partner and what's more his parents approved of me and I of them. Mother and Father approved of him, and he approved of Mother and Father (especially Mother). What more could any couple want?

Yet I told him I wanted to wait a while. That's always a downer of a reply, however you dress it up. It wasn't that I didn't love Willy – James – I did, and still do, but my love for Lionel was all-consuming. Strangely, it never crossed my mind that I could marry Willy and keep them both, because if I took the vows it would put everything into a new perspective. I never dreamt of playing by the dangerous rules of broken marriage vows. If I chose to remain Olivier's mistress, I'd never be able to hold up my head as Willy's wife. And I believed my Willy deserved the best, which at the least meant an upright wife. Should I talk it through first with Lionel?

No, because right then I wanted Mummy. Although I had never taken her into my confidence, it didn't take much wizardry to make all Lionel's phone calls to Barn Mead add up to four. If she had put two and two together I didn't want her 'four' being bandied around her Ingatestone cronies. Before saying anything to Lionel I should talk to her.

'Come to your senses. The Willys of this world don't grow on trees. You'll regret it for the rest of your days. He loves you dearly, you know that.'

'I'm in love with Lionel too.'

'It's impossible for a woman to be in love with two men at the same time.'

'But it's possible for men, is that it?'

'Yes. Men are different.'

'Has Daddy ever been unfaithful to you?'

'Not to my knowledge. It's simply not cricket. Besides, spreading it thinly over two makes it a pretty flimsy kind of love.'

That put me in a fury! The idea of my love for Olivier being described as flimsy made me see the truth for the first time, and uncomfortably clearly.

I decided to leave, collected up Addo's belongings, then kissed her goodbye. 'Thanks, Ma, you helped me see the wood for the trees.'

Mother rattled at the car window. 'Does Willy know about Lionel?' She leaned in, red with warning.

'Certainly not. Only you know.'

'Tell Willy, see what he says. He may accept it.'

'Yes, he might. And then what?'

Mother looked so deeply concerned for me. 'He's young, intelligent, beautiful and an exceedingly fine actor.' All that was true.

'Too good to deserve a thinly spread love,' I mumbled as the tears began to well up. 'No one must ever know. Ever. Willy deserves a clean marriage with children, and who can blame him?' I tried to break free before the tears spilt over, for I didn't want her catching them too.

'It's the hardest life of all, a mistress's. But that's your business, and you have my word your business will always be safe with me – not even your father will know.' As she raised her arm to wave me off I saw how sad she was.

Because of Lionel's schedule of running, directing and acting at the new National Theatre, I had to be ready to go to our new Waterloo watering-hole at any time. It had made a huge difference to our assignations for everything became more relaxed, which in turn had tuned more finely the strings of our *amour*. There was one little snag, however: our new watering-hole was hardly that, due to a noisy almost flowless cold-water tap and no hot water whatsoever. There was no denying it was a grim pad.

Until I met him I had assumed that if you were famous you were bound to have money. Not so. At this time Lionel was making neither huge, nor regular money in films, and a divorce from Vivien hadn't helped his finances. His National Theatre work, though prestigious and perfectly timed for his future ambitions, likewise wasn't bringing in sufficient revenue to feed his lifestyle. Neither of us had sufficient money coming in to better our Waterloo watering-hole. Although we had numerous friends who would have helped us out with cushy bedrooms, or flats, once you start confiding secrets and asking favours it can always backfire. 'Nothing is ever for free,' as Lionel always warned. (Except me, of course!)

One day with Lionel I was distractedly contemplating how to confide to him Willy's offer of marriage. It was important to tell him because it might come as a relief. I was always seeking ways to let him off the hook, for nothing would have insulted me more than for him to carry on for my sake.

'Willy wants to marry me.'

A pause the size of the Grand Canyon followed.

'And does that fit in with Dame Sarah's plans?' His wishes rang out so clearly in that one sentence that no more needed to be said. It was my problem, not his. He'd made it clear that I could have boyfriends, or marry if I wanted to. He wasn't stopping me, and neither was I – it was those confounded marriage vows.

He seemed restless that day, certainly not in one of his better moods. But gradually I dispersed the knotted-up anxiety of his troubles both at home and at work. 'Why in God's name don't you leave your new house free for us?' he mumbled into the pillow.

'We've been over this. Why should I live alone with a phone? Besides, we'd lose almost a whole hour in travel time.' He knew I spoke truth. I continued rubbing away his weary woes. He could be a complete bastard when it suited him.

He said, 'I feel guilt at home, guilt at work, yet no guilt whatsoever being here with you.' Guilt is a very convenient substance. It prevents us from attending to the root of the sin that lies hidden underneath.

'So?'

'So.' He turned over and whipped up my skirt without his usual peeling ritual. 'Don't you see? I feel so light and airy when we're together and that makes me feel horrendous guilt elsewhere.' He made love then, and how! Guiltily, dirtily.

CHAPTER FIFTEEN

M y IRISH FILM had been postponed awhile; another cock-up. My hopelessly planned career would have been running smoothly if I'd left it to Robin, but I'd thought I knew best, so I had to endure *The Rivals* being a great success at the Haymarket without me.

In the meantime I was offered a play opposite Nicol Williamson, at the Royal Court, one of those nitty-gritty northern jobs. This one, by Henry Livings, was called *Kelly's Eye*. It was pretty much a two-hander mostly set in sand dunes.

'I hear he's the flavour of the month,' I said to Robin, rather hoity-toity.

'He's much more than that,' scoffed Robin. 'He'll end up one of the greats. No, Nicol is with us to stay. His Hamlet up at Dundee was really quite extraordinary, I hear.'

I liked Henry Livings immediately and spent many a weekend up north in his hideaway, but Nicol Williamson was something else. He was the epitome of the angry young man. He was a tall bear of a man, with fine curly blond hair. I never managed to work out how much of him was a Scot and how much a northerner. The chip on his shoulder was so vast it dug right down into a great inner cavern.

Rehearsals weren't easy. Nicol, being such a powerful personality, repeatedly undermined the director's authority.

'He's an arsehole,' was all he said. The chemistry in the rehearsal hall grew worse and worse until Nicol began not to show up at all. This made me nervous, because I hadn't had much theatre experience. We both had whacking great parts and the first night was getting uncomfortably close. Sadly my character completely relied on Nicol's. Such is woman's lot.

Although I had a long journey ahead of me on preview night, I felt I'd done a fairly good job. I had a few friends in who thought so too. Henry Livings was delighted, and that gave me enormous encouragement. Nevertheless I wanted the first night out of the way so that I could relax into the character and start enjoying it. I was on my way in to see if Nicol had any notes for me when I saw him disappearing round the corner towards the stage door, arm in arm with Anthony Page, a clever young director. These two sneaking off together didn't worry me at the time; I knew they had worked together and respected each other's talent enormously.

On the following night, however, the first night, Nicol had a completely new character, doing completely strange business at completely different places all over the stage. I'd go to a particular spot to start a scene, only to spy Nicol on the opposite side of the stage, whittling some wretched piece of wood, for instance, or about some other business he'd never done before. What with my fear of crowds plus a full first-night audience to tame, I needed every ounce of courage to stop myself from wanting to bury not only my head, but my whole body in the sand dunes. How I got through I don't know. It was, without doubt, a most unfeeling thing to do to someone with so little experience. I closed my dressing-room door and wept.

I didn't bother to read all the reviews, having got the gist after the first few. They blamed the play more than either Nicol or me, but that wasn't the point, which was that I'd lost respect for Nicol. Whatever greatness he may have been blessed with was no excuse for what he'd done.

One night we must have been roughly five minutes into the first act when Addo sauntered onstage. Someone must have opened my dressing-room door. Even Nicol was non-plussed by this huge pure white godlike monster wandering all over poor Henry Livings's lines, sniffing away at those northern sand dunes.

99

'What a big dog,' I said, going over to Addo. The audience was entranced by him, never having been so attentive since the play opened. 'He doesn't seem to be wearing a name tag,' I said limply. Nicol stood there refusing to believe it wasn't a dream. If eyes could kill, both Addo and I would be dead. How I wished I'd thought of letting Addo out on the first night – that would've taught him! So skilfully was I able to blend Addo into the plot, though, that even Nicol began to enjoy the audience's delight in him. At the end of the first act our two characters had to move into a bedsit in the local town, so knowing the audience was now besotted with Addo I asked the Nicol character if we could take the dog into town with us.

'No,' said the Nicol character firmly. I heard sad sighing from the auditorium.

'But we can't leave him all alone – these dunes are miles away from anywhere, he'll starve.'

'I doubt it.' Was it his character or Nicol himself looking daggers? 'We're not taking him into town, and that's final.' The audience didn't like Nicol's character for being so cruel, but there was no time to argue. Besides, arguing with Nicol wasn't wise: he was more renowned for his muscle than I was.

'Who opened the fucking door?' bellowed Nicol in the interval. Silence. He came into my dressing room while I was changing for the second act.

'Lock your door this time, and keep it locked.'

'Nicol, I think it would be wiser to take him on with us otherwise the audience—'

'He stays locked in here, is that clear?'

My dresser made a timely entrance with an apology. 'As soon as I opened the door with your second-act clothes he shot out. I wasn't sure whether it was better to leave him or to come onstage and collect him.'

Nicol had thought I'd let him out myself.

When Act Two lights go up in *Kelly's Eye*, Nicol and I are

discovered back in town, entering the bedsit with our suit-cases. As we did so that night all we could hear were concerned murmurings from the audience.

'Where's the dog?'

'What have they done with that beautiful dog?'

'Fancy just abandoning him like that.'

It was almost impossible to continue with the play, because we couldn't hear ourselves speak. I was thoroughly enjoying myself. I felt I was getting my own back for his behaviour on the first night. I knew we should have brought Addo back for the second act, and judging by the sounds from the audience I wasn't alone. They began shuffling and coughing until we'd completely lost them by the curtain call.

Once Nicol knew I hadn't done it on purpose he warmed up a bit. He was a mysterious chap, such a mixture of contradictions, conflicting moods, emotions, and talent. It was partly because he pretended not to give a damn about anything – although he did hugely underneath – and partly because he appealed to the snob in me that I found myself, reluctantly at first, drawn to him. The early sixties were especially exciting times around the Royal Court Theatre. Not much to see with the naked eye, but the working-class revolution sent a buzz around Sloane Square that couldn't be ignored. Olivier had found it necessary to seek out the new kitchen-sink mode of drama, and I wanted to be part of it too. A couple of years earlier Robin had put me up for Arnold Wesker's *The Kitchen*. Before I went off to the audition, he warned, 'Pretend your father's a dustman or something.'

'Why?'

'Whatever you do, don't let them know you're a Roedean girl.' So off I went to audition, but even my nifty Cockney accent failed to pull their leg. I never gave up, though, and here I was finally with my toe in the door. Nicol was, of course, the embodiment of that intoxicating new wave.

'Why do you like me?' he asked one day.

'It's not you I like, it's your voice.' It was an honest

answer for he was blessed with a surprising singing voice. One evening he took me to the house of a friend who had a piano and there Nicol sang his way right through to my bones. Was I about to make Grandpa's fatal error? When he fell in love with Grandma he mistook her singing voice for her.

After his proposal, Willy, my choir of angels, and I gradually drifted further apart. I see now with hindsight that Nicol was my nest of demons. I let myself be wooed by his mellow singing voice. Such a magical sound that gradually it moved away from my ears, and down towards my heart, where it got tangled up with fashionable new-wave yearnings together with my inverted snobbery. A tangle so tight that it finally snapped the cord that had joined me to Willy/James so long and so lovingly.

CHAPTER SIXTEEN

I ADORED MY new home in Hasker Street, which nestled cosily between Walton Street and King's Road. It lifted my spirits to glimpse the comforting line of compact little houses, originally built in Georgian times for workmen and servants. I loved its position in the middle of a short, rarely used one-way street. Its chaotic hardware shop offered a veritable Aladdin's cave full to the brim with nineteenth-century smells; stuck in a time warp of genuine unpretentiousness it was quite out of place in poshest Chelsea, selling everything in the world except what I wanted.

Nicol had come to live with me because he had yet to find a flat of his own. I often wondered whether the discomfort I felt in living alone was due to the need for companionship, or from guilt at clattering about a three-storey house when so many people out there had nowhere. After our stint at the Royal Court, Nicol was never far from my side, content to focus all his energies – and formidable they were too – just on me. I found myself as bemused by his background as he was by mine, since everything I stood for was completely foreign to anything he'd known. To begin with, this ludicrously unsuited mixture of opposites created an undeniable frisson but though it paid dividends in the bedroom, it grew less effective elsewhere.

Our life was simple and uncluttered; I was as unsociable as ever, which was fine by Nicol since he too had no desire to mix with showbiz, the so-called establishment, or society. He was a surprisingly gentle lover, home-loving even to the point of making it up with Addo. But clichés aren't clichés for nothing and, like any other lovemaking, it could never reach its peak when he was pissed. Thankfully this was not commonplace during the first few months, so everything was as it should be with a new love – as long as I turned a blind eye to tantrums. Sadly these became more regular as the months passed and I found it disconcerting to be powerless while witnessing him either wrestling with his dark devils, who were hell bent on attacking the world, or encircled by angels, allowing him to be as soft and tender as a lamb, frequently even bordering on the sentimental. He was usually to be found in the kitchen in a striped apron, cooking some magnificent Scottish hotpot, spoiling me rotten – he was a great cook.

Given how much I'd loathed him during *Kelly's Eye* I often wondered, If he could change my mind so absolutely, perhaps I could tame that tempest of his? I don't try to change people any more – thank God! People only change for themselves, not for others. But I was young then, and didn't realize that I should have accepted Nicol for what he was rather than what I would have him be.

Nicol had some quaint habits. He must be the perfect expression of the term 'punch drunk': he'd have a few drinks, then go out and punch someone up. His knack for turning his mood round on a sixpence was scary. For no apparent reason he'd stop singing and abandon his apron and kitchen to get his fix of punch drunkenness, knowing that the power of his serenading would melt all doubts into forgiveness. He'd try winning me over with his hangdog-and-hard-done-by look. 'Can I take Addo for a walk for you?' he'd ask sheepishly.

Walking down a street with Nicol one day, pleasant weather, Addo heeling nicely, Nicol suddenly stops dead in his tracks. 'Did you hear what that man said?'

'Which man?' I could see no man.

'Him!' shouts Nicol, pointing to a couple holding hands quite far ahead. 'He was talking about me – I heard him!' Off he goes to accost the poor innocent stranger. An almighty row inevitably ensues in which Nicol decides to let him have it. Having thus battled and slain the mighty dragon, Nicol rubs his hands together and returns victorious. 'That'll teach him.'

On one memorable occasion, Nicol was walking up the street with Oliver, a good mate of his. Oliver had more reason than Nicol to be angry. When all's said and done Nicol was lucky. Because of his quicksilver temperament, his reputation as an actor could well have been in excess of his ability; also he lived free in a lovely house in Chelsea (with Addo and me!). Oliver, on the other hand, had a reputation for being that fine Irish actor with the mop of red hair. (Then out of the blue he got alopecia and every single hair fell from every part of his body – brows, eyelids included – never to return.) They were walking up Hasker Street one day when a builder, smoking a fag out of a top-floor window, saw them hand in hand and decided to comment to a mate, forgetting that the window was open. 'Look, Mick, a couple of poofters!'

Nicol looked up. 'I beg your pardon?' he said, arching his back for the oncoming battle. The builder backed away from the window, mumbling something like, 'I've got work to do.'

'I'll give you some more then.' Whereupon Nicol reached in the skip for a brick and threw it up at him. There was a mighty crack of broken glass.

The builder leaned out of the window.

'That'll cost yer, yer bastard! I want an apology – now!'

'You'll be lucky, old mate,' said Oliver, egging Nicol on.

'Apologize or—'

'Or what?' said Nicol, rolling up his sleeves. Even from my doorstep I could see that Nicol's complexion was changing to battle puce. I turned to enter the house. By now I had begun tiring of punch-ups; seen one, seen 'em all. Although I was still in adoring mode as far as the charming side of Nicol's character was concerned, I'd never had the slightest interest in the violence in him.

As I went inside I saw that Nicol had his usual audience. Most of Hasker Street's wives were on their doorsteps, taking a good sniff of imminent danger in the late-afternoon air, on the pretext of waiting for their husbands. The six o'clock rush was due back from the City, all stripes and bowler hats and armed with umbrellas at the ready for an Addo attack.

The builder was still leaning out of the window. 'You've broken this window, I want an apology.'

'Fuck off!' shouted Oliver.

'It's we who want the apology,' echoed Nicol.

'For the last time, I want an apology!' The builder was behaving quite well, I thought; his only mistake had been in calling them poofters. So what?

'Come down here and I'll whisper an apology in your shell-like ear,' said Nicol, rolling up his sleeves even further with the smell of blood in the air. When the builder finally appeared on the pavement he was the size of Arthur Askey. Nicol looked down at him and gave a great King-Kong-like laugh.

The builder looked up threateningly, stretching his neck backwards to stare Nicol dead in the eye. 'I'm giving you one last chance to apologize.'

King Kong found this hilarious. He and Oliver each put their hands on their knees and feigned a rather funny poofter 'quaking with fear'.

'OK. That's it,' said the builder. As he was getting his fists up, Nicol took a swing at him, but the builder was quicker, giving him a warning clout on the side of his head. Oliver made a run for it. Nicol, feeling the breeze of no back-up, panicked and lunged once more at the builder, who this time laid him flat. Housewives gasped as the blood ran from Nicol's face. They looked at me, as if I should do something. I had no choice but to drag him to the top of my steps, helped by a neighbour, where I threw a bucket of cold water over him.

Hasker Street, already past a point of no return with Addo's antics, now had Nicol's bloody battles to add to their ever so posh grievances. I wondered if he would start to punch people up at much the same rate that Addo humped them. Help! Addo was becoming so well known around London that taxi drivers occasionally brought him home in the evening. Imagine that happening nowadays! Addo gathered fervent admirers everywhere except in Hasker Street. But, then, one is never a prophet in one's own land. Coming from the High Pyrenees he didn't take kindly to being indoors, and had claimed the front doorstep as the rightful place from which to guard his domain. Restaurants all knew of Addo's good manners, for he promptly took up his position under the table. He was well trained, except for dry-cleaning fluid mixed with bowler hats and umbrellas. But we all have a penchant for something we shouldn't, do we not?.

One day with Addo off the lead I was walking through Debenhams. Maybe it was because we were progressing through the green carpets of the hat department, with many of the hats on stands, that I was reminded of the countryside and the Ingatestone Flower Show. Addo went up and smelt one of the hats. It was so ridiculous, with flowers, feathers, birds' nests almost, that even he did a double take.

As I walked on I heard a scream – the kind of scream ladies in movies made when discovering a murder. I turned to see a fearsome woman in navy blue beckoning me.

'Look what your dog has just done!' She pointed to the hat, slightly the worse for wear. A brief summer storm had drenched the flowers.

'It'll soon dry out,' I said, ever so sweetly.

'This hat's had it.' She was right, but I wasn't going to agree with her.

'I never saw my dog do it.' There was no other dog around, alas.

'We did,' said another even larger navy-blue frock, who had come sidling up.

'Addo never pees indoors, he just mistook all this for a real garden – can you blame him?'

'Yes, we can. That hat is worth forty-five pounds, it's a

designer model.' In the early sixties that was one hell of a lot of dough. But there was the price tag dangling before me with Addo's drippings, leaving me no choice but to pay up. As we left I put it where it belonged, on a skip.

Being so white Addo was oft times embarrassingly wary of its opposite. Late one black night we were walking home through Hyde Park, when I heard the clanking of a heavy dog chain. As it loomed eerily closer I noticed that the immediate area of the park was empty. Not till I heard a dog panting with excitement did I put Addo on the lead. The sound of confident laughter preceded a large black chap, who slid up beside me, right into my walking rhythm. Clank, clank goes his chain, straining to hold an equally big black German Shepherd. Finally he gibed, 'I saw you put your dog on the chain.' Why he found this so fiendishly funny was beyond me. I kept walking straight on, trying not to show the strain of holding Addo, who was chafing at his chain.

'Frightened ma dog eat him for breakfast, lady?' He kept this up for quite a while, inciting me to let Addo off the lead, and pissing his pants for some sort of confrontation. I was growing scared, and attempted to mask it by breathing as deeply as possible. 'You frighten your dog not fend for himself?'

I concentrated on my breathing and looked straight ahead as I marched on towards Knightsbridge barracks.

'You frightened ma dog kill white dog, eh?' He was close enough now for me to get a whiff of his breath. I tried to stay calm, but I didn't like where it was heading. The barracks were still too far away for comfort.

'Good night.' I smiled tightly, walking onwards as elegantly as possible. What a relief it was to pick out my cream Mini highlighted under a distant lamp-post. Just as I was thinking what a priggish Sloaney twat I must have looked, he leapt in front of me, blocking my view of the barracks lights.

'Stay here, lady, and let them fight.' His whisper festered with menace, and Addo was prancing at the prospects. To hell with it, I'll be safer with Addo loose, in case I need protection.

'OK.' I let Addo off his lead, he did likewise with his dog, and we watched them fight.

'Kill, Tiger! Kill!' What a nice chap he was. But not for long. Before I could say 'Black Robinson', Addo got a stranglehold on the German Shepherd, from his usual bear-hug-cum-humping position. It was a sight to behold, the ease with which Addo grounded his prey. But that's what they're used for in the Pyrenees – bear-killing.

'Get your fuckin' maniac off ma dog!'

I didn't. I just stood there watching him squealing.

'Get him off, woman, get him off!'

After long enough, I challenged him.

'Why?'

'He's gonna kill ma dog! Git him off!'

I let him squirm for a while longer before walking forward, grabbing Addo by the tail and hauling him off like a sack of potatoes. I put him back on the lead and headed for the barracks.

CHAPTER SEVENTEEN

I'D RECENTLY COMPLETED a television play by Jean Anouilh, *Ring Round the Moon*, with Keith Michell, to lovely reviews. My career was as healthy as it could be, considering I wouldn't go abroad, and lacked an overall vision, dreams, perhaps, but no steady solid ambition. Only later would this lack of sensible ambition become a problem. Meanwhile *The Servant* was still doing well, and Robin was still battling for me as an agent – upset though he was at Willy's and my parting. For that I was grateful.

Brother Chris had finished his two-year film course in Paris at IDHEC with flying colours. On his return to England, though, he found the lack of opportunities dire. In the early sixties you couldn't be a film director without a union card, and you couldn't get your union card without being a director. The industry was protecting its kind and closing its doors on new talent, but playing a waiting game didn't interest Chris. He decided to break a few rules. He had no choice: he could begin his career either illegally or not at all. He wrote a half-hour film, a pastiche, sending up how six different film directors would approach the same subject matter, wife and lover caught out unexpectedly by the husband. It gave the three actors involved a chance to play six different characters. The film was to be called *Six-Sided Triangle* and I was to be involved.

Chris found a stage in an advertising studio in Chancery Lane. We couldn't afford more than a five-day shoot, so each day we had to produce six minutes' worth of cut material. It was a tight schedule, but Chris and his team were well organized. He had plucked a real plum of a lighting-camera-man for doing documentaries for British Transport Films,

David Watkin, now one of the top lighting-cameramen in the world. If all went well, I was to play the wife, Nicol Williamson had offered to join our band of cheating players and was prepared to give us his daring lover, Bill Meiler, my husband, and Addo, the dog.

The Boulting brothers were supportive and said that if the film turned out well they would give us a distribution deal. Chris's future depended on this one week of risk. Mine, too, to a certain extent and that, perhaps, was why Robin Fox was adamant I shouldn't do it. 'As far as I can see, you're putting your newly acquired star status into a risky venture. Take my advice. Don't do it. It's an unwise career move.'

'How can it be unwise? I'd be playing six different FOs all within half an hour rather than trundle through a whole film playing just one.'

To hell with the right career move. I believed families were more important than careers, and for my brother to get his director's card was reason enough for me. My gut told me to commit myself to Chris's talent and the project. Besides, I loved a bit of a gamble, and it would be fun, like old family films. However, since Robin was so against it, I thought it best to talk it over with Lionel. We were between watering-holes, and, looking for somewhere more suitable for the same modest rent, had arrived at a seedy hotelette in Victoria, wearing equally seedy clothes. This time he was wearing a squalid little wig beneath his equally horrid trilby (fortunately no feather this time).

'Just for a giggle,' he said, producing a bottle of bubbly and smoked salmon. How I worshipped his capacity for wickedness.

'I'm not sure if I'm coming or going.' My sweet superman was working flat out at the National. How he summoned up even ten seconds' worth of energy to spend with his concubine was miraculous. But then his bad knee was giving him gyp and needed massaging.

'Do your brother's film. It'll be fun beating the system.'

'Is that why you still insist on playing this charade, so you can cock a snook at the system?'

He looked at me for a moment, then held me almost tighter than my heart could bear.

'Dame Sarah, if I'd met you one year earlier I wouldn't have had to beat the system at all. We'd be safe in each other's arms for good.' I felt it necessary to change the subject; my stiff upper lip was quivering.

'I think the chap at the desk recognized you.'

He brushed it aside like a flea.

'What utter nonsense!'

It always took a moment for us to peel away – how succinctly he'd peel – our personalities from the disguises – the protection from the brutal outer world and place them, as gently as possible into the inner womb of our brief eternity. Finally unwrapped and vulnerable, we evaporated into our lighter selves, softly drifting along ceilings of silken turquoise rainbows. From up there ceiling bound, I couldn't help but notice the sadness of the room beneath. I couldn't help but spy the clues of our deceit. I wish I hadn't looked down. Which was real? Our disguises or our lovemaking? Weren't those disguises there to ground me in reality? How absurdly forlorn and temporary they looked, hanging empty, slumped over the chair . . . Which was which, who was who? What was the truth and where were the lies? On the ceiling? Or were they there, hanging over the chair? Either way Lionel was right, this illicit pantomime sneaking had an edge that lifted us higher than ever. Finally, with the gravity found in gratification, we thudded back to earth, and later, much later, we began putting on our lies, our disguises once more.

Lionel spoke frequently about the sadness of life's timing. Timing was always on his mind. He had mastered the timing of both his craft and leadership, but often felt he'd missed out on the ultimate goal. 'Great sorrow can block the antennae, leaving you unaware of some of the deeper timings of destiny.'

The most spiritual of men underneath all the periphery of ambition, he reminded me continually of Daddy. Why is it that so many brilliant people pretend to be less spiritual than they really are? Are they frightened that their spirituality might make a mockery of their intellect? I think we clamp down on these major 'somethings' because society being riddled with fear dictates that we should. Though not brilliant, I was no better at that time. I was blocking out all childhood understanding of an overall great 'something' to which I was linked. In fact, so unreligious was I that Lionel called me his little heathen. His spiritual philosophy seemed more inclined towards reincarnation than Heaven and Hell, though this, he being a vicar's son, was always whispered, as if his father might be listening. Sometimes he'd seem a normal church-going Christian, the chameleon again, changing philosophy to suit the moment. Because his mother died when he was around twelve, a vital nurturing love was missing. There were times when the great loss he still felt, not only for his mother but for Vivien too, wrenched him violently away into atheism with a cruel and an unresolved loneliness.

Once again firmly grounded in the illusion of reality, we lay in a sadness that planted the seldom random kiss, intermingled with fiery fingertips gently stroking me (his tickling was coming on a treat). We fixed our eyes on the curled wallpaper puckering in the corner, with dappled shafts of evening sun, too damn low for my liking, nudging us that time was up. These thoughts of mine were always echoed by my dreaded thunderous rumblings.

'Your poor tummy. The parting siren.' The silence became too heavy. 'If your brother's film gives you a chance to be funny, take it. My chameleon needs to shine a little. But don't *try* and be funny.'

'How d'you mean?'

He told me a story about the famous American acting couple, the Lunts. 'They were doing a comedy on Broadway and each night Lynn got the biggest, surest, most robust laugh of the night when she asked Alfred for a cup of tea in the second act. For months it brought the house down. Then one night she came to that "would you like a cup of tea" line and there was hardly a titter. Perhaps it was a one-off, she thought, forcing herself not to worry as she dressed to go home. Tomorrow I'll get my laugh back.

So secure was she in the prospect of recapturing her laugh that she decided not to mention it to Alfred. Tomorrow night came and the next night, and the night after that, but her biggest laugh had gone for good. So, disillusioned, humbled and defeated, she had no choice but to share her anxiety with Alfred.

'Darling, you know in Act Two when I ask you if you want a cup of tea? Well, Alfred, I'm not getting my laugh any more.'

'I know, my sweet. That's because you're asking for a laugh and not a cup of tea.'

Lionel looked at his watch. 'I'd better be off.' It was Laurence Olivier who turned at the door before giving me a camp Archie Rice half-exit.

'Toodle-oo.' But who was I saying goodbye to? Sir Laurence, Larry, Lionel Kerr, King Richard the Lionheart, Heathcliff, Archie Rice, Hamlet, all the archetypes, or Mr No-man All-things? Chameleons linger when saying goodbye because their mouths fit so well together. I watched him walking briskly along the corridor to the rhythm of doubt fairly clattering in my brain. He'd never risk these tender trysts of ours once he was a lord, surely? But, then, wasn't he already risking everything *before* he was a lord?

While putting on my disguise to go out into the other life, I felt the familiar and welcomed warmth of knowing that the implicit trust we shared was bound to endure, even if I never saw him again. It had always been there between us from the very beginning, for we never spoke of 'not telling anyone', it was simply never on the agenda.

Years later, naively, perhaps even foolishly, I found

myself suggesting that Olivier write his own book, rather than have Kenneth Tynan write it for him. It seemed a good idea because their rows were becoming so raw that I didn't see why he should continue torturing himself thus. 'I can't write my own book,' he grumbled like a fifth-former over Latin prep.

'Of course you can – judging by your love letters.'

'They're different.'

'If *you* can't write a book, how come you insist I write a book about us?'

He'd continued to nudge me, reminding me to write about us when he died, for he was quite proud of our secret.

'I know Dame Sarah can write.' With that knowledge firmly intact, he left all the rest to me. He took my advice (but not mine alone, I hope) and wrote his own autobiography.

'Yes. I will write my autobiography,' he said, 'but I'll not mention you once.' He touched me on my special place. 'I'd be bound to give away the whole shooting match.' (He would've, too. And that's how we left it. That's what we did.)

CHAPTER EIGHTEEN

·

I BEGAN TO compare Lionel with Nicol; a dangerous occupation. Inevitably, tension in Hasker Street began to mount, so before everything turned poisonous I decided to take Nicol and Addo, my two bloodstained warriors, to Shag Rock, our holiday home down in Cornwall. It would clear the air, and give the occupants of Hasker Street well-deserved respite.

I rang up to ask Mother if I could go down for ten days or so. 'Not without a chaperone.'

I couldn't believe what I was hearing.

'Mother, I'm twenty-one years old – and still alive!'

She decided to ignore that. (Mother always warned me I'd be dead before I reached twenty-one.) 'We've already told them all down there that Willy was your fiancé, so you can't be seen in Port Looe with another man on your arm so soon. You'll seem a loose woman to them, and that's not good for the family name. So I'll come too, just to make it all seem above board.'

Mother hadn't met Nicol until that moment in the kitchen at Shag Rock the following weekend. She was polite to him, and to begin with Nicol was charming to her. But as the evening wore on, Nicol allowed the maudlin and cantankerous side of his nature to emerge – a tedious state of affairs, and sadly common among drinkers. Mother sat there stiff as a board while Nicol meandered on and on about his childhood. It might have been riveting, but neither Mother nor I could follow his inebriated gist. As soon as she could, Mother excused herself.

'Well, Nicol, it's my bedtime. Goodnight.'

Up in her room that night, she sat at her dressing table

brushing her hair right over her face. She had been brushing her hair that way since I could remember. It was certainly effective, giving her still glorious blonde hair extra bounce, fullness and gloss.

'I'm off home tomorrow.'

I didn't want Mother to go. I don't know why, but I didn't.

'What about my reputation?'

She gave me a bit of a look before getting into bed. Turning on her side to switch off the light, she said, 'Your reputation will have to fend for itself.'

Mother kept her word. From the window of her car, as I ran to keep up, she gave me instructions for Clarence, the gardener, and Olga, the daily help. Before finally shooting off up the cart-track she made some gesture with her hand against her face. Was she blowing me a kiss or blowing my brains out?

I didn't have to blow out my brains because Nicol was as good as gold for the next few days. Then Chris telephoned to say he'd got the money for *Six-Sided Triangle*, so we were off back to London to get our costumes sorted out.

Nicol wanted to be a movie star (what actor didn't?), though usually he kept this tucked well away. When I was on the phone with Robin sometimes I saw hints of dissatisfaction, which often ended with him openly begrudging me being one. I didn't see myself like that. To shine as a movie star you must believe you *are* a movie star and I didn't. Neither was I impressed with anything I'd done – yet.

With his show finally on the road, Chris was most impressive as an organizer, sliding into the director/producer shoes with ease. It's a great feeling, respecting the director, especially when he's your brother and appears to be just as popular with everyone else. The five days of filming would have gone well throughout if it hadn't been for Nicol not tipping up on the third day, with no explanation. It was the Margaret Lockwood/Michael Wilding type of Ealing comedy sketch (the only one with Addo in it). I think it was because he couldn't take having to compete with Addo.

Six-Sided Triangle got its Boulting release and was a huge success. It was nominated for an Oscar in the Best Short Film category and was shown all over the place. Alas, Robin wasn't interested in the film deal, having warned me off the project, and since I've never been able to understand money, I lost out. I chose two hundred pounds up-front rather than a slice of the profits – entirely my fault.

Addo and I clinched another job, *Those Magnificent Men In Their Flying Machines* (stick close to Addo and I'd be fine). Ken Annekin, the director, had seen a rough cut of *Six-Sided Triangle*, and was impressed enough to give me the lead.

Nicol, eager only to accept the best, wasn't getting the roles he wanted, or indeed deserved. Olivier thought he was an actor of spectacular ability, but was wary of Nicol's inability to work within a team. I naturally didn't repeat this in so many words, but tried to warn Nicol that he should change his attitude. This, added to my being offered *Magnificent Men*, with Willy Fox playing opposite me, ignited his rage to such a degree that I knew it had to be diverted. Fortunately Nicol had fallen in love with Cornwall, and since I had nothing to lose (now being known there anyway as the fallen woman) it seemed a good idea to return to more inconspicuous pastures.

Two miles from Shag Rock, in the village of Veryan, there was a great old pub with a piano. The publican heard Nicol singing there at lunchtime and asked him if he would like to entertain one night. Nicol jumped at this opportunity. What followed was a revelation.

Each night Nicol sang, and each night the pub filled up a bit more. He was the genuine article, blossoming into the gentlest of Pied Pipers, and mesmerizing all around him with his talent. Oh, to have that ability! To open your throat with such ease and let your sound come tumbling out. The whole village, having found its voice, joined in in one massively heart-lifting sing-song.

Why did those magnificent highs we experienced nightly in the pub have to be complemented with depleting lows? After the pub closed and we drove back to Shag Rock I found myself becoming scared as my Pied Piper disintegrated before my eyes. Why did Nicol want to be a movie star when he could sing like that? If I'd had the maturity to think about it properly, I would have understood something Nicol himself didn't comprehend or was unable to communicate. He wanted to sing, more than anything in the world, but didn't know how to harness his unique and awesome power. How ironic. Both of us wanting to sing more than anything else, and him with everything and me with nothing.

One day Nicol wanted me to get all dressed up. He wouldn't tell me why, only that it was a secret. He was looking particularly beguiling; all spick and span, oozing confidence and kindness. These moments, being so few and far between, were worth hanging on to, so, even though I loathed dressing up as much as ever, I acquiesced. Once he had me looking sufficiently presentable he ordered me into the car. (He couldn't drive properly yet. I was teaching him, that's probably why.) Off we went down to Veryan, and into the church. Nicol had set up a meeting with the local vicar. I didn't know what they discussed because I wouldn't go into the church. He never mentioned marriage in so many words, so I presumed he was merely testing the waters.

Another time, he mumbled into his glass, 'You won't marry me because I'm working class.'

'That's the only reason why I'm with you, you fool!' He didn't get it even then – neither did he question it, but went bumbling on. 'Want to remain a mistress for the rest of your days, when I'm here wanting to make an honest woman of you?' If he was as angry as this about not tying the knot, what if I told him about Lionel?

Things went from bad to worse. Nicol egged me on one day to do some water-skiing at the beach. Having never water-skied in my life I declined, not wanting to look an idiot in front of him.

'You go first,' I said. Let him be the first fool.

'I'll give you two quid if you stand up for ten seconds.' That two quid (quite a lot in those days) was enough incentive. And by now making a fool of myself was second nature. I listened to the speedboat chap's instructions, waved to Nicol who was sitting on the beach, and off we went.

I stayed up. Up and up I stayed. This was a piece of cake, I thought. It was miraculous! After about a minute I looked over to where Nicol was sitting. He'd gone. The bastard! Even then I didn't fall. For some reason I just stayed up. That first water-skiing day I was able not only to stay up but come to a halt standing on the sand.

I found Nicol up the beach; he was about to hand me an Italian ice cream.

'Why the hell did you go off?'

He looked at me with his baby-blue eyes. 'Go off where?'

He was going to play games. I'd be wasting my time doing a, why-didn't-you-stay-to-watch-me? routine. Hopeless to continue down that snake-infested path. 'It was your idea, not mine, remember that.'

'What idea was that?' he said, licking a hole in his chocolate ice.

I woke up one morning to find Olga knocking on my bedroom door. She was one of those elderly virgins, mistrusting anything remotely sensual or loving. Although she knew nothing of the world, never having been out of the village, let alone Cornwall, she knew everything. She knew clearly enough that old age was setting in and that somewhere along the way she'd missed out. This being so she had a tendency to look unkindly on my own goings-on.

'Miss Sarah, I'm sorry to bother you but your friend . . .

or is he your fiancé? Your Mr Williamson is all curled up on the lawn.'

'Maybe he's sunbathing.' Olga drew the curtains on another rainy day and, sure enough, there was Nicol all curled up, soaked to the skin. She gave me one of her specials: a withering look from the corner of her witch-like Cornish eye.

'Just take no notice of him, Olga.'

'The thing is, Miss Sarah, I went out to offer him a cup of tea, and he asked me to tell you that he's very ill.'

'He's all right, Olga, he's only dying of cancer.'

She gave me another of her searing looks. 'I've had a friend who died of cancer and she never lay on the lawn like that.' Olga picked up my socks, while giving Nicol another moment's contemplation. 'Maybe she'd still be alive today if she'd laid on the grass like that.'

'It's more the London way,' I said lamely. Olga, my Mrs Danvers, gave me one more reprimanding look before retreating to her domain.

I felt irritated. Probably a bit guilty, too, for I had a feeling Nicol was performing his dying-of-cancer farce because I had made him sleep in the spare room. But why should I feel guilty? I'd made it perfectly clear from day one of our relationship that I would not sleep with anyone who was drunk. He'd have to raise his life act to meet his pub act. However, Nicol stayed on the lawn for three days (except for his pub performances).

On the fourth evening he became violent (though he never harmed me), and when I asked him to sleep in the spare room the ensuing racket of objects smashing resounded around the house. A saint would have asked Nicol to return to the maiden's chamber, but I was no saint. The ultimate in house-proud, Mother wouldn't have taken kindly to the spare room being broken into pieces. She had some excellent antiques, two of which were in the spare room, so when I heard the mirror crash I knew I had to do something. I went to the door and banged on it. The raging continued.

'Give over, Nicol – grow up!'

'Fuck off!'

I remembered it was possible to crawl out of the bathroom window and into the spare bedroom via the roof. As it was a pretty safe journey, I decided to go for it. I had to stop him before there was nothing left. I crept out along the side of the roof, clinging to the bathroom window-frame. With an effort I was able to grab the frame of the bedroom window and haul myself in before he saw me. As I secured my footing inside the window, he turned and saw me. 'I said fuck off, woman!'

An enormous ego such as his, combined with fury, is a veritable time bomb. Losing all sense of what *he* was doing, Nicol charged at me like a raging bull. I fell backwards out of the window and went on a journey at some speed down the roof. Thank God for gutters, for without them I wouldn't be here to tell the tale. And only God knows how I managed accidentally to wedge my plimsoll in that gutter. Although it didn't save me, it broke my fall enough for me to grab the gutter. Which would cave in first, the gutter or my fingers? I also remember thinking how lucky I was to be an experienced tree-climber.

As I hung there miles from the ground and miles from the spare room, I looked up to see what Nicol was doing about my attempted murder. Even worse than committing murder, surely, is not checking to see if your victim's dead? There was no sign of him. He didn't even come to the window. As I looked down at the gravel far below, a great sadness crept up through me. Evidently he hated me more than I knew. I waited there a few moments longer, hoping that Nicol would come first to his senses and then to my rescue. He didn't, so I had to close my eyes and surrender to my fate. Thanks to a childhood not only of tree-climbing but falling off horses, diving and generally mucking about doing physical stuff, I'd had my share of practice landings. I landed, then got up and brushed myself off with a twisted ankle to show for it. I knew of Nicol's personal agony, a pain stronger than childhood memories, deeper even than an obvious lack of nurture. But I'd come to the resolution that my days as Florence Nightingale were over. (How wrong I was!)

At this thought, something shifted in me. Freedom came galloping up, stamping out and flattening the last glowing embers of passion. Sad, though, all the same, that moment when love dies. I'd hung in with Nicol because deep within him I knew there was a man worth pulling for, beautiful as the talent itself. But now all my pulling power was used up. I had failed to pull off the veil covering Nicol's lost self. Half-hearted as my attempts might have been, I never blamed him for what he did that day, and told no one apart from my family. How could I blame him when perhaps I was the villain, my heart in two places at once?

From the moment Lionel and I began our secret assignations, everything that went wrong for me was due to that damned double life of mine. Mother was right, loving two men at the same time had been bound to leave a trail of chaos. I decided that was it. Back to healthy Hasker Street's pure Chelsea air.

CHAPTER NINETEEN

URING THE FILMING of *Those Magnificent Men*, in late
spring 1964, Addo looked stunning as he galloped
beside me on my motorbike, totally at home with
his newly acquired star status. (The truth is, it was getting
too expensive waiting to get Addo *out* of shot and, time being
money, Ken Annekin gave up and let him stay by my side –
in shot.)

What a wonderful cast of comedians there was in that
film. And there was I topping the bill for merely being the
Fuckable Object. Almost everyone had some funny moments.
In my only comic bit, with Stuart Whitman (being the love
interest he got no funny lines either), Stuart is down on the
ground all grimy while doing something butch like mending
a biplane's engine, when my skirt gets caught in something
mechanical and – surprise, surprise – off it comes. Hard to
make that funny, and to make it even sadder I promptly
looked up to heaven and there was Lionel wagging his finger
at me! 'You're asking for a laugh and not a cup of tea!' I was
infuriated at being told that for insurance reasons the actors
were forbidden to go up in those glorious 1909 flying
machines. Before wistfulness turned to envy through watching the comedians doing their funny bits, I went to seek out
the French pilot (the only woman), whose biplane was by far
the prettiest. If I could just get her to take me up in her
biplane, for a moment or two I could forget all my frustrations
and be a flying object rather than a fuckable one.

'Hello!' I made it as warm and friendly as I could. It was a
pleasant day and she was strutting confidently about on the
wing. Most attractive she was, petite with glossy black hair.
'How come you're the only woman pilot?'

She gave an enchanting shrug. 'Usually women are not so stupid.' I do see why the French accent is so appealing – all that pouting.

Having exchanged names I thought it perfect timing to sidle up to the point. 'Would you kindly take me up?'

'Not unless you have special permission.'

'Oh, I have very special permission, that's why I'm asking you.'

She looked embarrassed, as if she should have known that I'd got the most special permission there was to get, being all dressed up in an Osbert Lancaster original. 'Hold on a moment.' She clambered off the wing, most elegantly I thought, changed jackets, put on a strange helmet, gave me one too, then opened the passenger seat for me. Though I wanted to check the time, doing so might have made it look as if I was playing hookey (which I was). I only prayed the current scene was taking a long time, because I was on next.

What a thrill to be up in the blue sky in a primitive wooden biplane. We were flying over the Chilterns. They must be the purest essence of picture-postcard Englishness that you're ever likely to see. The view just took my patriotic breath away. Beneath me lay the nooky little village of Turville, nestling between two hills, smooth and green with clumps of trees clothing their crevices. A sturdy windmill stood protectively on the hilltop.

'Can you fly lower? I want to see if there's a house down there.'

The biplane swooped quite suddenly and my stomach went blasting through my head. She hadn't flown lower, she'd just dropped. When I retrieved my stomach I spied with my greedy little eye, nestling in among some chestnut trees, a Chekhovian, battered Gothic rectory. My heart went ping. My dream house. Somehow, sometime I would earn enough money to buy that rectory. Everything was turning out perfectly timed, for my list of dreams was gradually coming true. My country retreat and a kennel/conservatory

were next. Must get a conservatory for Addo before I'm
finally booted out of Hasker Street, and I feared that time was
imminent. Yet I had a great deal of saving up to do if I were
ever remotely likely to afford that rectory, especially since
any hopes of sharing a country home seemed out of the
question. Just imagine living in that Shangri-la with No-man
All-things . . . I shooshed all such thoughts away.

The wind forbade me to talk too much to my pilot *en*
flight, more's the pity, but returning over the airfield I
suddenly heard one loud clear voice.

'Please land immediately!'

Was God talking to me?

No, the first assistant with a loudspeaker. 'Artists flying
the biplanes is forbidden.' My delicious French pilot was truly
upset.

'You very bad! No permission, eh? Terrible trouble
coming!'

It all turned out just fine, for I made sure everyone knew
I'd taken her up under false pretences. Having cleared her
name, all that lingered was the memory. Christ, the importance of building a life full of good memories. It's like filling
up the petrol tank for the great journey Home. The way my
heart soared that day adds up to a hell of a lot of gallons'
worth of juice for that ultimate exit.

Those Magnificent Men In Their Flying Machines was great
fun to make. Among all its immortal comedians, in the role
of my father was Robert Morley, another of God's innocents
simply littered with twinkles and someone I knew well and
loved greatly. But if the truth be known I found it heartbreaking to play the part of Willy's fiancée. Whenever we caught
sight of each other we smiled wistfully, inwardly sighing
regrets. If I hadn't still been in love with Lionel, I would have
longed to become Willy's wife. How mutually ecstatic we'd
have been, nestling up in those undulating Chilterns.

My antennae didn't let me down, but my timing did:
Hasker Street signed a petition wanting Addo chained up in

my back garden (patio). If not we had to leave within three months. I thought this absolutely rotten news. If Addo had been ferocious I would have understood, but except for lusting after cleaning fluid and window-cleaners, he'd never put a foot wrong. Without the wherewithal to contest the petition I began racking my brain as to where we could go. It would have to be a country cottage, I supposed, because my Chiltern dream rectory was financially well out of reach. How could I hold up my head coming home to Addo, knowing he was chained up in a dark, smelly patio? Simply too cruel after almost two years of front-doorstep heaven.

One morning I looked out of the drawing-room window to see Addo walking up Hasker Street side by side with an old man in carpet slippers. They were so deep in conversation that I thought I'd leave them to it. As the summer drifted on I saw them walking together regularly. Off they'd set on their meander in harmless rhythmic contemplation.

One warm afternoon, I opened the drawing-room windows to let out the heat when I saw the old man, still in carpet slippers, sitting on the doorstep basking in the sunshine. He and Addo were locked in silence as if mutually having discovered the secrets of the universe; then the sound of my opening window broke the magic spell. He turned around to meet my eyes, and in that instant I knew he was a flirt. It's funny how one recognizes flirtatiousness immediately. Age, colour, creed or sex has nothing to do with it. There it was, bubbling up in a man old enough to be my great-grandfather – and a most mischievous-looking great-grandfather at that.

'What a day we're having!'

'Splendid. You and Addo certainly hit it off.'

'We have . . . how shall I put it? . . . an affiliation.'

For a few moments all three of us let our minds drift silently through the afternoon's Indian-summer mellowness.

'Care to come over one afternoon for tea?' he said with a hint of challenge.

I still hadn't got used to tea-drinking, but I didn't want to hurt his feelings; afer all, he was getting on a bit. 'I'd love to.'

No sooner had I said the words when he punched back in with 'When?' and he meant just that.

'When?' I said, repeating it to gain time, but no time allowed.

'Yes. When?'

'At the moment I'm here most of the time.'

'Good, tomorrow afternoon. Five o'clock.' He bade his adieux to Addo, rose and crossed the road without looking back. I could feel his mischief brewing up even from across the street.

I was knocking on the door with Addo at my side exactly at five. I like being punctual. Maybe unruly, spoilt, clumsy, obstreperous, rude sometimes, but always (almost always!) punctual.

'Right on the dot. I am impressed.' His eyes dazzled with a friendly foxiness. 'Come on in and make yourself at home.'

It was a fascinating house. Just like I longed for mine to look like one day. Ancient furniture tossed elegantly into corners speckled with dust. Faded elegance fraying at those edges where curtains and carpets became too well acquainted. As I sat down to observe this delightfully tasty mayhem, my chair wobbled over.

He came to my rescue. 'Sorry, we're all a bit dilapidated in here.' He gave me another equally lopsided chair.

I watched him go through into another room – perhaps it was the kitchen. I didn't want to follow immediately. So much to take in, so many pictures, pots, and furniture and a mass of books. I guessed he came from some fine, ancient-blooded family, more brains than money probably, well educated, Bohemian tendencies.

'Don't leave me to make tea all on my own!' came a cry from the kitchen.

He was in profile at the far end as I entered and a shaft of sunlight opened from the sky, spotlighting his silky silver hair. Holding his head sideways, he reminded me of a remarkably alert mottled hawk, scrutinizing my every move. He cut the crust from a brown loaf on a wooden board. Beside him was a cucumber. 'I trust you'll take cucumber sandwiches with your tea?' His concentration was already back on the loaf, whereupon he held one piece up to the light, that rich pinky-golden light of an early autumn evening.

'Each slice has to be paper thin, enough to see daylight through.' He placed his hand between it and the window. You could detect a shadow, but from his sigh it obviously wasn't sufficiently thin.

'Hopeless.' He threw it into the bin, and then almost tried to catch it back as his thoughts moved on. 'Mustn't give it to the dustbin when Addo's here to mop up. Addo!'

Addo plodded in from the drawing room.

'Here.' Addo smelt the bread, looked at the old man as if to say, 'You're joking, I'm a red meat man,' and wandered back into the drawing room.

The old man was still at it. Slicing the bread, holding it up to the light and chucking it in the bin. We hadn't even introduced ourselves . . . or had we? Of course we hadn't, for we met through Addo, and Addo had forgotten to tell us who we were. I was curious. 'What's your name?'

'Someone told me you were a film star, yet I don't need to know your name.'

I'd like to have introduced my new Mr No-man to Mr No-man All-things, I think they would have got on great guns. Paper thin, he was, as he bent over his task, so determined to achieve the same in his sandwiches. On and on he tried, concentrating all the way.

The buttering was coming next. I could never butter thin bread without tearing it and told him so.

'Ha! It's all in the butter texture.' He made a gesture and fetched the butter which he'd left to soften in a sunbeam. 'Easy when you know how.' He beckoned me with the knife. 'Come nearer and watch.' There was something about him, a zest for life that so resembled Lionel – Father too, come to that. It was obvious he had his butter-spreading down to a fine art. He waved the cucumber in my direction.

'No fun to be had in a mean sandwich.' He gave me a look as if we were talking about much more private things. Dirty old man, I thought. 'Essential that everything be paper thin except the quantity.' Looking up at my breasts. 'Now for the cucumber. Here again there must be plenty of daylight.' He repeated the gesture with his hand between the slice and the light. Out of a whole medium-size brown loaf, only six slices had managed to pass the sunlight test, but it was different with the cucumber. On he went with the sunlight test. Each sandwich had to be healthily chubby, with equal amounts of cucumber in each.

'Ample. Three sandwiches each,' I said soothingly.

'Incorrect.' He was obviously no mathematician. He piled the great fat thin sandwiches on top of each other, and sliced twice through the lot of them diagonally with great aplomb.

'Six each.' Couldn't argue with that. He placed his finished masterpieces into a porcelain peacock dish along with matching tea-set on a silver tray. Such passion for detail gave me insight into how civilized the ritual of English afternoon tea can be.

I liked this unknown old-timer a lot, and not just because of his friendship with Addo. I think he took a shine to me, too, because he kept squeezing my knee under the table – not half-heartedly either. Robin Fox often called me Olive Oyl and, knowing my luck, the cucumber would probably turn into spinach, and with a flex of his muscles this pensioner would rematerialize as a randy Popeye. Fortunately I had protection – Addo was still snoring under the table. We made mostly small talk. He managed to ask all the questions, so I came away knowing nothing about him at all.

Next teatime was a week later. Again he asked all the questions. I realized that this was his way of distracting my attention, because while I was thinking up the answers he took many an opportunity to give my knee a nip, a tweak, or two or three. How does one tell a graceful old chap of ninety to leave off? It all seemed too lowering, so I let him get on with it. But only so far, you understand – besides, now I was a little wiser.

'I never knew you were Bertrand Russell.'

'You never asked.'

I wish I'd known who he was earlier, for even though I wasn't overly informed on why his name tolled such an impressive bell, he could, nevertheless, be a great influence on the Addo/Hasker Street petition. I wondered if he'd signed it yet. Looking as innocent as I could (not too bad, actually), 'Addo and I have to go away.'

'Go away?' His hawk-like noble head drooped in sadness, which touched me greatly.

'Did you sign the Hasker Street petition regarding Addo?'

'I live in Wales most of the time. I must have missed it.' I told him about my need to find a place in the country because of Hasker Street wanting Addo out.

'What utter nonsense, Addo wouldn't hurt a fly.'

'Tell them that, will you?' Stroking my knee was one thing, but my thigh . . .

'Worry not. Consider it done.' I don't know what action Bertie took, if any, but I never heard a peep from anyone in Hasker Street after that. Addo slept peacefully on the front doorstep and I let sleeping dogs lie.

CHAPTER TWENTY

O<small>UT OF THE</small> blue one morning in late October, there came a knock on the door. On opening it I found a girl I hadn't seen since RADA. I was quite taken aback, so frail and battered was she – just like her suitcase.

'Hello, Sarah, I'm Nona. Do you remember me?'

'Of course I do.' But a strained cobweb of her former self. If it wasn't for her amazing Pre-Raphaelite head of silky hair, I would never have recognized her. In the RADA canteen I'd spent many a half-hour whiling away my time *wishting* for hair like Nona's. *Wishting* is different from wishing. *Wishing* is the energy that I put out on dreams that *can* be realized. And *wishting* is wasting precious time and effort on dreams that cannot possibly *ever* come true. Nona was never one of my RADA gang, so except from *wishting* for her hair across a crowded canteen, I hardly knew her.

'I read about your lovely house in a magazine. It looks just as lovely in real life.' She peered in past me, giving me little excuse not to ask her in. Something told me I shouldn't and to stand firm. The sight of me blocking her from entering bothered her not a whit. She sailed straight on.

'I've been receiving shock treatment in a mental hospital.' I didn't know what shock treatment was, or how to respond, so I didn't. 'I can't take it any more, it's destroying me both physically and mentally.'

My heart still wasn't opening up to her, I couldn't think why.

'I'm very sorry, Nona, but—'

'All I need do is to give them the name and address of where I'll be so they can check up on me.'

Everything went numb.

'What do you mean?'

She repeated it all as if I was deaf. 'If they know where I'm staying I can leave the psychiatric hospital. Imagine, no more shock treatment ever again.'

'Haven't you got any relations, family, to stay with?'

'No, none at all.' Silence. In she came, barging past me into the drawing room.

'Nona, I have nowhere for you to stay.'

'Who's living here, then?'

'Well, it's all a bit difficult right now.' Of course! That's why I didn't want her here. Lionel! The house had been empty apart from Addo and me since Nicol left, so Lionel could come round when he had a couple of hours to himself. I couldn't tell Nona that I needed the space for my double life. The thought of this ex-RADA student, someone I only vaguely knew, living in my house and coming between us was a grotesque nightmare. Besides, I wanted no one but me picking up his calls. The desire to manhandle her back along the passage and close the door in her face was intense. Why, oh, why didn't I?

Nona knew what she wanted. She almost pushed by me as she made her way down to the basement, which consisted of the kitchen, dining room, cloakroom and garden room where her nose was already poking its way in.

'This is all I want. This'll do me fine.' She went upstairs to fetch her suitcase. Nona spoke English with a capital E. All very pleasant, plummy and perfect. Even through a tendency to whisper, she managed to round off her vowels with great precision. Down she came again, full of fresh hope which I hadn't the guts to trample.

She hauled me to the psychiatric hospital to let them see that all was above board. When I met Sister I was about to tell her I wasn't ready to take home a mental patient, not yet being sure of those mad/sane boundaries myself. Suddenly I heard a scream. It came straight out of a horror movie, but in the flesh it sounded like someone's soul being ripped away from their heart.

'What's that dreadful noise?'

'It's Belinda having shock treatment,' said Nona knowingly.

'Nonsense,' said Sister. As she escorted us to the exit, I got the definite feeling that she was in a hurry to get rid of me. 'Think of it, Nona, you need never have it again.' She patted Nona and stroked her infinitely strokable hair. 'Make sure she stays on her medication.'

I turned around to see who she was talking to. I was right about one thing: she obviously wanted to get rid of Nona.

Nona had won. Once she was ensconced in the damp but passable garden room, she went into a swift decline. In those days I hadn't a clue about madness, drugs, pills, so her attacks of manic depression left me baffled. All I managed to work out was that when Nona was happy all she wanted to do was fuck, and when her dark spells fell on her all she wanted to do was sleep. The sleeping part was no problem (till later) but when her ravenous fucking moods came upon her, life got a little tricky. Nona's lovers made an odd assortment. Half-broken men all colours of the rainbow stumbling down the half-broken cellar steps, groping their way through the kitchen and into her love nest.

One night I was dreaming that curtains of silky hair were brushing across my cheek. It wasn't a dream but Nona. Shame, because under different circumstances the sensation could have been a real turn-on.

'Lionel rang yesterday while you were out.' I kept my eyes closed and didn't move.

'Thanks, Nona.'

'Who is Lionel Kerr?' She was leaning over me, making a minky wigwam out of her hair, with me and her breasts inside. I remained silent and still. 'I'm not leaving till you tell me.'

'No one you know.' Nothing had changed between Nona and me. She still gave me the creeps and I still wanted her out. Difficult to contemplate, chucking her out, encased as I was in her wigwam with nothing but my absolute favourites, silky hair and breasts, but I was far from tempted. Things were getting dangerous.

How was I to get her out without shock treatment, suicide or her discovery of my secret love? I didn't trust her. *Why* had I allowed her to barge into my home? It must have been guilt. Guilt at living in a whole house on my own? I had always avoided it at RADA by living on everyone else's floor. Was I avoiding it still, by renaming it compassion for the homeless? Probably a bit of both.

Nona had sussed something was fishy, that was for sure. How much did she know?

'*Who* is Lionel Kerr?' Her breasts wobbled with stubborn curiosity.

'None of your business – Nona, please leave.' If I pulled away she'd think I was anxious, so I remained still, until she dropped her next bombshell.

'I was in love with you at RADA.' I knew that, I wasn't a fool. She was forever staring at me from the other side of the canteen, her gaze clinging to me as I left. That's why I thought I'd try and be kind, mention her hair or her periwinkle eyes in passing. No need to hurt her feelings as well as keeping my distance. 'I still am.' This was my first excuse to remove myself from the wigwam. I climbed out of bed and would have put on my dressing gown, if I'd got one – the towel had to do.

'It's wasted energy and all the more reason why you should leave immediately.'

'I'm not leaving.' Her robust stubbornness was only equalled by her robust buxomness. Having eaten me out of house and home her frail cobweb days were over.

'Oh, yes, you are.' I went over to her and led her swiftly towards the landing, where I said as firmly as I knew how,

'Nona. This can't go on. You have to find somewhere to live. You can stay here till you do, as long as you're gone within three months. Goodnight.'

'Who is Lionel Kerr?'

I was convinced she knew something, but how much? My terror of being blackmailed was, like all who are guilty, at the forefront of my mind. It mattered tremendously that Olivier and I shouldn't be found out. It was my only hope of keeping my head above the shame. 'A friend who is going to Brazil to live, and I shall miss him.'

She turned to walk to the stairs, then turned back. 'I shall miss him too.' I closed the door, sleeping not a wink that night. No fool, Nona.

CHAPTER TWENTY-ONE

THERE'S A BEAUTY spot in Sussex known as Chanctonbury Ring. I went up there once on an outing from
Roedean in a howling gale and the place gave me
the creeps. Ironically Lionel had chosen it for our next
rendezvous.

Today, however, there was no gale and I wasn't in a
school crocodile; Addo and I were climbing to the top alone.
What a clump of contradictions Lionel was. His supreme
confidence in the knowledge that he was the king of his
profession was forever jousting with a profound insecurity,
especially about reaching middle age. It was his fear of the
latter that had given birth to today's plan. Being convinced
that I was in love with Heathcliff, and not Olivier himself,
he'd wanted to relive Heathcliff and Cathy on the moors. We
couldn't trundle up to Yorkshire, so he'd decided Chanctonbury Ring was a suitable second best. I often wished he'd
stop playing these silly games. It was him I loved, wrinkles,
balding and all, not Heathcliff. Besides, he was still in fine
shape and I was never one for pretending.

As I panted my way to the top, there he was, standing at
the summit, my very own King of the Castle. He saw me and
waved enthusiastically.

'Cathy!' How magnificent he looked – as enduring as the
ring of trees themselves then seemed – most of Chanctonbury's ancient beeches were later taken in the great storm of
1987.

'Heathcliff!' I waved as cheerfully as I could. How was I
to tell him that poor old Lionel Kerr had pissed off to Brazil?
We levelled with each other, and stood still but not silent.

137

The combination of hill-climbing and lustful hankerings drove my heartbeat upwards, cracking at my skull. He held my head in both hands, and looked at me. Slowly he began tracing my body line with his finger. Oh! That middle finger of his!

'No! Not here! Chanctonbury Ring is a famous place, people come in droves all the time.'

He let my skirt fall and stood like Nelson on the bridge looking out seaward. 'I see no droves.' True, there was not a single drove to be seen. 'Addo! Guard the castle walls. *En garde!*'

He caught my teasing eye as he folded our clothes into two neat little piles. 'I learnt this from Vivien.'

'So you keep telling me.'

Catching the edge in my tone, he added almost apologetically, 'A clean pile of folded clothes is the sign of a clean, orderly life.'

'I must learn to follow both your examples.'

He looked up. 'Bitch,' he said, ruffling up his neat little piles to form an cushion; then he placed them on my huge squashy satchel and laid us down.

I wasn't up to playing Cathy that afternoon, if ever. Lionel eyed me forlornly. 'Is it all getting to you?' He searched my eyes for answers.

'There's nothing getting to me.' I couldn't share my Nona fears, for the look he gave me ricocheted straight to my cunt and back. He saw it, gently cupped my breast and opened my thighs *en route* to kissing my feet. He'd chosen my feet as a plaything after I told him my ears weren't mine. (Damn things still hurt.) How sad that I lacked the lightness to climb above us, way up on the ceiling of the downs that breathtakingly clear afternoon. Some explanation was needed. 'It's this place. I came here once before. It gave me the creeps then as well.'

'I'll give you the creeps.'

Lately Lionel's creepings were doubly lovely. 'Which creeps will win?' He sparkled, never able to resist a challenge.

Later.

'I concede. The other creep has won.' He perused our reclining bodies. Never being one to dally over misfortune, he rose and moved away. It was a wonderful sight. 'Stand at ease, old boy. After all, Chanctonbury Ring is only our first flop.' Moments later he was beckoning me over to a delightfully mossy knoll. There, spread out before us with as much flamboyant good order as Bertie Russell's sandwiches, were the Downs, one-time protector of the county of Sussex from French invasion. We stood there taking it in.

He nipped my bum. 'Barbaric but soft, like you.' As if from thin air he began opening a Fortnum's hamper. 'This'll fix it,' he said, offering me a smoked salmon sandwich. 'I do love thinly sliced smoked salmon sandwiches.' I laughed, for he reminded me of Bertie. 'What's up?'

I told him about Bertie Russell and he seemed uncomfortable. 'Have you given it to Bertie?' Both the expression and the idea of 'giving it to' Bertie Russell made me laugh. Also my pet cockerel was called Berty and this childhood memory kept bleeding through the image of Bertie 'giving it to me'. 'Beware! He's a man of action, is Bertie Russell.' I do believe he was serious. Olivier had learnt over the years to contain stray sparks of jealousy – he'd had to – and I'd certainly never encountered them before. Interesting that he felt more threatened by a ninety-year-old than by my young lovers.

'Lucky bugger! Fancy having you living opposite.' He was sincerely put out. 'You be careful – he'll be into your knickers in no time.'

'Does he go into ladies' knickers a lot?'

'A lot?' he roared. 'Bertie's knicker triumphs would stretch half-way round the world!'

'Have anyone's knicker triumphs stretched the whole way round the world?'

'Offhand I can only think of Errol Flynn's.'

'What was he like?'

'Everything he was – his strength, his flamboyance, his easy masculinity, in fact his whole charisma – stemmed from his dick. He was famed for it, the biggest dick in Dickendom. Wenches came from far and wide to follow his Holy Grail.'

'Did you unlock its secrets?' The champagne spilt as he released the cork, so he put it in my mouth. I sucked off the froth – and a bit more as well – I had to, Lionel was in command. Was he miming his relationship with Errol? Errol and Lionel together – surely not? The mind gawps. As he slowly removed the bottle from my mouth, I spluttered. 'You're a dirty old man too – just like Bertie.'

'Dirty enough to remove your knickers, but not, alas, to lift your heart. Let's hope the champagne'll lift it.' As we kissed between sips, an unusually mellow changing light caressed the Downs.

'Look out there, Cathy! Our Yorkshire moors.' How unbelievable life was! Sussex had been where I fell in love with him.

'Where's Brighton?'

'Over there to the right somewhere.' I cocked a snook in the general direction of Roedean as Heathcliff pulled me down to the ground.

'I'm going to count up to ten in Old Sussex for you.'

'Heathcliff talking in Old Sussex, how come?'

'Heathcliff knew about counting sheep.' Who could refuse him, precariously parked on the hamper and stuffing down smoked salmon as if it were pastie?

'One-erum, two-erum, cock-erum, shoe-erum, shith-erum, shath-erum, wineberry wagtail, derry, diddle, den.' He made it sound more beautiful than Shakespeare's sonnets.

'That's so pretty. "Wineberry wagtail."'

'Wineberry wagtail.' He knelt before me, brushing off his elbows.

'Now come on, concentrate.' Lionel was always strict when it came to my education. 'I'll keep repeating it till you've got it.' As I listened to his reverent whisper reverberating out across the Downs, gently coaxing me to learn to count in Old Sussex, I swore I saw a flock of wineberry wagtails glide silently over.

'By God, she's got it!' Mission accomplished, poor knackered Lionel collapsed in a heap with his head on his hands, gazing up at all those wagtails. 'Retain that for me and then pass it on when I've gone.' He said it summed up England for him and he didn't want it lost.

'I've done a stupid thing.' I took a deep breath and delivered my Nona saga.

He took it all in with a knowing smile playing upon his lips. 'All that sleeping and fucking is the same as Vivien.' He pulled at a tuft of grass, guiltily.

'What do you mean?' I was lost.

'It seems you've found a manic-depressive, schizophrenic nymphomaniac too.'

I was none the wiser. 'Are they bisexual or am I safe?' I told him about the other night when Nona came into my bedroom wanting comfort.

'Go on.'

I shrugged it off, not wanting to disappoint him, as he liked sexy tales.

'I awoke when I felt her hair on my cheek. She asked me if I still liked her hair, as much as I used to at RADA.'

'Did you ever flirt with her at RADA?'

'Only in passing; I smelt danger. She struck me as being tainted with torment.'

His features darkened considerably as he whipped his profile away from me. His voice became staccato and dark. 'Tainted with torment,' he quietly repeated. 'Tell her she's being paid to walk Addo, cook and tidy up – not to fuck. And if she doesn't stop fucking and start pulling her finger out then she must fuck off. Pronto.'

'If I turn her out she says she'll kill herself.'

Before my eyes, Lionel transformed into a veritable Falstaff, ranting as he marched furiously up and down. Addo thought it was a game and began joining in.

'Another fucking blackmailer!'

'She wanted to know who Lionel Kerr was.'

He stopped quite suddenly.

'I had a feeling. Once I saw her face in the kitchen as I climbed out of the taxi, and thought she was the char.'

'Long enough for her to recognize you?'

'At the time I thought not.'

'We must never let her know for sure.' I took another smoked-salmon sandwich for courage. 'I'm afraid Lionel Kerr has had to bugger off to Brazil.'

He took it very well, and immediately began racking his brain for another codename. Finally, as the sun was going down, he had a clever idea. 'I know. I'll say it's Robin Fox calling. That way if she keeps me talking I can have some fun giving her my Robin. Yes, he's a good character to play.' He was incorrigible.

It was arranged, then. He'd be Robin Fox on the phone, and Lionel Kerr everywhere else. 'As for her, she must go immediately,' he said, already practising his Robin voice.

'If I hadn't rushed her to hospital when she took an overdose, she'd be dead by now.'

'Well, stop rushing her to hospital. You'll be amazed how many overdoses they can take.' In a flash he turned more serious than I'd ever known him. With not a hint of Robin he said, 'Let's pray she kills herself before you kill her,' and then he told me how Vivien's sadistic streak had led him into the darkest corner of his nature, one that till then he'd never known existed. It was in their home in Lowndes Place. His exhaustion, coupled with rows that tumbled into fights, caused him to lose sense of everything and he threw Vivien away from him with great force. 'I'd had enough.' He looked washed out, depleted. 'She fell and hit her head.' His voice went quiet. 'She stopped breathing. I was convinced she was dead.' As he leaned over her, praying for her life, he knew he couldn't be responsible for his actions with her ever again. 'Dead or alive, I knew I had to get out. Get away and never return. For the next time around, she surely would be dead.'

'And that's when you left?'

'More or less. Met Joanie soon afterwards on *The Entertainer*.' Due to a stupendous lack of curiosity, I knew next to nothing about my Mr No-man's private life.

'How many wives have you had?'

'Three. Jill Esmond gave me my son Tarquin as well as my first leg up the showbiz ladder.'

'Vivien must have helped you up a few more rungs.'

'Socially, yes. She taught me the ways of the world.'

'How to fold your underwear, you mean?'

He stuck out his tongue at me.

'Joanie?'

'She's my Nicol, my third time lucky.'

Indeed Nicol was my new wave and my third lover, so I stuck out my tongue back. He smiled and looked thoughtfully at my thighs. 'I suppose, unconsciously, I used all my wives to further my journey up the ladder.'

'But wasn't it you who told me everyone uses everyone?'

'Yes, but something in me is lacking. No ability to love just for the sake of it.' He began tickling me thoughtfully.

Then as an afterthought, 'What *am* I doing up here with you?'

'God only knows!' He lifted me up. 'Be careful or I might remove the ladder altogether.'

He continued tickling me, and it wasn't gentle, not one little bit.

Our faces darkened as a cloud passed over the sun. Our manic-depressive schizophrenic nymphomaniacs were bringing us even closer together.

'What if I throw Nona out and she *does* kill herself?'

'Then she'll have got what she wanted. They all get what they want.' I wanted to argue, but didn't know how.

'Vivien didn't get what she wanted.'

'No.' He veered around the point to my nipple. 'Here's you refusing your Heathcliff while Vivien wanted to play my Cathy more than anything in the world.'

'Poor Vivien.'

He made a dismissive grunting sound deep down in his chest. 'I want to direct the film of the Scottish Laird [*Macbeth*], more than anything in the world, yet I'm cursed too.' Another silence fell over the hills. 'Most of us are cursed one way or another.' Suddenly he began laughing cruelly. 'Nona and Vivien had it made! No fools, either of them. Just sleeping and fucking! And when they tire of both, they head for the unknown.'

I held him tight. My thoughts flew off over my Chekhovian rectory in the Chilterns, with me and Lionel living there all alone, just sleeping and fucking. We were both distracted by Addo finishing off the smoked salmon.

'Addo! *En garde!*' This time, when Lionel began his irresistibly stealthy creeping, we both got caught up in a flock of wineberry wagtails with their flickering rainbow wings or turquoise and gold twirling up and over our sky-blue pink succulent heights.

'One-erum, two-erum, cock-erum, shoe-erum, shitherum, shatherum, wineberry wagtail, derry, diddle, den.' My divine Dragon of Dickendom back in *his* den.

CHAPTER TWENTY-TWO

NONA GAVE ME quite a turn.

'I have a son, Sam. He's coming to stay for a while, if that's all right with you?'

I was simply staggered at her nerve.

'Please, Sarah, please! He was so unhappy in the orphanage.'

I believe people who speak quietly do it on purpose as a kind of one-upmanship: Nona never raised her voice, never spoke in anything but a whisper, which drove me mad because I was always having to strain to hear, or cup my ear with my hand, or say, as in this case, 'What?'

'Little Sam is so unhappy at the orphanage.'

Something in the depths of Nona's eyes struck me for the first time. Where had I seen that look before? It was a look not of this world, as if there were a dazzling cornflower-blue protection over her eyes, keeping her from honest participation in the true world. Then it struck me. Of course! Vivien Leigh's were the same. Her eyes, too, were not of this world, brilliant, brittle and the greenest of green. Their mad selfishness was their protection. I never could argue with Nona. I let her win every round. Why was it that I had the guts to do almost anything except stand up to Nona?

Sammy didn't arrive because he already had. There he was, safely tucked up in her bed in the garden room. He was two and a half years old and sleeping when Nona first led me down to see him. I had to admit, while sleeping he exuded a positively angelic glisten.

Nona continued to be a hefty responsibility during her manic phases, in other words her waking hours. She was still usually failing her agreed daily tasks in return for her bed and lodgings. Often failing to walk Addo, forgetting to shop, cook, clean. She had it made and we both knew it. My double life was turning into a merry dance of charring and cheating – but, then, we all get what we deserve. *Serves me right*.

Was it brutal of me to begin to long for her depressive phases, because they signposted sleep? She could get up to little mischief snoring away on her pillow, and the men in her busy manic phase knew – by bush telegraph probably – when the depressive part of the cycle had arrived, so the through traffic was pleasantly minimal. Why did these depressive phases fill me with such guilt? Because it conveniently covered up my lack of courage to boot her out, son and all.

I only wondered what else I could do for her. She took so many different pills I couldn't keep up. I still took her to hospital when she needed to check in with her doctor, but when I mentioned this to him he said, 'She's coming along famously, you're doing a good job. Well done. Nonsense. You can always call me if things come to a head.'

'Is committing suicide what you'd interpret as "coming to a head"?'

'They rarely carry it through. It's merely a cry for help.'

I explained to him how in her manic phases she came into my room wanting to make love to me while in the depressive one she thought only the worst of me. He said that was the general pattern of her disease and that I wasn't to become entangled with either extremes of mood, just try to observe it from the centre. Who did he think I was? I was only in my early twenties, and not mature enough by any means to remain cool and centred. Nona wasn't getting any better. As far as I could make out, she was worse. A second time now, I'd had to rush her off to hospital after she'd overdosed.

Looking down into Sam's innocent little face made me more scared than ever. 'How will you manage to sleep the pair of you in one bed?'

'He's not sleeping with me, how could he?' she said coyly,

fluttering her lashes. 'I don't want to corrupt him, do I? Follow me.'

We climbed to the top of the house and into the box-room. I was astounded. Without my knowing she had turned it into a most presentable little nursery.

'What do you think?' she asked proudly.

I was at a loss for words. 'When did you do this?'

'While you were at rehearsals.'

Winter 1964 found me doing another play for television by Jean Anouilh, *The Rehearsal*, with John Gielgud, Martita Hunt and Alan Badel. Alan Badel took a dislike to poor Sir John. It was beyond my comprehension how anyone could possibly have anything against sweet Sir John. Rehearsing the play was a nightmare. Alan Badel had had a big success in a West End production of the play and was contemptuous of any changes, good or bad, in the television version. He knew best and he wanted all of us to do it *his* way. He knew, because not only had he done it, but he'd succeeded in doing it brilliantly and wasn't prepared to lower his sights for the ineptitude of a cut version for the telly with actors who hadn't a clue what they were doing. The director meant well, but had no control over him. Loving Sir John as I did, I stood by him, with Alan never far away, prowling around snarling.

By no means was the atmosphere conducive to the essential team spirit that I was so keen on: I'd had a sniff of what it was about while working at Worthing Rep, and on *Term of Trial*, and I desperately wanted to experience it again. So far, alas, it had eluded me.

In the plot, Sir John's character, the Count, had to come into my bedroom and seduce me as the young governess. This made Sir John so nervous that each time we came to rehearse it, he said to the director, 'We'll leave the love scene for the moment.' This made me nervous, too. He was embarrassed either to make love to me, or to any girl. If it was the latter, and I hoped it was, how had he managed in the past? This couldn't have been the first time Sir John was called upon to play stallion, could it?

I needed rehearsal time for the love scene. I wanted it to be choreographed a little, so that it wasn't clumsy, rushed or inept. Erotic moments rarely happen by accident, for true lovemaking is an art form, the antithesis of today's debasing expression 'having sex', which perfectly describes the function of mindless banging up and down. Erotica has to be well planned, patiently worked out to the finest detail, leaving nothing to chance. Sadly, it's a long time since I saw love scenes that didn't result in a lowering experience. I see erotica as praising physical love while pornography debases it. I did not want Sir John and me to fall into the latter category, but neither could I say I had high hopes of us achieving the former. The chemistry was wrong, added to which he hadn't even run the lines. 'We'll try it tomorrow, Aroon,' he said sorrowfully, when I suggested we go off on our own. (He called me Aroon after directing me in the famous flop *Dazzling Prospect*.)

In a confrontational scene to be played between Sir John and Alan Badel another heavy atmosphere was settling in. Alan kept putting off rehearsal until they met his demands for dialogue changes.

Martita Hunt was a real old Valkyrie. Her timing was excellent as she passed around her caustic wit with great panache, especially when witnessing Alan's attacks on Sir John. 'Horrid little hooligan – I'd box his ears.' She would have, too, and I'd have paid over the odds to see it. Martita continually wore black, travelling to and from rehearsals in a hearse. Always in mourning and expecting more deaths ahead, she must have had a good sense for endings because she died soon afterwards.

One one occasion Alan was ranting on and on about

nothing as usual, encircling Sir John while flapping the script about like a bat on heat. I couldn't resist asking, 'Have you upset him, Sir John?'

'Not that I remember,' replied Sir John, neatly letting himself off the hook.

Whenever things became too hot to handle, Sir John would say, 'Aroon let's go and see *Jules et Jim*.' Thank God for *Jules et Jim*. Without his passion for that film, we may never have got through *The Rehearsal* in one piece.

Things got worse. Alan wanted either to murder Sir John or fuck me, but the script called out for Sir John to fuck me, not Alan. One day Alan was in such a temper that he picked me up during rehearsal, carried me straight into the lavatory and locked the two of us in, as neatly as if it were all rehearsed. He dropped me on the loo seat and began wheeling and dealing through the lavatory wall for more scenes to be reinstated from the original version. Fortunately, being locked in the lavatory with Alan Badel was a piece of cake compared to being thrown out of one by Nicol – both men dangerously thwacky thespians.

From the loo seat I could do nothing but wait. The director, Sir John and Co., were outside the lavatory trying to strike a happy compromise. Alan banged the lavatory wall repeatedly, with his script, his hand or his head. I couldn't stop him; besides, I was merely the FO (not in the eyes of Sir John, alas). In those early days you rehearsed for a month or so and then taped the final performance over a couple of days. On the recording day we still hadn't done the love scene. All hopes of erotica with Sir John were well down the plug-hole. But he had to seduce the girl, otherwise there was no story, and we still hadn't even worked out the moves. The director asked us to rehearse it on the set. Sir John blathered on a bit, till the director said – firmly for the first time – 'We have to see what we're filming, Sir John.'

Sir John looked at us all and walked off set. As we all stood there contemplating what to do back he came, looking remarkably sleek in a *Private Lives* kind of silk dressing gown and matching pyjamas. 'How do I look?' he asked.

'Splendid,' I said truthfully, yet not sure how Sir John looking like an 1890 Noël Coward was going to help.

'Right,' said the director, 'let's play the scene please.'

While the gaffers moved the lights through, Sir John drew me to him. 'Aroon?' Turning me outward away from the gang, he whispered confidentially, 'What does one do? Kiss or embrace first?' Poor Sir John. I wanted to hug him just then and cry out, 'Check with your old mate Lionel, I won't eat you.' Then I saw what the trouble was. Alan Badel was standing there, attending to our every move, still as a panther about to pounce.

'Shall I ask the director to get him removed?'

'No. We'll have to get on with it. You lead.'

'I can't possibly do the leading, Sir John.'

'Why ever not?'

'Because you're seducing me, and proper young girls don't lead, they follow.'

'Enough chatter,' said the director.

Sir John paced up and down while he waited for them to readjust the lights, sweeping the floor with great swirls of agitated silk. 'Oh, God! I'm in a terrible muddle.'

How could I reassure this giant of a man that all would be well? 'Whatever you do I'll follow. Just close your eyes and think of England.'

'Hold my nose more like.' I was quite put out. Did I smell? He intercepted his *faux pas* before it crashed to the ground. 'Oh God, I meant England drowning, not you smelling, Aroon. Oh, my God!'

We played the scene: it was a print first take and so subtle as to be invisible. It wasn't remotely erotic by any stretch of the imagination; neither was it long enough to be inept, debasing or gross. Thank God!

Not such good news was coming from the taping of Alan Badel's and Sir John's confrontation scene. Instead of Alan coming up and hitting Sir John across the face with his glove, he batted him with a real thump, whereupon Sir John fell sideways to the floor, shaken up considerably. I could hardly believe my eyes. How could Alan Badel behave so to someone as upright and correct as Sir John? What was he trying to achieve? So destructive to witness such great actors at logger-heads. It couldn't have been competitive ego-tripping, for Sir John just didn't fit into that category: he was too refined.

About two months later Sir John and I were sitting alone in a screening room, watching the cut version for the first time. He remained silent, oft-times looking away from me. I think he may have been privately crying. Alan's sadistic nature was plastered all over the film. When it was over, Sir John stood up and said, 'God damn blast Alan Badel!' His upright walk took him swiftly to the door, he being too ashamed of his own tears to linger. Our *Jules et Jim* days were gone for good.

The three Knights. Ralphie, Sir John and Olivier. What a gang! We'll never see their like again. They made it hard for the likes of Alan Badel. An actor of equal ability, but not with the discipline or manners to go with it.

It's foolish to judge other people's bad behaviour because no one knows the depths of anybody else's private pain, which is the bedrock of bad behaviour. I'm nastiest when depressed, so forgiving Alan Badel wasn't too hard for me. If true brilliance isn't nurtured sufficiently, believed in, or lucky enough to sparkle in the sunshine, its owner's responsibility becomes too overwhelming to bear.

Whatever the fascination of great talent, people who aspire to match it with a graceful life interest me much more. Talent is unremarkable – so is life – if we don't attempt to turn it into an art form. To live as wisely, modestly, coura-geously and indeed correctly as possible is the highest form of art. But this crème de menthe frappée wasn't thinking about art forms then – no, just keeping my fuzz straight, Lionel and fucking. Alas, there's no short cut to Eternal Bliss through Fucking, for Eternal Bliss is found only in the Palace of Wisdom. Unfortunately I'd have to take the motorway right around, through Great Horrors and on through Learning Lessons. Turn left at the Endless Nature Faults public house, right into Nervous Breakdown, then straight down into Hell itself through the quagmire of Utter Exhaustion, refuel and climb up yet again into Lessons Still Unlearnt, finally coming to rest in Eternal Bliss within the Palace of Wisdom. Yes. If only I'd known then that there was no short cut through Fucking, I could have started my journey earlier, and saved so much precious energy. As it is, I'm gone fifty and only approaching Lessons Still Unlearnt – whereupon, fuzzy hair triumphant, I'll probably slip and drown in If Onlys. It's damned hard.

Out of the blue, Sir John telephoned me while I was in Cornwall with Mother and Addo. (I still owed Binkie a play even though our three-year contract was up.) Addo and I had just returned from getting ourselves completely stuck half-way up an horrendously steep cliff for well over an hour. (I'm ashamed to admit I suffer from vertigo, but Addo, being a Pyrenean mountain dog, should have known better. I should have jacked him in for a St Bernard.) Unable to go in either direction we stood still. Finally, Addo remembered his origins just in time and hauled me up by his tail.

I noticed I trembled still as I took the phone from Mother. 'Hello, Sir John.' I was delighted to hear from him.

'Oh! Aroon! Aroon! I'm in a terrible pickle!'

'You sound like you're in the Outer Hebrides.'

'Toronto, actually. Oh, Aroon. Aroon! I'm directing *Hamlet*. It's awful! Well, you know what a ghastly director I am.' Silence. 'Oh, God! *I* do, *I* do! I deserve the catastrophe swirling around me.' I asked him what catastrophe. 'Ophelia isn't quite right. Do you know the part?' I'd played her briefly at RADA. John's sigh of relief thudded down the phone as he asked me to fly to Toronto and take over. *Oh, Dad, Poor Dad* came flooding back, together with a feeling that this whole firing business didn't sit well with me – simply wasn't cricket. Besides, I'd made a vow not to leave because of Addo, and so far I'd kept to it. I turned a deaf ear to his enchanting billing and cooing down the phone.

'I'll have to think it over, Sir John.'

Later the same evening. Mother. 'It's only a limited run—'

'But—'

'I'll look after the damn dog—'

'Bu—'

'You're not turning this down. Over my dead body!' Off I flew to Toronto. Mother, as I have already hinted, was someone not to cross.

When I arrived I went straight to the theatre to see the production. The whole cast was in modern-day costume and I was able to get a whiff of Sir John's 'catastrophe swirling round him' that night. Richard Burton's Hamlet wasn't as energetic or as romantic as he was afterwards – to put it mildly. He welcomed me fiercely, clinging to his new Ophelia as if she was the one raft in stormy seas.

What with the long flight it was all rather too much for me. Sir John came to my rescue. 'We'll begin rehearsals at 10 a.m., if that's all right with you, Aroon?'

Next morning at 7.30 I had a very rude awakening. It was Sir John in a terribly new pickle.

'Oh, Aroon, Aroon, could you please come down to the Elizabeth – I mean the lobby – and Aroon – oh, God! Aroon, with your bags packed.'

All the way to the airport Sir John was unable to explain the new catastrophe swirling round the taxi. 'Oh, Aroon! Oh, Aroon! Oh dear, oh dear me!'

Since I had behaved impeccably the previous evening,

and having been denied the opportunity to display my craft, I hadn't a clue what was up. Sir John was either too much of a gentleman or too busy swooning to let on.

'You see, Aroon, you see – well – oh, God! You see.' He put his head in his hands. 'Oh dear, Aroon. Oh, God!'

I assumed it was a contractual problem, but Ma thought it was insecurities running riot, because Antony and Cleopatra had yet to tie their famous diamond knot. Whatever, I was home to Addo once more.

CHAPTER TWENTY-THREE

I WAS GOING through Hell and back at home, all right. Getting up all hours of the night for one's own child isn't the best part of motherhood, but having to do it endlessly for someone else's child was far worse. Nona slept in perfect peace down in the basement while I was in the upstairs bedroom, a stone's throw from the box-room's anguished blubberings.

'Nona, I can't sleep, Sam cries so in the night.'

'Close his door, he'll soon keep quiet. Come and wake me if you need to.'

'I can't do that, Nona.' Sam wouldn't sleep with the bedroom door closed. I had too many recollections of my own childhood dread of closed doors ever to go against Sam's wishes, so to begin with I had no choice but to endure, almost nightly, Sam's tortured insecurity. As if that wasn't enough I found myself running him to his kindergarten near Hyde Park. (Yet when Nona was up to it, she was a devoted doting mother.)

The phone rang. I thought it was Robin Fox at first.

'Hello. I want you to be in my *Love Show*.'

'Who is this?'

'I'm doing a show about love and I want you to be in it.'

There was a catch to this somewhere, I could smell it a mile off.

'Who is this?'

'Willy Donaldson.'

Could I admit that I'd never heard of him, or was he too famous?

'How did you get my number?'

'Robin Fox. I'm an impresario, I put on plays.' (Which Robin? Robin or Lionel Robin? We were going to have to change the telephone code, this 'Robin Fox' idea of Heathcliff's simply wasn't working. Whenever Nona said, 'Robin Fox phoned,' I was left-footed with confusion all day. Often Robin would reprimand me for not returning his call.)

This Willy Donaldson had an intoxicating telephone voice. 'You can check me out at the Grade Organization. If all proceeds smoothly I'll take you to lunch at the Ivy.'

'But—'

'Next Tuesday, twelve forty-five. You're perfect for my *Love Show* – it'll be spectacular!' With that he hung up. A cultured voice. I soon excused the charm from being almost studied, thanks to the one-offmanship of his wit.

Telephone voices had always deceived me in the past, but not Willy's. (Another one already!) He was a 'one-off' all right. I'm a real sucker for those, because it's only people with a few bats in their belfry who interest me – bats being brilliant creatures, swiftly becoming extinct. I resembled Lionel in that respect, finding life always tastier on the edge. The other side of this is that I'm still close to all my beaux, because one-offs endure like a good wine. Willy Fox was fair and slim, so too Willy Donaldson, but there the resemblance ended. Willy Donaldson was more refined, yet oddly decadent-looking.

Our lunch at the Ivy turned out surprisingly romantic. His manners matched his quickness of tongue, and though he flirted outrageously it was all subtle, tongue-in-cheek, leaving me in doubt as to how he really felt. Was he just another prankster? His ideas for the *Love Show* were as spectacular as they were unformed. No script, no scriptwriter, no director, no theatre, no actors. Was it all merely a wheeze to get into my knickers?

Nona was running out of lovers, because she kept coming

up to my room and waking me. First she would creep upstairs to check on Sam and then come into my bedroom. I found these visits a trifle disconcerting. One night having awoken yet again to find myself inside her wigwam, I whammed my way out, utterly furious. Holding her face between my hands, I looked into her lonely gaze. Just as Lionel had cupped my head, with his eyes full of warning, 'Get rid of her, get rid of her now,' so I held Nona.

'Nona, I cannot live my life—'

'That's not my fault, I'm not stopping you.'

I became dead serious and dead cold.

'Nona, you and Sammy have to find somewhere to live by the end of the week. Willy Donaldson is coming to live with me.'

Nona's whisper was venomous.

'If you push me out, Sarah, you'll regret it till the end of your days.' With that she gave me a look that still pierces my soul, and left the room.

I was frightened. Whatever move I might make, the outlook seemed bleaker than bleak. But I'd had enough of Nona's satanic blackmail, so I made myself a promise that if she attempted suicide once more, I'd pack her bags and push her out, suggesting that if she really wanted to kill herself she should grow up and *jump* next time.

All these black thoughts had given me a headache. I went down to the kitchen to take an aspirin.

'Nona, where have you put the aspirin?'

'They're on the sideboard in the kitchen,' said Nona from her garden room. While stuffing them down my gullet something niggled me. I'd never taken aspirin in my life – come to think of it I'd never had a headache, before Nona. She came into the kitchen rubbing her head. 'I think I'm catching your headache.' She went to another bottle on the side table. I ran to stop her from swallowing them but she held me back. 'What's the matter?' She showed me the label. 'Look, aspirin not cyanide! See?'

I saw all right. She was taking aspirin, the bottle said so. What had I just swallowed? I went back to the other bottle and my fears were realized. The label read: 'Addo. One every evening with meal.' Crumpets! I hadn't eaten for donkey's years. This wasn't good news. I'd swallowed two of Addo's pills from the vet to stop his cock from dripping. (It wasn't a pleasing sight, always detracting from his godliness.) I felt quite odd for days and kept checking, but I was lucky, my cock didn't drip once.

No, things couldn't go on as they were. It was I, not Nona, who needed protecting. And what a divine bodyguard Willy (D.) would be for this new Willy was dapper, no two ways about it, he had a unique style. Robin Fox told me that he was responsible for bringing together Peter Cook, Dudley Moore, Jonathan Miller and Alan Bennett for *Beyond the Fringe*, yet typically he never mentioned it, being a truly modest man. Willy probably had more fingers in more pies than any other impresario in London. After he moved into Hasker Street it gave me a real buzz to hear him on the phone with his great nose for business shrewdly sniffing out the greatest acts in town. It was equally impressive to hear him on the doorstep trying to talk his way out of another hole he'd dug himself into with one of his many creditors. No doubt about it, I was full of admiration for Willy D. – not to mention gratitude for his divine presence as a buffer against Nona's suffocating nocturnal visits. (She still hadn't gone.)

Willy would rise at nine thirty, my debauched Burlington Bertie, and dress with hurried precision – while still at it, standing there in a striped shirt, tasty tie and pukka grey suit. How I loved it. I seemed to spend all my Willy D. era more or less naked. He'd pull his fingers away so reluctantly before wrapping me up tightly in my towel. Then he'd kiss me as only a debauched Burlington Bertie could, before sauntering off like a toff. Willy liked making love, a lot, and, no two ways about it, so did I.

Walking through the park, Addo and I would gossip about Willy and play guessing games. What did Willy do at the office all day long? Addo felt neither one way nor another about Willy, their passion for each other being lukewarm.

I drove him down to Barn Mead for the weekend. Poor old Wil, very brave he was to come, considering the Miles Mafia. When my boyfriend and I (whoever he was, we were never allowed to sleep together, but there were always ways round the rules) entered the dining room on the first morning of the weekend, the family would give a sign, newspapers up or down according to their interest or indeed approval. There had never been a beau yet to gain the family's full attention.

'He's a dark horse, your Willy,' said Daddy. A most accurate description, for Willy fell between a choir of angels and a nest of demons, in the valley where dark horses graze. 'That chap of yours spends the whole damn weekend holed up in a darkened room. Get him outside – away from newspapers and on to the tennis court.' This went on weekend after weekend, but Willy didn't come out.

Until Father decided enough was enough. All dressed up to kill, tennis racquet in hand, he marched into the sitting room. 'Meet you on the court in five minutes, young man.'

'He doesn't play tennis, Father.'

'A Wykhamist not a tennis player? Nonsense! In five minutes, is that clear?'

'Yes, sir.'

Off went Father, leaving Willy in a state.

'I loathe tennis.' He hated all sport.

Half an hour later I went down to see how my brave Willy was faring, and there he was slaughtering poor Father. Daddy turned seventy a few weeks previously, and on that day he did the quaintest thing for such an unostentatious fellah. He hired the palatial River Room at the Savoy. There we sat, the six of us, Mother, Father, Chris, Chuzzer, Vanessa and myself, marooned right in the centre with fifty waiters quietly hovering in gilt corners. No one dared utter until Daddy struck up quite loudly. 'Reminds me of two waiters looking at a chap guzzling a fillet steak. Finally one turns to the other smugly and says, "He's eating it!"' Father begins to laugh narrowly, for waiters are now looming in on us with huge gold-encrusted menus.

'Shoosh, John,' reprimands Mother,' that's quite enough. They have ears, you know.'

'Care to order some fillet steak, sir?' inquires a daring waiter.

Yet playing against Willy at seventy didn't mean he wasn't still of a pretty high standard. However, I did observe Daddy's joviality dissipate somewhat as he failed to judge his usual winner of a dirty drop shot for the second time. He lit his pipe before wiping down the sweat of losing.

'You really are a dark horse!' he said, strutting back to the safer territory of a nice hot bath.

'It never occurred to me that tennis is the same as riding a bicycle,' said Willy, attempting to sit modestly on a heap of astonishment. That was Willy. Quiet and modest. He never raised his voice.

'I'm proud of you, but Father will never be the same again.'

He didn't seem bothered. Then, under his breath, 'Come with me quickly behind the summerhouse.' He was only testing me, otherwise he would have dragged me. No, my Willy was too cultured to turn into Mr Caveman. But he had me there later, in his own time, in his oh-so-mannerly way. 'Can we go home now?' He reminded me of a Wykhamist fag looking round towards the prefect's study. 'I'm frightened.' He was, too. The Miles Mafia frightened him a lot. Yet he moaned fearlessly as he locked us back together again.

CHAPTER TWENTY-FOUR

LIONEL WAS FAIRLY bad-mannered on hearing that Willy Donaldson had come to live with me. Understandably he felt much more secure with me between lovers, so he swore a bit, then dwindled into semi-petulance. 'Couldn't you do without?' So busy was he with championing the new Chichester Theatre, simultaneously acting, directing and running it, plus the new National Theatre, which was off to a flying start at the Old Vic, plus commuting from Brighton, plus another baby on the way, plus, plus, plus that it meant he had no time to take a quick gander at my life. If he had he wouldn't have begrudged me my Willy. At the time my love for him completely eclipsed the thought that he might be using me, yet he, none the less, lacked awareness when it came to the lives of others. This isn't a complaint since such blindness is inexorably tied in with greatness. Genius rarely sees much but its own, and it had been that monumental greatness that had drawn me to him in the first place.

Times were hard for Lionel, though, and he needed sympathy. Not just from me, but from all those who loved him, for he was about to lift off into the journey that would lead him to become the first lord of the theatre, and which needed all his concentration and devotion.

I often wonder what would have happened if I had never met him. Those 'once in a whiles' with Lionel were more than merely precious moments – they were my raison d'être. But they were also surreptitiously poisoning the rest of my life. I'd become reclusive and wary, never going out on the town, never going to discotheques – and I loved to dance – never mixing with showbiz, turning down every invitation to make contacts, to be seen. But I had no choice. I had to be home in case 'Robin Fox' was to call. It wasn't only that: I wanted to keep this double life of mine as single as possible. The more I went out, the more I'd have had to cover up the truth, and the more lies I'd find myself telling.

'Am I a mistress or a concubine?' I asked one grey afternoon between watering-holes in Victoria.

'Neither,' he mumbled from the pillow. His back was playing up badly from a pinched nerve that was pressing on his buttock. I believe most of his pain stemmed from a knee injury incurred while playing Coriolanus, when he's insisted on showing off with one of his magically effective, yet none the less foolhardy stunts.

'What am I then?'

He turned over, opening his arms, looked at me with acres of love, then held me enduringly. 'I want you to be mine and mine alone, but I haven't the money.'

How dare he? I slapped him hard across the face, but I mean really hard. He looked astonished. 'You asked me what you were. Both mistress and concubines receive *something* in return.'

I got dressed and left. I walked around for hours alone. Yes, I thought, I was indeed nothing but an unpaid mistress. How a secret love can kill. *Serves me right*.

Willy D. was a home body, too, which was convenient, for he never questioned my desire to stay in. Fortunately there was no need to change the codename 'Robin Fox' – Lionel had it down to a fine art. Not only did he have Willy and Nona completely fooled but sometimes me too. I doubted if even Robin would have known the difference.

So there I was sandwiched again, this time between two impresarios. The great lord to be of the National Theatre, and Willy Donaldson's Theatre of Embarrassment. As a devotee of the latter, Willy got off on people's naked moments – like me in my days as a peeping Tom. Willy brought out the raunchy in me, gently tugging me further and further – but though his appetite for erotica bordered on the pornographic, he was careful never to bring the latter home. That's why I wondered what he was doing all day. Dark horses have to give their dark side fresh grazing ground. Was my shady dark horse deceiving me, too? It was the only time in my life that I had brief twangs of jealousy. With hindsight I can see that when love-making becomes obsessive it can tarnish the spirit with negativity. It was as if we were channelling all our daily frustrations into our nightly rituals. I knew this new form of over-indulgence would inevitably ruin us. But how dare I question his office hours when I was having secret assignations with Lionel? Double standards, double set of rules, double trouble.

Although Willy was forever fleeing financial difficulties, he never lost his enthusiasm for discovering new acts. He was proud of his boys, The Alberts, and their *Evening of British Rubbish*. They had an act in which they blew up machinery and themselves on stage, after which they'd all camp down on Hasker Street's drawing-room floor for the night, pissed out of their minds. I could never fathom why they hadn't blown themselves up yet, but I kept hoping. On one occasion, they *did* blow up the theatre. 'They're about to make the big time, this time, I promise you, darling. It'll soon be striped shirts and chicken on Sundays.'

So never-ending was that divine optimism of Willy's that he suggested I cut a disc. 'If Marianne Faithfull can then so can you.' However wispy Marianne's voice used to be in those early days, it could never reach the depths of my incompetence. Willy wouldn't hear any doubts, so we went ahead. I can't remember on what label; probably it was called 'Truly Abysmal'.

Hal Prince, the famous New York producer, telephoned me one day to ask if I would like to be in a musical on Broadway. 'It's the musical version of Chris Isherwood's *I Am a Camera*. It's called *Cabaret*.'

'Really?' I said, not knowing how to break the news about

my singing. I told Robin I could sing, because all actors lie to their agents about their accomplishments. If we're asked to ride a horse, we say, 'Of course,' and fall off later.

'Sally Bowles could have been written for you,' Hal Prince said. 'I spoke to Binkie Beaumont and he says you're far and away the best bet.' He seemed so enthusiastic, I hadn't the heart to let him down. He arranged for the musical director, John Candour, and composer, Fred Ebb, to come down to Barn Mead. Hal Prince liked the sound of Daddy's Bechstein grand as much as a trip to the English countryside.

Before they arrived Daddy was pacing about, most agitated. 'What the hell are you playing at, Pusscat? It's not cricket to bring them down all this way – poor wretches!'

Sitting around the piano, listening to the score of *Cabaret* for the first time (indeed its first airing ever), I was happier than I'd felt in ages (away from Lionel, that is). What a wonderfully uplifting, catchy score. The best I'd heard since *My Fair Lady*. Funny, isn't it, how we know within seconds when something's got what it takes? And within those same few seconds they knew that I hadn't. But I had to try, don't you see? Miracles happen all the time – so I'm told.

Singing was still where my heart was and I went to quite a few singing teachers who all said in some polite fashion to pack it in. One sweetly told me that since I was a movie star perhaps it was better to let sleeping dogs lie, as she looked down at a sleeping Addo. So after that spurt, I had to tuck that dream away again . . . for the time being.

CHAPTER TWENTY-FIVE

NINETEEN SIXTY-FOUR and driving home from our new watering-hole after a quick assignation with Lionel – lately they had to be quick – he'd asked me to join his National Theatre. 'It'll be fun working with me as a director and indeed Noël. It's an experience you shouldn't miss. Besides, I can always find you down the corridor,' he said, nibbling at private squashy bits.

I was to play with him in *The Recruiting Officer* with Maggie Smith and Robert Stephens. Also as Abigail in Arthur Miller's *The Crucible*, which Olivier would direct himself, and Sorel in *Hay Fever*, written and directed by Noël Coward. Noël had been such an important part of my growing up, 'Mad Dogs and Englishmen' echoing across the tennis courts and croquet lawns of childhood. I was tempted by Olivier's offer, but knew myself well enough by now. I was still no pack animal, though I admit to being flattered that Lionel was so dead keen for me to say 'yes'.

I couldn't help but compare his overture that afternoon with Sir Ralph's when he came wooing me in St Pancras for *The Rivals* at the Haymarket. Ralphie knew how to charm, but when in doubt you need to be seriously wooed. If Ralphie had pursued me in the same way as Olivier, more seriously focused and brimful of technique, I might have ended up at the Haymarket. Lionel wooed me superbly that evening. 'You'll love it, we're a real team at the Old Vic, we'll all make you feel at home instantly. I promise.'

So, feeling very wanted, merry and feminine driving home, I stopped at the traffic lights in Eaton Square, and there beside me, winding down the window of his taxi, was Peter Finch. We'd never met, but that didn't seem to deter him one whit. He leaned out of the open window and gestured for me to follow him. He was a handsome fellah. But I kept my face in profile and shook my head. 'No.'

'Where are you going, young lady?' His 'young lady' line made me sure he had no idea who I was.

'Home.'

'I'll follow you.'

'Oh, no, you won't!' I said haughtily, putting my foot down on all that Mini Cooper S's power, and shooting off. Men! To him I was just another tart. Wouldn't he get a shock if he knew where Olivier had been just now when he asked me to join his National Theatre?

It was late when I arrived back at Hasker Street, even though it was only about fifteen minutes after I'd left our new watering-hole. I was getting out of the car when – Bob's yer uncle – there was Peter Finch paying off his taxi. The scallywag! Addo was there too and obviously liked his dry cleaner.

'Get this dog off me, please!'

'Where do you get your suits cleaned?'

He looked at me, bewildered. 'I haven't an idea, just get this dog off!'

I wanted to find a dry cleaner using Addo's aphrodisiac, for his relationship with Willy still needed pepping up.

I pulled Addo off by his tail.

'Please may I come in?' He looked drunk, dishevelled, enchantingly battered and bruised.

'It's too late. Besides, my boyfriend lives with me.'

'I haven't come here to fuck your boyfriend – or your dog.'

I was full of Lionel, both literally and emotionally, so to flirt with Peter seemed somewhat redundant. 'Truly, not tonight, it's almost twelve and I know it would end badly.'

He pushed past me and looked back at me from inside the hallway. 'Just one for the road.' He was in a bit of a state.

I could see him now under the hallway light. His eyes were bloodshot and puffy.

We sat and talked for a long while – rather, he talked and I listened. He poured out his heart while I poured the whisky. What a lonely man he was. He shared his grievances with me, his unrequited longing for Shirley Bassey and how he couldn't live without her. The only thing as repetitive as his broken heart was his determination to get his lips on to mine or his hand up my skirt. Another Bertie Russell. I'd have to lengthen my skirts. I'd noticed a short skirt on a shop girl in Oxford Street. It was the first one I'd ever seen, so I'd accosted her and asked her where she'd bought it.

'I knocked it up myself,' she'd said with pride.

So I asked Mary Quant, who had a boutique at the time called Bazaar in the King's Road, to raise my skirt three inches. I'd been wearing them just above my knees ever since *Term of Trial* – but now, with half my thighs showing, I was the bee's knees! I wore it with little white socks and flat pumps. 'It suits you,' said Mary. I'm not taking credit for the mini-skirt. All clever fashion entrepreneurs steal their ideas from the streets. I often wonder though what happened to that little shop girl.

None of Peter's flailing drunken passes were an insult, for he was too unhappy to warrant my asking him to leave. Just a lonely middle-aged man wanting a bit of skirt and tender loving care, who'd come to the wrong place. I was in no mood for mercy fucking – after all, I was to be a National Theatre player. But to Peter I was just another crème de menthe frappée in an extremely short skirt and a Mini Cooper S.

'Did you love Shirley while you were having it off with Vivien?'

He looked taken aback.

'Certainly not. What do you take me for?'

Crumpets! Had I been indiscreet? Peter and Vivien's affair was common knowledge, surely? Lionel had told me about their love affair, a romance that he wanted to last and last, from what I could gather. Too late to back-pedal now. 'Did you love Vivien?'

Peter looked a little furtive. 'You look a bit like her, you know.' He dwelt on my features while sipping his drink. Old news, Lionel had said the same, yet, alas, a miss is as good as a mile. He took another sip of whisky. Sighing, he added, 'Did you know the Japanese have at least fifteen words for love?'

'Sounds enormously sensible to me. Another whisky?'

'I'd love one. How can one word *love* describe another drink *and* what I feel for Shirley?' He added as an after-thought, 'And Vivien, of course, too . . . obviously.' It wasn't at all obvious to me.

Each time I got him to the front door, he decided against it. Willy was upstairs, all meek and sleeping, and I wanted to join him. 'I'm going to show you a game. It's a short cut to finding out what kind of person you are.' He perked up at his brainwave. 'All I need is some paper and a pen. I have to draw a little map.'

'Then after that you'll let me go to bed?'

He swept me up on to his lap. 'You can sleep right here and now, my sweet little princess.'

I wiggled off him the way fuckable objects tend to wiggle: purposefully.

He saw this and got pissed off again. 'Paper.'

I fetched him some paper.

'Pen!'

I went to fetch him a pen, but he'd already found one and placed the paper on the coffee table where he began drawing with great concentration. He'd occasionally look up in thought, and then down to the page again. Finally he straight-ened his back, took a sip of whisky and as he did so he scrutinized the pen.

'Oh, my God,' he whispered on an outward sigh, before turning ashen.

'What's the matter?'

He sat there quite dazed for a moment or two. 'You? Oh, my God!' It was eerie. He stared ahead of him for a moment or two, then rose from the sofa, pulled himself together into a new persona, put down the pen, crumped up his complicated map, put it in his pocket, and made for the front door. 'I really have to go now.'

I opened the door for him. He was stiff as a poker, quite unlike the man whose pliable body had been flirting a moment ago. I waved him off into the night wondering what on earth I could have said wrong. It couldn't have been Vivien because she'd been mentioned earlier.

I went back into the drawing room to tidy up. As I was putting the pen away, I realized what had brought about the sudden personality change. Peter had seen my name engraved on the pen. The American producer Hal Wallis had given it to me the year before, saying how sorry he was that the part of Anne Boleyn in *Anne of the Thousand Days* had gone to Genevieve Bujold. (I'd refused to test because of leaving Addo.) My consolation prize was this golden pen with a blackamoor standing on the top wearing golden bananas on his turquoise turban. A hugely expensive, heavily tasteless pen with my name across it. It was a constant reminder that I should have tested for Anne Boleyn. But that's life. *Serves me right*. Why, though, had Peter been so ashamed of himself as he left? He had done nothing wrong in taking me for the tart I really was.

CHAPTER TWENTY-SIX

A T THE LAST minute Olivier gave me a single ticket in the second row for the opening night of *Othello* at the Old Vic, Waterloo, a stone's throw from our new extravagant watering-hole. As bedsits go it was cheap, but because of Lionel's workload we rarely used it. When I asked how he'd found it, for it was a little less gloomy than the last, he shrugged. 'I just knocked on the right door and inspected the basement bedsit to let. 'It's for an actor coming over from Canada on a modest grant. He requires a private basement room with complete privacy,' I explained to the non-resident landlord.' Shrewd, he was.

That glitzy first night was so choc-a-bloc with the best, brightest, most beautiful members of the theatre world and its hangers on that all I can remember was the thrill of spying Noël Coward a few seats away. When the curtain went up there was a hush in the auditorium that I'd only experienced with Edith Piaf in Paris. I wasn't able to look up at Lionel often because he seemed too close, too large, too overwhelming. His body, which he'd been working on diligently, paid off a millionfold under the lights, so much so that I had to hold back the vapours. Imagine having to be hauled out because one had fainted at one's lover's animal magnetism, though I wasn't blind to the occasional hint of the blackamoor on the tip of Hal Wallis's pen – bananas and all! What resounded more truthfully within me, however, was the plot. Jealousy is a quaint illness. Fancy killing someone, especially someone you love, over a small white hanky. I wondered whether Joanie would react in such a way if she found out about us. I would have despised myself if through clumsiness Joanie had found out, for I wouldn't have wanted to hurt her.

Hurting people is the easiest thing in the world, whereas mature loving demands the best of us. (Joanie found out well over a decade later, but through no indiscretion on my part.) I wonder if Othello had mistresses or concubines? It has always been mysterious to me why mistresses are held in such low esteem by both sexes. For surely all through history they have been the glue sticking dodgy marriages together? Nowadays families are crashing asunder all over the shop. I'm certainly not advocating that every married man has a mistress, each married woman a lover, just a rethink, perhaps. Is true love about absolute possession? Does a bit of flesh-poking warrant no forgiveness and the destruction of family? In letting the one she loves swim free, the true mistress secures her only hope of holding him. Learning to love without possessing is fiendishly hard – as I looked up to see my love ranting, raging and spewing with jealousy. Desdemona certainly had to practise unconditional love with all that going on.

I almost ducked as great globules of spit came showering down upon us in the stalls. Christ he looked beautiful up there! Lucky Maggie Smith to be embalmed in his gargantuan passion. Even luckier Desdemona, for I would gladly die for him. Towards the end, I have to admit, I found my reaction to the play's message a little frail. Perhaps I was cut out to be a mistress, because finding even a speck of compassion for such a blinkered, vain, obsessive love as Othello's isn't within my humble orbit of comprehension. It was slightly unnerving, though, to recall my mother's warnings. Is it because my love *is* so thinly spread that I'm unable to enter the demonic depths of jealousy?

His curtain call was the circus of adulation he must have known it would be. What an ovation! I wanted to leap up onstage and bury myself in that hairless black-velvet barrel of a chest. Hard to conceive it was the same chest I'd first encountered in Paris, with the few straying grey hairs peeking out beneath his loose Garrick tie.

Olivier had phoned a few days earlier. 'Come round to my dressing room afterwards?' Leaving the theatre I realized I couldn't. Too many posh people all trying to tell him how moved they were, how magnificent he was. I wouldn't know how good he was until I'd managed to assimilate the clashing emotions he'd roused. No. My love for Olivier wasn't thinly spread. It was because of its limitless dimensions that I couldn't go backstage, to be pinned against the mob, walled in with grim deception. I'd see him one day soon, hopefully, which would give me an opportunity to swoon in private.

Arriving for my first day of rehearsal at the Old Vic Theatre I got the collywobbles. We would have to be so careful, never to let anyone guess how well we knew each other. The insane recklessness of the situation was turning me to jelly. Had either of us thought this madcap scheme through properly? It was going to be hugely tricky, and I would need my wits about me if I was to fit in at all. Waiting in dressing rooms longing to be ravished wouldn't help my concentration one little bit as I climbed into character.

I liked the overall feeling backstage at the Old Vic, though not the atmosphere hovering over actors. I'm not paranoid by nature, but right then I felt so alienated that I could have sworn Olivier had given away our secret, for as soon as I turned to anyone and smiled, they looked away. I became infested with memories of school, riddled with doubt and insecurity. I wanted to run home to Willy. That feeling of wishing I'd never come began to fill the corridors, dressing room and canteen, making every day more difficult.

When two people try to hide their intimacy from others why do they always go to such extremes? Olivier managed to keep his distance publicly – and how! He could be cruel at times, especially since he knew how vulnerable I was feeling. For days on end he'd ignore me, then call me into his office to squash me in his arms while he profusely apologized for his lack of attention. It made me feel like a yo-yo. Couldn't he see I was terrified and only wanted him to show me the same respect and kindness that he was showing everyone else? 'Darling one, it's because I have to fight off the demons of lust.'

I didn't believe him for a second. 'I feel as if I'm from another planet. Have you said anything to anyone here, like you certainly did with Ralphie? And don't tell me you didn't because—'

He tried kissing me to stop my ranting. 'They can't stomach your sexiness, Dame Sarah. Theatre actors will always be theatre actors.'

'What do you mean by that?' What bullshit! 'And stop calling me Dame Sarah – it's ludicrous!'

'You're the only film star among them! They all want to be movie stars at heart, so just get into their hearts like you got into mine.' By now he was an old hand at winning me round, just like he did the whole world. That same knack was going to make him first lord of the theatre.

I enjoyed being directed by him, even though he was still hitting me over the head so to speak with a lustful sledgehammer. Oddly, he didn't give me much direction during rehearsals for *The Crucible*. Mind you, I'd done a lot of work on my own, having become pretty well word perfect before rehearsals had even begun. Abigail, my character, is supposed to be in league with the devil, so late one afternoon in bed, Lionel suggested it would be fearfully effective if I flew across the stage. 'Then wire me up.'

'No, I mean really fly. I know you can, you do it in my arms all the time.'

I asked him why Arthur Miller never came to rehearsals. He shrugged. 'It's probably to do with our little problem on *The Prince and the Showgirl*, but he'll be here for the opening, I hope.'

During rehearsals of *The Recruiting Officer*, Olivier wanted to know what I'd be wearing on that night.

'I haven't had a fitting yet.'

'Ask for a low-cut dress with plenty of cleavage.'

When it was being fitted, they asked why I wanted so much cleavage. 'Ask Sir Laurence.' It was his idea for me to have this mole on my breast which he would kiss off on stage. I was convinced they had no removable moles for actors to kiss off, but then what did I know?

'What kind of sticky surface would they have used in the eighteenth century?'

'Don't ask me,' he said.

'Aren't you asking for a laugh rather than a cup of tea?'

'You hold your tongue, young lady.'

'Isn't the mole too small to pick up?'

'Of course it is. But how is any healthy man to get through a whole scene without kissing your breast?' he said, cupping them. I'll give him that, he liked my breasts.

One evening I was in the wings waiting to make an entrance, my first at the National. I could hear the roar of that first-night animal and I didn't like it one bit. A roaring full house waiting to eat me for dinner, and me standing there unable to breathe, hardly able to function at all. Frozen with terror, aching with fear. 'Cheer up, old gal, it's not the end of the world.' If you think your sweet little virgin fear is bad, wait till you get to my age.'

'You mean it doesn't get better?'

'Better, my arse! My fear is thirty years worse than yours.'

'Stop bragging.' He looked left and right, and kissed my breast. I looked down nervously.

'Just think, my whole future depends on that silly little mole coming off my breast and on to your cheek.'

'It'll come off, all right, my business always comes off.' He was right, it came off beautifully. I don't think many people saw that piece of business, but it was fun having him kiss my breast through the chronic fear.

Next time I saw Lionel he was as usual kissing my cleavage upstage, while Maggie Smith and Robert Stephens were playing their scene downstage. What a downstage act they were playing too. They were falling in love, all over the place – most dramatic, with him a happily married man and all. That was my first time on stage with Olivier, and the last.

We were in his office one day when he said, 'If someone comes in we're discussing your main scene with Colin Blakely [my father in *The Crucible*].' I'd get the gist and go to his beckoning lap. 'How's it going with Noël?' I'd begun rehearsing *Hay Fever*.

'So far, so good. I like Noël. He's a good egg.'

'I told you so. Just enjoy it. That's my only note.' With that note attended to, we had a bit of a cuddle. Those cuddles being so rare lately, they hurt.

A sudden commanding knock coincided with Noël Coward in the doorway, transfixed. I could feel Lionel's knees start to tremble; I'd better think quickly. If I remained seated, would I erase any suspicions? 'Excuse us, Noël, but I must get this finally drummed into my thick skull.' I turned back to Olivier. 'But that way won't work either. He has to say the line first and then take me on his lap.'

Olivier returned to the land of the living. 'One moment, Noël,' he said politely before turning back to me. I almost giggled with nerves. 'Try sitting before the line once more for me.'

Noël interrupted our brilliance. 'Could I just say my little piece and then trot off?'

Hard to tell from his delivery whether he'd been taken in or not. I thought it best not to hang around to find out. 'I'll have a go with Colin, Sir Laurence, and we'll show you later.'

'See you after lunch, Sarah,' said Noël as I left.

The really witty, well-written roles in *Hay Fever* were being played by Dame Edith Evans and Maggie Smith. Derek Jacobi played my brother, and being the two juveniles we didn't get any funny lines. (This time I wasn't even the fuckable object!) Prior to Noël's appearance in Olivier's office, rehearsals for

Hay Fever had been going splendidly. Noël had been terribly pleasant, continually encouraged by my sparkly interpretation of the rather dull Sorel and everything was hunky-dory. But after his rude entrance things went downhill swifter than an arrow from Cupid's bow. A decline that I found exceedingly disheartening. Judging by his new attitude towards me, I began to suspect that he not only smelled a rat, but was jealous. No doubt about it, from then on Noël's attitude towards me was that of a spurned lover. When I mentioned this to Lionel, he gave a strange bird-like twist to his head as if he were secretly flattered.

'Noëlie likes his friends safe in their little boxes where he can keep an eye on them.'

'Has Noël any reason to be jealous?'

He brushed it off like a fly.

'None at all. Noëlie's passion for me is long gone – such as it was.'

'What do you mean, "such as it was"?' Lionel, being thrilled with my own bisexual relationship with Sylvia, my whore in Half Moon Street, shared with me many things that perhaps he wouldn't have otherwise. He had no feeling of shame. If what Lionel said is true then Noël was after a wee bit of hanky-panky during *Private Lives*, and where's the harm in that? I'm sure Noël didn't rape Lionel with a gun at his head.

On top of Noël being hell-bent on seeing me as the *femme fatale* in this new melodrama, almost overnight Lionel, too, began acting strangely. Had Noël said something to him, or was it because he was too immersed in Othello? Either way, he had problems for which I felt only sympathy. 'Noëlie' was another lorryload of monkeys altogether. When I feel I'm being unjustly got at, I retaliate.

'I didn't write Sorel to be funny, Sarah,' said the maestro.

'I realize that, sir.' I went all meek and mild.

'Then just play the lines.'

Brushing dust off his shoulder I asked admiringly, 'Is it

really true you wrote this play in three days, sir?' with all the adoration I could muster.

'It is.' He put his finger down the back of his shirt collar to hide his pride.

'I'm not at all surprised.' I walked away, smiling sweetly as I went.

Lionel had asked me into his dressing room. His concentration was locked into painting his winkie waddle and balls black. It was his ritual, he did it for every performance of Othello.

'Noël's being unfair to me in rehearsal. Couldn't you tell him to lay off?'

'I'm sure, Dame Sarah, you'll give as good as you get.'

'I just have. I was rude to him.'

'He can take it, he's a big boy now.' He was a complete blackamoor, not a scrap of white anywhere. I couldn't get the figure on Hal Wallis's gold pen off my mind.

'He's not being too kindly to me either.' He was scanning his back for any tell-tale white blotches. 'Have I missed anywhere?' He hadn't. He never did.

'You're perfect. Do you think he knows about us?'

'We failed to fool him for a second, he knows me too well; so I told him everything.'

'How come? We made a pact to tell no one.'

'Noëlie won't say anything. He's simply terrified I'll ruin my life again.'

'I trust you informed him they were my fears, too?' Noël and I were both aware of what he stood to lose if anyone found out. That's why we were both so scrupulous with our planning. But Olivier was a stubborn bastard, with a spirit that would not be crushed by what he *should* be doing, and what he *could* be losing. Besides, he knew by now that I wasn't after any glory, merely the ecstasy of his close proximity. He made me feel trusted, and quite right too. I prided myself on being trustworthy above all things – except perhaps our lovemaking and massaging. To have Noël coming between us was both infuriating and insulting. Who the hell did he think he was? Just because he might have been Lionel's lover – still might be for all I knew or cared – and just because he'd written some good songs and a few frothy plays didn't give him the right to use me as he did.

I became rebellious. I couldn't stop myself. Had I been in a position to get those two silly camp louts together and ask them why they were sticking me with whipping boy as well as piggy in the middle, things might have been different. But girls aren't allowed in prep school yards. No, I was only the FO. That's certainly the way Noël treated me from then on. I didn't take to it. Shame, for under different circumstances I think we could have got along just fine. I loved to watch the rehearsals. Dame Edith was even more of a character than I remembered from seeing her lecture at RADA. Though the beauty was still there to be conjured up at will, underneath her blisteringly robust front I felt she was rather sensitive, much more nervous than Maggie Smith, who had the knack of rolling up her sleeves and immediately getting the bull by the horns. She was the National's prize star and she'd won hers – Robert Stephens. Her power was at its height, forcing me to keep well clear. I always made sure I was at a safe distance from her magnificent swooshing skirts. There was, however, the one time when she spoke to me. We were in the wings waiting to enter during *The Recruiting Officer*.

'Guess the colour of my pubes,' she said. I was at a loss, not having given the subject much thought. 'Are they red like my hair?'

I was relieved at being able to agree. 'I'm sure they are, Miss Smith,' I said as I watched her entrance. That was the high-light of our relationship. What an entrance it was. Her timing off an audience was a joy to behold. Edith was aware of it too.

But how could I practise, let alone improve, my timing

with a whole lot of dead, silly lines? Derek Jacobi said them well, really got into them, which was amazing since he was so miscast. There lay the difference between us: Derek was an actor and I wasn't. Yet being Noël's flavour of the month must also have helped. Derek had other advantages too. He wasn't caught on Olivier's lap and I was.

Olivier burnt his foot quite badly one night while walking from his dressing room to the stage. He liked walking it barefoot, it helped him to get earthed in his blackamoor. It must have been difficult playing the whole of Othello with a burnt foot. Later he gathered us all together. 'Since I'm walking barefoot to the stage, I have no choice but to ban cigarette smoking in the corridors.' That little episode didn't sit too comfortably, so when he next called for me I took along a handsome brand-new pair of bedroom slippers.

'What's this?' he said, opening his present.

'I bought them for you, sir, to walk to the stage in.'

'But I choose to walk barefoot.'

I decided to take a breath and give it to him. 'Is it correct to ban everyone else on your team from smoking, from doing what they love to – need to – do just so that you can walk barefoot to the stage? I expected to find a team here, sir, because I chose to believe you when you told me I was coming to work for a team, yet I find only wolves fighting over glory rights. Everyone trying to stay on top, or stamp on who they can to get to the top—'

'I'm sorry I missed your Worthing St Joan. I should have liked to have seen you playing yourself,' he seethed sarcastically.

One morning, I found a genuinely funny way to say a couple of lines from Hay Fever while still remaining loyal to both Sorel and the play. Many of the company laughed. Hooray! My Sorel was finally coming to life. The only trouble was that Edith felt none too overjoyed.

'Is the gal going to play it like that on the night?' she boomed across the rehearsal room. Sadly this didn't help the relationship between Noël and me, which had disintegrated even further.

'Come here, Sarah, a moment.' Noël took me aside.'I know you don't like the part as written, but you'll have to lump it. Just play it.'

The man was a writer, wasn't he? If he wrote it in three days, surely he could sit down for a fourth? There are areas in *Hay Fever* which I, the actor, felt the writer had no interest in whatsoever. 'Sir, are you happy with the writing of the brother and sister?'

He gave me a doubly wary look. 'I beg your pardon?'

'If you were to reread the play from the point of view of Sorel you may find more understanding for what I'm saying.'

Another wary look while clapping his hands. 'All right, everyone, teabreak over. I'll have a read, Sarah.'

'Thank you, sir.'

In his office later, Olivier turned to me, truculently. 'Why have you been so cruel to Noël?'

'I haven't been cruel to Noël, he's been cruel to me.'

'A mere snippet of a thing, yet you dare tell Noëlie to rewrite his play?'

I became fierce. 'I'm damn well not going to be his, or your, whipping boy.'

'But to rewrite his play?'

'I think he should mull through it from the point of view of Sorel.'

'I've been doing some mulling of my own.'

'How did it go?'

'I give you one last chance before I fire you. Play Sorel as written.'

'Did you play kissing a mole off my breast as written?'

'That's entirely different.'

'How is it different? I see it as an actor trying to make a part work, or as in your case trying to draw as many laughs and as much attention to himself – without a cup of tea to be seen – as he possibly can.'

He knew I had a point, that was the best part of Olivier, his great sense of justice. 'I ask you one last time. Play the part as written.'

'Only if you do. It's not my playing of Sorel, is it? It's because I'm your mistress that all this rot's set in.'

I went home angry with everyone. Angry, above all, at Noël's attitude towards me ever since his fateful entrance in Olivier's office. People should never knock while entering, it isn't cricket. Othellos and Iagos wherever I cared to look. That evening the whole experience made me want to vomit. So, finding it foul throwing up on an empty stomach, I quickly cooked dinner for both Willy and me, pork chops and grilled tomatoes. I wolfed down my meal. A rather large bone from the side of the chop jammed in my gullet. I couldn't speak, but, what was worse, I couldn't breathe. Because Willy wasn't too keen on the physical side of humanity apart from the sexual, it was no turn-on for him to see me sprawled over the chair trying to spew up on a chop bone. Finally, 'Come on, I'd better take you to hospital.'

Off we went with Willy driving my car for the first time. I thought he couldn't drive, and I still don't know. After all it isn't every day that one's gagged, unable to breathe and about to depart to pastures new. Strangely enough, I was taken back to my childhood, breathless from the fear of death. At St Thomas's Hospital a surgeon looked down my throat and said, 'Get her on the operating table, anaesthetic – quick!'

When I returned to the land of the living I was told I mustn't speak for ten days. 'But that's impossible, I'm in a play—'

'I'm sorry,' said the sister. 'Those are the specialist's orders. The throat is badly scarred. You must rest it.'

I was determined to look on the good side. Perhaps I'd be able to sing at last. Back in Hasker Street I slept as peacefully as I did when I finally escaped for ever from Roedean – though it wasn't long before Nona was whispering at the door, fluttering her eyelids, like some coy virgin. 'Sir Laurence has brought you some flowers.' She let him in, and went to find a vase – or did she? I nodded in the direction of the hallway, he went to check.

'She's gone.' He came to sit on the bed. 'We've had to recast with your understudy. Noël is most upset.'

'Bullshit,' I whispered.

'It's all for the best. You were as unhappy as I've ever seen you – you still haven't healed from the school experience yet, my little one.' He looked in my eyes. 'You're still smarting from the pain of being institutionalized.' There was no hint of patronage.

'Are you telling me as politely as poss that I'm no actress?'

'Far from it, you have it all but—'

'But what?'

'It's your reluctance to enter the arena.' His eyes reached for something far, far away. 'It's fear.' That pissed me off, for I was fearless. (Or so I thought, then.)

I retaliated. 'We're all frightened – and according to you it gets much worse. So I haven't a hope.'

I laughed, but it hurt. 'My father told me it was only temperament that prevented me from becoming a tennis pro' – I thought I'd let him have it as it was – 'yet it's *your* temperament, *your* lust that prevented me from becoming a National Theatre player.'

He looked at me a moment, before ducking the challenge. 'Remind me never to play tennis with you.' As an after-thought. '*Our* lust.'

'Who knows? Maybe just Noël's.' He tickled me so sweetly, evading a response.

Later. 'Lack of temperament is a very British desease.'

'And how can I get to grips with it?'

'Discipline. Discipline alone can win.'

'How does one get to grips with discipline?'

'No good getting to grips with it. Aspiration is all – follow your lodestar.'

I personally had no aspiration whatsoever to become the

first lordess of the theatre. 'What do I do until I find that lodestar?' He looked so concerned at that moment.

'You have the capacity to fly higher than flock because you are a free spirit.' (I'm forever being called a "free spirit" but have no clue as to what it is.)

He gave me a cuddle, then kissed me very gently, as if the chop bone were still there.

'Be careful.' I indicated the door and Nona. 'She doesn't knock.'

'If I were not so incurably selfish, I'd let you go. But I can't. I can't.'

Maybe he was right, perhaps I was still smarting from the pain of school as well as the pain in my gullet. Smarting with regret that I'm simply unable to function within a group. Smarting with the ache of this No-man All-things in whose arms I needed to rest for long enough to heal. I wanted to stay like I was, snuggled up against his, by now, world famously handsome chest.

Noël came to see me three days later, bearing flowery gifts. Lionel had sent him. 'Do be careful, the pair of you. Promise?'

'If you'll promise not to open doors while still knocking.'

'You're a tyrant, did you know that?'

CHAPTER TWENTY-SEVEN

I WAS GROWING nauseous watching the Irish Sea roll ferociously beneath me. It was 1965 and Addo and I were drawing closer to all those beautiful memories of my last Irish venture. How time flies! When I'd declined *The Rivals* at the Haymarket with Ralph Richardson it was because I wanted to do the many-times-delayed film of the lyrical Irish tale *I Was Happy Here*. (The only quality film being made in a country where I could take Addo.) At last it had its finance together, and we were off. Desmond Davies was the director. Julian Glover was to play my husband, Shaun Caffrey my lover, Cyril Cusack my father, and Edna O'Brien had written the script, a sequel to *The Girl with Green Eyes*.

A few weeks earlier, Willy and I had gone to a dinner party at Edna's in the splendid house she had then on the river at Putney. I liked Edna a great deal – a horny, secretive kind of a woman. But a real woman, that's for sure, reminding me of Simone Signoret, which warmed me to her even more.

While we were both in the kitchen after dinner, clearing away the dishes, she drew me closer. (Edna always has to bring one to her because she speaks in a low whisper.) 'Sarah, can I ask you something?'

'Fire ahead,' I said confidently, putting the plates in the sink. She drew me even closer.

'Which do men prefer, the taste of soap or cunt?'

Rather like Maggie Smith and her pubes, it came to me right out of left field. I had no idea how to respond, this issue, too, never having crossed my mind.

'Which?' said Edna, leaving me no room for manoeuvre.

'It'd depend on the cunt' – since she'd called it that – 'and to some extent the brand of soap.'

'What kind of an answer is that?'

'I suppose the truth is, neither. It should taste of you.'

She didn't listen to my last remark, merely turned back to the sink. I realize, with hindsight, that she wasn't interested in the answer, only in my reaction to her question. She was pleased to have left-footed me.

I was going to get a 'thing' about it now, I could tell. Soap or pussy? Like the old grandfather with a Father-Christmas beard who was asked by his great-grandchild, 'Grandad, do you sleep with your beard in or out of the sheets?' He paused, scratching his head. 'I'll tell you in the morning.'

Grandad sleeps with his beard out. This doesn't feel right, so next night he sleeps with his beard inside. This feels just as awkward. So the next night he sleeps with his beard out again, which still feels strange. On and on he goes, trying to find the answer, in, out, in, out, night after night, until one morning he's found dead with exhaustion, his beard neither in nor out.

I wanted to take in the approaching coast and I stood on deck looking out at the grey sea below, lashing memories at me, mostly messy ones. All through history whenever there are unanswered questions, unresolved problems, financial chaos, men go off to war. The same with relationships. Let's go away and hope that the problems vanish in that fickle wind of separation. That's what Willy and I were doing, I suppose. Hoping that being apart would make our hearts grow fonder. Money had come between us, because of Willy's pride. It didn't matter to me one jot that Willy had no money. How could it? If money was important I could have chosen someone who was rolling in the stuff. It was impossible to persuade Willy that I loved him not because of what he might become, but for what he already was. But he thought I deserved better and would never take a penny off me. So there we both were, Willy convinced that he was a failure and me thinking myself a two-timing whore. Not a good climate for blossoming.

Willy was heir-in-waiting to the once famous Donaldson shipping line; the heiress was his rich Scottish granny.

'When Granny dies it'll be striped shirts and chicken on Sunday for the rest of our days.' Willie's recipe for success.

'How old is Granny?'

'She's getting on a bit nowadays. In fact, I have a little plot afoot.'

Willy's plot was to ask Granny down to London, and then to walk her off her feet.

His plan had a pitfall. On the appointed day Willy went off, looking spruce and crisp, to collect Granny from her hotel and take her on this marathon walk. About four hours later he arrived home in a taxi, looking thoroughly the worse for wear. 'Granny walked me off my feet. She put me in a taxi, because she had a dinner party to attend.' He collapsed on the bed, exhausted. Willy wasn't at all fit. He never walked further than the office round the corner, across the road to the newsagent's, then home again.

His creditors were becoming a menace. Often he'd be at work and I'd be left to face them alone. I wasn't too keen on this new role. Most appeared tough, businesslike and shady. I never asked Willy what he owed money for, or how much, but it was always hanging over us, this urgent need for him to get some funds together. I wished I could have helped him more, but I wasn't interested in becoming the world's greatest earner. Besides, I still had Nona and Sammy eating me out of house and home.

The Irish coast was looming into view. Because I had to sound Irish for this film, the producer, Roy Millichip, had sent along an Irish girl, who came from the required area, the bogs. She had an almost clichéd Irish look about her, I thought. Dark with a keen Irish eye that danced around the drawing room of Hasker Street, sparkling merrily. She came regularly for a month, until, after a great deal of effort, I had a passable County Clare accent. 'Our month is up, my task is done and I'm proud of you,' she said, rubbing her hands.

'Let's have a cup of tea to celebrate,' I said, rubbing mine in sympathy.

'That would be heavenly,' she replied in a most cultured lah-di-dah London voice.

'Say that again?'

She slapped her thighs as she delivered her upper-class hoot.

'Your producer wanted someone who came from the bogs, so that's me.' There I was thinking I had the genuine article when I find a budding Sloane under her County Clare.

'Hello. Don't look as if you've seen a ghost. My name's Sally Mates.' (Michael Mates's sister.) So impressed was I with the way she had me completely fooled that we've remained firm friends ever since.

Lionel and I met before I left. As I watched him in the dusky light in the strange unused room, I could feel my heartbeat ricocheting against my ribs. It was true. I *would* happily die for him, run and stand between him and the bullet, for that would be far less painful than the walk into his arms at that moment.

'Do you want to get married?' he asked sadly from the shadows.

'No. Not yet. I haven't found anyone I want to keep the vows for.'

'You believe in the marriage vows, do you?'

'Yes. I believe there's no other reason for getting married.'

'Wait till you are,' he said sadly, taking off his mac.

'Yes. I suppose marriage takes quite a bit of discipline.' Except for our breathing there was a silence as we stood there, at either end of the room.

'Come here.' Slowly, so slowly I went to him.

'I don't want you marrying, not one little bit.'

CHAPTER TWENTY-EIGHT

THE COUNTY TOWN of Ennis wrapped me in a new, calmer frame of mind. Although I missed Willy, it was good to put some space between us and our over-indulgent lovemaking. Being away from Nona and Sam gave me a wonderful sense of freedom, too. However hard I tried, and believe me I had, I simply couldn't get rid of her. Sammy was a healthy little chap, which meant demanding, nudging me with uncomfortable daily signs that motherhood and I might never hit it off.

Fortunately the part demanded that I get a sense of what it would be like as a girl again, free of the chains with which I'd weighed myself down of late. The director, Desmond Davies, was a sweetheart, giving me an easy passage into the bicycle-riding, sand-and-sea-loving colleen, and I enjoyed every minute of it. No funny lines, alas, but you can't have everything.

I looked around me at other girls of my age and I felt apart, I suppose because I had no friends, either girl or boy. I'd always felt I didn't need any because I'd found family totally sufficient. I'd cultivated no actor friends except for the recently discovered Sally Mates. Friendship takes patience and nurturing, and perhaps I was simply too selfish to want to share myself, so ashamed of a double life.

One night after I'd been revelling for a couple of weeks in my new-found freedom, Nona turned up without Sammy, at the hotel in Ennis. She wore that oh-so-sweetly-defiant smile, tempting me with the familiar need to smash her face in. I wanted to send her packing, but hadn't the heart. Living quietly in Ennis with Addo had been therapeutic, and I needed to continue. Luckily there wasn't too much cause for grief, because a few days later she bundled herself off to Dublin with some burly lorry driver.

I found Julian Glover, my husband in the film, healing from a private life, that seemed to be beyond repair. He was estranged from his wife of many years. He claimed she had given him the brush-off, and because they were living apart he was sad and lonely. Julian made me feel safe. Lying in his arms was as healing for both of us as it was easy, for he seemed strong, uncomplicated and correct in a most unboring way. Just what the doctor ordered. Sanity, safety and a little moment of peace.

Although Julian was tall, blond and handsome in a craggy kind of way, he had a stiffness that smothered his natural charm, a stiffness that comes from damage. I fear it was the old need to play Florence Nightingale that made me yearn to direct Julian's sunshine back on to full beam and in so doing perhaps take a moment of respite myself and put my other life – my two other lives – on hold. Yes. I needed all to stop for a moment; because I'd lost all sense of life's direction.

By the time we left Ennis, Julian's sense of self-worth had been somewhat restored, and it was I who had to return to face the music.

Home again and good old Hasker Street. Julian, who had been staying with me for the past week, was down in the kitchen making tea one morning when the phone rang. Would it be Willy Donaldson, Robin Fox, or the real Robin? I wasn't up to it being anyone. Owning up to Willy about my affair with Julian hadn't been my favourite task and I felt a real bounder even though things between us had been deteriorating before I left.

It would be difficult for a man to comprehend the way I felt about lust and love, and probably most modern women, too, for I am a deeply old-fashioned girl at heart. Each time I make love to someone a whole commitment automatically has to follow. I don't love lightly. Why couldn't I grow up and become an Edith Piaf, simply plucking them off the streets for the night, giving them all the love I had and then waving them off with no questions asked? There was no doubt my capacity for loving was immense, but whose isn't? Why didn't I lighten up and enjoy playing the field?

I didn't want to answer the phone.

'Hello?'

'Is that Sarah?'

'Speaking.'

'You whore, you bitch, you slut. How does it feel, stealing husbands? Can't you keep your filthy hands off?'

Shock rose within me as the phone went dead. It had been a classy voice. Joan Plowright? I didn't recall Joan speaking such handsome English. No, I believed, though I couldn't be certain, that I was listening to the tones of Eileen Atkins, Julian's ex-wife. It's usually quite easy to tell an actor's background, but not Eileen's. Her working-class roots were immaculately missing.

Oddly enough, that it had been Eileen Atkins and not Joan Plowright made me feel even worse. I'd never purposely destroy a marriage – it's too easy a game to play, well below the belt. I would never have allowed Julian anywhere near me if I'd had an inkling there might be the smallest spark of hope waiting to be rekindled within his marriage. Was Julian playing a double game with me? I sat up in bed. What was the truth?

Although Julian reaffirmed his original story, declaring that all sparks had indeed gone out ages ago, I began to think. To hell with that, what about the great spark that had gone out of my heart? Huge doubts niggled every time we were together. What's worse, I found myself hopelessly lacking in self-esteem, given the inner knowledge that Eileen was right. I *was* a whore, a bitch, a slut, even if these feelings of disgrace had little to do with *her* ex-husband.

*

Out of the blue my dream house, at Turville, in the Chilterns, came up for sale. My Chekhovian Gothic rectory could be mine. I was unable to believe my luck and immediately took Julian down to see it. It didn't let me down. Everything about the house at close quarters was as perfect as it had been from the sky. Perhaps it was a sign to grow up, settle down, get wed and start a family. This house and all the mature, nurturing dreams that Julian and I would be putting into it would hopefully save my soul.

On the phone with Mother. 'No, darling, you must let me vet it for myself – I bet they saw you coming.'

'What do you mean, Ma?'

'I bet you told them you'd fallen in love with the house from the sky. Which is no way to buy a house. Arrange for me to be there and don't sign anything.'

Mothers will always be mothers. She found the damp, the rot in the attic, the broken floorboards, the rickety stairs, the rusty boiler. 'The window-frames are splitting all over the shop!' She breathed in deeply. 'Dry rot riddled with damp. Can't you smell it?'

'I've never seen such fine copper beeches.'

'They're out of their minds if they think they'll get half the asking price.' It was about thirty-two thousand. I'd bought Hasker Street for eleven thousand. 'You can't afford it.'

I let Mother's negativity wash over me, and told her to attend to her own dreams rather than destroying mine.

'When dreams are playing at damp and rotting family games with Julian Glover, then money is everything. This is no reflection on Julian's ability to make you happy, but on your ability to do the same for Julian. Whereas sharing all these responsibilities with the man you should have married in the first place is something else altogether.' I didn't argue. She was biased towards Willy Fox, who was now going great guns as a movie star and could therefore have helped with the damp.

I watched Mother's mouth moving. How I loved that mouth of hers, so generous yet refined. I watched her nose puckering, those famliar willow-leaf nostrils quivering as she whispered with an all-knowing confidentiality. 'How's Lionel Kerr?'

I had to think quickly. 'He's gone to live in Brazil.' Ever since that time I needed her advice when Willy Fox asked to marry me, I had never spoken of Lionel Kerr. But she knew from the word go, insisting she saw a possessive look in Lionel's eye that time we all ate together in Ireland. 'Once I've taken the marriage vows, he'll be no more.'

'Then be sure you'll be able to keep them with no doubts whatsoever. One little niggling doubt can grow astonishingly swiftly, niggling away until your whole world tumbles in, leaving Turville only a stone's throw away from Brazil.'

What did she mean? She had done her usual slick job – I believe, purposefully – of mystifying me. Driving back to London, my brain was a swarm of nigglings. First I visualized Julian and me living in the rectory. Then I pictured Willy Donaldson there with me, which made me chuckle. Not much wheeling and dealing in Turville – no, he would go mad. Mother was right, Willy Fox would have been my ideal life partner. Hell and damnation! I couldn't help revelling in the fantasy of Lionel and me together in my rectory – only to find myself splattered with the pain of common sense. I could never afford the place, even if I accepted another film abroad. No, I had to release myself from that particular dream.

'It'll be a great millstone around your neck, you mark my words.'

Back at Hasker Street I had an urge to ring up Willy Donaldson, just to hear his dry wit and sexy drawl. Once Willy had got over the initial shock of our parting, he'd regained his balance and found a new bird to feather his sexy nest, and in no time she was begging Willy to marry her. Whoever she was, she had immaculate taste in men. But

Willy being a secretive soul, I knew nothing of this from his own lips.

'How are you, Smiles?' he said cheerfully.

'Would you like to live in the country?'

'Not me, Smiles.'

'I miss you.'

'Ah, little thing, do you?' he snorted. Even his snort had a drawl to it. 'Are you phoning me just to play cruel games with your old Wil?'

Ever since Eileen's phone call and what I suspected was Julian's incorrect colouring of their relationship, I seemed unable to choose between Julian and Willy. Therein lay the answer.

One Christmas, years later in LA, Carly Simon asked me to her home for carol singing. Because most of the élite in the singing world were to be there, and with me still song-struck, I went. Who could resist going carol singing with Joni Mitchell, James Taylor (Carly's husband), Joan Baez, Bob Dylan and Linda Rondstat? Carly Simon turned out to be a stunner and her husband had a handsome poetic face. They looked the kind of pair that dreams are made of and seemed blissfully happy together.

Yet it transpired that Carly had asked me over because she was besotted with Willy Donaldson and wanted to check me out. 'I loved him more than you will ever know.' I was astonished, and completely unprepared for her confession after she'd dragged me into her funky-chic kitchen for privacy. She obviously wanted me to resolve some dark unfinished business lurking within her tormented breast. Some of her obsession for Willy had unfortunately dribbled over into an absolute turmoil of bitterness towards me. Who can blame me for having no women friends when they all behaved like this? Her voice was hard and edged with pain, similar to Eileen's during that horrendous phone call.

'Why did you ask Willy back, merely to chuck him again?'

'It wasn't like that – he never once mentioned your name.'

'He's secretive, Willy. at the time I thought my life was ruined.' She meant it.

Apparently when I made that phone call asking Willy to come back, Carly was packing in her old life, including her romantic poet of a husband, to come over and marry Willy. I checked it out with Willy later. It was all true.

CHAPTER TWENTY-NINE

IT WAS THE first time I'd been back to the National.
During the interval in Congreve's *Love for Love* I quietly
snuck out to digest what I'd witnessed. I was angry.
Too angry in fact to stomach any more of Lionel's idiotic
'asking for a laugh'. (His role was Tattle, the poncy fopsy
gossip.)

Later in the watering-hole we were skipping furiously.
This was a regular discipline, which was why he had chosen
another damp basement – no one above us. He had been
seeing me in his gym time because things were getting ever
tougher at the office. So we'd skip for a while before I took
on the mammoth task of deknotting him. That day he was
doubly furious: not only was I able to skip for a much longer
time (being the school champ!), but do bumps to every one of
his singles.

'Bitch!' he snarled.

'Dirty old men must have some price to pay.'

He snarled even more disgustedly and, after skipping for
a while longer, went rather thoughtful. 'Having a name,
however measly, makes it obligatory to stay till the curtain
call. It's one's duty.'

I laughed, astonished at having been missed. 'Who told
you I'd walked out?'

'Don't be naïve!'

I decided to let him have it since I was still smarting from
my *Hay Fever* injustice. I would never have got that chop bone
stuck if I hadn't been unfairly treated.

'What the hell were you doing up there – asking for
laughs all evening long?'

'Apparently you weren't there all evening; besides, Tattle is a part that calls out for—'

'Scene stealing? Who but thee could get away with fiddling false calf muscles throughout almost the whole of someone else's scene?'

He went on the defensive.

'All fops wore false calf muscles beneath their tights in those days.'

'Irrelevant. I'm talking about justice!'

He grew so out of breath that he collapsed on the creaking bed. 'I'm getting old.'

'Too old to be dishing out different roles for different fools – and I've been fooled!'

'Come here.'

I did another decade of bumps.

'Come here,' he said with such sincerity that I did just that.

He was in fine shape, overwhelmingly so. What discipline it took to keep a figure hard as iron in one's late fifties. I did my bit with the lumps and bumps till the tension began to melt.

'You're right, Dame Sarah, I must watch it.' He went silent, then said, 'I suppose I'm leading my own private revolution. Against the coming age of the clone, when acting will disintegrate into forging realism.'

'I hope not!' One can watch realism in the coffee shop all day long and it's free.

'"Art" stems from the word artifice, which in turn is artificial.' Lionel didn't go overboard with the Method School of Acting. He saw it as artless, self-indulgently mumbling and minuscule, but to my mind his style was just as indulgent, being unsubtle, full of tricks and overbearing. To me great acting would be roughly mid-Atlantic, somewhere between Olivier and Brando. 'How I'd love to see you on the screen with Brando!'

He liked the sound of that idea immensely. 'Let's try and

196

set it up. *Julius Caesar*, with him as my Antony.' He made a camp gesture, turned over and there we are . . .

Coming home one afternoon with my love life still messily unresolved, I went down to the kitchen to find Nona with three shady-looking characters. One Rastafarian, a black girl and a blonde hippie. Nona introduced me and, while I was making everyone a cup of tea, from the corner of my eye I noticed her handing over some money. Although this was none of my business I couldn't help but note that it was my money she was handing over.

She saw me looking, so she beamed one of her dangerously bright smiles.

'I wasn't expecting my friends over so early. Would you go and fetch Sammy from school for me?' How I longed to return one of her coy eyelash flutters with a lethal left hook.

It wasn't the request to fetch Sammy that bothered me – I did that most days anyway – it was the urgency behind it. I was in no doubt that she wanted me out of the house. Her eyes were glazing over with that too familiar frenetic zeal, the dreaded first signs of a manic phase. I'd seen it with the Irish lorry driver, so perhaps she wanted to take on the three ragamuffins all in one fell swoop.

Sammy and I watched Addo take his usual dip in the Serpentine followed by his usual refusal to come out again. There was another dog, a red setter, swimming about beyond the bridge leading from Hyde Park into Kensington Gardens. I hauled Sammy after them, to find Addo doing something strange to the red setter in Kensington Fountains. I became a little concerned because of the red setter's continual disappearance under the surface. Were they making love or fighting?

There was no option but to leave Sammy sitting on the bench while I took off my trousers and waded in after them.

Looking around I saw this chap on the edge. He was one of the sprucest young fops I'd seen in a long time. Floppy silk hanky with tweedy country clothes, and muddy brown leather boots. 'I can't get my dog off yours, sorry.'

'It's not my dog – my dog's over there.' He pointed to a huge Pyrenean mountain dog. A great idea came to me. I waded out and ran over to the Pyrenean in an attempt to make Addo jealous. I took this horny gentleman Pyrenean to the water's edge, and once we were firmly focused in Addo's sight line I uttered abandoned love groans.

'What's his name?' I asked the owner, who looked on a wee bit spellbound.

'Beethoven.' To each his own.

'Give us a kiss, Beethoven,' quite loudly, using all the notes in my voice that I used when Addo and I were feeling amorous. It worked. Addo looked up, and I swear he did a double take, for he was off that poor red setter, out of the water and over to Beethoven in a flash.

As I saw the red setter greet an elderly couple in the far distance, I heard that gentlemanly voice speak again behind me. 'Has your dog got a lead?'

I turned back to find Addo about to do something strange to the Pyrenean.

'He won't hurt him.' But I undid Addo's lead (which I also wore as a belt) from my drenched waist and threw it over.

'Thanks.' The fop caught it with ease, while indicating Addo.

'He's a lovely specimen.'

'So's Beethoven.' He put the lead on Addo and hauled him off.

As I was wringing out my shirt tails, 'Oh! My God! Sammy!' How could I forget Sammy?

The fop kindly took Addo from me while I ran around like a blue-arsed fly, not settling anywhere long enough to look. Having made sure that Sammy wasn't to be seen towards the Serpentine, my panic rose to chaos point. What was I to do? I'd get Addo and then find a policeman. Yes.

No Sammy to be seen anywhere. Returning through the Serpentine Tunnel, headed once more for Kensington Gardens, I found myself shivering. Yet all was safe. Indeed not only safe but fruitful, for there stood the fop with the two Pyreneans, now the best of friends, and Sammy, bold as brass, sitting astride his shoulders.

'Thank you so much,' I said weakly, trying not to let him see how hysterical and unfit I was. 'You deserve a cup of tea for saving the day.'

'Not now, but one day I'll knock on your door, if I may? Perhaps we could walk together if you were sufficiently in the pink?'

'Excellent,' I replied, taking Addo from his calm hand for the third time. 'Say goodbye, Sammy.'

'No!' he said, pointing to the fop. 'Name!'

'My name is Johnnie Windeatt.'

'Bye, Johnnie Windy,' said Sam, rightfully triumphant while Johnnie shook me pleasantly but firmly by the hand.

'I'm Sarah.'

'Yes, I know, I've seen you and Addo many times round Hasker Street. In fact I know you're number eighteen. As I say, I'll knock on your door, one day.' He smiled and walked off most mysteriously.

Nona was lying on her bed when Sammy and I got back. 'I'm just having a little rest. Could you give Sammy his tea and put him to bed?' Her voice sounded weird, so I thought I'd better check her out in case I found a mass of pills all over the place. After our return from Ireland, Nona had achieved yet another suicide dress-rehearsal, this time choosing to flirt with death on my drawing-room carpet, leaving me to feel all the guilt, exasperation and failure while a neighbour helped me get her into the car. Off we went to St George's Hospital, a journey that I could probably have made with my eyes closed. Once she was off the danger list, I was allowed in to see her. As she lay there, a veritable Ophelia on a great pile of white pillows, I am ashamed to admit I found myself, for the first time, shaking with almost uncontrollable fury. 'Nona, no more rehearsals! Jump next time.'

This time it was neither a suicide rehearsal nor the real thing, and I was about to start ripping out her lashes one by one – just to compare her screams with the one I heard in the hospital. I consoled myself with the fact that she was still breathing, sighed, then went and gave Sammy his supper of cornflakes, milk, with banana, and a quick bath followed by a bit of *Rupert Bear* in his nursery. I then tiptoed downstairs to make myself something before getting an early night, it being one of those rare occasions when I could have a moment to myself. That's the one thing about love affairs – and deceit – they do take it out of you.

Lovers tend to suffocate the spirit. Suffocation eventually strangles the love. Long-lasting lovers respect each other's space. By space I don't mean separate castles, but different interests and moods. Freedom within trust. I was thinking such thoughts while still gobbling my dinner of baked beans and grilled tomatoes when Nona came lilting in looking like Isadora Duncan.

'Those beans, they look like frog spawn.' She picked up a handful – messy things to get hold of, baked beans – and quietly scrutinized them. Nona was either on something, or had forgotten to take something. I had no idea which.

'Go on, Nona, take the whole lot.'

She knelt down on the floor beside my chair. Looking up at me like the Virgin Mary, weeping, she said, 'I love you, Sarah, I love you.'

I quickly changed the subject. 'How's Manny?' Manny was her lover these days. In fact he'd outlasted all her others by a mile.

'He hasn't been round lately.' Nona wept buckets all over my Serpentine-wet trousers, which I hadn't had time to change.

'Take them off, they're soaking.' Nona was tough when she wanted something, as I had found out over the last two years, or was it three? How come she was still there, still tough, with a son who was learning fast?

'Are you frightened of me?' she said, as she tried to persuade me to remove my trousers.

'No, I'm frightened *for* you.'

'What's that supposed to mean?' She was pulling at my trousers. 'Nona, please don't!' I meant it. Nona had a faraway look. Her pupils were the size of Addo's.

When it came to drugs I was as innocent as a babe in arms. I'd only ever consumed alcohol and tobacco, both in small amounts. Even marijuana hadn't come into my consciousness. I was having a tough enough time grounding myself to Mother Earth without thinking up ways of getting higher off her surface.

So it confused me somewhat to see Nona seeming to perform a feverish version of Ophelia/Isadora, quickly to be forsaken for a flushed, sweaty manifestation of Mrs Danvers. Where, oh, where, was Mr de Winter?

'Nona, please leave off. Are you on something?'

She started wiggling her hips. 'Come on, Sarah, discard your gloom and dance with me.'

We did, we danced together. It was nerve-racking looking into those eyes at such close quarters. It was the vast hopeless darkness in Nona's eyes that repelled me. Something was pulling at Nona from somewhere else. Whatever it was, it was trying to suck me in too. I fell against a crooked kitchen chair and, as I slipped, she tried to pull down my trousers. Not wanting to take them off in front of her, I lunged up the stairs to my room. It was strange, my physical attitude towards her. Nona had the most wonderful hair and breasts, yet I didn't want her to touch me. How much more powerful it is, the spirit compared to the flesh. To think Lionel had been jealous of Bertie, whose flesh had mostly turned to bone. Just goes to show.

Nona was in my bedroom like a weasel and collapsed on my bed, sobbing to her very soul. Not wanting her to wake Sammy I closed the door, leaving myself no choice but to observe her mood changing direction, lust evaporating into fear and back again.

'Nona, what have you been taking? Should I get a doctor?'

'LSD.'

I hadn't heard of LSD so I was none the wiser. 'Is it dangerous?'

'Just a bad trip. Hold me.' She began to shake. Her body was sweaty yet cold. If it hadn't been for the godforsaken look in her eyes, and her clamminess I would have thought that the whole evening's exercise was to remove my trousers. She buried herself in my breasts (such as they were) and occasionally rose up wailing. 'No one knows what it feels like to have devils inside.'

'I know what it feels like because I can see them in your pupils.'

Nona's face lit up. But then she turned around again. 'Be careful, they'll take you too!'

Nona forsook my breasts and danced her way over towards a more reliable turn-on – wallowing in her own reflection. She put the light on and gave her pupils a long look. Why do most of us pout our lips in the mirror, in a way that is totally foreign to the onlooker? Every one of us must regularly give our bathroom mirrors reason for a merry hoot.

Nona stood back to get the effect of her silhouette in the mirror and with great effort managed to breathe in her stomach while pushing out her breasts. With nothing living up to expectation she expelled a raw sob, ran back to my lap and wept again. Her staccato shakes got so bad that I filled up the bath and guided her towards it. Shaking quite severely now, she sat among the steam, fluttering her lashes. 'I think I'm in for a bad night,' she whispered with rounded modulation.

'What can I do?'

'Wash me all over.' We were back, swift as a twirl on a hatpin, into one of her ravenously lusty phases. I wasn't sure I could cope.

'Nona, I'm going to finish off my cold baked beans, I'm starving. Do you want anything?'

She looked away from her swelling breasts, bursting forth from the water's rim. Breasts can look good in the bath, if one lies in the right position. 'Would you kindly bring me some ice cream?'

'We haven't—'

'I always keep some for Manny.'

Downstairs I rang up Manny to ask him about LSD. He told me just to see that she didn't harm herself. 'Be patient with her.' I was to call him if her condition deteriorated. He was with his wife so it wasn't easy for him to get away. He said LSD wasn't his particular tipple, confirming that the culprits were, as I suspected, the gang I met earlier.

Just as I was about to go back up, she appeared in the stairwell, wet and naked. If I wasn't going to undress for her, she was surely going to undress for me; it had all the signs of being a bumpy night. As I feared, so it came to be, and at one point she became frighteningly violent. I couldn't stop her banging her head against the dining-room wall. Finally, confused, and terrified at being so ineffectual, I opened my still-wet shirt and pulled out my breast. She grinned at me as her mood pirouetted on a pinhead back to the raunchy domain of her devils, where they wanted not one breast but both. She placed my hand on her breast too, wanting all four hands to be touching breast. 'The miracle of these things!' She peered down at our breasts like a chimp looking for fleas, fingering them just as she had done earlier with the baked beans. Finally bored, she dropped mine, just as the Spanish fortune teller had dropped my hand, forgetting it was joined to my wrist, and collapsed on her bed. 'Oh, Manny! Oh, Manny! I love you so.'

Why is it that women ever start an affair with a married

man? Why did it take so long for the penny to drop that I, too, was in that category? Why did I pretend my affair was different? Yet in a way it was. For instance, Nona had been round to Manny's house, pleading to be let in. I thought of me going down to Brighton and whining like a puppy to be let into Lionel's house on Royal Crescent, and chuckled – but not for long.

It was an important night for me. I knew I'd never want to be taken through Nona's realms of darkness again. Never had I delved so deeply into the dense power beckoning on the darker side of life. I'm reminded of the film *Blue Velvet*. It had a smell about it, the stench of raw naked evil leaking out from armpits and crotches, forcing me to look at the same dark potential inside myself. People walked out in droves. Not only did Nona point the way to that, but she also put me off wanting to take hard drugs. I was never tempted, even when I lived in LA and they were on offer at every turn, because I immediately saw Nona being shaken like a rag doll by the omnipotent power of those dark forces. A sight to put anyone off for life.

Late one afternoon with Lionel in Hasker Street, he kept saying, 'Get her out, she's ruining your life.'

I couldn't make out why Nona should be so disturbing to him. 'I think there's something else bothering you, not just Nona.'

He leapt out of bed and swished a white towel around his waist. It wouldn't join in the middle, not because he was fat – on the contrary, he was looking particularly dashing still – but it was a mean towel.

'It's all Nona. You're letting some manic-depressive, schizophrenic nymphomaniac come between us.' A real tongue-twister and he loved saying it rapidly, for it exercised his already formidable elocution.

'How come?'

'How come? Use yer brains, woman. We could be meeting here every week.'

As I thought this through, I got the giggles.

'What's so funny?'

'It could turn into a Feydeau farce.' He loved a bit of farce, did Lionel, and began twisting his imaginary villain's moustache as I told him about Julian and Willy alternating.

'Fine for men to behave thus, but a woman – my woman?'

'You mean your mistress.'

He held me. 'Everyone's mistress more like.' He buried himself in what fleshy bits he could find, but as always it would have been too brief even if he had held me till the nuclear bomb dropped.

'Have you ever taken an aphrodisiac?' he asked with a hint of oneupmanship.

'No, never knew there was such a thing.'

'Oh, yes, there is. You pick a fresh coconut from the palm tree at its moment of ripeness. Then you inject it with half a bottle of Napoleon brandy 1902. Finally, you bury it three feet in the earth and leave it to mature for twenty-two years.'

'Shall we get Lionel to carry out the experiment for us while he's in Brazil?' Then it dawned on me. 'Twenty-two years?'

He laughed. 'Patience is the essence of an aphrodisiac.'

I got the message, took hold of his haunches and patiently blew him right off to Brazil. He loved it.

CHAPTER THIRTY

'**S**ARAH, HAVE YOU accepted that invitation to Leslie Caron's *soirée*?' asked Robin Fox on the phone.

'Why, are you going?' I was puzzled how he should know that I'd been invited.

'No, I'm not, but you are.' Could it have been Lionel giving me his by now wizard Robin impersonation? Because if it was Robin his voice sounded unusually strict, over-peppered with seriousness.

'It's none of your business whether I go or not.'

'It is my business if I'm to remain your agent.'

'What are you saying?' Was he trying to dump me?

'You've got to put a stop to all this hiding away. It's not what you *do* in this business, it's who you know.'

'Then I'll just not work because if my talent isn't sufficient – fuck the lot of you!' I put down the phone feeling truly insulted. How could Robin lower himself even to hint that I should go sniffing around like a hooker after work?

Later that same evening there was a knock on the door and in barged Robin with Ros Chatto, who was now a partner of Robin's. They hardly spoke a word to me, just pulled me up the stairs and into my bedroom.

'Cinderella is going to the ball after all,' said a cynical, thoroughly pissed-off Robin. I was put in some dress they pulled out of my cupboard. And resistance would have been futile, for they were both hell-bent on carrying out their task.

'There, now, you look fine,' said Ros, looking at me in the mirror and putting more rouge on my face. 'That's better. Cheer up, you may meet your knight in shining armour.'

Outside Addo wanted to come too. 'Sit. Good fellow,' said Robin sarcastically. 'Let Mummy step out of your shadow for a moment.' They hailed a taxi at the end of the road. Hauling me in, Robin said, 'I cannot help your career any more if you don't get out to meet your employers face to face. When I tell them you won't film abroad, they look at me as if I were mad. So do me the favour of telling them yourself.'

'Is that where you're taking me, to meet my employers, looking like this?'

'No, but it's a start,' said Ros, flattening her skirt with a sigh as the taxi rolled on down Beauchamp Place.

'You must be seen out more. If you don't . . .'

'You're giving me the sack?'

'Don't be silly, you sack us, but the answer is yes, if you don't change your ways.'

'It's true,' said Ros, sitting there all small and sharp as her mongrel. That's why I loved Ros, because of the way she loved her mongrel, Blacky. 'We can do no more than get the ball rolling. The rest is—'

'I know,' I groused.

'And it all begins here,' said Robin, taking me by the arm, with Ros on the other side so I wouldn't escape. It reminded me of childhood, as they hauled me by my armpits up the steps of Montpelier Square. They rang the bell. The door opened and in I went with my bodyguards.

The maid took my coat. 'Follow me, please.' As I climbed the stairs Robin waved mischievously and made his exit with Ros. There I was, trapped.

What a magnificent drawing room – a feast for the spirit! What breadth of vision these eighteenth-century houses offer when architects stay loyal to the golden mean. The setting was pure Cecil Beaton. Three or four long french windows sweeping the floor. Outside, the backdrop was a floodlit Montpelier Square with a communal garden centre-stage. What else could one want in life? Warren Beatty, by the look on Leslie Caron's face as she stood near her fireplace, pouring cocktails from a silver decanter. The whole room was straight out of Noël Coward – cowardly Noëlie.

She turned and saw me gawping at the splendour from the doorway. 'Hello, Sarah, welcome.' She was warm and friendly. Warren walked up behind her, looking me straight in the eyeballs. No, I tell a lie, that little eye of his was still straying a little.

'Remember me?' Warren managed to say that line with innuendoes flying wild all over the drawing room. We had starred together in *The Roman Spring of Mrs Stone* with Lotte Lenya and Vivien Leigh. (Actually, I was only a walk-on.)

'Drink?'

'Bloody Mary, please.' I would like to have asked for a crème de menthe frappée, can't taste the alcohol in those, but felt it best not to risk it. Warren had been to visit me in my dressing room during the shooting of *The Servant*. He'd been in one of his amorous moods, like a puppy playing with a ball of wool. I saw no harm in his need to flirt, for it was plain that he simply loved women. It's just that my love was elsewhere.

He and Leslie monopolized me for a while. Both were charmingly open with their new-found lust, grabbing at each other whenever the opportunity arose, though Warren's straying eye was after something, I could tell. 'Stay on after, why don't you?'

I hedged. 'I couldn't find my dog when I left home, and I can't leave him roaming the streets too late.' Sounded pretty convincing, I thought.

Ros had put me in a high pair of Pinet shoes, which had pinched like hell ever since I bought them because I'd never bothered to try them on, so the mounting agony in my big toe forced me to make a bee-line for one of the sofas. Everyone looked in keeping with the elegance about them, and I observed for a while. I watched Leslie offering nuts with a flourish. She certainly was a superb hostess; could even be in the same category as Vivien Leigh. Lionel said once, 'Some women are born to the kitchen, some to the bedroom,' and kissed the top of my head.

'Vivien, I suppose.'

'No, Vivien was born to the drawing room. There was not a hostess to come near her.'

How hard it was, always having to stop thinking about Lionel. Here were Leslie and Warren both giving me strange looks, and me thinking about nothing but Lionel. I was sick, that's what it was, no hostess with the mostest or even with the leastest, no hostess at all – if I wasn't prepared to change my ways.

I took a tiny sip of my Bloody Mary. Why couldn't I have been brave and asked for apple juice? Just as I looked out upon the glorious square, a bird flew across the window. I suppose it could have been a pigeon, but it being dusk I wasn't sure. I thought I'd play a 'count the birds' game. When trapped in public I always find something to play to distract me from the noise of gossip.

From the moment I decided to start counting to when I noticed the chap on the sofa beside me light his pipe, I never saw a single bird. He was different from the rest, with no jacket or tie and his shirtsleeves rolled up. I hoped he might be a breath of fresh air, but I couldn't strike up a conversation with him, because Madame Caron had overlooked our intro-duction. Though even *I* had to admit his bare white arms were a titsy bit common in such elegant surroundings. After all, this was no bingo hall, racetrack or pub, or a party, not even a dinner party – this was a *soirée*. He leaned forward as he puffed on his pipe, looking way beyond Montpelier Square, as if tomorrow might never come.

'Why are your shirtsleeves all rolled up?' I found myself saying rather haughtily. He turned to me slowly, and with a northern twang sprinkled with undeniable common sense, replied, 'Because I'm hot.'

Couldn't argue with that, thought I, my nose still in the air. He reminded me of an old bull mastiff, energetically puffing on his pipe. As he rubbed the hair upwards at the nape of the neck with his free hand, I couldn't help noticing, apart from the apparent sweat, how sweet and delicate it was, like a Boy Scout's, all smooth and vulnerable. He had a surprisingly noble profile, I noticed, as he puffed away, his pipe bobbing with serious contemplation. His thoughts wafted back to their place beyond Montpelier Square, so I returned to counting birds. After a moment I felt his eyes upon me again, appraising and flickering with the blinding blue of curiosity. 'You look like a debauched Alice in Wonderland.'

With my nose even higher, 'Since I didn't dress myself, I cannot be held responsible.'

'It wasn't your clothes I was looking at.'

Still, I didn't want this stranger to think that I always dressed like this, and not liking the sound of 'a debauched Alice in Wonderland' I told him about Robin and Ros forcing me into my clothes.

'Better to have you sitting here debauched than not at all.' He waited for a response, I gave him none. I thought I recognized his face. Was he someone I should know?

Once, in a similar situation (the only grand party I'd even been to), I'd taken my drink and sat on a sofa, where I saw this strange young man beside me, also looking lost. I finally plucked up the courage to talk to him. 'What's your name?' I asked, demurely.

He turned to look at me full in the eye. 'Ringo fucking Starr,' he replied, not demurely at all. It was at a time when the Beatles were known, but unless you were hip you wouldn't necessarily recognize them individually. He'd obviously thought that I should have realized. But then I was always last to know of any modern trend. Just because I'd copied the mini-skirt off a shop girl didn't mean I was part of the swinging sixties.

I looked over towards my hostess, but came into collision with Warren's eyes instead. Come to think, I'm sure Vivien's hostessing wouldn't neglect an introduction.

'What's your name?' I asked, looking as debauched as poss.

'Robert Bolt.'

It rang a bell, but I couldn't swear to it, so thought it best to keep mum. A strong, firm name, Robert Bolt. I know what he became – my Bolt from the blue, my Bolt of lightning, my Bolt on the door, my Mr always Bolt upright, each other's Bolt holes – but who the hell was he? I'd heard that name often. While the name Robert Bolt was still ringing through my head, I could have sworn that a big bird flew past the window again, a pigeon, maybe . . . or was it a wineberry wagtail?

I can remember nothing more about the *soirée*, except just after cheese and before coffee, I knew I had to leave. Not that I wasn't having a good time, I was. But I simply had to go. Something was pulling me away. Perhaps it was to do with this man. He was a fine raconteur, quite a character, was this Robert Bolt. He had us all in stitches, with such timing it's a wonder he wasn't an actor.

We spoke about *Dazzling Prospect*, my first play in London. How it waddled into the Globe Theatre, Shaftesbury Avenue, bringing off his great *A Man For All Seasons* (playing to full houses, I may add). He remembered and laughed. We spoke of the way he wrote Omar Sharif's entrance in *Lawrence*, and the effect it had on Omar's life from then on. We spoke of so many things, and he never failed to make me laugh – but I had to go.

'Do you have to leave so soon?' asked Leslie.

'Yes. I'm driving down to the country.'

'I thought you'd lost your dog.' Warren's eye might stray a bit, but not, alas, his memory. Forgetting my own lies and continually putting my foot in it were the very reasons I chose to remain at home.

'I'll be off to the country after I've found Addo.'

As I rose to leave, this Robert Bolt chap leapt to his feet

like a jack-in-the-box. Although I found his total lack of *savoir faire* immensely endearing, I also wanted to be rid of him. Why did I find him so disturbing? Probably because I knew he was after me, and I had too many complications in the loving department already. He was a threat and I needed to get out in the air to cool down.

'I'll drop you off,' he said enthusiastically.

'Oh. Have you got transport?'

'Yes.'

I noticed, while I was saying all my goodbyes, that Mr Bolt from the blue never left my side. I gave him ten out ten for keenness.

His form of transport, cheekily enough, turned out to be hailing a cab. He took me to the Pickwick Club, where with great confidence he gave all those present the wonderful gift of his gab. It was easy for him to take centre stage and keep it for as long as it interested him so to do. Miraculously he never came across as a show-off, more of a wise and witty Leo. Home once more I thanked him. He kissed my cheek on the doorstep. 'Can I take you out Thursday night?'

I hoped to be seeing Lionel that evening. 'I'm afraid I'm having a dinner party.'

'Saturday, then?'

'No, because I go down to my parents in the country.'

'Next week?'

Why was I denying to myself that of course I wanted to see him again? I left it safely noncommittal.

Since Nona was away with Sam, staying with her mother near Worthing, Lionel and I had planned it that he should come to my house. Yes! It turned out that naughty Nona had a lovely mother in Worthing and a gorgeous brother in London. How I'd been duped! The phone rang. It was Lionel. 'Hello, darling. Can't come tonight. Make Tuesday teatime possible, about four thirty?' Lionel was overworking and his health was suffering. It was mainly *Othello* that had taken his life blood. I could tell he still needed our rendezvous because they gave him a respite from National pressures and, indeed, from real life. We never spoke about acting, careers or showbiz, except that Kenneth Tynan had got under his skin: his was the only name that ever crept regularly into our world. Sometimes the sun shone out of Tynan's arse and at others Lionel was thinking up ways of killing him. Whether they did anything about their insidious attachment I doubted, unless Lionel was a complete sex maniac, which I also doubted. But then all things are possible.

The next evening, feeling sad, stood up and rejected, I began to count the times Lionel had cancelled me. I could only recall five, and over a six-year period I thought that was pretty damn good, giving me few grounds for complaint. But it didn't help that evening, because I needed to be curled up with him.

The doorbell rang.

'Hello,' he said, chirpily. What the hell was Robert Bolt doing here?

'Can I help you?' I found myself asking.

'Can you help me?' he said, pushing his nose in the air with his finger – and quite right, I could hear myself being fearfully snotty.

'I thought you said you were giving a dinner party.'

'I am.'

'What, dressed like that?'

Since I resembled a scarecrow, I couldn't go on with the lie. 'Pax.'

He came up the steps and I followed him in. There was no food in the house what with Lionel cancelling and all – no appetite. Didn't want to eat, being in a bit of a moody. To be honest, my moodies weren't very pleasant – Addo sniffed them coming and headed straight for Swiss Cottage.

Robert took me to dinner and with great aplomb swept

my moody under the table before the melon had even arrived. During dinner he had me laughing all over again and in no time at all we were back on the doorstep of Hasker Street.

'Hello, Addo,' he said as Addo came down to greet us, having returned from Swiss Cottage. (Robert and Addo got along like a house on fire, and that helped Robert's case considerably.)

'Aren't you going to ask me in?'

I wanted to say yes, but I had to sort everything out with Lionel first. With all my lovers I always talked it through with Lionel. My heart was so full with love for him that it feverishly desired fidelity. It was horrid telling Willy and Julian. I wish I could have remained loving them all because I didn't want to lose any of them, but that would have been greedy and frightfully unladylike. No. To have made love to Bolt that night would have been a careless, faithless, lowering thing to do. Also I wasn't as easy a lay as that. Even *I* have to insist on a healthy period of courtship (the best bit). 'Not tonight.'

His kiss was lovely, I thought, as Addo and I waved him off.

Later in Hasker Street, Lionel and I were taking full advantage of Nona's absence, leaving the final coming together as long as we dared. I watched him looking round the drawing room – snooping, really.

'Like a drink?'

'No.' He began pulling me towards the staircase. 'Seems old Robert impressed you, the bugger.'

'Well, he is impressive, don't you find?'

'His screenplay of *A Man For All Seasons* certainly is. It's a cracker.' The film had just starting shooting down at Pinewood, with Fred Zimmermann directing. Robert Shaw was giving his Henry VIII, Paul Scofield his mightily subtle Sir Thomas More.

'I was offered More after Burton turned it down, but I wasn't free.'

'I hoped you'd say you turned it down because it rightfully belongs to Paul Scofield.'

Lionel snorted arrogantly and added as an afterthought, 'Not playing Thomas More will probably end up one of my main regrets.'

I thought I'd give my question one last crack of the whip. 'So you don't think that if an actor makes a great job of a part in the theatre, the film should be his by rights?'

'By rights, yes, but there are none. It's all down to piggy banks and dog eat dog,' he growled and began to eat me with enormous skill – he'd had enough practice. Above the ceiling, among the rainbows, we lay cloaked in silence watching wineberry wagtails winging their way through eternity, drenched in turquoise and gold. Ecstasy! It was such a telling time, when I lay there guessing how many breaths he'd take before our parting. How counting those seconds dug into me.

'Joanie will be waiting,' said Lionel, imitating Joanie waiting, before looking at his watch and leaping out of bed. I never rose to his Joanie moods. I pride myself that they remained brief only because I didn't take the same journey, not because I was a saint, but because the pain forbade it. I remained businesslike about keeping our lives separate, never bringing up Joanie, or wanting to know about the state of their marriage. Yet with *my* lovers, Lionel really got off on being nosy. He looked at me sideways – quite spooky, considering his next question.

'What's going to happen to your other *amours*?' He was ahead of me on this one. 'You want to live with Bolt.'

'What would you do if you were me?'

'Live with Bolt. But . . .' The 'but' hung in the air, painfully. We both knew how I felt about the marriage vows: if I took them I'd do my damnedest to keep them.

'How dare I feel what I feel?' he whispered, flinging himself over and putting his face in the pillow. His voice

215

hardened a little. 'What will you do when he pops the question?'

I'd only just met the man. 'That's a long way off. It's only you who can see it from here.' After I'd turned over on to my tummy to join him, along came his tongue gently licking stray tears with wondrous care.

I had to turn away for a moment – the old stiff upper couldn't take it. 'I'm not strong enough, alas, to live my whole life through without a safe haven.'

'I am your safe haven.'

As usual, time and reason melted into the safey of his smile.

CHAPTER THIRTY-ONE

ROBERT ASKED ME to come over and be with him in his flat on Chelsea Embankment. I've never understood why it's meant to be élitist to live down there. It's noisy, dirty and unfriendly. But since it was early days and we were still only courting, I didn't want to seem ungrateful, snobbish, judgemental or pushy. Yet I continually felt an intruder, never able to settle. Since acquiring Hasker Street, my own home, bought with my own money, I wanted to be in it day and night.

I have been most fortunate during my life, with all those fellahs out there who liked me enough to want to be with me. All my lovers were such perfect teachers. Willy Fox showed me loving-kindness. Anthony Blond showed me the high life. Nicol showed me power capacity, singing capacity, but more importantly the necessity to untangle myself, or stay for ever strangled and static. Julian showed me balance. Willy D. showed me style. Olivier showed me my heart capacity (eternal) together with the faint possibility of turning my life into an art form. My Bolt from the blue pointed out the possibility of my having a brain, however modest in capacity, hidden back there somewhere, and patiently dug his way in. He never bothered, however, with the possibility of life being an art form, he merely picked up his pen. How privileged I have been.

I never wanted to be far from Robert – in fact, I had to be as close as possible, because once his day's work was finished, I could grab him for the rest of the evening. Robert was my world encyclopedia, pure jewels spun from his lips. I learnt something every time he opened his mouth (except when kissing, of course).

'So that's our next move?' he said one day, getting dressed to go and work.

Fortunately Addo didn't like our Thames Bolt hole at all, so finally I made him persuade Robert to come and stay at Hasker Street. He did. Poor Addo nearly got himself run over on the Embankment.

One day I knew Addo was doing something terrible, for I could hear his brand of mayhem out of the window. What would it take, I thought, to make Robert's typewriter change rhythm? The businesslike knock on the door brought me face to face with Johnnie Windeatt. Addo was proving himself extremely athletic, with poor Beethoven not knowing how to keep his dignity.

'Addo – off!' I dragged him by his tail. 'He has no pride, I'm afraid, none at all.'

'Care to come for a walk?' said Johnnie keenly.

'I'd love to.'

I called to Robert over his typewriter, 'Robert!' Nothing. Using my considerable lung capacity, 'I'm off for a walk.'

Still no change in the typewriter's rhythm. 'I won't be a minute.' I left Johnnie to go into the drawing room where I found Robert far away in distant lands. I knew about those distant lands because I'd often had brief glimpses of them, but I had no clue how to call them to order. 'I'm going for a walk, won't be too long.'

Again no response, so I left, knowing I'd done my best. We set off towards Hyde Park. I liked Johnnie Windeatt from the beginning. Maybe he had me fooled, and he went home and did the most despicable acts, but I doubted it. His craft was landscape gardening, but temporarily, to earn some money, he was a valet to an extremely rich businessman. That was the only part of the tale I was allowed to know, for quite a while. He was always dressed like the bee's knees, crisp, clean, shiny dark hair with a healthy glow, sparkling eyes, good teeth and a pink tongue.

Dig those awesome lashes! When we were all very
small my brothers warned me that the mole on my left
wrist would gradually spread all over my body.
They were right – it has!

Enter Robert Bolt, the eighty-a-day man. Fiercely probing the unknown, with swirling smoke for company.

Hours and hours were spent in the Old Mill itself which we turned into a games room. Competition was fearsomely heated. On and on we went until Robert finally won a game!

Above: Looking rightly dubious about being asked to stand next to my poster for publicity photos at the San Sebastian Film Festival 1967, even though I won Best Actress.

Right: In Bombay, collapsing under the strain of too many floral tributes, Bombay belly and early-morning sickness. How I wish the film had happened for Moti's sake (the one beside Robert). It was his dream.

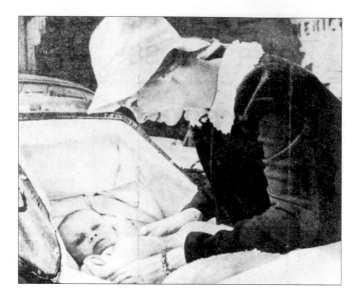

Left: The arrival of the Tomcat. Pusscat's the one wearing the hat.

Below: Tom aged two.

Fermoyle House, County Kerry. Off walking with the menagerie: Addo, Betty, Arthur and wonderful Gladys.

Left: The street we built for *Ryan's Daughter*. When filming was complete, we asked the locals whether we should bulldoze the village down. 'Yes,' they replied unhesitatingly. Once flattened they realized their mistake and asked us to re-erect it.

Below: The school house they allowed to remain. It brings in good revenue from tourists so imagine what the street with its own pub would have brought in.

Trevor Howard, the priest, and Johnnie Mills, the village half-wit. Note the innocence in Trevor's eyes.

I'd undone all his buttons but look at mine. I'm trying every trick of the trade to stop Christopher nodding off on me.

Right: Mohammed (David Lean) and the Mountain (Robert Mitchum) and Her Nibs, the goddamn go-between.

Below: Mitchum was so like my brother Chuzzer. On their good days there was no one better.

Right: Home again and Tomcat's first show. Flattering the judge got him from eleventh to fourth place.

Below: Hunting my palomino stallion Cavalier was never dull. He was the one who humped Robert. My leg is in a cast as per usual. The photo was burnt in a fire we had in our conservatory.

Once in Hyde Park Beethoven became immediately interested in a haughty Weimaraner.

'She's not having it,' said Johnnie, as we watched the Weimaraner walk straight by poor Beethoven, who so wanted her to catch his perfect leg-cocking. All that beautiful balletic peeing and no one to heed it – but, then, that's life.

'Where's Addo?'

'He's probably on his daily cleaning-fluid hunt.' Johnnie dusted off a bench before offering me a seat.

'I long for the country.' I found myself loathing the echo of that stupid sentence. If I so longed for the country, why didn't I damn well go there and finish ticking off my list of dreams?

'I'm going to start the search,' said Johnnie, as he rose to look for Addo.

I suppose that since I'd become a sort of movie star – certainly nothing to write home about – now was the time to settle down. Had I found my Knight of Wisdom? Would we, could we, live happily ever after? Would we buy a country home and paint it all colours of the rainbow? Would our children's wellies be strewn about the hall?

I went into reverie, and began again to tick off my dream list. The atmosphere would be an elegant chaos, rather like Bertie Russell's home, with crackling fires in every room. I'd want a big homey kitchen-cum-dining-room, the womb of the house; a kindly cook, maid, groom, and gardener, and a chauffeur for my Rolls-Royce convertible. Next, an efficiently run stud farm on the same property for breeding quality palominos, a well-equipped stable yard, and a Land-rover and trailer plus enough money to keep the happiness going. My mind was made up, I was definitely going to accept Robert's idea of looking for a place to live in the country, as long as we didn't get married. Neither Robert nor I felt ready for the marriage vows. Yet Addo's kennel (conservatory) hadn't been ticked off yet, and I was twenty-four years old.

Bolt had recently (nothing to do with me, I didn't know him then) broken up with his first wife, so for him, coming from a marriage with three children, it seemed natural for the married state to have soured somewhat. He divorced his wife for her infidelity. Robert felt strongly that marriage vows are there to keep.

His eldest daughter was called Sally. She was a buxom wench at the ripe age of fourteen when I first met her. Her eyes were almost as blue as Robert's, yet the other two children had brown eyes, like their mother. Robert's son Ben was tall, handsome, quick-witted and quite divine. The first time we all met was in a restaurant, and I remember standing while waiting for Robert to indicate where we would sit, when Ben said, 'I'll sit here, next to Sis.' I liked being called Sis. Thirdly there was little sister Jo-Jo who was about seven when Robert and his first wife separated, a dangerous age for losing security. In some ways Jo-Jo reminded me of my mother, beautiful yet expert in keeping everyone at a distance.

Johnnie crashed into my daydreams. 'I think I saw Addo over there, you stay here.' He wouldn't find Addo. Addo would return only when he wished to, and there was not a single thing Johnnie Windeatt could do about it.

I took Robert down to meet the parents one weekend. What an occasion that turned out to be, for when I came downstairs with Robert on Sunday morning, all the newspapers were down and everyone seemed a bit in awe of this new beau of mine, old enough to be my father. Robert was eighteen years older then me, which automatically made my father feel better about being over twenty-three years older than Mother. No wonder Daddy was so forthcoming, even to the point of liking him,

Robert is a Mancunian, a Salford boy who had to go to Methodist chapel twice a day come rain or shine. He came from a poor yet good family, his father having to scrape and save every penny to send both Robert and his elder brother,

Sydney, to Manchester Grammar School. Robert was a real tearaway, stealing from shops, playing up relentlessly and generally making the whole family's life a misery. His time at Manchester Grammar was fairly brief, thanks to Sydney's brilliance, for Robert, unable to step out of his brother's shadow, flunked his exams and became an office boy. After serving in the air force during the war he retook his exams, passing with flying colours, and began teaching English at a little village school in Devon. An appalling motorbike crash put him in hospital, where he saw a vacancy for an English teacher at Millfield. He applied and got it. While he was teaching there his first play was put on by Binkie Beaumont, *A Flowering Cherry*, with Celia Johnson and Ralph Richardson. It was such a success that it allowed Robert to move to Richmond and stop teaching altogether. *Tiger and the Horse*, with Michael and Vanessa Redgrave, was another hit, and there also followed *Gentle Jack* (Robert's favourite), with Dame Edith Evans and Kenneth Williams, *A Man For All Seasons*, the screenplay of *Lawrence of Arabia*, *Doctor Zhivago*, and now the film of *A Man For All Seasons*. When all the family newspapers went down that breakfast time, was it because of Robert's charm or his impressive track record?

It was during that weekend that I came across Daddy in the garden watching Luigi (his Jack-of-all-trades) precariously placed up a huge oak tree. Luigi was about to saw off a large branch which was rubbing against the woodshed roof.

'That's the ticket,' said Daddy. 'Saw it off right there.' Luigi, who wasn't a large man, looked lost up the tree brandishing the saw like a child with his father's sledgehammer.

'Watch him, Pusscat. Watch what he does.' I was thrown both by Daddy's conspiratorial wink, which I hadn't seen for a while, and by where Luigi was – at the wrong end of the branch. 'Just watch him, Pusscat. Just watch.'

'He'll hurt himself,' said Chuzzer, my brother, having come to join the afternoon's activities.

'Yes, let's see if he notices.' Luigi didn't. He meticulously sawed through the fair-sized branch and fell, just missing the woodshed. Fortunately not much more than pride was hurt. My father was becoming quite wicked in his old age.

'Why did you do that?' I asked, askance.

'We have to knock some sense into him – just like you as a little girl. We had to shake you into waking up because you wouldn't open your eyes and see the real world. Luigi's just the same but, being too old for the hairbrush, he has to be shaken up some other way.'

Perhaps I should have climbed the oak tree and fallen off in Luigi fashion, because I knew I hadn't woken up yet. Stupid as my brain was, my inner body heard what Father was saying. I shuddered and got goose-bumps. Nearly twenty-four, and I still needed a thrashing. The sound of 'twenty-four' was repellent enough without adding the bitterness of that particular truth. All I did was walk Addo, watch people, take care of Sammy and Nona, sleep and—

I wasn't a bit interested in politics. I didn't read the papers, and rarely opened a book (reading was, of course, still an enormous effort). I had no interest in the showbiz side of acting. Just in the process itself. I can scarcely even remember eating during those six years in Hasker Street, either in the kitchen or the dining room – or out on the town. Nona was meant to help with that side of things, but I can't recall her doing so. I have three memories of eating. The first was the only dinner party I ever gave. My guests arrived and I went into the kitchen to bring in the roast chicken, to find Addo had eaten the lot in one minute flat. Second, Nona scrutinizing my baked beans in her hands. Third, the chop occasion. But surely those weren't the only times I ate anything? Agitated by having no more food memories, I did my first bit of research for this book. I rang up Willy Donaldson from my publisher's. 'Shall I come to you?'

This made him nervous.

'Don't be frightened. I promise I won't rape you.'

'I wish you would. No, it's this place – even you'd be shocked.'

I wasn't too keen on the 'even you', but I let it go. He'd had great success with his Henry Root character, so there had been a few striped shirts and chicken on Sundays at last for old Wil. 'I'm going to put a string out from my flat window for food, so I need never go out again.' Since he lived at the Fulham Road end of Park Walk, a mere twenty steps to both the paper shop and Cullen's for food, I thought the thing a wee bit redundant.

'Meet you at the Macmillan coffee house in ten minutes.' The phone went dead.

Why did I feel so nervous walking across Fulham Road to Macmillan's? Perhaps because I hadn't seen him for some years. How had those years hung on him, I wondered. Then I saw him, crouched in the corner smoking a cigar and looking exactly like Howard Hughes. Long pale hair sprouting over his collar, longish fingernails, with skin tones bereft of any sunlight whatsoever. Apparently he'd just lost the love of his life – she'd run off with a millionaire – so Willy was in the process of purchasing a gun and going down to Cornwall to shoot the millionaire's brains out.

'Doesn't sound as subtle as your usual ploys.'

'That's precisely why I'd never be suspected. It's not my thing.' Dear Willy. I felt so comfortable with his thoughtful, overly bred manner.

'Did we ever eat at Hasker Street?'

'Except for your chop bone my mind's blank. Strange, isn't it? We must have never eaten anything. We never gave a dinner party in two and a half years.'

'Nor did you take me out. Not once.'

'You would never come.' That was true. 'You did nothing but walk Addo and . . . play with me.'

'Did we ever watch television?'

'Of course. That's why it was in the bedroom. We never strayed far from the bedroom.'

It seemed my father was right. I still needed that jolt, for I hadn't yet opened my eyes.

I watched Johnnie Windeatt returning from across the Park, Beethoven at his heels.

'You won't believe this.'

'What?'

'Addo. I just saw him over there.' He pointed towards Kensington Palace. 'He was getting into a taxi.'

'He likes riding in taxis.' I wasn't sure whether Addo stopped the taxis or the taxis stopped for him. Strange, three or four times Addo arrived home in a taxi, yet I never caught the moment of their coming to a mutual agreement.

CHAPTER THIRTY-TWO

MY KNIGHT OF Wisdom took over everything in a masterly fashion. A twenty-four-hour-a-day safe haven. Life was shaping up a treat. With Robert Bolt I knew I'd never feel suffocated again, for I'd found the magic formula, to feel cocooned in safety amid a spacious terrain. Within this perfect combination I felt free to do whatever made me happy. And I was happy, in a mature sense, feeling hints of domesticity, even of housewifery, sprouting up. Most of all, though, I felt supreme contentment in being able to hold up my head without the shame of deception.

February, and we were off to the Canaries, the island of Lanzarote, for a pre-honeymoon in the sun. On Tenerife, a mass of concrete high-rises, and human flesh indenting black sand, greeted our arrival – not a canary to be seen. But Robert promised me that on Lanzarote the tourists hadn't yet arrived. I believed him. Yes. That's it. To be able to believe. What a blessing to lie down upon a bed of truth you can rely upon.

Robert was my Snow Goose, his wings so soft to cry upon.

His promise came true, as I felt sure it would even though I didn't yet know him that well. I had never imagined such a paradise. We stayed at a place called Playa Blanca at the furthest tip. No hotels, just the one dilapidated, ramshackle guest-house right on the beach, with nothing but chickens and a cock who resembled my childhood Berty, amid elderly locals playing chess and backgammon all day long.

Our first day, and there lay the ocean. Wow! Above it, the translucent dance of the etheric and beneath, a silky transparency of aquamarine. How swiftly we threw off the stench of travel and stood at the water's edge (the only swimmers around), poised, aching to revel within its shimmer. I remember Robert challenging me on that first day.

'Ten quid to the first one on board that fishing boat out there – see it?' I saw it, a plain wooden one about two hundred yards out. Ten quid was no chicken feed in those days, more like a hundred quid today, but then Robert always had a penchant for excess and therein lay my victory. I could tell he was a little too fat for any speed.

'OK. You're on. Ready, steady, go!' I tingled with the pre-glow of winning as we both plunged in (no doubt I was the better plunger), and then – heavens a Betsy! I hadn't bargained on Robert being such a superb swimmer! He crawled with unexpected ease and power, the water scuffing round him as the wingtips of a snow goose might scuff the sky. Way up ahead, he was abandoning me to such thoughts as, how can he glide like a snow goose with the speed of a gazelle? He's too fat, fuck him! I watched him skimming on ahead, leaving nothing behind but the back end of snow goose. Having to abandon all hopes of winning was a real downer – I wasn't used to losing at sport. *Serves me right*. Swimming along immersed in the slump that follows the acceptance of losing, I spied approaching a wee glimmer of light. There before me were decks too high for hauling up the great belly of Bolt. Early days though they were, I already loved Robert's fat squashy bits three times as much as a mass of clunking bones, but never so much as then. From shore the little boat's deck didn't seem so high out of the sea. Hugely comical it was, the close-up view of a snow goose's bum flailing to and fro as I slithered past and up the little boat's high wooden ramparts just like the Chinese snake that I am. Once on board I was safe to leap about with returned cockiness.

'I'm King of the Castle!' Peering down the steep ramparts of my walls, I glimpsed my valiant Knight of Wisdom breathlessly heaving and wondered (a) Would he ever make it – up or down? (b) Would I ever receive my ten quid of glory rights?

'I won really.'

'You distinctly said, "First one *on to* the fishing boat."'

He collapsed on board at long last, tossing me a look and a half before bowing his head in defeat. I followed suit, and with our little wooden fishing boat being the only castle out there upon the translucent glimmer, I bowed down in reverence to the belly of the Bolt.

Both my father and brothers played a great deal of chess, but I never went near it – only for intellectuals, I thought. But on that holiday, under my black umbrella, Robert insisted I learn, and took me through the fundamentals of the game, step by step. When I'm being taught anything new, that familiar silver screen with black edges from childhood slots over my eyes, blinding and deafening me to what is being taught. But after two days of Robert's Job-like patience, I finally got down the elementary rules and moves sufficiently to participate in a game. Our very first, and I beat him.

'Beginner's luck,' he said. So it was, but he's never been able to beat me since. This might sound as if I'm bragging but I promise you I'm not. Robert happens to be a brilliant teacher but an appalling chess player.

The next day of that idyllic pre-honeymoon Shangri-la, Robert, with his wary sensibilities, surreptitiously placed Jane Austen's *Emma* into my hands. 'Go on, try her, she's an easy read, witty, too.' I took it, shattered by page after page of small print. Could I ever read this whole book? Was I perhaps finally growing up! Were little bits of me crying out, 'Wake up! Wake up?' No doubt especially about it, I was beginning to feel academically inadequate, during conversations Robert had with other people. What had begun to accumulate was a strong need to broaden my horizons and master the art of reading. Robert was too canny to suggest that I should; never once did he draw attention to the palace of inactivity that was my cerebral department. I found myself none the less with a desire to kick the lazy habit of bluffing out my lack of knowledge.

It wasn't like being with Olivier, who wasn't notably well educated. He just happened to know every play containing a good part for him that had ever been written as he skipped gaily through his life, not living but acting out the whole spectrum of human potential (the twelve archetypes). This is why his relationship with Danny Kaye was so profoundly important for him. Both he and Danny Kaye were able to conjure up all the twelve archetypes at the drop of a hat. They were both entirely at ease accessing the fool, joker, magician, slave, child (though towards the end, Olivier had difficulty tapping into his child), actress, old woman, warrior, enchantress, patriarch, observer and last but not least, Mother Earth. We ordinary mortals complacently spend our lives stuck in maybe two, three or four of our twelve-part arche-typal potential, but for those two magicians, Danny Kaye and Olivier, living out those twelve roles regularly might have prevented them familiarizing themselves with their true nature. So Danny and Larry (subconsciously, perhaps), both secretly craving for some *inner* nourishment, a deeper recog-nition, spied each other's predicament across a crowded room and made a beeline towards their mutually lost souls. Once united, they clung desperately to their – up till then – neglected true natures. Does it matter whether they clung to each other as long-lost lovers, or innocently, like twin babes in the wood? Neither surely deflects one whit from the joyousness of their coming together. Within the mystery of intuition they found the key to a magic formula. Two people, whoever they are, simply making each other happy is no crime.

Next day, lying on the beach under my umbrella, immersed in the romance of *Emma* and lazily comparing Lionel with Mr Knightley, I looked up to find Robert gone. An elderly peasant lady dressed in black noticed my concern.

'Papa gone that way,' she said, pointing to the horizon. That was the first time I realized the age difference. It had me wondering about Lionel: what were receptionists thinking in those seedy hotel lobbies? 'Grandpa gone that way?' Robert looked a mere teenager compared to Lionel. From then on wherever we went I referred to Robert as Papa. I liked it, but I don't think Robert was overly keen.

It was a blissful holiday, one of those rare jewels. The place had been unaltered through the centuries; it offered memories of primitive simplicity. My brother Chuzzer went back to Lanzarote a few years later and apparently Playa Blanca was unrecognizable. A whole beach full of red bodies and soulless high-rises. How lucky we were to have found it still in God's hands, and the lacy spider-webs of chickens' footprints in virgin sand.

CHAPTER THIRTY-THREE

O N OUR RETURN to England Robin Fox asked me if I was prepared to do an Antonioni film without a script. I'd admired *L'Avventura* a great deal but, then, I was biased because the film was brimful of Monica Vitti's all-encompassing femininity. 'Only problem is, without a script, you'd have to just surrender to him,' said a dubious Robin, knowing I wasn't the surrendering type. I went to meet Antonioni and found him quietly intelligent and sufficiently gentle for me to give it a go. David Hemmings and Vanessa Redgrave were also participating in the so-called geniuses' London location dance.

The film was mainly shot in west London, and my part mostly in a photographic studio in Holland Park. Once the film got under way, Antonioni's quiet, gentle, intelligent ways were coaxed by a formidable creative energy into something else. I tried to get into the ritual of his megalomania, but I wasn't too keen on it. Nevertheless, to begin with I turned a blind eye, putting all of my concentration that first day into surrendering as sweetly as possible, and the next day and the next. I was being a very good girl. On about my fourth day of shooting I noticed Antonioni never mixing with the actors or crew. Each day he had a Fortnum and Mason's hamper and champagne delivered to a room at the top of the studio where he would remain all through the lunch-break. It would have been nice to have had some contact with him, especially with no script to bring us all together. Wanting everyone to be a family while filming is perhaps a little twee, but I was still hankering after team spirit. (Or was I the element that made it so elusive?!)

In spite of the apparent lack of teamwork, for some reason

the film became the epitome of the swinging sixties. I believe I lack sufficient intellect to see what Antonioni was really trying to say. *Blow-Up*, for me, was a cluster of clichés bundled up in fashionable emperor's new clothes. I saw little truth in it, but I never remembered the sixties as being Utopia. Doubtless *Blow-Up* titillated the tastebuds of those who swung old London yet, alas, I never found the swing.

Perhaps I'm prejudiced. One day Antonioni asked me to do a lovemaking scene. I asked him what he wanted. 'Get into dis bed and make love to dis man.' He pointed to a complete stranger. 'Den David Hemmings come into di flat and find you vid dis man,' pointing back to the stranger in the bed, 'you about to climax vid dis man, so you signal to David Hemmings to wait and watch – vid your eyes only, of course. OK?'

Robin had warned me not to argue the toss with Antonioni, and so far, now the seventh day, I had obeyed. I was left no choice therefore but to take off my clothes and dive under the sheets. The other man got into bed with me, and there we were, naked except for the hefty weight of two rampantly nervous hearts. How humiliating it all was, this acting lark! What was I doing in bed with a complete stranger, whose name I didn't even know? In terms of the story line, was this fellow on top of me my husband, my lover or a one-night stand? Whose flat was it? Was David Hemmings about to enter *my* flat, or was I living with him in his? What was David Hemmings to my character? My fiancé, husband, brother, ex-lover or simply lover? Wouldn't I be able to give a truer performance if I was to know who was who and what was what?

After two takes of surrendering to Antonioni's genius, I became convinced that I was acting by numbers, something I swore I'd never be a party to. If I was to muster courage to bare my soul and act from a place of truth, and if I had to open my legs to a complete stranger, then I had a right to know what my relationship to that stranger was. I was still unsure of who *I* was, let alone anyone else, as during a take

David Hemmings entered the bedroom. Right at the point when I'm meant to ask him with my eyes only to stay and watch while I climax, I suddenly called out, 'Cut!'

'Why?' Antonioni was furious.

'May I ask you something, Antonioni?'

He came over to me, and as sweet as pie said, 'Don't call me Antonioni, call me Michelangelo.' Even more a mouthful.

'OK, Michelangelo.'

He must have smelt trouble because he put a towelling dressing gown around me, guiding me to a quiet corner across the studio. 'What is your problem, Sarah?' he asked, a hint patronizingly.

'Is this man on top of me a one-night stand, an acquaintance, husband or lover?'

Antonioni looked at me as if I'd asked to be escorted to the moon, so I ploughed on.

'And David Hemmings. We've already played two scenes together and I haven't a clue as to his connection to my character. Is he my husband, platonic friend, or my lover – ex-lover?' At which point Michelangelo shrugged his elegantly dressed Italian shoulders at me, and said, as if scoffing at my need for clarification, 'It does not matter.'

I tried to remain as sweet as I knew how, even though I was boiling inside. What effrontery! Would he climb into bed with a stranger, cameras rolling, completely naked and with no script to quell the storms of doubt as a hardly acquainted bunch of crew members watched? 'What d'you mean, "it doesn't matter"?'

'All you need to do is listen to my directions. When I tell you to turn to David, do so. When I tell you to turn back, do so. Within that, play whatever you want. It does not matter.'

'If the actor isn't given some truth with which to clothe his nakedness, then truth doesn't matter – therefore, nothing matters!' I went to the bed, said goodbye to the sweet chap therein, put my clothes on and left. I'd bowed and scraped for long enough.

I packed up never to return. Having no script, Antonioni could write me out of his head with no problem. He could easily replace me with some model girl, because that's all he really wanted. In the finished film, if you notice I'm suddenly no more, that's because I did my own bit of scriptwriting.

Why is it I behave as I do? Why can't I simply shut up when I witness the abuse of power? Forgiveness evaporates as I feel the rebellion rising, leaving me unable to bend toward tolerance. I often think about this conundrum because it's been so destructive to my career. Perhaps it all stems from the rough ride I was given at school – maybe even further back than that. I'm certainly not proud of it, and neither is it the least bit saintly as Lionel insinuated – it just *is*.

When I returned home to the safety of Robert's bear hug, he didn't reprimand me too much. He seemed to understand. 'I only hope you'll work again,' he said, thoughtfully.

I heard through the grapevine that Antonioni was shooting the final scene of his film in a nearby park and that it was a tennis match with painted trees and no ball. My curiosity got the better of me, and I went to have a secret snoop. Lo and behold, there were the two tennis players balletically miming their game. So intrigued was I that I crept a bit closer. The trees had indeed been painted, and the whole effect was pretty arty stuff. I chuckled to myself and dared to come right up to the camera. Antonioni saw me.

'Hello, Sarah.'

'Hello, Michelangelo,' I said sheepishly. 'What's all this about?' I indicated the trees and miming tennis players. Antonioni looked me straight in the eye and shrugged. 'It's for the critics.'

I was amused. My attitude towards this man spun right round. Suddenly I was filled with respect, for he had finally come clean . . . or was he saying what he believed I'd like to hear?

CHAPTER THIRTY-FOUR

ONE MORNING, COMING out of the bedroom, I misjudged the top step of the stairs and bounced and bumped all the way down. *Crash! Bang! Wallop!* The whole house vibrated as I landed in a thudding great heap and groaned. Luckily I could tell all was well. Years of falling off Mischief, my pony, had made me a tumbling expert. Lying at the bottom of the stairs I looked through into the drawing room, where I could just see Robert's typing retaining its reliable rhythm. This man was certainly allowing me breathing space – after all, not to be suffocated was what I'd yearned for.

'Ouch!!' I gave one last cry of agony, to no avail for the typing continued as if nothing had happened. I got up, rubbed myself and having had a dubious whiff of this yearned-for freedom, took Addo for a walk.

I bumped into Jill Bennett as she came stumbling out of La Popote, the local restaurant regularly frequented by Robert and me because its strawberry, raspberry and gooseberry fools were pure elixir nirvana. I was familiar with that curious secret smile of hers, so knowing and devoid of curiosity, and often saw her wandering along Walton, Ovington, First and Hasker Streets. She wasn't married then but was always to be seen in close proximity with a particular waiter in La Popote. Watching Jill stroll elegantly up Ovington Street in her often too large hat, overshadowing too high a heel, in my imagination I used to follow her home. Once my mind was firmly there, I'd get morbid feelings of something lonely and unresolved. Broken fragments of unhappiness were all around her, defiantly at odds with the outwardly rather harsh, yet well-held-together persona. What a great act she was having to put on to be that liberated woman. I could have been wrong, but that's what I thought.

Addo and I walked on towards Hyde Park. I used to get my clothes designed at Deliss in Beauchamp Place. Mrs Deliss was a clever businesswoman, and initially she'd thought she might get some useful PR out of me. 'Sarah, why you never go anywhere special to show off my clothes?' she moaned. Poor Mrs Deliss. I led her a merry dance, helping her to design outfits for which she charged me half price just to leave them unworn in my cupboard. Lately, though, since Robert had come into my life, they were being seen a little more because I wasn't forced to stay home waiting day and night for Lionel's phone calls. This was my attempt to ease him out.

Thankfully Addo was always excellently well behaved in Harrods. He seemed to know that neither humping, nor pissing nor fighting would have been welcome. Holding his mighty head aloft, he'd sway his wonderfully bushy tail to and fro, padding along at my side with a real Harrods dignity. In the piano department, playing the only tune I can, 'Some Day My Prince Will Come', I realized I had two princes now. I had found my safe haven, my Bolt hole, yet I was still Olivier's crème de menthe frappée. Although I hadn't yet taken the marriage vows, I felt committed to Robert. I was frightened of seeing Lionel again, in case . . . well, in case.

I don't know how long I sat there day-dreaming away when I wondered why there was such a silence. I got up to find Addo asleep under the piano. The place was empty and the far entrances had steel gates dividing various departments. I didn't wear a watch so I had no idea of the time. Memories came flooding back of that fearful train journey when I was seven and Daddy put me on the train at Liverpool Street station. Mummy was going to meet me at Ingatestone, but I got stuck in the loo and ended up a bundle of terror at the end of the line in Colchester. 'Help! I've been locked in!' Not a sausage.

While hunting for a lift I thought what a good film this would make: two different kinds of people, from different cultures, getting stuck in Harrods for a weekend. They meet at the phones, decided not to call the police and go to town with great zest, playing getting-to-know-you games in all the departments that gave them pleasure. Black, white, pink, green, male, female, it makes no odds because by the time the weekend was over they just couldn't give a damn, having broken through to a deeper understanding

Thanks to my powerful lung capacity a man in uniform arrived with some keys, looking grumpy. 'How did you manage to get left behind?'

'Day-dreaming.'

Out under the open blue sky again, Addo and I trotted up the north side of Hyde Park to my agents, the Grade Organization. Always good to see Robin and Ros – and, after all, they had brought Robert and me together. They were both delighted to be responsible for the meeting between Robert and me in Montpelier Square. 'You two seem to be turning into pretty serious stuff,' said Robin, giving me his usual elegant peck.

I enjoyed going into those offices, not for the heady whiff of success and the plush of the establishment, but because of the Boss, Leslie Grade. Everyone had a particular soft spot for Leslie. A koala bear, always merry, always looking at the best of life. I sometimes went and sat on his knee, which he now patted for me. 'I hear you're looking for a place in the country, Sarah. Lovely old house in the *Country Life* this week. All on its own on an island in Surrey – have a look.' Addo and I said goodbye and wandered through the park, splashing our feet in autumn colours, and savouring the fresh nip in the air. We went and sat at the edge of the Serpentine. 'I won't be long.' said Addo as he plunged off into the deep.

After he returned we went to buy *Country Life*. Walking home, I noticed the cover: what a beautiful simple house. Was it William and Mary, Queen Anne or early Georgian, I wondered. I put my money on early Georgian. Looking inside, I realized it was the house Leslie had talked about. All on an island with twenty-five acres, river, woods – but where was the church? When I was seven years old I had a vision and saw Home in the palm of my hand: this house wasn't old enough, and there was no church. Shame my Chekhovian rectory wasn't on the market now that I'd found my Prince Charming. Twenty years or so later, when Robert Bolt and I got married for the second time, we'd been looking for a place in the country when the rectory popped up on the market again. I had been dreaming about the place over the years and had inveigled myself into the owner's life by making my love for the place known to him. He was a fusty old rotter, but took a liking to me because of our mutual affection for the house. On top of which, with no knowledge of this long *amour*, Robert's oldest friend from their days in the RAF, Tony Quinton (now Lord Quinton), had come to live right across the lane. Sadly, though, we were outbid.

'Lucky for you,' consoled Lord Quinton's wonderfully exotic American wife, Marcelle. 'The whole place was rotten through and through, they had to start all over. It's cost them heavy.' Shortly thereafter Peter Hall fired me from the National Theatre, for which I am most grateful. Without time on my hands, Robert and I would not have lucked upon the house we live in today. My childhood vision, returned to reality. An unspoilt ancient house with a church, river and woodland. My own piece of England, ours and for ever.

The phone rang as Addo and I approached the front door. I could hear it ringing as I put the key in the lock. Was it Lionel? The door wouldn't open! God damn it, why didn't Robert answer the phone? It was at that moment that a new feeling flooded over me. Did it matter if Robert answered the wretched phone? As I stood there fumbling with the lock, I hoped he wouldn't. Was my love for Robert Bolt expanding at such a rate that it was making inroads into those achings for Olivier? Finally the key turned and I shot into the drawing room, where as usual Robert failed to look up from typing. I just got there in time. It *was* Lionel, I knew it. 'Hello, Robin. Yes . . . Yes . . . Yes. I've got it, thank you. Goodbye.' I hung up and went upstairs to run my bath. I was to meet Lionel next Thursday afternoon. The thought frightened me. Lately I'd become unusually apt to take long hot baths, and it was always to do with Lionel: the knowledge that we would have to part was unbearable.

It's miraculous how warm water soothes the aches of love.

'Sarah?' said Nona, entering the bathroom and sitting on the loo. (Nona came regularly to sit on the loo, trapping me – a captive audience at last. I kept reminding myself to get a lock on the door.) She ranted on and on about how Manny abused her love. I remained silent. I knew Nona's dark patches. She needed professional help and that was that. She rose from the loo seat and stood in the doorway, gently fingering her lavish curtains of silken mouse, which trailed over her greeny blue kimona.

'I only know one thing.'

'And what's that?' Attempting to stifle my impatience.

'I can't live without Manny.' Another suicide threat.

I could be brutal when called for. 'So you'll fuck up his life instead?'

'Just because *you* don't know what love is!' She looked daggers at me as she stalked out of the bathroom. Was she right . . .?

Roughly a week later Robert and I were having a drink in the drawing room. Nona was there too. We were all trying to make a go of it. Sammy was down with Nona's mother, and Nona still hadn't heard from Manny. While I was wondering whether Lionel would take on another crème de menthe frappée in my stead, Nona spilt her coffee on the carpet. She sat there hardly looking at it, so I dashed downstairs to get a cloth. When I got back Nona was delving into her private depths, so I cleaned up the spot. I got it all up, I think. 'Thanks, Sarah,' said Nona from far away.

Next evening Robert and I were alone. 'Is she a friend or what?' he said, puffing his pipe with vigour.

'You know what she is. Stop mixing it.'

'I know bloody well what she is – but do you?'

I kept silent, because I didn't have a clue what my relationship to Nona was. I suppose I was a kind of guardian against her suicide attempts.

'She's my friend from RADA.'

'If she's your friend she'd go to her mother's for a while. She won't because she's insensitive to our needs – and that's not friendship. Tell her to leave, this evening. Just say you want to be alone with me. Is that too much to ask?'

Robert never raised his voice, never got angry. Well, that's not quite true, but his buttons had to be well and truly pressed first. I think I pressed them twice, but not till much later.

'I can't tell her, I'm a coward.'

'You, a coward?' he said disbelievingly.

In three days' time Lionel would probably be telling me the same thing. Could he and Robert both be wrong? But I knew that unless Nona's bags were packed and thrown out along with her, I hadn't a hope in hell of removing her or her son. I said, 'I'm going to bed. *You* wait up for Nona and tell her. You have a better gift of the gab.' I kissed him goodnight, 'Please', and went upstairs.

Half an hour later he came in, switched on the light and whispered, 'I've done it.' He kissed my hair. 'I told her.' A brave man. I turned over to him, feeling protected and cherished. Robert's eyes had the same blue intensity as Nona's but hers were glazed with the familiar shallow brittleness, Robert's radiated benevolence and wisdom.

Next evening Nona was playing her 'packing' act down-stairs in the dining room. I went through into the kitchen and she followed. 'I'm going to stay with Mother.'

'So Robert said.'

'I do think that you should have told me yourself.' That was unforgivable, but Nona always knew how to get a rise out of me.

'Nona, I've been telling you for two years.' I got myself an apple, and went to the stairs. 'It's for the best. Besides, that's what mothers are for.'

Next morning the phone rang. It was Nona's brother, Carey. 'Hello, Sarah. I have some bad news, I'm afraid.'

'What's that?'

'Nona jumped off a building.'

'Is she dead?'

'As soon as she made contact.'

I felt a giggle, that first sign of hysteria, rising up uncon-trollably. Searching for a way to dampen the flames of shock, before they burst out all over the shop, I sat down on the floor.

'Sarah?

I was too full of suppressed mortification to reply. I tried to breathe. 'Carey, I'll call you back later.' As I put down the phone the hysteria lunged upwards from my innards. I couldn't get up off the floor. The only thing securing me to the here and now was the familiar rhythm of Robert's typing. Please God, fill my lungs with breath!

God came to the rescue.

'Darling?'

'Yes?'

'Get me a cup of coffee,' asked Robert, oblivious of all the things in this realm. Making the coffee saved me (but then service to others is the only way *to* be saved). I waited till the coffee cup was safely down beside him, and then I waited some more. Mesmerizing it was, the coffee coiling beneath my nostrils, its potent smell allowing me at last to breathe more calmly.

'Nona's dead.'

He actually looked up.

Lionel had lit the gas fire. Waiting for the room to warm he opened his briefcase on the dusty, rickety table and proudly laid out before me a whole lot of architect's plans. The familiar silver screen with black edges came down in front of my eyes, taking me into the realms of inadequacy and fear. 'I've never understood maps.'

He gave me a peck on the cheek. 'These are sacred. The plans for the new National Theatre.' So many, and all of them making him agitated. Their presence seemed to reawaken the bees in his bonnet, driving him buzzing mad. 'No one listened to what I wanted!' He began marching up and down. From what I could gather, there was strong opposition to those particular plans. The more he tried to explain to me, the more feverish he became. 'My way was the only way it could, would – *will* ever work!' It was all too late since construction was well under way.

These attacks troubled me. He was overworked and overburdened, with Ken Tynan waxing fickle as a fairy queen instead of providing the bedrock of reliability that Lionel not only deserved but desperately needed. It was bound to play havoc with his health. Periods of losing his breath, followed by profuse sweating and disorientation, had become sinisterly regular, undermining his sense of destiny. He swore that if they didn't go away soon, he'd have to give up acting on stage altogether. 'I saw nothing but black the other night, nothing but black. Lost all sense of who I was, let alone who I was playing' (the Master Builder). He confessed his fear as if betraying his dearest love. For the first time I shared with him my silver screen with the black edges and he held me tight as if we might drown together. Perhaps my removal from the scene was perfectly timed.

'It's no more than exhaustion. Giving up your crème de menthe frappée will take care of everything.'

'You're part of it, bitch. I need—'

'My free massage.'

This time it was he who slapped me across the face (gently).

I cursed myself for not comprehending those plans for they were the design for that plebeian, hefty terminal so forlornly lacking in hope, that maudlin mud pie overshadowing the Thames. Was it part of some conspiracy to stifle the human spirit? Surely England's National Theatre should be a sparkling, uplifting space for weaving magic spells? I confess there were times when Lionel's taste went for a tiny totter, and the National Theatre is a sad example of this. In my more compassionate moments, I put it down to him having the vapours at the time.

Later, in the little warmed-up room, I wanted to love him till the end of time, but instead, it was our own time that had come to an end. I looked down at his noble head. I'd grown so fond of his bald patch. Why are men so afraid of losing their hair? He said sadly, 'Dame Sarah has finally sown all her wild oats.'

Perhaps our heartbeats knew too, because I could never remember them being so out of sync before. He noticed. 'Listen to us, everything's gone haywire.' We lay there, quite still. 'Must be quite a chap, this Bolt.' I said nothing. 'A mere spring chicken, only eighteen years your senior.' He'd worked it out, the bugger. Age never interested me.

'He got rid of Nona.'

I do believe he was miffed, for he turned away, thrusting his back at me for a massage. 'So all your worries are over.'

I imitated him as best I could. '"Get rid of her before she either kills herself or you."'

Quick as a flash, he knew.

'She's jumped.'

As my tears welled up he kissed them away. 'She *had* to jump, for that was your suggestion. She had to get her revenge, don't you see?'

'What revenge, for God's sake? I did my best for her.'

'I did my best by Vivien too. But they wait, delivering their wild card at a time when they know it'll choke us with guilt for the rest of time.' He held me tight. 'Where's little Sammy?'

'With her mother, where he should have been all along.'

Silence fell as he held me tight. 'Come, sweet, it's not yet your wedding day.'

Neither of us felt inclined to even reach the ceiling that Thursday afternoon. His body hinted at a paunch (not yet in Bolt's league!) but was still in magnificent shape. His touch was now blessed with perfection. No one would ever stroke me as tenderly again, but then no one would be so determined to get it right. What was it that made it so exquisite? Was it tenderness combined with a stubborn knowingness? Or daring intermingled with care? Whatever it was, Olivier's fingertips scorched me more than ever before, lighting the candle to my soul, tipping me into the realms of the divine.

CHAPTER THIRTY-FIVE

I'LL NEVER FORGET standing there on our first visit to the old Mill House, Byfleet, in 1967. Addo felt at home as soon as we arrived and plunged into the river only to be chased out again by three unfriendly swans. Poor Addo! They weren't at all like the Serpentine swans. He was going to have to learn like the rest of us that the natives weren't friendly.

I'd just been round the house, and some rooms were a bit creepy. I wasn't sure what I meant by creepy in those days because I didn't believe in ghosts then. But I knew it was something weeping in the mortar. Probably no more than just centuries of human pain.

'It's the most beautiful place I've ever seen,' said Robert, fishing for his pipe.

'Didn't you find the house is a bit spooky?'

Robert's reply teemed with hopefulness. 'Our love will overcome all.'

Observing him standing there so straight and strong, always itching to move on once his mind had been made up, made me realize what joy it was continually believing in him. He couldn't stay still for more than seconds at a time and if he found himself a moment too long in already conquered land, out would come the cigarettes or pipe.

I looked up at the Old Mill House. Should we buy it? Take the plunge? What was it that I had felt inside so acutely? A shiver went down my spine, so I turned to watch Robert, striding along with that comical, enthusiastic bounce to his walk. He had better dress sense than Lionel, knowing perfectly what suited him.

*

I'd just been to the American Embassy with Robert to get his visa. He was off to New York on business and would be gone at least a week. Meanwhile Addo and I waited for him on the grass of Grosvenor Square. As I sat there wishing that he didn't have to go he reappeared looking mightily chuffed. 'Guess what? I don't have to go!' He threw me up into the air. 'I'm blacklisted. For being a communist, and I suppose going to jail with Bertie Russell didn't help.'

I remembered Robert taking me over the street thinking to introduce me to Bertie.

'We've met,' said Bertie, giving me a bedroomy wink all for Robert's benefit. Later, when they began reminiscing over the table, there was something about their conspiracy that reminded me of schoolboys playing truant.

Robert had just returned from being in China for a month. He'd felt honoured to be one of the first British party allowed there since the beginning of the Red Guard. Bertie was keen to know all about it. There were only four in the party. One of them was Hugh Trevor-Roper, who'd grown fed up with forever being spied on, his every deed and word scrutinized. He began to get bolshie, so much so that one day he dragged Robert away.

'Where were you?' asked Bertie, sitting there like a fine speckled hawk.

'Somewhere in the countryside outside Peking,' said Robert, shrugging. Having escaped from their party he and Trevor-Roper climbed to the top of a hill and hid. 'Wonderful it was, Bertie, to smell a bit of freedom in that Chinese air. And absurdly childish, because we could hear the secret police calling out our names in the valley below. We left them to it. Thought we'd wait it out.'

'How long did you stay up there?' Bertie moved his elbows further on to the table to prop up his interest.

'About an hour, I suppose,' said Robert, fishing in his pockets for his pipe.

'Were you nervous?'

'I just puffed on me pipe and Hugh smoked his fags.'

'How did they respond once they'd found you?' Bertie couldn't get enough of the Red Guards' ways.

'We all played "Hail Fellow Well Met", but they kept a closer eye after that.'

After Robert's party returned home, an official close to the British ambassador was murdered in the British Embassy in Peking, which started fresh hostilities between our countries. Robert had been lucky to get in when he did, and, more important, to get out.

Not long after, Bertie asked Robert down to Wales to do an interview with him for the BBC. The 'two old jailbirds get together once more' routine. It was the last interview Bertie gave, and how endearing they were, talking about dying and death. I might have been biased, for Bertie had stolen my heart, even before I knew who the hell he was.

Back to the Old Mill House. I worked out that Robert must be walking the perimeter of the property, so I went down to the bottom of the garden. The river Wey divided at the south end marked by the two giant cedars of Lebanon, the most luxurious examples of these trees that I had ever seen. Their generous branches formed a loving mantle over the swing and trapeze, protecting great areas of lawn from all weathers. Once the river divided around them, it wound its way round both sides of the house, passing rose gardens and old brick walls, lawns and box hedges. Our own moat – excellent for security.

Robert came into view on the iron pony-track bridge to fulfil his circular amble, past the Manor and up Lover's Lane. He saw me watching him and stood there, centre bridge, captain at his helm, waving at me just like Christian in *Mutiny on the Bounty*. So warming that Addo had taken him to heart without humping him to death, a real turn-up for the books.

As I waved back, I felt all was going to be well. Perhaps the spooks I felt were simply aftermath-of-Nona spooks poking fun at me.

'I'm just going this way back!' cried Robert from across the river, the other side of the hedge.

He'd recently taken me to watch filming on *A Man For All Seasons*, purposely choosing a time when Orson Welles, who played Wolsey, would be in action. He looked fearsome in his great puce robes, sitting at a royal desk with a quill in his regal hand. If Sylvia, my whore of Half Moon Street, was right, Wolsey had a pretty fine member, for his middle finger entwining the quill was quite a monster. I couldn't make out whether his puce face was painted to match his robes or whether it was natural. He gave the impression of being determined to steal the film from under the noses of both Robert Shaw and Paul Scofield. Jolly hard luck it must have been for Welles, striding through life on the back of his first film, 'The man who made *Citizen Kane*' echoing forth between every step. He cushioned the agony of never making it a second time by stuffing himself to the gills.

'Boo!' Robert made me jump right out of my skin. 'Let's go round and see where we'd put the tennis court.' Robert wasn't a tennis player but he'd be playing in no time, and beating me in a year, I wouldn't wonder. We found the perfect spot and another for croquet, my palomino stud farm, and a conservatory (Addo's kennel). The perfect spot for Robert's study above the mill race, another for darts, in the cellar, wellies to be strewn about the hall, and table tennis and handball in the lower decks of the Mill. There was a perfect spot to build my homey kitchen and a perfect cottage for the gardener and his wife. A perfect place, in fact, for ticking off the whole of my dream list. As we kissed again, back under the cedars, we both knew this was as good a home as we'd ever find.

*

'Mother, I'm ringing up to—'

'You mustn't marry him yet.'

'Exactly. We're going to live together, buy the house half each.'

'I forbid any child of mine to live in sin.' (What I didn't know at the time was that Mater and Pater had been living in sin for yonks, making me the bastard that I am.)

'You won't let me marry or live in sin. What do I do, Mother mine, become a nun?'

'Nuns have to take exams, you'd never get in.' Mother liked bringing up my lack of education, it won her the point. 'Don't sign anything until I've been down to vet it.'

'We're going halves. The house is £40,000, £20,000 each, and hey presto!'

'Get Michael Simpkins [my solicitor] on to it, otherwise you'll end up – hey presto – with nothing.'

'Mother, Robert isn't at all like that.'

'They never are.' Mother was mellowing through her right-wing Gestapo period, to merely right of right. Daddy, too, was mellowing. No longer a communist, he was in a perpetual no man's land. It was amazing how mother had surrendered to liking Robert. She didn't mind him being blacklisted in the USA or even going to jail with Bertie Russell, but when she found out he came from Salford, she stroked her rising feathers. 'Still . . .' she paused for a moment, 'he *did* write *A Man For All Seasons*.' Nothing like a dazzling track record to bulldoze the class barrier.

CHAPTER THIRTY-SIX

MOVING HOUSE DIDN'T take long because I was also rehearsing a new play by Michael Hastings for the Hampstead Theatre Club. Peter Coe directed, with Alan Dobie as Lee Harvey Oswald, and I played Marina. Reading the Warren Report for homework was riveting stuff. I passionately believed that Oswald was an innocent victim caught up in something overpoweringly corrupt. The amount of witnesses who were conveniently bumped off convinced me of the conspiracy theory. I enjoyed playing Marina, cultivated a passable Russian accent and had myself a ball, bouncing around in a feeling of team spirit.

Robert, Father and Mother came to the first night, plus an old friend of Robert's, Anne, Marchioness of Queensberry, who often came to visit us at the Old Mill. She was down in the dumps because her marquess had cruelly trotted off with another. In my dressing room afterwards, I caught a glimpse of Mother in my mirror giving Anne Queensberry, whom she'd never met before, a strange long look. After Robert had driven off with Anne, I asked Mother what the look was about.

'You be careful of that Anne, she'll take your Robert from under your very nose.'

I laughed, brushing aside the idea. They'd known each other for years, and I thought Robert would have gone off with her by then, if he was going to. Almost fifteen years later Mother's prediction came true: Anne and Robert got married between his and my two marriages. My mother, as I keep saying, was some mother.

Hardly had we got used to calling the Old Mill home when Robert, who was revamping an old play of his and renaming it *Brother and Sister*, was asked to do a film of *Gandhi*.

A delightful Indian called Moti Katari came forward, asking Robert if he would write the script for a penny, for the Gandhi Foundation. How could Robert refuse? So there he was being invited to go to India, to visit Gandhi's ashram and meet all the people still alive who knew Gandhi, ending up in audience with the Prime Minister, Mrs Gandhi, who had lived with Gandhi when she was young.

Still stubbornly uninvolved in any mind-expanding activities, I didn't want to go one bit. I was just getting the stableyard in order, having bought a fifteen-hands-two-inch Irish mare, pure chestnut heaven from Mr White who owned the Roehampton riding school. Daisy and I had fallen in love at first sight. It wasn't her slender flanks, for hers were those of a bull; it wasn't her thoroughbred head, for hers was more Roman than Anglo-Saxon; it wasn't her slender feet either, for hers were great hairy dinner-plates. Alas, no silky tail to flip the flies, for Daisy's was cruelly docked. Mr White had scratched his head.

'She must've got that tail of hers stolen on the boat coming over from Ireland.' Tail docking was illegal by this time.

'How old is she?'

'Judging by her teeth, she's about seven.' I had a good look at her teeth, too, and I thought she was nearer eleven. But age is no deterrent between genuine lovers, and her tailless mystery added a certain piquancy. What I had fallen for was her great arched neck, straining at the bit; her elated jaunty gait, matched only by Robert's; her keen Roman eye always on the alert for any excuse to charge towards the wind and enemy. Everything about her had enormous will, a gigantic spirit pushing her onward with mighty strength and power.

Holding in Daisy's desire to charge needed all the concentration I could muster. She had a habit of flicking the reins loose when I was least expecting it, and in that split second between changing grip – charge! She'd toss her head victoriously to and fro, too far away for me to grab back the reins. Even when I put her in a double pelham and martingale she still managed to play Houdini. She was brilliant at galloping off with everyone, and in next to no time had the reputation of being totally off the wall. Bob, my enchanting epileptic stable boy, saw her trying to climb a tree once and rushed to get me. I couldn't believe my eyes: She had reared up against it!

The odd thing about Daisy was that although she let no one ride her but me, as soon as our son Tom arrived she allowed him on board and was as good as gold. Also whenever harnessed to the trap she never played up once, but did all the right things first time off, as if she were born to it. (She probably pulled a milk float in Ireland.) Off we'd trot, either through the bridle path and on to the common the far side of the woods, to the pub for a game of shove-halfpenny, or up towards Weybridge to collect someone from the station. Such fun it was, Daisy being as perfect as a hackney when it suited her. Clippety clop, clippety clop. Mad as a hatter and wise as Aristotle.

'But we won't be going for long.' Robert was half talking to me about the Indian trip and half watching the Indians shoot it out in some corny American cowboy film on TV. He'd spend most of his free time watching such movies on telly, just like all other intellectuals, no doubt. 'Only about six weeks.'

'Six weeks! I've never left Addo for that long, not since Larry Harvey's film in Madrid.'

'You do whatever you feel you must. I have to go, and I'd love it if you came too.'

I was left to make up my mind. How could I leave my new home, Addo, Gulliver, our new Yorkshire terrier, Daisy and Fred the goose for six weeks? I'd been offered some good films, but I just wasn't interested in leaving my own stable-yard now that I'd finally got it back again. I was a groom at last – so snooks to you, Mother mine!

Mother and Father had been down. She fairly liked the house, but said we had an awful lot to do to make it how we'd want it. They were both impressed by the garden. 'It reminds me of your father,' putting her hand gently on Daddy's shoulder, for she was the taller.

'How d'you mean?' inquired Daddy.

'A miniature estate. Everything perfectly proportioned and in its place.'

'I've never seen ancient trees placed so sensitively – could well be a Capability Brown,' Daddy said. How I loved him. Still on his pedestal – then, anyway. The last of the Edwardians, as rare as country lanes. 'Not a building in sight.' He took my hand and kissed it.

'They'll probably go and build London's ring road right through here,' warned Mother. She was right, naturally. We would spend most of our time in future years fretting as to where the damn motorway would go, in constant fear of paradise lost.

'Aren't you glad it isn't that smelly damp Turville Rectory?' said Ma, triumphantly.

The mill was separate, on four floors, crumbling beautifully, yet still almost all intact, except for the peeled-off pale-yellow-painted planks. The sluice-gates were operated from the side of the house. We were responsible for working them, which became quite a task in flood times. 'What if you're both off making a film when the next flood comes?' asked Mother while I demonstrated the effort needed in turning the great handles.

Well worth it, to see the trapped water plunging forward into its new-found freedom, splashing up between the walls of the ancient mill.

'It's listed in the Domesday Book and I'm going to build Robert a surprise study in there, over the mill race.'

'I can see you being happy here,' said Father, busily parting with us to drive back home to Ingatestone. He always forced an air of business over possible sentimentality.

'Especially since you hardly ever go in houses anyway,' Mother remarked, settling into the driver's seat. 'Except, of course, in London when you never went out.'

'I did. I pretty well knew every tree in every park.'

'Precisely.'

'I'll be back in the house once the new kitchen and conservatory are finished.'

Mother looked at me strangely, as if trying to shrug off something eerie.

'Hmm. Do that, and then you needn't go in the rest of the house at all,' Daddy rolled down his window so I went round to give him a kiss. 'T-t-take care of your man, P-P-Pusscat, he's special.'

Off they scrunched purposefully up the drive. It was true: since arriving at the Old Mill I would spend all day, while Robert worked, in my stableyard. I never went in the house, especially since we had found the perfect housekeeper and gardener, Francesca and Fernando, who had previously worked for Lady Antonia Fraser. (Don't fret, Antonia, your secrets are safe with me!)

As I watched them driving away, I realized I would have been happier closer to Barn Mead and the family, but I suppose we all have to grow up. However much I failed to see eye to eye with Mother, and however much I got on her wick, it never stopped me from wanting to be near her. Daddy, too. I greatly missed our croquet matches, ping-pong and tennis.

Apart from the importance of continuity, if I really try and work out why I wanted to be near them, it was because they had such integrity. To me they were what the word 'marriage' was all about. (They weren't married in the beginning because Daddy couldn't get a divorce.) It was their togetherness that rooted my strength. How vital it is, a good role model. Would I ever have a marriage such as theirs? I didn't want to fall short, not for them or for me. I had witnessed a perfect union between man and woman, so I knew marriage *could* work. I would do my damnedest to make it work too.

What a spoilt brat I was! I wanted all this and heaven too. And I was getting it. Everything except Lionel. However much I still loved him, the feeling of moral correctness made me want to give my marriage vows a good crack of the whip. I thought it might somehow bring dignity to an up till then rather messy and deceitful life. Nothing is more important than being able to hold up one's head without the weight of inner shame, I find. The task was made easier in that my witty and wise Bolt from the blue had such innocence (whenever I caught a glimpse of him, that is).

Although the sound of wedding bells was out there on the horizon, my need to see Lionel one last time became paramount, for the parting ache was still rampaging against my need for self-worth. I knew I finally had no choice but to put our affair safely behind me, and the sooner the better . . . but just once more. (The word 'affair' perhaps belittles us, for there was a mysterious synchronicity, whose same magnetic pull brought him back to me out of the blue one evening in LA seven years later.) I had to pretend that I was no more than Lionel's crème de menthe frappée, and that any minute now I need no longer share my life with the phone.

We were able to meet at Hasker Street, because Johnnie Windeatt had accepted a landscaping job and was in the process of turning Mount Etna into paradise – another veritable Capability Brown. He wrote to us, enclosing photos of the extraordinary work he was up to out there, all of which seemed impressive. I believe he went up Etna to escape from his employer.

Johnnie also worked as a pimp. Young boys. This was a hard one for me to embrace, so I suggested that if Johnnie decided to give up these wicked ways he could move into Hasker Street at a minimal rent. It was good to see his face light up with glee. 'Thank you, Sarah. I promise you, I'll love it as my own.'

And that was that. It was best to keep Hasker Street lived in, and Johnnie seemed to have a few bob, judging by his lovely suits, Rolls-Royce and silky lifestyle. I had taken a real shine to him, even finding a motherly side popping up for the first time. I think it was his carefreeness coupled with his kindness that drew me to him. Besides, Addo, having spent so much time with Beethoven during our dog-walking days, was missing him too – they, like Johnnie and I, had become great mates.

Lionel didn't consider 'getting his end away' the main reason for meeting; and since he didn't want to talk shop or be massaged that last day, I took it to mean that what he said was true. I was able to rekindle his belief in the better part of his woefully complex nature. He was in one of his Notley Manor moods. He'd often say that he loved Notley Manor more than any of his wives or lovers. 'Not more than Vivien, surely?'

'Of that I'm sure . . . but you?' He took me to him, burying his head in me.

'That's what you say to all the girls.'

He was a devil when he wanted it. Compliments flying all over the shop, but even when all was quiet again the compliments lived on – my very own Cyrano de Bergerac, sans nose (usually!).

After a while his thoughts wafted home again, to Notley Manor. 'When I walked the gardens alone for the last time and saw my modest efforts paying such worthwhile dividends, I hoped the next owners would nurture it as I had done.' His voice had a timbre which I hadn't heard before.

'You knew it was home.'

'As clearly as I know I'll never find it again.' Whenever he was really close to me, looking me dead in the eye, I could feel my heart pulsing upwards through my irises.

'Lucky to come home – even once in a lifetime.' We knew our time was up, and sat for a long time at the edge of my bed. Half off, half on, half clothed, half-heartedly looking at the time, whole-heartedly wanting time to stop.

'Is your new Mill House home?'

'I couldn't call it my Notley, but who knows? It's early days yet. We're off to India.'

'Off to India?' He jumped.

'Yes. Robert is writing a film on Gandhi.'

Quite suddenly Lionel vanished and Laurence Olivier came into being, right out of left field. He looked at his belly. 'Tell David Lean I've already begun slimming.' He swirled the sheet around his head, and began to walk round the room barefoot, giving a magnificent rather than a humble Gandhi with morsels of Othello and a speck of Lawrence of Arabia, but jolly good all the same, before disintegrating back into the comfort of Archie Rice. Every bit the actor he painfully was, yet he had something else, too, that something which held us suspended in each other's bliss. I never knew if he was joking or not.

And that's how we left it. Had it all been a joke or what? What had it really been to him, our time together? One thing is for certain, our mutual happiness was never forced, never questioned, it just was. What would happen next between us? Was I ever going to see him again? He kept saying that it was merely *au revoir*. I didn't believe him. I should have known better, his psychic antennae were always alert. But, at that moment, having watched him dress with his familiar economic precision, combing his hair (still hanging in there), holding out his arms for me to place them into his oh-so-familiar raincoat and then on to those fiendishly familiar shoulders, something way down deep pinged at my gut. Surely that familiarity could never be severed? After he'd kissed me on my most sensitive place, the back of my neck, I knew, too, that it wasn't goodbye. He turned his back to me. '*Au revoir*,' he said, blowing one last kiss. As I watched him on his way, I noticed that the bounce in his step had temporarily vanished.

CHAPTER THIRTY-SEVEN

I SAT VERY still, cross-legged under Gandhi's fig tree, which conveniently lent its shadow as an umbrella to all weathers. It grew right beside his ashram, overlooking a sweeping expanse of arid riverbed. Although everything seemed hopelessly cracked and dry, something intangible oozed from that same fracture in the earth, spreading its calm not only about the ashram, but blanketing the whole area in a balmy benevolence. Even with my insensitivity and indifference to energies in those days I could feel it in the air.

Robert was off somewhere talking to some saint or other, but I wanted to stay still for a morning because I'd done too much standing around and smiling at strangers. I had been meeting too many people. Over the past weeks everyone we met who had known and loved Gandhi hadn't a bad word to say about him, compliments flowing through an adulation of tears. Was it too much reverence that was making me want to throw up? One night Robert, puffing away on the edge of the window ledge of our hotel in Bombay said, 'Doesn't bode well for a film script. Moving stuff though it may be.'

I wished he smoked less, not for my sake, for I smoked occasionally at that time, but for himself.

'Can't find any conflict.' Robert needed to uncover something that brought out the weaknesses in Gandhi. All humans have failings, thank God. How boring we would be without them. Even saints must get a day off sometimes. Robert was becoming more nervous. No inner conflict, no man. No man, no drama.

Something else was making me throw up, too. I thought perhaps I might be pregnant. I knew Robert would be outwardly thrilled to bits, but inwardly he might well feel that three children were enough. We had never discussed babies, and here I was, sitting under Gandhi's fig tree, having to make earth-shattering life decisions, all of them born of ignorance, laziness and stupidity. I had no clue as to how many weeks pregnant I was, but I felt hugely relieved that Lionel and I hadn't made love on the last two occasions. Just cuddling. If we had made love, I wouldn't have had a clue as to whose baby I was carrying. It was time for me to get hold of the reins of life and finally take control.

While walking round Gandhi's ashram, I became convinced that there must have been *some* hanky-panky going on, for he had so many beautiful women followers. Surely if a beautiful, youthful, double-barrelled English rose offered you her private swelling places, you'd not reject them, not even if you were a saint? One of those classy English girls, by then in her eighties, came to visit us at the Mill House just before she died. Sadly, neither Robert nor I can recall her name. She spoke of Gandhi with such a raunchiness shining in her eyes that I presumed my suspicions were justified. Looking back, though, most probably I had mistaken a fecundity of love for lust. There are more satisfying ways of playing with that all-consuming loving energy than merely poking away at the flesh. Inner places where fornication pales by comparison. I didn't know any of this then. I wish I had, there was so much I could have learnt. I curse myself for waking up so late in life.

We went to see Gandhi's prison. Before he went into prison there was little crime, but once Gandhi was a prisoner and saw the living conditions, he decided to do something about it. He did, too: arts, crafts, weaving, carpentry, silent places, music rooms – indeed, the word spread far and wide that Gandhi's prison was the 'in' place to be. Petty crime went up, at least that's what a friend of Moti Katari told me.

We took a few days off to go to Agra and surrender to the Taj Mahal by moonlight. I have to admit I wasn't prepared for it. What a woman she must have been to inspire in her man the desire to create such a mighty, shimmering, pearly being! Not satisfied that this white-marble monument was sufficient to honour her. Each facing each other, throwing off great sparks of love igniting the Ying and the Yang, the life force thrusting the centuries forward. Soft echoes of affirmation whispered through the moon-lit marble, reflecting my own fertility and approaching motherhood. Robert and I were being drawn closer and closer, as if being pulled into something – by something everlasting. Yet it felt completely different from the love I felt for Olivier. I recalled Finch's fifteen different words for love in Japan. I was certainly falling in love – but if not while embalmed in the soft curves of the Taj Mahal's most exclusive moonlight, then when? While we were climbing the Taj Mahal's moonbeams together in the Agra Hotel bedroom that night, I looked up towards the ceiling and, instead of seeing Robert, I saw a little golden water baby, half winking at me with eyes as transparent as his wings. This time it was no flamboyantly colourful wine-berry wagtail, or faithful Snow Goose, no, it was my coming baby and he was going to be Tom. Tom from *The Water Babies*.

Afterwards, while lying there watching Robert search for his cigarettes, 'What shall we call him?' asked Robert, relieved at pulling out one last fag from the corner of the packet.

'Could be a her,' I replied lamely, anxious to keep water babies on ceilings from him.

'I'm sure it's a him,' he said over his shoulder, fishing around for some matches before finally settling back to puff away at the fruits of his labour. 'Let's call him Tom,' he suggested, inhaling zestfully. And that was that.

We went to see another of Gandhi's followers the next day, the most interesting of all so far, though when stories go through a translator one risks embroidery. Apparently Gandhi wanted some of his own special goat cheese and there was none left. This was bad news since they were hundreds of miles away from Delhi, where it came from. Gandhi threw one of his hot little moody numbers, ordering a train to return to home base, where more supplies were to be loaded on board immediately. That must have been fearfully costly cheese. We all have our idiosyncrasies.

Back at the Agra Hotel next night at dinner, Robert noticed David Lean sitting alone in the far corner of the restaurant. He thought he was seeing things because he hadn't set eyes on David since *Doctor Zhivago*, three years previously. Just as Robert was refilling his pipe along with raising sufficient courage to go over, David saw us. He, too, couldn't believe his eyes. Robert rose, crossed to David's table, and after a moment pointed at me. They were obviously filling each other in with their news, quite a bit of it in three years. David rose to come over to our table. I'd never met this man before, this giant, this legend in his own editing room.

What struck me first off while being introduced were his devilish pointed ears, formidably straight no-nonsense countenance and enormous hands with huge thick fingers. 'I know you,' said David, giving me a piercing stare. 'I wanted you for *Doctor Zhivago*, but this chap wouldn't hear of it.'

Robert looked a trifle hang-dog, and changed the subject. 'Shall we order?'

I wasn't going to let him skim over this one. 'No, tell me what happened.'

David thought we ought to order first because the service required it. Afterwards he went on, 'I said to Robert, "That girl Miles is the only one who acts with her eyes."'

I turned to look at Robert. 'And you said?'

Poor Robert wasn't enjoying the retelling of this tale one little bit. 'I said,' he squirmed, while delving for another fag, 'I said—'

'He said,' David snatched the tale back, delighted to mimic Robert's northern twangs, 'She hasn't got the class for the part. I've seen her films, she's just a north-country slut.' Robert had obviously only seen *The Servant* and *Term of Trial*, and formed his opinion never having set eyes on me.

'I was so taken in by her acting,' said the Bolt, clearing his throat sheepishly.

David peered up from over the menu. 'Quite a compliment, but it lost you the part.'

During the main course David confessed all. He was there at the Agra Hotel because he had fallen in love. Up until this meeting he'd been living with Barbara Beal, who'd been continuity on *Doctor Zhivago*. Before Barbara, David had had an Indian wife, Leala, whom he left shortly after. The reasons for this bizarre behaviour remained obscure. Which was a good job since Leala was to keep up her telephone calls to the Mill House, year after year after year. 'Hello, Sarah, vere's David? I must speak to him. It's urgent.'

I am ashamed to recall how often we were commanded by David to buffer him from her cries of despair. He was a deeply mysterious man, and grew more so as time went by. But right then, as he sat scoffing his meal, he resembled a public schoolboy, with that first flush of romance that deepened as his story unfolded.

'She brought me up my afternoon tea here one day. Usually I got one of the Indian girls, but that particular afternoon I got Sandy. I asked her to stay and talk to me. She's only eighteen and has never set foot out of India.' He leaned in to sip the best wine of the menu. 'She's called Sandy Hotz.'

Her parents owned the hotel, but David didn't know that when he first fell in love – well, that was his story and he was sticking to it. She seemed mature enough, even a touch matronly for her eighteen years. Eventually, unbeknown to her parents, David stole her away into the world of showbiz. Poor Sandy had no idea what she was in for, but it wasn't the end of the world, for those German-Swiss are relentless survivors.

Over that first dinner David hadn't known for sure that Robert had accepted to write the script and seemed genuinely excited about filming *Gandhi*. Talking shop, those two became halves of the same whole, each having what the other lacked. A partnership made in heaven. David had only one reservation about the film and, that was his fear of returning to India because of Leala. The problem with Leala seemed to give life to David's pointed ears – they were verily quivering with anxiety. He had an eagle-like arrogance similar to Bertie Russell's, in fact there was a physical similarity between them. Bertie had softer edges however, a lustiness where David had ruthlessness.

Back in Bombay, my morning sickness was 'Bombay appalling'. Why couldn't I be one of those lucky women who never suffered it and therefore didn't really believe it existed? Because I'd had a pretty Bombayish night, Robert went off to the Gandhi Museum leaving me to follow on later. As soon as he left the suite I did a bit of Bombaying from both ends. Much relieved I pulled myself together, went out and hailed a taxi. 'The Gandhi Museum please.'

The Indian taxi driver looked most puzzled.

'De vat, memsahib?'

'The Gandhi Mueseum – you know Gandhigi—'

'Ha! Gandhigi!'

'Yes. You know – the Gandhigi Museum?'

He shrugged so I got out. I had roughly the same line of questioning with all the taxi drivers I hailed. Only two had heard of Gandhi and they didn't know where any museum was.

When I finally arrived, having telephoned the British Embassy to get the museum's whereabouts, Robert was watching Gandhi on a small Moviola machine.

'Come on, let's go.' He was off to meet some more followers.

'Can I stay here and watch him on the Moviola?'

'I'll see you back at the hotel this afternoon, then.' Robert left with Moti Katari.

I've always found watching real people in real-life situ-

ations infinitely more hypnotic than drama. I became transfixed for hours by the documentation of Gandhi. As he peered
out from his flowing robes and obvious goodness, I was
pleased to encounter an occasional staccato wiliness reminding me of Donald Pleasence's bird-like sly glance. Not a
heavenly being – far from it; those sandals kept him earthed
in reality. His eyes occasionally had a harshness, his mouth
at times a sullen bitterness. Perhaps he was secretly aware
that he would fail in his mission? Later I was lucky enough to
meet Krishnamuri (who renounced his role as the new chosen
Messiah) at one of his schools in Ohi, California. He also felt
that he had failed. 'I was unable to penetrate through to the
layman, only the semi-enlightened.'

Although I was in no position to judge him on that score,
a hint of bitterness at the corner of his mouth mirrored that
of Gandhi. I believe they both knew the world was not for
changing – not in their lifetime, if ever. But both had sufficient
humility to recognize that. It's not what one good man does,
surely, but the accumulation of all our better efforts down the
centuries that will eventually bring about the turn. When the
moment is right, why – a child could turn it on a sixpence.

Gandhi's wickedness seemed to blossom as he got older.
Watching him lead his men barefoot into battle, I was relieved
that it wasn't I who'd had the task of telling him the bad
news about his goat cheese. No doubt Robert had seen his
potential naughty side too, so I came away relieved. But what
will remain with me were the last few frames on his last day.
He had already made it known he was going to be assassi-
nated that morning. There was no trace of the sly fox to be
seen, just stillness, with his dignity held high as he faced his
destiny head on.

When I phoned Robin Fox I discovered that I had been
offered a quite amusing West End comedy, a two-hander
called *World War Two and a Half* opposite a fine actor called
Roy Dotrice, directed by my old mate Peter Coe. It sounded
fun and I was longing to return to comedy, having taken such

an unwarranted detour into crème de menthe frappée sex symbols. The image that the media had decided to lumber me with had finally got me in a stranglehold, preventing me from being light of heart. It was decided that I would return to England, after I'd thrown up all over the Red Fort, my early morning sickness being now at serious odds with my Delhi belly. We had arrived in Delhi to see Mrs Gandhi, the Prime Minister.

'Try not to throw up all over her,' said Robert, giving me a kiss as we and Moti Katari were ushered in to an anteroom where we were told to sit and wait. We did. On and on we waited. After what seemed a decade, she swooshed in, her sari swishing and shimmering as she crossed between us to sit at the end of a sort of high coffee table. A fine figure of a woman with a fearsomely angular contenance and, at that moment, agitated, impatient, even. The overall effect was so daunting that there followed a most embarrassing silence. It should have been Moti Katari's job to do the introductions but he just sat there, presumably spellbound. Robert, who usually has no problem in any social situation, was similarly struck dumb. Perhaps neither had experienced a woman in power before, and weren't sure of the etiquette. What was clear was that she had no intention of bailing them out. With every second expanding the silence's embarrassement, I was left with no option but to speak up.

'It is very kind of you to spare us some of your precious time. My husband', I gestured towards Robert, 'is writing a film on Gandhi.'

She snapped with contempt, 'I know nothing about films, I never watch them.' Her disdain was as if the whole business of filming left her with a bad smell under her nose. Robert finally said, 'It's very good of you to see us, ma'am. I understand you lived with Gandhi during part of your childhood, is this so?'

'Yes.' Her tone was far from drooling. That one word suggested all hadn't been peace, love and light between the two of them. She wasn't going to offer any information of her own free will, we would be pulling teeth every inch of the way.

'Can you share any of your memories of him?'

She shrugged in a negative way. 'I remember his temper.'

I perked up no end.

'Was he prone to lose his temper?'

'Sometimes. I remember one occasion. I was turning into a young woman and had just returned home from finishing school. Like all my contemporaries, I was keen to be coming of age and so wore a little lipstick, powder and what have you. When Gandhi saw me thus he lost his temper, literally dragging me upstairs to my bedroom and making me wash it all off again.' Silence. 'This happened repeatedly.'

'Make-up upset him, did it?'

'All things of which he didn't approve upset him. He was unable to find sufficient moderation over certain matters to see clearly without prejudice.'

This was the side of his nature I had observed on the Moviola, and the same stubbornness that ordered another train to bring him his special goat cheese. I have this theory that all so-called saints have to be sinners on their day off to become saints over the long haul. Anyone with a burning sense of purpose is bound to have a degree of tunnel vision, just as anyone born with a harmonious mellow goodness has difficulty in achieving anything spectacular.

Robert would now be able to put the pieces of the jig-saw together and write about Gandhi the man, rather than Gandhi the saint. Knowing this, I was able to leave India breathing easy. Robert would return in a couple of weeks, by which time I would have started rehearsals. All would be well.

CHAPTER THIRTY-EIGHT

JANUARY 1968, AND how I enjoyed the process of rehearsing comedy again! Roy was a terrifically energetic actor who knew the ropes, so I had to keep on my toes. The play was a success at the New Theatre, St Martin's Lane, and it was good to feel a team spirit once again. I had to remember to throw up before my entrances, because one night I concentrated so hard on not throwing up that I almost dried.

I so longed to get home to the country after the show that each evening I attempted to break my own record. I still had my Mini Cooper S, and I once got the journey down to twenty-four minutes, door to door. One early evening I was homeward bound on the dual carriageway (now the M3) when a clapped-out shooting-brake, doing thirty in the fast lane, forced me to slow down. More infuriating was that its rear window was too filthy for the driver to see me flashing my lights. Every now and again it would scuff the grass verge down the centre. Was its driver drunk? Since no notice was taken of my flashing lights or my impatient horn, I passed illegally on the inside lane, giving the driver, a woman, the victory sign. I regret dreadfully what I did next: I looked into my mirror. Holy Moses, I caught her old shooting-brake topple over the central reservation, turn a somersault and come to rest amid the oncoming traffic. Perhaps she had never seen a victory sign before? Watching the tragedy unfold in my driving mirror was so horrific that I thought I might miscarry there and then. Gathering my scattered guilty wits I parked precariously and made my way back on foot to the scene of the crime. I was roughly four months pregnant and Tom was wiggling inside me as if to say, 'Make a run for it,

Ma, before they nick you!' I was tempted to do just that. After all, if I hadn't looked in my mirror I'd never have known. I'd like to understand more about why our conscience pricks us, and what happens on other levels that inhibits us from 'getting away with it'. It's the good part of us, that I do know. As I grew older, I was to find through meditation that digging into that conscience area was strange at first, producing an 'out of bounds' sensation, but later I found it part of the centre of my nature.

By the time I arrived at the shooting-brake there was quite a to-do. The traffic was stationary for what seemed miles, and there were police cars, winking, and an ambulance.

'Is the woman all right?' I asked a copper.

'And what business is it of yours?' he inquired in the way that coppers do.

'I was the one who caused the accident.'

He grabbed me by the arm and took me over to another copper. After they'd taken all my details, I tried again. 'Is the woman all right?'

'So far only a broken leg, but that's not official. Off you go, and we'll see you in court.'

Luckily I had Michael Simpkins representing me in court, but it turned out that I didn't need him: the woman who climbed into the witness box was too good to be true, a perfect witness for the defence. She stood there apologizing for her dirty car, for being in the fast lane at twenty-eight miles an hour and for being under the influence – drunk in other words. Her story let me off the hook and the other two witnesses backed it up. I gave a sigh of relief. A delighted Michael Simpkins leaned towards me, whispering, 'I'll just go and phone Robert to give him the good news.' Off he went.

Then I was asked to take the stand.

I got up, dressed seriously prim, and stepped up into the witness box, whereupon I was told to tell my side of the story, which complemented hers. When I had finished there was a pause.

SERVES ME RIGHT

'You are an actress, are you not?' the magistrate asked. He said the word 'actress' as if I were a tart.

'Yes, that's correct.'

'Actresses are emotional creatures, unreliable on our roads, so I'm going to secure our safety by taking you off them. I'm removing your driving licence for a year.'

Michael Simpkins re-entered the courtroom – too late.

On many occasions after that (because I felt a great injustice had been done), I took profound pleasure in going to Kingston in the trap with Daisy, walking to and fro on the main street in front of the courthouse as slowly as possible. I became the slowest-moving vehicle in Kingston, clogging up the traffic for hours, and the coppers could do nothing.

World War Two and a Half was still bringing them in and I was enjoying it more and more. Roy Dotrice used to come into my dressing room and check himself out in the mirror, rubbing his chin regretfully. 'If it wasn't for this pathetic little chin, I could be a new Ronald Colman,' he said wistfully.

'You have a sweet chin.' And I meant it – his chin was perfect the way it was.

'But I want to be a movie star and make some money.' This yearning for a Ronald Colman chin remained a constant echo all through our modest run. Modest because one matinée I experienced a searing pain in my stomach, so unbearable that the whole theatre spun round and round taking me down and down until I must have fallen to the boards, unconscious.

I came round on the sofa with Roy shaking me and spouting the play's familiar lines at me. I don't know how long it took me to realize that the audience was still present and that I must continue acting, but gradually, with Roy's determination, it dawned on me to say the lines. He was a true professional the way he refused to bring the curtain down. Although I was still in excruciating pain, I managed to brave it out till the curtain call.

During the interval the doctor was called. I'd had a

268

threatened miscarriage, and he warned me that if I didn't rest the chances were that I'd lose my baby. I didn't want to lose Tom now, because we'd already been through quite a bit together. Besides, we were mates, so it was decided that I'd have to call it a day. The whole company knew that I was pregnant, and I'd hung in there for over three months, so I wasn't completely covered in shame.

A few years later, I came across Roy at some function. He smiled at me and then pointed to a scar beneath his chin. 'I had a false chin put in, but it slipped, so they had to remove it.' . Destiny hadn't got him cut out to be a new Ronald Colman, but then I thought he was smashing in the first place.

CHAPTER THIRTY-NINE

B EING PREGNANT DIDN'T suit me one little bit, neither
did resting. Some women blossom, others don't. I
wish I'd been a blossomer. All I did was eat mashed
potatoes and O.K. Daddies sauce, then threw them back up
again. I never went to the doctor, or birth classes. I never ate
vitamins or did any conscious exercise, even though I was
still riding like a maniac, playing tennis and swimming. I felt
the need to give birth in the same manner as my horses. Just
keep gently grazing until the baby plopped out. I must have
been living in Never-Never Land. Although regret is a waste
of precious energy, nevertheless I regret my ignorance about
the way I chose to have Tom. I would have given anything to
give birth with the dolphins thirty years ago – if only I had
known about water birth thirty years ago both our lives
would have been completely different. But I didn't. And in
my clumsy way, wanting to have him purely and simply, like
an animal, ignoring all human fads and fashions, I was
stumbling up the right track, but still missing by a long chalk.

'We'd best get married,' said Robert, looking at my belly.
It was hard to know what Robert really thought about Tom's
oncoming arrival, for he never mentioned him unless I did,
his mind always being elsewhere. When I'd given him the
news that I was pregnant he took it in his stride, made all the
right noises, but I never felt that wonderment of having
created a new life together, or the bliss of sharing in the
intimacy of childbirth. I'd often find myself comparing his
attitude with how Lionel might have responded – a dangerous occupation, so I firmly pushed such thoughts away.
Besides, I'm sure their responses would have been similar,
both having had children before and both being relentlessly

committed achievers. Had I wanted my spouse to be billing and cooing, embalming me in mashed potatoes and devotion, I ought to have chosen someone different to sire my offspring. I knew I couldn't change him, nor would I want to, so I had to content myself with undertaking the process on my own.

Because my nature is full of contradictions, being both stupidly open and deadly secretive, it was important for me to keep our humble little wedding absolutely private. I went to enormous lengths to do just that, secretly booking us in at the Woking register office with no fuss. When I saw a drive full of paparazzi it upset me more, perhaps, than it should have. Their presence ruined an uncluttered simplicity intended to echo the marriage itself, though as it turned out, neither was to be so. Nowadays I heed the signs and symbols around me, and, again, if I'd known then what I know now, I might have realized what a monumental role the press would play not only in gatecrashing our wedding, but in crucifying any lost vestiges of hope when our marriage broke up a few years later.

What better time for preparing the nest than when pregnant? The kitchen had been modernized, and the chap who had the Mill before us had turned our main bedroom into a dressing room/bathroom *en suite* using flush, smooth-grained rosewood partitions. We christened it the Hilton Brothel. It had thick fur carpets and taps of tasteless splendour. 'It cost me a bomb,' he'd said proudly. To remove it all would have cost another. I suppose fashions change because fashion means spending more money. No one, thank God, has the same taste, but it was surely inexcusable to attempt to turn an early Georgian foursquare classic house into a fifties den of iniquity. What with renovating the Mill, adding on a huge, ancient, womb-like Aga kitchen/living/eating room plus an equally enormous conservatory (another dream ticked off), the bedroom *en suite* would have to wait, for we were financially over-stretched, to put it mildly.

Summer was with us and I painted Tom's bedroom deep autumn yellow, similar to Pip's beak. Pip was my first childhood toy, a penguin knitted for me by Grandma, so yellow is a colour I still associate with happiness – I hoped Tom would too. I found myself in the bath or swimming in the river most of the time, because only when immersed in water did I get any respite from Tom's ferocious kicking. Such peace it was too, except when the swans thought I was about to steal their young. Swans are enigmatic creatures. Some days they would float up to say hello with such grace and charisma that I felt we were mates and the next day, for no reason that I could make out, they'd head for me making a noise like a jet plane about to take off. Addo would accompany me on my swimming jaunts. I felt he knew I was pregnant because he had become much more protective lately, as if he were my man. But, of course, he was, since my real man was up there in the mill typing away a fourteen-hour day.

One morning, out of nowhere my dark horse was standing on the doorstep of the Old Mill looking a trifle upset. Willy Donaldson.

'The police are after me, could I lie low down here for a moment or two?'

I was delighted to see him. It had been well over a year since we'd last met. I went to ask Robert.

'Of course. Tell him he's welcome to stay as long as he likes.'

I took Willy up to a spare room. 'Do you want to come down to the kitchen, or do you want to stay up here?' Poor Wil, he looked so harassed and wan, as if he never saw daylight – but, then, he never did. 'You can hide up here for as long as you wish – do you want me to bring your meals up on a tray?' He looked at me with gratitude. 'Everyone has their ups and downs,' I said, giving him a hug.

At the door I turned back. He was opening his case, whereupon a mass of newspapers fell out. He began skimming through for headlines.

'Have you murderd someone?' He looked back at me in

shock and then downwards towards his shoes. 'Come on, Willy, come clean.' He lamely changed the subject, looking sheepishly out of the window at two Highland cattle locking horns in the far meadow.

'What fearsome horns they have.'

Oddly enough, Willy's and my Capricorn horns had never locked. I realized then how treasurable my time with Willy had been and how I'd always love him, no matter what he'd done. Still, I wanted to know.

'Have you murdered someone?'

He looked at his shoes once more. They were covered in dust from the asphalt jungle. 'I have a play on its pre-London tour starring Moira Lister, called *Dial N for New Castle*, and I can't pay Moira or indeed any of my actors.'

I laughed. He never had any money. Suddenly I remembered him trying to kill his grandma by walking her off her feet. 'How's Grandma?' I asked nervously. Again I got a funny look. 'Still alive and kicking. But it makes no odds since there's no money left now, anyway. I'm going to have to go abroad – Ibiza, maybe.'

The next evening Robin Fox and Ros Chatto were coming for dinner. I asked Willy if he wanted to dine with us. He turned ashen. 'Good God, no! I'll hide here until they've gone, don't mention me at all.'

No sooner were the four of us seated for dinner when Robin asked, 'Have you heard from your old pal Willy Donaldson lately, Sarah?'

I almost dropped my napkin. 'No. Why?'

'He's missing. He must return and pay off his cast otherwise he'll leave a terrible stink behind him.'

Robert gave me a look, put his eyes upward in the direction of Willy in the spare room and shook his head, while Robin put two and two together. Why was Robert such an ace at letting the cat out of the bag? He'd descend from those far distant realms just long enough to let out one or two big, fat furry ones. Since the game was almost up, I put

Willy's dinner on a tray and handed it to Robin. I had to – I couldn't bear the thought of the police arriving and taking a handcuffed Willy away on an empty stomach. 'Take it to the guest room at the top of the stairs on the left.'

Although Willy was grateful for the advice Robin had to offer, it didn't stop him leaving England for Ibiza. He bought a glass-bottomed boat and took tourists to see the underwater sights. I have as much difficulty in picturing that as I do Noël Coward playing baseball, or, indeed, Henry Root meditating.

After two months Robert felt that all this resting was becoming as tiresome for him as it was for me. 'I've hired a yacht for the children's holiday down on the Mediterranean. Do you want to bring any of your lot with us?' Robert was a boat lover but, alas, boats and I didn't get along terribly well, since I'd already capsized with him out in a sailing dinghy on the Solent. The reason he didn't panic, and knew exactly what to do, was because he had spent most of his boating life doing just that, capsizing. The thought of spending two weeks in the summer heat of the Mediterranean while eight months pregnant should have been daunting, but strangely it filled me with joy because Tom and I could merge into one single water baby.

It was fortunate that I'd grown very fond of Robert's children. I was thrilled that my sister Pooker, now called Nessie, her real name being Vanessa, had decided to come along, too. Nessie was a prefect before graduating from Benenden with flying colours, and found herself greatly admiring Princess Anne who had recently eased herself into the role of new girl, instantly becoming one of the gang, and a real brick plus a bit of a devil all at once. A hard row to hoe, particularly with the burden of princess to lug around.

As fate would have it, Nessie, having just stepped off the train with Benenden finally behind her, had come round to Hasker Street and fallen in love. It was while I was still living there with Willy Donaldson, that Willy discovered a Welsh singer, Ceredig Davies. Ceredig was a good-looking blond lad with an undeniably special operatic singing voice. Willy was convinced he had at last found the magic key to success, his sixties Pavarotti who would finally bring us striped shirts and chicken on Sundays. When Nessie fell madly in love with Ceredig, Daddy was a trifle wary, Ceredig being pretty well the first man she had ever clapped eyes on. Mother, on the other hand, wanting only Nessie's happiness, showed surprisingly little concern.

Nessie was thrilled to be coming on the yacht with us, because Ceredig had got a job singing on some luxury liner (marking time while waiting to become Willy's Pavarotti) and there was a chance that we might bump into him mid-Mediterranean if we timed it correctly. Robert thought the chances were slight but agreed it would be a most romantic rendezvous. Some miles off the South of France our little yacht caught sight of Ceredig's great liner at anchor. Approaching it was formidable, for it seemed like some massive beast about to devour us. We sailed by, waving and shouting, trying our damnedest to catch someone's attention. I went all tingly watching Vanessa stepping out of our little ant to climb aboard that great dinosaur and into the awaiting arms of her lover. There he stood on deck, so high above us, a tall eager shadow against the setting sun. (Not, alas, for Ben Bolt, Robert's son. He was miffed at witnessing this romantic rendezvous because, being only a few years younger than Nessie, he had fallen for her passionately during the holiday – quite right too, for Nessie had become quite a dish.)

The whole holiday turned out just as we dreamt it could. Mastering the art of water-skiing in a bikini while eight months pregnant wasn't nearly as bizarre as the sight of Robert whose stomach was even more flamboyant, repeatedly crashing towards the yacht with skis flying in all directions. Robert would never give up. He had to conquer all things, and he did. It's called will.

CHAPTER FORTY

UNLESS MY CALCULATIONS were wrong I was ten months pregnant. Just as I thought I was about to pop I began labour pains. This was good news indeed because I was keen to have the whole birth business over and done with. Robert drove me to the maternity wing of the Woking hospital. There the sister welcomed me, saw that I was in labour, called our local GP, and between them they confirmed that all was well and that I'd give birth before dawn. It all sounded easy as pie. With the pains coming only every five minutes, sharp, regular but bearable, there was plenty of time between for Robert and me to settle down to a serious game of chess. (I think he thought he might stand a better chance of beating me in my present condition.) We must have played three games at least (they never took too long!) before he saw I was tired, and kissed me tenderly. 'I'll be here. I'll stay until he arrives, now you get some sleep.'

I know it was my fault that I'd chosen to give birth in ignorance like the animals. I know it was my fault I'd decided to have Tom at a local hospital rather than at Queen Charlotte's or somewhere equally posh. Therefore I had no one to blame but myself for the fact that he didn't arrive that dawn, or the next, or the next after that. No, Tom didn't show himself for seven dawns. I became used to having a drip secured to my arm for a bedfellow, for it was thus for three days. By the end of the week Robert was reeling round the hospital with a bottle of whisky and a lot more than mere designer stubble.

It's hard to say what went so wrong. Partly my stupidity, partly that Mother kept telephoning, hinting that if the baby wasn't in danger (and he wasn't) it was best to fight on; to have a Caesarian might be fashionable but one misses the ecstatic joy of the real birth experience. But the main reason, I believe, was Tom himself. I'm pretty strong and athletic, with a high pain threshold, and although I have narrow hips, I was perfectly capable of pushing out my son. But it gradually dawned on me that he didn't want to be born. 'Why don't you help, Tom?' I'd shouted as he clung on even more relentlessly. 'Let go!' He'd respond by clinging even tighter.

We certainly had the doctors flummoxed. Back in the sixties there was no such thing as an epidural to numb the spine from the regular onslaught of agony and because I was determined to have Tom naturally, I had no choice but to ride the waves of torture, which grew worse as the week wore on. It wasn't that I thought having a Caesarian was wrong, or cheating or failure, because I didn't and don't. But in my ignorance I felt that since my son wasn't in any danger, I had no alternative.

After the seventh dawn the specialist decided to intervene. I was wheeled into the operating theatre where he removed Tom with forceps. Poor, poor Tom. He came out screaming, all 7 lb, 8 oz of him, on 20 October 1968. Being utterly drained by the week's activities I receded into a stupor for three days, too exhausted to bring forth any enthusiasm, milk or indeed motherly disposition. During those three days I believe the natural bonding process between mother and son was damaged. Not irrevocably because we are very close now, but it took over two decades.

Welcoming us back home was the biggest teddy bear I have ever encountered. The blue ribbon around its neck could easily have fitted around Robert's waist. 'Love from Sam Spiegel', it said. I was bemused by the generosity of a man I'd never met. 'Rubbish,' said Robert. 'He's been embezzling great lorryloads of profits from *Lawrence of Arabia*.'

We employed a special nurse because Tom had digestion problems, never once bringing up wind like a normal baby. His colon was dysfunctional, which meant endless projectile vomiting. Just when we thought he'd have to be operated on, it miraculously righted itself – the colon, not the vomiting, alas. But the nurse, who'd brought over two thousand babies into the world, said she had never met such a case as Tom. He was hyperactive, and hated sleeping, eating, and being bathed with a passion. He only liked riding on Addo's back, or with me on Daisy, bathing with me, speeding along in the Land-rover or snuggling up in our bed. Because I was never allowed in my mother's bed I might have swung too much the other way to compensate. All I do know is that I found myself eating, sleeping and bathing with Tom because it was too much hassle for him to endure these functions separately from me.

Robert, not caring to participate in 'baby' issues, must have felt subconscious twinges of guilt because he took his love for me into his study, where he began writing the screenplay for *Madame Bovary*. I didn't have the slightest clue what he was up to at the time. I thought he was still struggling with *Brother and Sister*. Not until he showed me the script, before sending it to David Lean to see whether he would be interested in directing it, did I realize what he'd been up to.

'You are a great actress, you deserve a great part.' He handed it to me with such love in his eyes that all my secret cursings at having to deal alone with Tom problems vanished into shame. I found the plot dangerously near the knuckle. Thank God I hadn't even seen Olivier since the day I took the marriage vows. That mattered to me very much. However I might have prided myself on being a discreet and selfless mistress, I felt more comfortable and much lighter of heart being a faithful wife. I wasn't yearning for him either – well, once in a blue moon, perhaps, when I hadn't been noticed for days on end. But Robert compensated for his lack of attention by writing what he thought was a great part for me. How could I tell him that I'd rather be sharing a few hours of the day with him than receiving the writer's gift of a great role? I've always thought life much more important than a career.

Besides, all through those first years of having to cope while Robert was forever up in his study, I remembered that day in Hasker Street when I fell down the stairs and he simply continued typing. That's what drew me to him, made marriage with him a possibility – that he would never suffocate me. Robert hadn't changed one bit; it was I who had. I was needing more comradeship, and blaming him for his lack of attention. A quick shiver of shame pricked my bones. Never try and change the one you love; change yourself to grow in a sympathetic direction.

News came back from David. He didn't want to do a remake of *Madame Bovary* but was keen to do an original screenplay with Robert. David was living happily with Sandy Hotz in Rome, trying to dodge the taxman. He had left England about twelve years previously after *Bridge Over the River Kwai*, because the Inland Revenue had given him an unnecessarily rough time. Vowing never again to pay tax to anyone, he packed his suitcase, put it into his Rolls-Royce and drove away, never to return. (Until knighthood beckoned – it pulls them back in the end!)

Robert went to join David for a week at the Parco di Principi Hotel in Rome. The week turned into months and thus began our year of living in Rome. I went back and forth because of the dogs and horses. On my first trip out there with Tom, who was seven months old, I glimpsed an unusually thin book at the airport (I like thin books!) called *Baby Hints* or some such title. I bought it.

The first Hint that I tried out was the most appropriate because Tom (now known as Tomcat) was the perfect age. It stated six or seven months old, and the hotel had a wonderfully warm outdoor swimming pool. One morning, before even the sun had properly awoken or the dolly birds had decked the place in their chic Italian bikinis and with shiny oiled limbs, filling me with inferiority, Tomcat and I made our way down to the cool shade of a palm tree in the pool garden where I learnt the instructions almost off by heart. We had to move fast if we were to achieve our objective. With my courage sufficiently plucked, my little book in one hand and Tomcat under my arm, we moved swiftly to the edge of the pool. I opened the book at the appropriate page. It stated: 'Baby must be thrown in from the edge, not, repeat, NOT put in gently.' Because it was printed in a published book I never doubted its knowledge or authenticity.

> Baby might disappear for a moment or two, but DO NOT PANIC. DO NOT GO IN TO SAVE HIM. Baby will resurface, come up for air in his own time. He will no doubt be gasping for air, but DO NOT PANIC and DO NOT go in to save him. He may disappear again and yet again, but DO NOT PANIC. Gradually baby will recall the knack. After all, it's only a matter of remembering the womb which wasn't too long ago, was it? Gradually he will get his sea legs and become a real genuine WATER BABY.

I think it had been reading that last line that clinched it.

I gave Tomcat one last, lingering kiss and threw him in. I wasn't expecting the gasp from what, till then, had been an invisible audience. There's nothing so frightening as a group of baby-crazy Italian mamas creeping out of the woodwork, screaming in at you in the most murderous of fashions.

'*Mama mia! Bambino!*' I stood firm. It wasn't easy, keeping my eyes on both book and a vanished Tomcat with these self-important Italian nosy-parkers taking me to task. I pointed to my book, as if it were the Bible, while attempting to hold back the oncoming masses. Tom was not to be seen. I found the place in my book. 'DO NOT PANIC' stared back, giving me fresh courage.

Tomcat came up for air! How relieved I was to see his face, my sad little drowned rat, even if it only had a moment before disappearing to a chorus of '*Mama, mia!*' This time I had to be ferocious, for some of the women began climbing into the water to save him. 'Don't you dare!'

They knew I meant business, so reluctantly gave Tomcat

the space to reappear on his own. He did – thank God! There he was, his sparse white curls flat upon his noble head, paddling for dear life. How glorious it was to witness Tom-cat's transformation from panic through the slow blossoming of possible buoyancy, followed by an incredulous flowering of that first joy of accomplishment. The women stood there, gagged with awe, for it was truly a miracle.

From then on, for the whole year, Tomcat was never wholly content until he had crawled down to the pool and tossed himself in. He couldn't walk yet, but by God – hadn't he turned into his namesake – a truly triumphant Tomcat, the Water Baby! I hugged my little book as I shouted up to David's balcony, hoping Robert might witness this magnifi-cent feat. David had been in the hotel so long it was easy to pick out his suite for an exuberance of greenery had burst forth over his balcony, exotic creeping plants making their way in all directions upon the bare stone façade. David adored his balcony plants, and I found it sad that he'd chosen to deny himself the fulfilment of tending his own garden.

Out of the blue David gave us a beautiful Lamborghini for a belated wedding present. It was a humdinger! Being a speed freak I quickly became addicted to opening it up on the autostradas. Travelling at 165 mph, I found that the traffic directly in front of me in the fast lane seemed to zoom backwards. I found this all the more disorientating with a silent engine giving me no impression of speed. Doing 40 mph in the Land-rover felt much faster and more exhilarating. Driving through those damned Roman 'senso unicos' was a farce because I could never get it out of second gear, nor was I able to find the hotel again. But daily outings, as long as we were going hell for leather, kept Tomcat quiet. He'd sit there in the front passenger seat all strapped in, peppering me with toffee-nosed looks whenever the engine belched its fury at slow speed, or whenever I mistook 'senso unico' for the street where we lived. Only when we were breaking yet another record on the Rome to Naples autostrada was his concentration dead straight ahead. My old school chum from Crofton Grange, S.P.J. – every Roman's idea of heaven, being almost six foot, stunning and a natural blonde – came over to stay. Wherever we went, men followed, gawped, whistled and hooted horns. If I'd gone stark naked with a feather up my arse I'd still have been invisible, dragging along in her wake. But I knew my place, thanks to childhood with a similarly eye-catching mother. S.P.J. had an immovable 'bee' in her bonnet for the German movie star Oscar Werner (*Jules et Jim*) and insisted that I arrange a dinner. I didn't know him from Adam, but that didn't deter her one whit. With her Oscar finally located, the four of us had dinner together. What a profoundly dull evening it was! Her Oscar never stopped talking and his blatant arrogance swiflty removed the bee from S.P.J.'s bonnet – serves her right.

Robert and I knew we would never settle into hotel living, so we found a rooftop studio off Via Babuino, overlooking ancient ochre rooftops and the park with the Piazza d'Espagna beyond. It was pure heaven, except there was no lift. Yet even having to climb hundreds of steps lugging a pram as well as Tom was worth it every time. Gradually high summer was upon us and Tom and I decided to return to the cool trees of the Old Mill House and all the animals for a couple of weeks' respite.

As I was rowing the boat up-river one day with Tomcat, Addo, Arthur (an Old England sheepdog) and Gladys, a Skye terrier, a swan suddenly came zooming straight for us. The shock was too sudden for the younger dogs: the rowing boat tilted suddenly to one side and we all fell out. Now the river was indeed cold compared to the warmth of the Parco di Principi swimming pool, so Tomcat lost his breath with the shock of it. Nevertheless he was still afloat, whereas Gladys had disappeared – probably drowned in that spectacular coat of hers. Addo was swimming ashore, Arthur's face was vaguely apparent. Checking once more on Tom, I duck-dived to try and find my treasured Gladys. As I came up for air I

noticed Tomcat gasping yet still splashing about on the surface, Arthur likewise. Assuming all was well for a few
moments longer I duck-dived again in the dwindling hope of
rescuing Gladys. (All this seemed to lost hours but took only a
few seconds.) My hand touched something furry. Hooray! I
hauled her out with all my might and threw her into the
rowing boat. Then I got hold of Tomcat and put him in on the
floor while I went to rescue Arthur. Hauling a sheepdog into
the boat was too much for me, so I had to swim to the bank
with him, praying that Tomcat, who wasn't quite walking yet,
would be all right alone in the boat for a few seconds more.

When I returned to the boat Tomcat was still sitting on
the floor, purple with fury. Gladys, on seeing me return,
proceeded to cover Tomcat with ecstatic kisses, but he was
wanting none of them, pushing her away with as much
muscle as he could muster.

Life is fascinating in what we choose to remember. When
Tomcat could talk he was able to recall that near-drowning
episode. However many times I assured him that he was
swimming when Gladys had nearly drowned, he still
wouldn't be budged. I find it sad because for him it remains
the day I apparently showed my true colours, and proved to
him that I loved Gladys more than I loved him. But if he had
also been drowning, how come he was able to remember me
saving Gladys first? I think the problem was that they were
always rivals. They grew up together and Gladys, being a
Skye terrier, was a one-person dog, and didn't like anyone
coming too close. To cap it all she never changed her ways,
and chose to die under the table on Tomcat's sixteenth
birthday; he was blowing out his candles at the time.

'Typical!' said Tom grudgingly. 'Her last chance to steal a
great chunk of my glory.'

Towards the end of our two weeks at home, I was out in
the long meadow when I saw one of the visiting mares
prancing in the sunlight. She'd come to stay for a few weeks
while being served by my palomino stallion, Roundhills

Golden Cavalier. The sight must have echoed a part of me that yearned to be prancing too, so I came up to her and leapt on her back. That is without doubt one of the stupidest things you could do. Never leap onto an unknown steed, especially when she's full of the joys of spring.

She couldn't believe I had done it and galloped up the field rearing and bucking, determined to get rid of me. I'm used to riding bareback, but on a mad horse with not even a halter I didn't stand much chance, so I decided to bail out. Being slightly out of practice I misjudged my fall and went over on my ankle. Rule number one: if you are fond of your riding boots remove them immediately on impact, because by the time I'd stopped writhing around in pain it was too late: the ankle had already swelled up. I'm not sure which pain was worse, the injury or knowing I was about to lose my favourite boots. As I was hauling myself up the steps to the house the phone rang.

'Are you all right?' It was Mother. Was it coincidence, or were Mother and I inexorably linked on some deeper level, because in moments of crisis she never failed to contact me.

I went down to the local hospital and was told by my GP that the ankle miraculously wasn't broken and that I could still go to Rome, but to keep off it as much as possible. Because the sprain was severe it had to be tightly bound up for six weeks, so for the time being I hobbled to Rome without Tomcat. We had a wonderful girl called Pat, who helped both with the horses and with Tomcat. She would be bringing him out as soon as I'd solved the problem of living accommodation for I doubted my ability to climb the hundreds of steps to our rooftop studio flat.

I hobbled around Robert's office at the Parco di Principi, excited to be with him once more. Our love was still young and sufficiently urgent to make partings painful and reunions utterly delightful. He didn't notice my leg, but then why should he? He was still working. Finally he looked up. 'Pour me a whisky, will you, darling? I won't be long.' His head was bowed in work when I handed it to him.

'Thanks.'

About an hour later David came in. 'What the hell have you done to yourself?' he exclaimed immediately.

'It's not broken, it'll be fine.'

About a week later the pain in my ankle was unbearable. I put it down to the Roman heat and healing pains. I didn't want to cause a fuss, and didn't feel up to sharing it with anyone. One day David came over and began to feel it. He became quite concerned. 'Unwrap it and let the air get to it.' I complied, because it's always best to obey the likes of David Lean.

'Looks funny to me. Who told you it wasn't broken?'

'The hospital – they're very good, they even took X-rays.'

Robert was still bowed over his work, taking time off to gulp some whisky. David gave me an old-fashioned look while bending down to smell it as if I had gangrene. The whole episode seemed out of character, for since when had David Lean had any compassion? Mind you, I was bowled over by how swollen it was.

When he'd finished examining it, he made a phone call to some private specialist. 'Come with me, I'll give you the address and put you in a taxi.'

We had quite a bit of trouble with misdiagnoses, at one time and another. Robert was driving our Land-rover one day, with me and baby Tom, when he decided to pass another Land-rover and trailer, going rather slowly. As he did so the trailer swung out and clipped us.

'We'd better stop, I suppose,' sighed Robert.

We pulled into the side. In no time, a tall dark gypsy type rattled his hand on the glass. Robert politely wound down his window. The gypsy began using swear words that even Olivier never used. I couldn't believe the spleen shooting from his lips, and concluded he was mad. Robert went quite white, for the whole episode lacked any link to sanity.

'Do you mind not swearing like that in front of my wife?'

The gypsy took no notice, so Robert, being the gentleman that he is, stepped out of the Land-rover. As he did so, the man grabbed him. 'If my ponies had been in there, I would have done that – and that!' He made two rapid gestures indicating that he would have slapped Robert across the face, but he wasn't using any force. It all happened so fast that I was unable to see what really happened. The result was Robert pouring blood from his mouth all over his brand new and now newly ripped double-knitted Harrods cashmere cardigan that I'd bought him – it had cost an arm and a leg. How could he be bleeding like that, the man hadn't touched him? The gypsy got back in his car and drove off.

'Take his number!' cried Robert, blood still pouring from his mouth. I couldn't do much to help him because Tom, smelling the tension, had started screaming. Somehow we got to a police station and reported what had happened.

The doctor said the X-ray showed Robert's jaw broken on one side. They bound up his whole head, so he could only suck food through a straw. In London one day he went to a specialist because it didn't seem to be knitting together too well. I didn't like the look of it at all. After more X-rays the other side of the jaw was found to be broken as well. Had we not gone to the specialist his jaw would have been paralysed for life, leaving his face lopsided. The gypsy type turned out to be a black belt judo expert and apparently it is seriously frowned upon if black belts practise outside the ring. This bloke was never, as far as we know, allowed in the ring again. (So God help all of us outside it.) Robert got some compensation, though handsome it wasn't.

At last Robert had his heart's desire: Betty, our miniature Staffordshire bull terrier. He'd been hankering after another Staffordshire ever since his dearest pal Billy had been put down for killing another dog on Richmond Green, back when he was living with his first wife, Jo. Robert really missed his Billy so I hoped Betty would fill the gap. But alas, Betty and Gladys didn't get on well. I warned all who came to stay that if they were found fighting they should be left to it. One afternoon, Ben, Robert's son, went into the fray, and got bitten. As

I was washing his index finger under the tap I saw that it was half hanging off. Our local National Health doctor sewed it back on in his surgery. After a week or so, although Ben's finger was heavily bandaged up, it exuded a strange smell.

'D'you think I've got gangrene?' asked Ben, sniffing at his bandage. Since he was going home to his mother we decided it best if she took him to a doctor down in the New Forest. She later rang to tell us that our doctor had sewn a dog hair into the wound and that his finger would have to be amputated. Robert thought this a little extreme, and decided to send Ben to a specialist. We found only one surgeon who was confident that the finger could be saved; and so it was.

David's doubts were justified in the Parco di Principi Hotel in Rome that day, for my ankle was found to be broken in two places and put into a plaster cast for eight wretched weeks. We'd paid six months' rent in advance on the studio flat, so we lost a lot of money. There we were back in the bloody Parco di Principi, much to David's glee, since he preferred us all under one roof.

Eventually I went home again because Robert was deep in work almost twenty-four hours a day, leaving me with nothing to do. I'd seen most of the magnificence Rome had to offer; besides it was still baking hot, especially in my plaster cast. One can indulge only so much in expensive restaurants without getting spoilt. Rome was full of beautiful spoilt women, and I wasn't about to become one of them. Besides, my tastebuds respond to simplicity. I'm a cheap date, not liking wine, spirits or meat. How time dragged while David sat each evening choosing with such relish what he was going to eat, and Sandy, too, who was becoming particularly well padded, competing favourably with Robert who was fatter than I'd ever seen him. How he adored that kind of life! To work all day and eat all night held the keys to the kingdom of heaven as far as Robert was concerned – and there's nowt wrong with it if that's your bag.

One night, however, I remember well. We were at

Augustia's, a deeply serious gourmet eating place. David was telling a story about his Quaker upbringing. Apparently his family were aboard a boat to Calais and it was a first trip abroad for both David and his brother.

'Father stood on the bow and as soon as he spied land ahead he said . . .' David's story petered out. He went quite red and searched for his napkin, which had dropped to the floor.

'Go on, David,' I urged, always eager to hear stories about people's childhood. I find them hugely engaging, just like family photos. It makes no odds how well or little I know the owner of the album. Even with family photographs of complete strangers, I can sit immersed for hours on end. But on this occasion David remained flummoxed. He attempted to continue the story but seemed flustered and confused.

'What's up?' said Robert.

'I'm so sorry,' said David sheepishly, returning to that schoolboy I'd witnessed way back in the Agra Hotel – all pink and embarrassed with his scarlet pointed ears shimmering in the candlelight.

'Are you ill, man?' Robert got to the point with his usual bluntness.

'No, no, but Fellini has just walked in.' David hadn't much time for film directors generally, sitting pretty secure in the knowledge that he ranked with the giants of movie history. All but Fellini, that is. He thought Fellini was a genius, and apparently had never before seen him in the flesh.

'Go over and say hello,' urged Bolt, his concentration fixed on his menu problem: whether to have Parma ham or giant shrimps for a first course.

'I couldn't possibly,' said a shy David, his shoulders sheltering him from the idea.

'Think what it would mean to him hearing that you admired his work,' said I.

David mentally straightened up, drawing himself inwards

in search of courage. 'No, I can't,' he said finally. Robert ordered his usual Parma ham and we ate in silence, occasionally looking over to Fellini's table where he sat, rotund and guzzling.

'What happened to the days when artists used to meet up and discuss their ideas?' I enquired, as butter from my asparagus dribbled on to the white tablecloth.

Bolt mumbled, with his face in his plate, 'I don't think they ever did.'

'I don't want to embarrass him, that's all.' David shrugged.

After we'd finished the main course, David buoyed up with wine, wiped his mouth and rose from the table. It was fascinating to watch those two giants. David did the slightest little bow to Fellini, who seemed more interested in piling as much spaghetti on to his fork as possible. David didn't stay long, and Fellini never gestured for him to sit down. Two great egos confronting each other – why couldn't it have been two great artists embracing each other's brilliance? When David returned he was silent. I don't think it had turned out quite like he had expected.

'I think I made him feel awkward,' is all he would say.

'You showed great guts going over there at all,' Sandy said firmly. I thought it required humility rather than guts, a quality I never witnessed in him again. David, like most powerful men, was more at home playing Muhammad, demanding the mountain come to him, as I was to discover a year later on *Ryan's Daughter*.

I broke into the atmosphere hanging over cheese and coffee. 'So there you were, with your father and brother on the bow of the boat heading towards Calais. What did he say?'

'He said, "We're approaching Calais. Remember, these are foreigners, and if there's anything you don't like – spit." This line wasn't delivered in Fellini's direction, however.

CHAPTER FORTY-ONE

A T LAST ROBERT was back home in England and having a well-deserved holiday. He had been working long hours with David in Rome, and needed to rest. He decided to build a streamlined wooden sailing dinghy to his own design in the bottom part of the mill. He spent most of the day playing boat builder, shaping wood with a skill that had me dumbfounded. Robert was also determined to be a worthy horseman and with his formidable mind power, he made it. He became a *most* worthy horseman – until he hit his daily branch. Robert rode well with no reins, totally at two with the horse, while believing himself to be at one, having inches to spare between him and the saddle. I'm sure God would have kept him safely cradled in his precariousness if it weren't for all those wretched protruding trees. It wasn't only on Daisy that the end of the ride was a certain crash to Mother Earth. Whichever horse he was riding knew damn well that the quickest way home to nuts and hay bag was a low branch or two. None of my horses were fools.

His croquet wasn't half bad either. Robert, like Lionel, was committed to anything he did. It would have been pointless to take him to task over his use of muscle power rather than accuracy. An infuriating manifestation of this was his failure to see a croquet hoop straddling his path. He'd clout me into the long grass, having ricocheted off a hoop. A cracked ball would inevitably follow (new balls aren't cheap). I wonder if Lionel played croquet at Notley Manor. Or tennis. How strange to have been so intimate yet of mundane daily matters know nothing about him.

On the tennis court Robert was a spectacle. He simply

would not be beaten, without a bloody fight – and I mean bloody, bleedin' knees. When a tennis shot is placed out of reach of an opponent, most players concede the shot, but not Robert Bolt. He'd run to wherever I'd placed the ball, even if it meant crashing into a swallow dive like Olivier did in *Henry IV*. Happily Olivier was caught, but Robert came both to earth and harsh reality on the prickly asphalt, skidding across the court in a cartoon crunch as his whole bodyweight smacked into the wire netting boundary. Not once but time after time, just like a naughty boy after the school bully had done him over in the playground.

Early in the evening he'd come into the sitting room, put on the telly and often fall asleep with Tomcat on his lap. Tomcat's favourite word was 'gun'. Although he could say a few essentials, like 'yes', 'no', 'Ma' and 'Da', 'gun' was his masterpiece. How could it be otherwise, sitting with Father watching cowboy films all evening? Robert would eventually change channels, searching for the shoot-outs. He loved the killings more than the talking bits, and so did Tomcat. I find violence incomprehensibly old-fashioned and boring, but it was worth forgiving their foible for those were good times indeed, having Robert to play with, as well as exciting new Irish adventures up ahead.

In our village a silver and black gun twinkled at the front of the sweet-shop window. Tomcat had noticed it a few months back but I ignored his unending demands for it. I wanted Tomcat *not* to notice such things. I bought him a tricycle, a teddy bear – anything – but I was *not* going to buy that damn gun.

'Gun! Gun! Gun!' Tom never let up when he wanted something. His stubborn perseverance drove everyone who knew him straight up the Polly Tree. It was impossible not to surrender, just for some peace and quiet. For months on end his last word at night was gun and his first word in the morning was gun.

291

Down in the village one afternoon, taking some shopping back to the car, off he went as usual, pointing to the gun. 'Gun! Gun! Gun!'

Now I don't know what was weak within me that day, but something snapped. I had reached breaking point. Thanks to Tomcat's ruthlessness, I was to reach it time and again.

In we went. The shopkeeper looked at Tomcat. 'Ah!' she said, bending forward to flirt with him. Everyone flirted with Tomcat and he knew how to deal with it. It's hard for me to explain his flamboyant good looks, being his mother, but many would stop in the street and simply stare which didn't bode well for later years. I always did my best to deflect the compliments.

'Gun! Gun! Gun!'

'Those lovely blue eyes haven't lost their enthusiasm for that toy gun, have they, Mrs Bolt?'

I wanted to shake her, but instead paid for Robert's Benson and Hedges.

'What sweets does my favourite boy want today, eh?'

'No sweets today, just the gun in the window, please.'

She looked at Tomcat and they both shared their triumph openly.

'I knew Mummy wouldn't be able to resist those blue dazzlers for much longer.' She tossed this silly sentence behind her as she reached in for the gun.

'Gun! Gun! Gun!' Tomcat seemed to swell with victory before my eyes. Once the gun was clasped in his hot little hands, he ran to the door.

'Wait for me, I haven't paid yet.'

'Gun! Gun! Gun!' He was shouting it from the top of the step, peering down the street both ways, shooting anyone in sight. I'll kill Robert for this gun business. What corruption. I felt beaten.

'You'll never regret buying him that gun, Mrs Bolt, you mark my words.' My head was hung in failure. 'Don't you want any caps?' This stopped me dead in my tracks. I'd never thought of caps. It reminded me of my brother Jukes shooting me in the thigh with his air gun. That was probably a lot to do with why I'd held out so long against Tomcat's gun. I checked to see if Tomcat had heard. Fortunately he was too busy shooting everyone dead in the high street.

'No caps just now, thank you. Goodbye.' As I walked back to the car with Tomcat still killing the high street with one hand and clasping my shopping basket with the other, I couldn't help noticing how relieved I felt that 'Gun! Gun! Gun!' was gone for good. Tomcat might have won the battle, but I, surely, had won the war.

We noticed a small, rather morose little chap in pebble specs coming towards us; he too was holding on to his mother's shopping basket. He'd been crying. His mood matched his mother's: both looked grey and soulful. Tomcat held out his gun to show him. 'Gun? Gun? Gun?' he said, making a gesture as if offering up his newly acquired prize. I couldn't believe my eyes.

'No, Tomcat. That's very nice, but the gun is yours.' He looked daggers at me, then turned back to the little boy.

'Gun? Gun? Gun?' Neither the little boy, nor indeed his mother, had any idea what was going on. 'Gun? Gun? Gun?' Had my eyes been deceiving me? No. Tomcat was adamant that the little fellow take the gun.

'What's your little boy giving my Derek his gun for?' asked the bewildered mother.

'I don't know. Why don't you ask him?'

She bent forward towards Tomcat. 'Why are you giving your gun to Derek?'

'Gun? Gun? Gun?' The gesture was as clear as day. Derek was being given the gun. What could I do? Forbid Tom to be generous towards others?

'I think Tomcat wants you to have his gun, Derek.'

Derek held out his hand and Tomcat gently placed the gun in it. It was a most touching gesture, I felt deeply proud.

'There now, say thank you, Derek.'

'Thank you,' said Derek, unable to believe his luck. As we watched them walk on down the high street, Derek waved back with the gun in gratitude.

I turned to Tomcat. 'That was a very kind thing to do, Tomcat, I'm full of admiration.'

His dazzling eyes looked up into mine, all hot and glistening with fresh wanting. 'Gun! Gun! Gun! Gun!'

Tomcat's bedroom has always been empty, most of his life. Everything he has demanded has been passed on to others, left or lost, and on he went, demanding. He's stopped now. Such a relief.

CHAPTER FORTY-TWO

MADAME BOVARY TURNED into *Ryan's Daughter*. Those who are familiar with both will know that they are one and the same. But no one knew at the time and no one guessed later. Packing up to go to Ireland for a whole year, though traumatic, was made a little less so because I was able to take the four dogs with us. Addo, Arthur, Gladys and Betty.

We'd let the Old Mill House to Robert Redford who seemed a nice enough chap during the brief time I met him. He was about to start work on *The Great Gatsby* but, unlike many superstars, seemed to have his ego well in check. I felt a sadness in him all the same. All that fame, fortune and wonderful family, yet still a sadness. Later while living in LA I'd recognize that same sadness over and over again with many of the successful and famous movie stars.

Ryan's Daughter was to be shot on Ireland's magnificently gnarled, wild and woolly west coast, in a terrain of barren purple-heather mountains, way out on the Dingle peninsula, in County Kerry. Houses were found for the actors and crew, dotted about all over and around Dingle. The little town had never had it so good and was finally to be put on the map. *Ryan's Daughter* meant there were going to be jobs for hundreds of out-of-work Irishmen, so the whole place was celebrating. The town boasted as many pubs as weeks of the year, and they were usually all full to bursting.

For some strange reason Robert and I had been put in a house right over the other side of the Connor Pass, which wound through a mountain range on the Tralee road about twenty minutes from Dingle and the rest of the actors and crew. It was a handsome grey stone building, late eighteenth century, and stood a little back from the road, enjoying amazing views of the sea, all alone in its own bay, where people – mostly Germans and Americans – came to try their luck in catching the biggest sea bass ever. The whole crew and the actors, including Trevor Howard, John Mills, Leo McKern, came out fishing one day to see who would catch the most. Robert Bolt was the only one not to land a bass that day. Johnnie Mills caught three. Robert was the only person unable to catch a single bass in the whole year we were there and it wasn't for lack of trying.

I was in two minds about being so far away from the rest of the team. Mind you, there weren't many landlords, I suppose, who would put up with our menagerie. I had to get up so much earlier than the rest, and with my character being on the call sheet every damn morning, come rain or shine, I sometimes regretted the twenty-minute journey. We had taken our new Spanish couple with us, José and Trina, and perfectly cast they were too. Francesca was a little too grand for the Irish bogs and thought she'd move back to London and find someone in the Antonia Fraser league. Our entertaining, rare as snow in summer, blocked her creative flow.

Leo McKern, John Mills, Christopher Jones, Robert Mitchum, Trevor Howard – a veritable cartoon of colourful characters, clustered together for *Ryan's Daughter*, and never again would Dingle put up with so many eccentric goings on scattered within so small an area.

Meeting all the actors would have been wonderful but for the vulnerability I felt being the writer's wife. Maybe I was too sensitive, but I felt it put me at a gruesome disadvantage for every day I'd have to prove myself doubly able. No actor, I might add, ever gave me reason to feel this way. When David offered me the part, I asked him to test me along with anyone else who would make a good Rosy. 'Nonsense, testing would be a waste of time and money. I want you, and that's that.' All through the year in Rome I never dreamt I might be starring in the film, for I didn't even know what it was about. This might seem strange; none the less I'd never questioned what they were up to because they had made it clear from the outset that they wanted it kept a secret and I understand secrets.

Meeting the great Robert Mitchum was no let-down – in fact it was much more than I'd bargained for. He waddled into the production office, doing that famous puffed-up-penguin roll on bandy legs that's etched in gold within every film buff's heart, wearing huge sunglasses and carrying a red rose. 'For you, my Rose, with all my love.' The way he handed it to me struck me as so romantic, so delicate – most endearing for such a huge man.

'Thank you.' I couldn't think of anything else to say. Why was I so struck? I suppose because few people are better in the flesh than on the screen and, towering above me, he certainly had more than his share of presence, charisma, and pure animal magnetism. Later on in LA, when I'd met most of the great Hollywood idols, there remained only Mitchum, for my money. Perhaps that's because he's not so much an actor, more a human being. When not too much under the influence he knew all there was to know about everyone, his green eyes never missing a trick.

As I stood struck dumb with my red rose in my hand, his mood suddenly altered. He snarled, 'We were meant to work together on that *Mr Moses* film in Africa, but you never clocked in. Why?'

'I couldn't leave Addo,' I said apologetically, pointing to Addo lying on the floor of the production office. 'I tried to smuggle him over, but I turned out unlucky.'

Mitchum grunted disapproval. 'Women and their fucking hounds.'

With that he left and I had my first inkling that Mitchum's mood swings were going to keep us all on our toes.

Meeting Trevor Howard was another big moment. *Brief Encounter*, David's classic with Celia Johnson, was one of my all-time favourites. David once gave us a telling account of the time he gave *Brief Encounter* its first public outing. He was keen to get an average provincial audience's reaction before giving it to the Establishment's in-crowd and the critics to chew up and maybe spit out. A few moments after the film had begun to roll in a Devon cinema, a large lady in the seventh row began to laugh. Laughter tends to be irritating if the film you're watching is no comedy, but this lady's laugh was so infectious that it spread through the audience. By the time the end credits came up they were falling about in the aisles and David was convinced he had a disaster on his hands. He went up to the projection room, grabbed the reels and went for a walk through the quiet Devonshire streets telling himself the whole enterprise had been his *folie de grandeur*. He became obsessed with the idea of returning to London immediately and destroying the negative. Thank God that only Devon so far had been given the opportunity of ridiculing his precious new baby. He was determined it would also be the last. Such can be the power of one laugh. How steady and convinced the artist has to be with belief in his newborn.

Trevor, like Ralph Richardson, had an aura of innocence about him. It was at fearsome odds with his alcoholic overload. Trevor's wife, Helen Cherry, was a rare bird. She had his measure, and loved him as much as he loved her. Theirs was a poignant story. The patience and unconditional love that Helen had to dredge up on occasion was formidable, but she lived secure in the knowledge that Trevor was worth it. They taught me a great deal about love, those two.

Johnnie Mills was again completely different. A dapper little chap, disciplined, healthy, ambitious and professional. Because I was roughly the same age as his daughters, Juliet and Hayley, I sometimes felt that both he and his wife, Mary Hayley Bell, thought that either of them should have got the part – but they weren't married to the writer.

Leo McKern, who played my father, the publican, was already a good friend of Robert. He had recently played the robust and boisterous Baron Bolligrew in Robert's enchanting children's tale *The Thwarting of Baron Bolligrew* at the Royal Shakespeare Company as well as being the Common Man in the original stage version of *A Man For All Seasons*. He was a fine, honest, no-nonsense individual, straight as a die, with no dark undertones; qualities I found to be a freshwater stream when all else seemed to be conspiring against us.

Christopher Jones was a law unto himself. I like him a lot, though I think he was having personal problems at the time. Playing a leading part in a David Lean epic – that of an upper-class English major, a shell-shocked First-World-War hero, no less – isn't the ideal thing to combine with being an American who has very little film experience and an identity crisis. David Lean alone was responsible for casting Christopher. David, Robert and I had seen him in a film called *The Looking Glass War*, directed by David's usual artistic director, Johnnie Box. Chris stole the film playing a very James Deany, sexy Polish boy, who said little and did little except to throw a ball in the air and catch it again. This he did with great authority and a sensuous dark presence. No doubt at all, he simmered. Being blessed with such a doom-laden persona was what made him ideal for the part, though I found him more pretty than handsome. Christopher had been married to Susan Strasberg, the beautiful, intelligent daughter of Lee Strasberg, who was famous for giving birth to his Method School of Acting. He never really explained why they broke up, but why should he?

When filming began and Christopher did not attempt an English accent, David rightly became anxious. Then when it was brought to his attention that Christopher's Polish accent in *The Looking Glass War* had been dubbed. David felt duped and his anxiety turned to panic. He shared his concern with Robert. 'What the hell can I do?'

'Just be patient, David. It's early days, after all.'

'Patient?' said David, choking on his cigarette holder. 'He's incapable of hitting the mark and smiling simultaneously.'

Although this might have been true, I didn't think he was stupid, far from it. He may have been on something, but what, we never found out. 'I'm trapped in my own casting nightmare.'

'I'm afraid you are, unless you fire him immediately and start again.' Robert had a ruthless streak, too, when it suited him, seeing every problem black as black or white as white. No muddy grey waters for Bolt.

'He can't do that!' I was appalled. 'Just let him know you want him to succeed, let him know you care.'

David looked at me as if I belonged on Mars. 'Let's hope he falls over the cliff.'

Knowing David quite well already, I wouldn't have been surprised if he'd hired a hit man. Instead, he ran away and pouted in Killarney for a week.

Christopher had two characters in attendance at all times, flanking him, guarding him. It was quite eerie. They were his managers, apparently. Although they were pretty camp, it still took quite a leap of the imagination to visualize Christopher getting up to any hanky-panky with either of them; but when I shared my doubts with Mitchum, he gave me a withering look. Was it because I was such a romantic that when Olivia Hussey came out to join him I experienced a sense of relief? She would come out for weeks on end just to be with him. What a beautiful pair they made – or would have made if one ever saw them together. She was always alone at the hotel; never once did anyone see them doing what normal lovers do. But surely a girl as pretty as Olivia, she of Zeffirelli's film of *Romeo and Juliet*, wouldn't hang about Dingle unless there was something in it for her. If not in Christopher's arms, then what?

Nevertheless I was determined to see her and Christopher as lovers and no gossip was to change my mind.

After we had cut our baby teeth and the film was just about in full swing, Robert and I thought it would be both decent and correct to give a party. We were in a sense lord and lady of the manor, living in the gracious Fermoyle House, the biggest of anyone's, except for Mitchum, of course, but he'd hired a whole hotel right on the shore of Dingle Bay. We invited all members of the production team, crew and actors. News of our party must have travelled the length and breadth of Ireland because on the day the crowds were similar to those at the opening of Buckingham Palace to the public. It was too early on in the film to recognize everyone by name so I had no choice but to let them all in.

Apart from David, who declined, everyone showed up. What with most of them being sloshed in no time, something told me I had to keep my wits about me. One thing I forgot to mention about Mitchum. For some reason violence was drawn to him like a bee to honey. Echoes of Nicol Williamson – except that Nicol was the aggressor whereas with Mitchum there was always someone spoiling for a fight. He couldn't walk alone in Dingle for fear of someone coming up and picking one. Walking down a street with Mitchum was a different kettle of fish from doing so with Olivier. Mitchum would be recognized wherever he went; passers-by did double-takes while quickly sussing who he was. The same thing happened in London. He couldn't go anywhre without a hubbub of excitement, while I can't recall a single second look with Olivier. What is star quality? Why has Mitchum got it when Olivier hadn't?

As the party wore on I became aware that things weren't as they seemed. A subtle dance was being played out before my eyes and I was too slow to see the danger signs. It all began when I noticed Mitchum appear from behind a pillar in the drawing room. He saw me perched on the arm of an empty chair talking to one of the wardrobe department, and came to sit beside me. 'How's it going, Mitch?' I asked. He gave an equivocal grunt before submerging himself in his whiskey. I looked up to see a rough-looking red-headed Irish labourer appear in front of the same pillar. He stood there for a moment perusing the drawing room, spied Mitchum, licked his fat lips and gave a strange leer.

'Is he one of the crew?' asked a surly Mitchum.

'You're the one who remembers faces.' Mitchum was blessed, or cursed, with a photographic memory.

'Then get the fucker out of here,' growled Mitchum gently, again into his whiskey.

I stood up between the approaching giant and the seated Mitchum. 'What is your name?'

'And who are you?' he said, leering in towards my face, reeking of beer, fags and havoc.

'I am your hostess. Are you one of the crew?'

'Nah. I'm a Doblin man meself. Would ya move out of me way, I'm wantin' a wee word with Mr Mitchum.'

I loathe telling people off. Whenever I find myself in a position of power I run, like Dracula on seeing the dawn. 'Since you've gatecrashed this party, I'm asking you to leave.'

'Fine, bot not before I've had a wee word with Mr Mitchum here,' he replied politely, before shoving me sideways. An Irishwoman appeared from nowhere. She was big too. I gleaned that she might be the wife. She was dressed like a gypsy with grey roots that would have given her a kindly, matronly look if a vivid bronze hair dye hadn't clashed with her natural pink cheeks. The big Irish chap stood in front of Mitchum who remained sitting (bless him), sipping his whiskey as if no one was there.

'Would you mind standing up, Mr Mitchum, and showin' my wife Doris, here, that I am in fact taller than yerself?'

Doris pushed her great weight forward, landing on my big toe – some weight, like my stallion Cavalier, who was always treading on me.

'Sorry, miss,' she said, moving right in front of Mitchum while her husband introduced her.

'This is Doris. Doris, meet Mr Mitchum.'

Doris's pink cheeks decided to have a field day.

'You see, Mr Mitchum,' she said, attempting to smooth her stiff bronzed hair, 'Brendan here and I have a bet. He says he's taller than yourself and I say he's not.'

Mitchum wasn't impressed, and looked sideways into the fire.

'I'm sure you can't deny us such an innocent request?' said Doris, bending her already abundant cleavage further into Mitch's face. I tried to defuse the tension.

'How much is on this bet?' I asked lamely.

'Big enough to break the bank if I'm wrong,' said a flirtatious Doris, wiggling her hips now in Mitchum's face. Poor Mitch – the ladies opening their legs in front of him and the men hell bent on a punch-up, all drawn like a moth to his potent flame. I wouldn't want his life. He went on sitting there, quietly in charge of his space.

'Get me another whiskey, Rose.'

I felt nervous leaving him alone with these characters, but took his glass and went in search of whiskey and Robert. Where was he? I hadn't seen him all evening. Just as I reappeared round the pillar I saw Mitchum get up and stand straight. Bless him, he was letting them see his great height for themselves.

'Y'see, I'm taller – I told you, I'm a good inch taller!'

Doris swigged her gin and tonic. She didn't like losing the bet.

Brendan, on the other hand, with the adrenalin of triumph pumping through his veins, began feigning a boxer in the ring, jogging to and fro on the spot with his arms up ready to do some damage. He was puce in the face with cockiness and booze. 'Give us a punch, Mitch. C'mon, now, let's take a look at yer true colours – or can you only do it in yer fillums?'

He was really baiting Mitch so I stood between them like a peremptory school-ma'am. 'Pack it in, Brendan. Mr Mitchum wants to be quiet tonight.'

'Excuse me, but it's none of your business.'

He pushed me aside as if I were a gnat rather than the hostess whose party he'd gatecrashed.

'Doris, would you mind taking your man outside for a bit of fresh air?'

'I most certainly would.' She too pushed me away. She began to wind Brendan up – not that he needed it. Doris, wanting blood, said, 'C'mon, Brendan, luv, show him who's boss.'

Brendan obeyed and took a swipe at Mitch, but Mitch ducked and, handing me his whiskey, clenched his fist and went for Brendan's jaw. He mistimed it, allowing Brendan to give an evil smirk followed by a little skip before coming back, purposely aiming his thumbnail into Mitchum's eye-socket. No doubt the aim was to gouge out his eyeball. It was a ghoulish act.

Doris and Brendan scarpered from the room as Mitchum roared. On seeing his eye so badly gouged I called out for Robert. He joined me at the door as we both witnessed Mitchum quickly making his way out to his Porsche, where he reached in and produced a large, no-nonsense knife. Seeing it glistening in the moonlight made me realize how swiftly cantankerous drunken rubbish can escalate into the irreversible bedlam of violence. 'I'll get you, you evil mother-fucker!' shouted Mitch, unable to see much in the dark.

'Did they leave?' Robert indicated over his shoulder towards the house.

'I'll go and search.'

As I turned, Robert shouted back to Mitchum, 'They left, I think.' I wasn't sure why Robert said that – he hadn't even seen them. I started to walk towards the house, but Robert grabbed me back. 'They might be still in there and we don't want any more violence.'

'He could have destroyed Mitch's eye.'

Robert looked at me as if I was making a mountain out of a molehill. Mitchum, unable to find anyone out there, returned up the steps. I caught a glimpse of violence simmer-

ing in his one open eye as he pushed us aside, like heroes do
in movies when they have unfinished business to attend to.
Maybe Robert was right.

The energy level of the party had risen a few notches as
news of a wounded Mitchum spread. People started to panic
and who could blame them, with Mitchum by now crazy with
pain, scaring them all to death as he plunged half blinded
from room to room with that great knife poised for action?
Where on earth were Brendan and Doris? No car had driven
away and they couldn't walk because there was nowhere to
walk to. What if Mitch came across them hidden somewhere?
He'd kill Brendan, for sure.

I knew something had to be done before the mayhem
spiralled out of control, submerging any last vestiges of
common sense. I went into the large hallway, the centre of
the action, and in a loud, authoritative voice, mysteriously
dredged up from some part of me I never knew I had, said,
'Will everyone, and I mean everyone, please collect their
belongings and leave this house immediately.' A hushed
silence followed and people actually began to collect their
belongings and leave. Never before had I spoken up in such
a fashion, so I was stunned to be taken seriously. It even
impressed Mitchum, seeming to sober him up considerably,
because he got his coat, gave me a funny look through his
one eye and returned to his Porsche.

I ran over to his window. 'Mitch—'

'Thanks for nothin'.' His eye was puffed up and oozing
badly.

'Do you want me to drive you? That Connor Pass—'

I felt bad watching him drive off. None of it had been his
fault. That eye looked as if he wouldn't be able to film for
quite some time. Oh dear! Why do all my good intentions
turn into catastrophe? Robert said, 'That was most impressive, you cleared the house.' I pondered a moment or two.
Would Vivien Leigh ever have allowed such a disaster to
befall her elegant parties at Notley Manor? Having stood

politely and apologetically on the steps saying goodbye, I wanted to be alone to assimilate the whole mess. Where *were* Brendan and Doris? If I found them I'd kill them, too.

'I'm just going to get some fresh air, I won't be long.'

'Don't catch cold.' Addo, Arthur, Gladys and Betty all accompanied me. On reaching the bottom of the drive, I saw a car parked. I didn't recognized who it belonged to. Was it them? And if it was what would I do? Moving forward tentatively, I recognized Mary and John Mills having a quiet little snog together in the front. They looked up and saw me.

'I'm so sorry!' I felt embarrassed, it was so unexpected.

'Doesn't worry us. Thanks for a lovely party, you really put on a frightfully good spread. Good night!' As they restarted the car, I found myself full of warm feelings for the pair of them. They'd been married for ever and a day, yet still found time and the need for smooching. I saluted their car as it sped off, evaporating like Doris and Brendan into the night.

CHAPTER FORTY-THREE

'WHAT HAS HE done to his eye?' Mother asked. She had come over for a few days on a wee jaunt with Father. They had a good time, I think, meeting all the actors, but found the filming rather dull. Johnnie Mills and Mary gave a dinner one night and kindly invited my parents along too. Mitchum showed up with quite a bit of marijuana stashed around his personage. His eye had been so severely gouged that he hadn't been able to do any close-ups for six weeks. It started a surly mood in him that didn't disappear for the whole year.

'You ask him,' I said to Mother, putting her on the sofa next to Mitch so he could recount the story of the fatal night. He enjoyed telling people about it, as if it somehow exorcized some of the need for revenge, for although the police were given descriptions of Brendan and Doris, it seemed no one knew them locally and Dublin is a big place, so they got away scot free. As Mitch finished his tale, Mother gave me one of her looks. 'Of course it *would* have been at Sarah's party.'

'The first party I've ever given,' I riposted, defensively. Mitch handed Mother a toke from his spliff. Never until that evening had I smoked any pot, or taken drugs of any kind – neither indeed had Father and Mother (to my knowledge!). I'd only ever heard of the stuff when poor Mitch had been sent to jail for smoking earlier in his career. (He claims he was framed.)

'What's that?' said Mother, her nose quivering.

'Have a toke,' said Mitch. 'It'll ease you out.' He really was a wicked old flirt. The way he seduced Mother that night was classic. I pinched myself to make sure I wasn't dreaming as Mother inhaled her third toke. Father couldn't quite find his role: should he intervene or was he man enough just to sit there and watch the experience unfold?

'It isn't having the least effect on me.' I believed her at first for she gave the impression of holding together better even than she did with her gin and tonic. She never got drunk. (Not in front of us children, anyway.)

'Do you want to try, Daddy?'

'I will if you will.' So Mitchum, the diabolic imp, had corrupted the Miles family within the space of about fifteen minutes. Mary and Johnnie Mills watched, amused. I'm not sure whether or not they indulged. Suddenly Mother began to giggle. It started with her nostrils quivering more than I'd ever seen them quiver, and then she was off. Splitting her innards she might have been, yet never once did she lose her ladylike manner. That evening was the nearest she ever came to being out of control and it was positively Victorian compared to most of us. Although I took hardly any that first night, I became giggly too – but not Father.

'I can't feel a damn thing.' Of course he couldn't. He sat there, puffing away but never inhaling. I think he wanted to be fully alert as Mitchum and Mother began hitting it off rather too well on the opposite sofa.

What was that magic that Mitchum wove around women? His hotel became renowned as the Dingle Brothel. Whenever Dorothy, his long-suffering wife, flew home to LA, how the mouse would play. It was convenient that all the rooms had a number because it was a useful way for him to remember who was who. He'd often say to me on set, 'Number eleven's hot, she flew in last night.'

There's no doubt I found his power fascinating and if I wasn't careful I might get hooked into it myself. It was a kind of drug, maybe dope was what it was, for Mitchum had the best – perhaps only – stash in town. There are those who believe that Jesus's disciples dropped their fishing nets and followed him for the same reason.

Mitch's dolly birds would fly in from all over the place.

What I couldn't fathom was whether they came of their own volition, having paid their own fares, or whether Mitchum got them to come over and footed the bills? Were they simply dope carriers? The quality of most wasn't particularly appetizing, some of them being no more than scrubbers. Did Mitchum, like he'd have us all believe, really sleep with a different girl every night, or was it all bravura PR? I once asked Mitch's stand-in, Harold, who also lived with him, if he knew. 'It's none of my business, Sarah. Them that asks no questions is never told no lies.'

I found myself with a great deal of time on my hands, either waiting in the impersonal production office to be called on to the set or in my caravan. Because of the rain most of us actors would find ourselves meeting up in Mitchum's warm hotel living room to pass the time. An excellent cook, he was usually to be found in the kitchen with an apron on, cooking up a storm. Was his food really as good as I thought, or could it be that I was ignorant of the wickedly habitual 'munchies' that followed getting high? Whatever the reason, his cooking tasted better than anyone else's.

My own Robert rarely came over the Connor Pass into Dingle, unless David had specifically called for him, being well stuck into his next project. But one day he came over, to persuade David not to fire Trevor, who was without Helen for a few days. Dingle isn't the kind of place for someone like Trevor to be alone, especially when it's submerged in endless greyness, so he drank his way back into a little alcoholic sunshine – and why not? But because the rain didn't stop he was suddenly called in for cover shots and, not expecting to be on call, wove his way on set drunk as a lord. David, whose patience was fraying with the rain, decided to fire him. I thought this was well out of line, especially since Trevor had been hanging about not working for weeks. Robert, who respected Trevor, came over to put things right. Thank God, because Trevor's performance was the best in the film, I thought.

While waiting one day in the production office as usual, I overheard a phone call between Trevor and one of the producers. Trevor was trying to get permission to go for a donkey ride, but the production office were loath to let him out of their sight, even for a moment, so I stepped in on his behalf. 'Excuse me, but what possible harm could befall him riding a tired old donkey on the soft Dingle sand?' There was a silence while they contemplated this, so I went on. 'Less, surely, than sitting all alone in his cottage getting blind drunk?' This seemed to do the trick and Trevor's request was granted.

A delighted Trevor and tired-out old donkey were plodding along, doing a most sedate walk. Half-way down the beach, however, a slight hiccup could be detected in their togetherness. Was it because Trevor and his ancient mount both suffered from a temperamental nature? Having reached the far end of the beach in one piece, Trevor yanked on the reins to turn the donkey round and come home again; but the donkey turned round the opposite way. This was hard luck because daylight began to appear between their togetherness, widening in slow motion until they inevitably parted company. Trevor fell with such a thump that he broke his collarbone and couldn't be shot for at least three weeks. Only the likes of dear Trevor could fall off a retired donkey at the walk.

When we first arrived at Fermoyle House, on a rare morning off I was walking Addo over the moorland when he saw his first sheep. He couldn't believe his luck and, thinking it was another Pyrenean mountain dog, chased it. 'Addo!' I shouted, praying there was no farmer around. 'Addo! Come back here!'

I saw him corner the sheep, get behind it and begin shagging it. Surely Irish sheep weren't sprayed with his special cleaning fluid? By the time I got to the scene Addo had done his thing but the sheep just stared ahead, all stiff and still as if dead. I'd never seen anything die standing up

before. I put Addo on the lead and took a closer look. It didn't
bat an eyelid when I waved my hands in front of its eyes. Just
as I'd thought, it *was* dead. I had to act fast and take it to a
vet, dead or not, so I ran back to the house to get the Land-
rover but it had been bagged, to take Trina, Jose and Tomcat
shopping in Tralee, leaving me no choice but to take the
Lamborghini. Back at the scene of the crime the sheep was
still standing up, dead. How the hell was I to get that huge
great lump into the boot of the Lamborghini? Luckily Lamborghini himself started off designing tractors, so it wasn't
accidental that the car trundled over the moorland with ease.
I was also lucky with the boot, which was fairly near the
ground, and the sheep put up not the least bit of resistance –
but, then, how could it, being dead? After much sweating
and straining I managed to get most of it in and could nearly
close the boot, though not completely, thanks to its great fat
dirty bum. I was about to drive away, when what resembled
a scallywag of a farmer approached me.

'Good day to you! What's up?' Had he seen anything?

'My car stalled.'

'So you steal a sheep to while away the time?' His eyes
crinkled with craftiness.

'No, you don't understand, I found the sheep dead so I
was taking it down to the vet.' Opening the boot, he threw
another artful look before hauling the sheep out again. It
transpired he knew exactly who I was.

'And, Miss Rosy Ryan, I saw that dog chasin' my sheep
two days ago.' I did indeed go all rosy. 'So the next time, I'll
take my gun to him. Is that clear?' I liked his sparkling eyes.

'Yes, that's perfectly clear. I'll make sure he never does it
again.'

Once he'd got the sheep out of the Lamborghini, he
placed it back on its four legs.

'Can I pay for a new sheep?'

He tossed me another twinkly look, went behind the dead
sheep and gave it an almighty kick up its arse, whereupon it

flew off at twenty miles an hour. I couldn't believe my eyes – or my ignorance.

'They go into shock, y'see, miss, so next time you'll know what to do.'

'But there's not going to be a next time.'

'We'll see about that, won't we?' I do believe he was flirting with me – but being so steeped in blarney and innuendo, it was hard to tell.

We were shooting a scene on a beach down near Dunquin, which faces the renowned, doomed Blasket Islands. The islanders had mysteriously fled in the twenties, leaving a ghost town of ruins. I heard many conflicting stories of why they had chosen to evict themselves. What remains certain is that they never returned. 'Too haunted,' was the only explanation, given to me by a fisherman, but he wouldn't elaborate and I could find no one who would.

Maybe those Blaskets are cursed – or was David Lean the curser? Lacking sufficient respect for his actors, he was forever testing them, getting tremendous kicks out of discovering each one's breaking point while secretly laughing at them. He nearly caused Johnnie Mills to drown – and Trevor too – after forbidding the stuntmen to scruff up the sand while Johnnie and Trevor were shooting a currach (Irish boat) scene in the water. Both disappeared into the rough sea, but David refused to say, 'Cut!' The stuntmen finally pulled them to shore, where they were rushed off to hospital either stunned or unconscious, and Johnnie with a gash to his skull.

On another occasion Leo McKern finally got rescued from the stormy depths while David stood there fuming at a life being saved without his permission. The shock of Leo's soaking appearance was most macabre if you weren't expecting to see a mass of sand oozing out from an empty eye-socket. No one had told me Leo wore a glass eye. Shooting was again held up because his glass eye was impossible to replace – the eyemaker had gone to pastures new.

Having reluctantly sent Leo home, David had me kneeling in that February sea the rest of the afternoon. As he stood beside the camera waiting for the right formation of seagulls to fly past before giving that yearned-for word, 'Action', I knew his sadism was hell-bent on breaking me. And as I knelt there, iced up, it was mightily clear to me that filming is a frustrating unfulfilling process, only made bearable by those few minutes a day, five maybe, of genuine creativity between 'Action!' and 'Cut!' A paltry five minutes out of twenty-three hours fifty-five minutes of 'Hurry! Wait! Hurry! Wait!' As evening drew in, I cried seaward, privately, to myself. Just when I knew my body could bear the excruciating numbness not a moment longer, I heard those blessed words, 'It's a wrap!' He had failed to break me.

CHAPTER FORTY-FOUR

A   s spring approached and the weather slowly
                 improved, the relationship between Mitchum and
                 David deteriorated. Compensated with insurance
over Mitchum's eye incident, David decided to reshoot Mitchum's scenes again – all of them, mostly of long shots.
Apparently he didn't like Mitchum's hat. So with a completely new hat off we went again. Of course, this was an
insult to Mitchum's intelligence. David must have thought he
was talking to just another actor, but whatever the reason,
Mitch lost respect for David after that.

'Fuck it. If he can't tell me my performance is shit to my
fucking face then fuck him,' said Mitchum, while filling his
considerable lungs with almost a whole spliff in one great
blast. Mitchum's blasphemings were as frequent as Olivier's,
I noted.

On set, my modest caravan sat between David's gigantic
mobile home and Mitchum's, reminding me of Nepal
squashed between India and China. Neither would go into
the other's caravan, so I became the go-between, passing silly
messages back and forth until one day I decided I wasn't
going to play any more.

'Tell Mitchum not to take off his hat until—'

'No, David, you tell him yourself.'

David smiled up at me. I noticed he was usually
impressed whenever an actor stood up for himself. 'Tell him
to come in and see me.' I went into Mitchum's caravan,
letting out a sigh as I realized that here I was, playing piggy
in the middle again.

'David wants to stop playing funny buggers. Go in and
have a word with him?' I asked pleadingly.

'Tell him I'm sitting here, good as gold, waiting for him.'

'But he's the director and he wants to make amends.'

'He's never set foot in here for the whole ten weeks. It's his turn to come to me.'

'When have you ever been in to him, pray?'

Back we were at square one, so I washed my hands completely having assured myself I'd done my best. But things went from bad to worse, India squashing Nepal to stand guard against the onslaught of China. Added to which – interminable rain.

One day on Inch beach, Mitch and I had to shoot the long romantic meeting, the shot which became famous for all the seagulls, and the vast expanse of sand, brolly and sea. Shooting on sand is tricky, as David found out on *Lawrence of Arabia*. Once you've walked across it you have to wait for the tide to wash away the footprints, which could become expensive, time being money. So on a cold spring day, for well over two hours, we stood about twenty yards apart in a howling gale waiting to be cued on the walkie-talkie to start walking towards each other. Mitchum gradually became legless, not from booze for a change but from sinking further and further into the sand. All part of the humiliation of the actor's lot. 'Fuck this for a lark,' he finally shouted across at me, ankle deep in sand and sinking fast. 'I'm calling it a wrap.'

'But he's waiting for seagulls,' I called back across the void of dreary waiting. 'We'd better hang on,' shouted the writer's cowardly wife.

'No way! C'mon, honey, let's blow this joint.' It's important to mention that we were still in the sixties, and the way Mitchum spoke was completely new to me. Indeed, virtually no American used such expressions. For example, the expression 'no way' was Mitchum's. It gradually crept into the American language and then into ours. But Mitchum's 'no way' was his trademark. My son learnt it on the second day he met Mitch and from then on 'no way' was Tom's way out of everything – still is.

'Come on, Rose, I'll take the blame.' He came and took my icy hand, I was wearing only the brolly, straw hat, thin white jumper and skirt. 'You've got pneumonia.' We headed back across the sand towards the camera crew.

'There's professionalism and then there's downright stupidity. I only hope it turns out to be stupidity rather than sadism.'

He had a point for we had waited over an hour and a half.

When we got back to base there was no camera crew or anyone else in sight. We scoured the desolate landscape, but in every direction – nothing anywhere. Mitchum was turning white with rage. His jaw muscles had stopped flexing and were now clenched tight. Just as he was about to go up the Polly Tree he saw an assistant coming towards us.

'What's going on?'

The assistant didn't seem perturbed.

'Oh, they moved location. Sorry, I thought you'd been informed.'

As I looked at Mitch's granite profile I knew David Lean would have to pay for it. And if I were a superstar like Mitch, I might have been as furious, but I wasn't. No, I knew my place. The writer's wife.

His opportunity for getting even showed itself sooner than I had anticipated. There was precious little filming that week because tides and weather were calling the shots. Therefore Mitchum, though not on the call sheet, was suddenly called upon to perform a poignant dawn scene on the rocks. In the movie it is when his character – Charles, my husband – is distraught, for he knows I've been unfaithful with the English major, Christopher Jones, and has come out in his nightshirt to find me.

I was standing beside the camera, watching this great hunk of Hollywood movie star climbing over the grey rocks at grey dawn, dressed only in a grey nightie, looking equally grey and vulnerable as he missed his footing while scrambling towards us. When he was level with the camera, he stopped, looked round as if searching for his beloved Rosy – heart-rending. Turning towards the camera lens, he gave a wonder-fully regretful look, those fine features displaying his own misery, then, with no warning whatsoever, lifted his nightie and peed. David was struck dumb. That's what I admired in Mitch, his subtlety in revenge.

'Cut! We'll go again immediately,' said a well pissed-off David, albeit hiding it immaculately. 'Turn over,' he said scanning the skies for a patch of blue. 'Action!'

With the writing on the wall for the two of them, the wet weather fell in step, heightening the agony. The production office was desperate. I had to be there every morning at five-thirty, in case there was a moment's gap in the grey. Here's a typical morning with the production manager asking Dublin for the weather forecast.

'Dublin, hello.'

'Hello. The top of the morning to you!'

'Can you please tell us what kind of weather Dingle can expect today?'

'Hold on a moment while I find you. Now let me see . . . Dingle, Dingle, Dingle – ah – here we are! Dingle, I've got you!'

Pause. One of the production team clenches his white knuckles on the desk top, as he marches up and down as far as the telephone wire will allow. 'Well?' He's losing patience now.

'What's it like with you in Dingle?'

'It's raining, of course!' We all peered through the window at the hopelessness.

'Can you see any gaps anywhere?' asks the Dublin mete-orological office, hopefully.

'No, there's none to be seen in any direction.'

'None at all, eh?'

'Not a sausage.'

'In that case I'd bet me bottom dollar you're in for another rainy day.'

The Irish are a wonderful nation, and I was falling in love both with them and the place. My desire to go over to the Blasket Islands gradually became urgent: they drew themselves to me in a most mysterious way.

Robert felt the same. 'Go down and find a fisherman to take us over – book him for next Sunday.' Down I went to the cove one lunch break – and there he was, the perfectly weather-gnarled fisherman working on his boat, covered in nets, waders and what-have-you.

'Hello,' I said.

He dropped his net when he saw me, bursting all over with blarney.

'And the top of the morning to you, miss.'

'I'd like to hire a boat for three of us this Sunday and go across to the Blaskets.'

He licked his finger in the wind, looking up at the sky. 'This Sunday will be a perfect day for the Blaskets, we're set fine for this·Sunday.' He seemed a really sunny kind of chap. I'd struck lucky for once. 'What time shall we say, then?'

'How about noon?'

'Noon seems fine.' He was a splendid character, I liked him a lot.

'What about food?'

'Take a picnic, why not?' He was a big man, so I asked him what he'd like in particular.

'Well, now, let me see . . .' He scratched his stubbled chin and looked at me with his healthy brown skin glowing. 'I'm not fussy. How about chicken, ham, maybe, baked potatoes, salad, cheese, I'm a Cheddar man myself – and a few bottles of white wine would be excellent, why not?'

'Why not?' I found myself echoing his accent. I must stop – ghastly habit.

'I'm very partial to treacle tart myself – and a bit of Dingle cream.'

'Treacle tart and Dingle cream.' I hoped I could remember everything.

'It'll be a perfect day, that I can guarantee. I'll take you out to the shoal of herrings north of the Blaskets before lunch, they're a mass of tangles out there just now.' He was getting excited, rubbing his hands together with anticipation. 'You'll love it, and I'll have a bet with yer – it'll be a perfect day!'

'Till Sunday at noon, then.' I was just about to walk off. 'Oh, I don't know your name.'

'I know you, Rosy Ryan,' he said with a hint of coquetry, or more of the bleedin' blarney, but what the hell? 'I'm Pat.'

'Fine then, Pat, I'd best be getting back. Goodbye and thanks.'

'It's only *au revoir* – till Sunday at noon.'

I hadn't walked more than about twenty yards before I heard him call back to me.

'Rosy!' I turned back. 'Yes?'

'One little thing.'

'What's that, Pat?'

'I have no boat.'

CHAPTER FORTY-FIVE

HAD SPRING TURNED into summer? Hints that time was passing became certainties, made evident by the stupendous flourish of Mitchum's marijuana plant growing like Jack's beanstalk in the greenhouse at the back of his hotel. The rain affected us all immeasurably – and when boredom sets in, lethargy follows close behind, tripping the weak into corruption. If it hadn't been for Mitchum's efforts to keep us all happy, with a warm fire always in the grate, endless spliffs, pasta and hash cakes, most of the company would have been in much lower spirits. We hung on to Mitchum's hotel like the only raft in stormy seas.

Because of the ceaseless rain, one Tuesday in May Mitchum and I were called in suddenly for weather cover. So it was that we found ourselves hanging on to each other as we waited nervously to begin shooting our wedding-night sequence. In the story, Rosy is about to lose her virginity to her schoolteacher husband, Charles Shaughnessy, a man twice Rosy's age, previously married and stuck in his ways. He doesn't serve Rosy well that night, his technique being swift and mundane, leaving Rosy to wonder, 'Is this all there is?' Meantime, the whole village is celebrating in the traditional fashion of the times, throwing rice up at their window (the symbol of fertility), dancing, and drinking as only the Irish can. I was nervous, never having lost my virginity on screen before, and although Mitchum bluffed it out well, he was hardly his usual laid-back self.

I couldn't help thinking, as we lay in our double bed, me in my nightie, and Mitch in his long nightshirt, what a weird pair of lovers we made, both stiff from the strain of having to wait so long before acting out such an intimate scene. What would Lionel think of me now? No doubt he was in bed with someone else, yet I felt no pangs of jealousy, only love. Yes, it was still there, sometimes excruciatingly piercing, but I managed to shove it aside. The thought of returning home to Robert always did the trick.

Abracadabra! In he came, obviously needing to check out how his missus was faring between the sheets with Robert Mitchum. Watching Robert puff nervously on his pipe as he spoke to David, I realized how ill at ease David was, too, as he pulled away wildly on his cigarette holder with no cigarette in it. Freddie Young, the lighting cameraman (the best), ordered the gaffer to bring in some different lights. Meanwhile Mitch and I huddled up warm and had a natter.

'Gee! I need a toke, but I'm too lazy to get out of bed.'

'Doesn't it distort one's timing to smoke marijuana before performing?'

'I don't perform,' he said lazily, giving me his arm as a higher pillow. No, I thought to myself, Mitchum just *is*. He was well aware of being trademarked sexy. A real groin-grinder with that puffed-up penguin chest of his. He knew it worked for him, and I found out how. Whenever it was possible, just before '*Action!*' his dresser sidled up, discreetly handed Mitch a toke from his spliff, and Mitch spent the rest of the take holding it down. Hence the legendary barrel chest forever expanded, and the voice pushed even lower to hang on to any precious escaping smoke.

'Though I'd never take LSD before a take.'

'I'd never take LSD!' I said adamantly, and when he asked why, I told him all about Nona's bad trip.

'That'd do it. Though Tim Leary swears it opens up the gateway to God.'

What he was saying might be true, because before we left for Ireland there had been a programme on the telly about some girl taking LSD. She experienced some really interesting stuff.

'Do you take it a lot?'

'Nah. It isn't my bag. Worth a try – once, at least.'

'Do you have any?'

'Come round on Wednesday and I'll have some for you.'

'Can I bring Robert too?'

'Sure, it's best to experience it with someone you trust.' There was a silence. Did he think I didn't trust him?

With the lights at last in place, David came up to the bed. 'Now, I think we can pretty well stick to the script, it's most explicit, wouldn't you say?' We both lay there, quite still.

'So, Mitchum, just turn towards her and take her in your arms and then . . . play it by ear.'

His great pointed ears were twitching, from that Quaker upbringing stifling his vocabulary.

'Are we ready for action?'

'One little thing, David, what about my nightie? It's very long?' asked Mitch.

'Pull it up.'

'What, now?'

'No, we must see you doing that, it'll be effective.'

'After I've taken her to me?'

David took the script and looked at it. 'The script doesn't mention the nightie, but I think it's a good touch, don't you, Robert?'

'As long as it doesn't become a scene about a nightie,' warned Bolt.

'Perhaps I could have it off already?' said a hopeful Mitch.

'No. We must see the awkwardness, don't you think so, Robert?'

'Anything that helps the audience understand the failure of the man.' He gives the word 'failure' a definite ring.

'OK. I'll pull up my nightie after I've pulled up hers. Make sure you have a lot of film in the camera,' Mitch warned, snidely.

'All right, let's go,' shouted Lean with a couple of chomps on his still-empty holder.

'How long do I hump her for?'

David didn't know how to respond to this, and so nervous was he I feared he might have trouble digesting the ever-diminishing holder. 'What you do is to pull up both your nighties, and then . . . and then get on top of her.'

'Couldn't she climb on top of me?'

'No, of course not, she's a virgin. Just do it the conventional way.'

'Everyone has a different conventional way, David.' Poor David, Mitch was winding him up something rotten.

'Well . . . I mean, you get on top of Sarah . . .' He was lost for words.

'Yeah? I'm fucking her on top. For how long, roughly?'

'Roughly about a minute, and then . . .' He dried again. 'And then you, you – you—'

'Shoot my wad?'

I hadn't heard that expression before, and I could tell David's ears weren't too familiar with it either, for they turned deep vermilion.

'That's right, you – you – you – climax too soon and slowly roll off her.'

'Let's go for it,' sighed a reluctant Mitch. 'Let's get this fucking show on the road.'

'OK,' said David, while Robert had the sensitivity to remove himself from any embarrassment.

'*Action!*' commanded the chief. I felt sorry for Mitch, unable to take a toke with everyone being so near, forcing him to begin the nightie struggle sober. What a task it turned out to be. On and on, he hauls away at great lengths of material.

'*Cut!*' said David. 'What the hell are you doing under those covers?'

'Playing canasta – what does it look like?' Mitch replied, still fiddling under the sheets.

'Cheat both nighties up a little,' said David impatiently.

Mitchum pulled mine up. 'All the way up to your cunt?' he whispered in my ear into the pillow.

'All right. *Action!*' This time all went well. Mitchum was

behaving himself, and pulled up both our nighties with great aplomb, mounted me with as much again, then gradually speeded up the rhythm, and just as I'm thinking how brilliant we are and how realistic it must be looking from the camera's point of view, Mitchum shouted, 'Cut! Careful, honey, or you'll crease my nightie!' I believe he did that because he was embarrassed at simulating a climax, then falling off with a hard-on. Nevertheless David was furious as ever. Being merely the FO, all I had to do was hold my nose and think not so much of England, but of tomorrow and experiencing my first LSD trip with Robert.

'OK. Let's go again, Mitchum, and bugger the nightie.'

'How I wish, David, how I wish,' said Mitchum, grabbing hold of my lower cheeks. He was a mixer all right. He knew that any woman who had an ounce of lust within her would find it hard to resist his bearlike proximity, and I was, after all, apart from being the writer's wife, also a woman.

Finally tomorrow arrived. I'd been shooting beach scenes all day and Robert had agreed to come over the Connor Pass for the occasion. I was full of excitement waiting for his arrival.

'Sit down and get warmed-up, honey.' I did so. We were alone. Mitchum poured himself a brandy, and took a toke after offering me one.

'No, I want the LSD.'

'It's here, in this sugar lump, suck it slowly.' As he put a sugar lump in front of me on the coffee table there was a knock on the door. 'That'll be your old man, I have a sugar lump for him too.'

I ran to let Robert in, but was astonished to find a policeman standing there instead. Mitchum's toke was leaving a mighty frisky pong in its wake as, no doubt, the police officer was finding out. I stood there, transfixed.

'Excuse me, Miss Miles, but is Mr Mitchum in, by any chance?'

'Just wait there a moment.' I panicked. Mitchum was in there, all right – smoking pot.

'Well, miss?' The officer just stood there, like me. I couldn't possibly invite him in.

'Well?' he repeated patiently.

'Just wait there a moment.' I ran into the sitting room. 'It's the police!' I whispered hoarsely.

Mitchum didn't turn a hair, merely exuded a grand gesture of welcome.

'Bring them in, bring them in.' He made no effort to hide the pot.

'Good day to you, Mr Mitchum,' said the copper politely.

'How I wish we could have even one good day, officer. We all want to go home.'

'Is Dingle that terrible, then, sir?'

'It is after the novelty wears off, and the rain wears thin.'

'That's some novelty you've got there growing in yer back garden, wouldn't you say so, Mr Mitchum?'

'How did you see it?' inquired Mitchum, bemused. Why wasn't he freaked out with panic. Surely he could go to prison again?

'You can't miss it, sir, it's grown higher than the wall this past two weeks.'

'Well, well, well,' is all Mitch said as the officer cleared his throat.

'Shall we go out and take a closer look at it, Mr Mitchum?'

Mitchum rose. 'Let's do just that, if it would get yer rocks off.' The nerve of the man!

'That would be excellent, Mr Mitchum.' Out we all troop to the greenhouse, where the plant had come on a treat, no doubt about it. And it gave forth such an exquisite harvest, though I was no expert in these matters.

'It's a real beauty, Mr Mitchum, that I must admit.'

'That it is, that it is.' Mitchum imitated him.

'What would you be calling that plant then, Mr Mitchum?'

Without drawing breath Mitch replied, 'We call that pot, officer, POT spells dope – here, have a toke.'

The officer drew back almost eagerly. 'Oh, I couldn't possibly do that, Mr Mitchum, that would be against all the regulations.'

'Are you sure it's in the book of regulations?'

The officer looked this way and that, like a trapped weasel.

'Then come back when you're off duty and cool out.'

'It isn't that I'm on duty, sir, but that stuff's illegal.'

Mitch bent seductively inwards towards the officer, just like he flirted with Mother. 'I'll not tell on you, if you don't tell on me,' he whispered in the officer's ear, while offering him another tempting toke. This time, with the smell wafting up so divine, I could tell the officer was sorely tempted.

'I can't, sir, I can't.'

Mitchum puts the smoke under his nose.

'You can lead the horse to water, but you can't make it drink.'

What with the seductive smell of the stuff, plus Mitchum's irresistible laid-back charm, the horse gently went to the water. Mitch gave me a triumphant wink. Within a few minutes he was stoned out of his mind, and after a few days – or was it my imagination – many of the Dingle police force were to be seen in a cooled-out, much less cantankerous frame of mind.

Still no Robert, so I rang home to be told he'd just left.

'Start without him, why not?' Mitch lifted the sugar lump to my lips. 'Suck it, lie back and relax.'

I did just what he told me. Within seconds – well, perhaps a few minutes, it was hard to tell – the room took on a different shape and colour. It had more depth, more dimensions, yet I couldn't quite put my finger on what was different. Mitch gave me an orange. I'd never before seen a real orange in such detail. The resplendent colour was so kissable, so exquisite, lifting my heart as I perused its shiny, yet matt texture. Everything was a benevolent, sparkly fairy-land. I walked over to the window and there was familiar Dingle Bay before me, looking as I'd never seen it before. Through a tango rhythm of rain dancing on the window-ledge, the indigo and pink sky was a mass of rainbows, shooting colour downwards towards the ocean, catching the white horses spraying their offerings to the shore. Why, it was as if each rainbow had its own tale to tell, its own white horse, and each white horse its own funnel of silver light straight back up to a rainbow. Though fleeting, these freshly created patterns all melted into the one magnificent whole, as if somehow knitted together with ecstasy. Everything knew me and I knew everything. This was what the world was really about, if only I was able to see, yet up till now my eyes had been tightly closed in one-dimensional separation. That evening other layers of consciousness kindly opened up to me and they were real, as real as I was. For I was able to see through this reality/illusion into other planes, through all the realms of nature.

Mitchum struck me as a much kinder man than I'd previously thought. His eyes, though far greener, were so sad, full to the brim with aeons of elusive truth-seeking. What a gorilla, a giant of a man he was! But it was the orange that I was drawn to most. As I picked it up and spun it round it seemed to reflect the wholesomeness all around me. The smell was so subtle, so fresh and pure. As I peeled it slowly, I swore it let out a high-pitched, almost ultrasound squawk. Perhaps its nakedness embarrassed it, like I'd felt with Mitch during our wedding-night scene. When I'd lovingly peeled it completely, symmetrical nakedness, I stuck my finger down the tight little hole at its top. What a feeling that was, poking away into the deep, squelchy flesh. As I tenderly prised it open to watch its innards leak out over me, a thought suddenly struck me. Nona and the baked beans – yes, of course! The reason why she picked them up from my plate with such painful scrutiny was because she was able to comprehend the universe from the baked beans' point of view. I felt the orange surrender as we both drew closer to the ultimate union, it to sacrifice, me to nourishment and fulfilment. I could feel it aching for me to eat it. As its juice dripped down my wrist we both dissolved into a sacred moment of mutual satisfaction.

'That'll be Robert.' Mitchum's voice made me jump. Who the hell was Robert? I thought. The dripping juice felt cold against the sensitive skin beneath my throat. I looked up to find my husband staring down at me. What was Mitchum saying to him to make him burst out laughing? Were they laughing at me?

'No, I'll have a whisky – you tell her.'

What was he going to tell me? Was my shirt undone? I went over and held my husband's face in my hands. What a beautiful man he was. I hadn't really noticed before. And those blue eyes. Apart from the Queen Mother's when she visited Roedean, they were the bluest eyes I was ever likely to see. In them I saw Thomas More, Lawrence of Arabia – all his characters came alive in Robert's eyes that evening. That is, until Mitchum sat down beside me, and looking at me with compassion, delivered his bombshell.

'Honey, I played a dirty trick on you. There was nothin' in that sugar lump.'

Later, it became obvious that Mitch had been speaking the truth. The humiliation bit deep, into that private area where the Fool does his mischief. I felt a real 'Proper Charlie', but the Fool makes his appearance in all of us at some time or another, and that was to be the evening my Fool raised his cocked hat and pricked me with his feather, while demanding that I laugh it off. Unconsciously I had chosen to follow every detail from the LSD television programme – and probably bits of the Nona experience too. Why had I been so gullible when normally I was accused of being sceptical, a cynic, even? I found myself stunned that the power of auto-suggestion could have led me on so. But was it so alarming? Having proved I was able to go to such places thinking I was on LSD, surely there was no end to the beauty I could find through those same dimensions again and again *without drugs*? It was some lesson I learnt that night. Yes, that night I had my first genuine proof that all is illusion.

CHAPTER FORTY-SIX

EVERYTHING WAS GREEN and full – and squelchy, that summer of 1969. But not today. This was our day off so the sun came out. I was beginning to feel sorry for David, because whenever he gave us time off, the sun shone. Tom and I were at a children's birthday party given by Freddie Young, the lighting cameraman, and his wife, Joan, for their little four-year-old son, David. It was a glorious afternoon as I sat chewing grass under an old sweet chestnut tree, watching all the children playing games on the lawn. Tomcat, aged two, was minding his own business and quietly picking daisies. He was apt to muddle them with buttercups, repeatedly charging up and twirling a daisy under my chin, looking for butter.

'You need buttercups for the butter test, not daisies. Go and pick me a buttercup.'

It fills me with the better part of being alive, listening to church bells and children's laughter intermingling with their games as they dance across those summer shadows that gradually stretch longer into the rosy hue of evening. But I looked at my life, and it concerned me no end that I had finished ticking off my list of dreams. What was I to do now? I tried to push away those fears of 'Is this all there is?'

One thing I knew, I was content with just one pair of children's wellies strewn in the hall. Besides, the world was bursting at the seams, and by the turn of the century Britain would probably have 60,000,000 on its small surface. This decision filled me with a certain sadness because I would have loved a little girl, but it was only my own vain, selfish

needs crying out, nothing more. Robert, after all, had two
girls already.

'Where butter, Ma?'

I took the buttercup and placed it under my chin.

'See? All the butter?'

'Me have butter?'

'Let's have a look. Oh! You great enormous lump of
butter!' We hugged some more before he went off to pick
more white 'butter' flowers. I watched him as I lay there
dreaming the nightmare of having no dreams left. Silly,
really, because all I had to do was surrender to my fate, live
in the moment and let God take care of the rest. But I wasn't
aware of that then. I knew only the void left by dreams
having come true. Oh, why was the need so urgent to forge
on like some robot, to reach the winning post? There *is* no
end. Advance is not the only answer. For thirty years I
wiggled blindly through, never looking left or right, into a
tunnel-visioned cul-de-sac. Because the blueprint of my fate
was merely pencilled in lightly, I now tend to see destiny's
clues only from the view over my shoulder. My one deathbed
dread is to witness that sadly moist, reverent creature 'if only'
bearing down on me with great gifts of hindsight . . . all too
late.

'No darling, that's a poppy.' I looked around, but I
couldn't see another poppy. I wonder where Tomcat had
found it. After changing tack and counting all my *good* luck, I
noticed a small boy of about four creep up behind Tomcat
bearing a long bamboo cane. Tomcat, dancing alone among
the buttercups, was facing in the opposite direction. Suddenly
the small boy thwacked him hard across the back of his bare
legs with the cane. Tomcat turned round in shock. Just as I
was about to get up and take away the cane, Tomcat, seeing
him standing there, slowly approached, looked him straight
in the eye, bent forward and kissed him on the cheek. The
little boy with the cane didn't know what to do, so he backed
off gingerly till he was a good distance from Tomcat – and

scarpered. What a mysterious creature Tomcat was, a bundle of contradictions. A wilful little saint.

The climax of *Ryan's Daughter* is the love scene between Rosy Ryan and the English major. Just my luck therefore that Christopher Jones didn't want to play it. This vitally important scene was the centrepiece of the plot: it is the first time Rosy Ryan understands not only the power of love but also its fulfilment. Her husband came too soon, but with the shell-shocked English major her clash with the cosmos was to be cataclysmic. So far we'd shot up to the point where we dismounted, let out horses roam free, knelt down on the mossy ground, and (so the script states) he unbuttons me slowly. 'Cut!' sighed David. 'We'll do the rest when the sun comes out again.' It never did.

So there we were, David, Chris and I, in David's caravan waiting for Chris to join me on the floor on his knees, so we could continue rehearsing the scene from where we left off in the bluebell woods. To be fair it was rather tricky continuing an intimate love scene that we'd shot outdoors the previous week and were now, because of weather problems, being forced to finish in an old barn. Eddie Fowley, of the art department, had the unenviable task of transplanting all the bluebells, butterflies, dragonflies, grass, moss and trees, and making an exact replica of the woods inside it. The transformation was a miracle, because on the close scrutiny of the finished film, I never saw any seams.

'Come on, Chris, the barn bluebells won't last for ever, so get on your knees on the floor and let's choreograph the love scene with some sort of precision and then go in the barn and get it over and done with.'

I was kneeling on the caravan floor (oh, what a good girl am I!), waiting for Chris to get off his arse and on to his knees opposite me. But he didn't, he just stared vacantly out of the window.

About a month earlier Chris had gone up to David and asked him if he could bring over his Ferrari. David looked really pleased. 'Yes, Chris, of course you may, if it'll make you happy.'

As soon as Chris was out of hearing, David turned to me and said, 'Hopefully he'll kill himself in it.'

I could have sworn he meant it. Their relationship had never been convivial, but lately it had been dire. David was unable to find sufficient compassion for the mess that Chris was in. He was totally uninterested in trying to win Chris over his side, or in pumping up his ego with the confidence he so desperately needed. Chris was crying out for help, but David's ears weren't pointing in his direction. Could his reticence, perhaps even fear, be because he was lonely? Earlier in the film one of his managers had had to leave him, to fly back to LA being the owner of the house where Sharon Tate had been murdered by Charles Manson. (Mitchum was in a state when he heard news of the murder, because his daughter Trina had intended to go there that night. Eventually Trina rang, telling Mitch that at the last minute she had decided not to go.)

'Get on the floor, Chris, opposite Sarah and play the scene. We haven't got all day.' David's legs were shaking and his great big knees were twitching: he was in as much of a state as Christopher Jones. I was wondering what was wrong with me that Christopher was so desperate to skip the love scene altogether. Mind you, he wasn't the first . . . I suddenly remembered old Johnnie Gielgud, so quietly asked, 'Is it me, Chris?'

He looked down at me, kneeling all alone on the caravan floor. 'Fuck off, woman, it's not that!' and returned to look out of the window.

'Then what is it?' I said as gently as I knew how.

David was twitching madly now. 'This isn't a psychiatric ward, we have a dying bluebell wood out there, so for Christ's sake, be a man for a change and get down on your knees!'

I wasn't sure that David's technique was going to bring home the bacon. Judging by the way Chris simply continued staring out the window, I thought perhaps the gentle approach might bring forth more fruit.

'You read the script before you accepted the part, did you not?' David demanded.

'Yeah, of course I did.'

'Did you skip over reading the love scenes?'

'Of course I didn't.'

'So you know you're contracted to play this scene and that if you don't we'll be forced to take legal action?' Absolute silence. 'Chris, for the last time, get down on your knees.'

My knees were beginning to hurt so I got up off the hard floor and took the opportunity to play earth mother, putting my arms around Chris's shoulders, and saying nothing. We both just stared out of the window at his caravan.

'This is all very touching, but we have to get a move on!' David's state was as gnarled as his cigarette holder, the third new one now down to the quick. He had some lean ways all right. He never threw away old pieces of soap but treasured them right the way down though paper thin to invisibility. On your head be it if you threw away any transparent slivers of soap. I liked David's lean ways; without them perhaps we'd never have been given a Lamborghini – incredible generosity. My son Tomcat mocks me for similar economies, claiming I even hang my tea bags out to dry. (A trifle unfair, that one; I none the less feel that each tea bag will be going towards his Harley Davidson.)

David must have caught the tone of his own fury because he suddenly changed tack, recrossed his legs to stop his oak-tree knees from wobbling, and lowered his voice. 'Chris, will you tell me why you won't play the scene?'

Another endless silence. 'There's a whole crew out there

waiting to work, a beautiful young girl here who must be
feeling very unwanted right now, so why will you not go to
work?'

More silence. 'Chris, answer my question please.'

Chris didn't move his position, he just continued to stare
out of the window. And then, very softly, he replied, 'I don't
work on a Sunday.'

This came as a big surprise to both of us. I had had no
idea he was a religious man, neither obviously had David.

'You've never mentioned this before.' Silence. 'In future
we will never use you on a Sunday.' Silence. 'We'll call it a
wrap.' David wanted to strangle the boy. So did I. It was
disgraceful behaviour. David went to the door of his caravan.
'It's a wrap, everyone. Christopher doesn't work on a
Sunday. He's a religious man, so please forgive the wasted
day. Be here first thing in the morning and we'll shoot the
scene then. Have a good rest of the day off.'

The whole crew knew Chris was being a jerk by refusing
to play the love scene, and knowing how unwanted I must
have felt they all let me know very sweetly that if it'd been
them in the caravan . . .! Cor!

Robert didn't believe the story. He thought there was
some other explanation. 'There isn't any. He just doesn't
want to make love to me.'

Robert took me to him and made love to me that night. A
host of bats who had made their home in a hole above the
windows came swooshing down every time we were thus
united, adding a certain *je ne sais quoi* to our nocturnal
activities. The terror of bats getting caught in your hair
provides an extra frisson or two to any orgasm. They never
did – alas. Perhaps they weren't bats. Perhaps they were
snow geese or turquoise and gold wineberry wagtails?

Next morning it was the same story. Chris arrived, white
as a sheet, refusing to participate in the love scene. Poor
David, what could he do? He couldn't fire him now, it was
too late, we'd shot too much footage on him. He hadn't, alas,

killed himself in his Ferrari – so far. He just sat there in David's caravan refusing to become involved with us.

'Right. Let's go into the woods and shoot the damn scene any old way.'

But Christopher remained sphinx-like, staring out of the window. Perhaps I did smell after all? It tried to sample my breath by catching it in my cupped hands. I've always been lucky with my smell, never having had to use deodorants in my life. Perhaps right then was the time to start?

In came Eddie Fowley. 'Sorry, David, but we only have one more day left and then it's elbow bluebell woods. The butterflies and dragonflies are dying too and I can't find any more.'

'Do you hear that, Christopher?'

Not a muscle moved, absolutely no reaction.

And so it was that another day bit the dust. That afternoon I went to talk it over with Mitchum, who was frustrated, edgy and grumpy because he was all keyed up to play another of our bed scenes straight afterwards and had been waiting for three days now.

'I'm all sprayed, douched, powdered, manicured, shaven and polished. What the fuck's his problem? Talk about coitus interruptus!'

'He doesn't want to touch me.'

'Bullshit, he just wants you to bugger him, that's all.'

I thought that a bit crude. 'Is there such a thing as an aphrodisiac?'

'No.'

He being so sure, I told him about freshly fallen coconut injected with a 1902 bottle of Napoleon brandy, then placed in the earth for twenty-two years.

'I'm not walking up and down this fucking room all douched, powdered, manicured, shaven and polished for the next fuckin' twenty years!'

With Chris's behaviour still as perverse as ever, David and I concocted an equally perverse little plan. David was well 'in' with the local chemist (you could get almost any drug straight over the counter in those days) and got him to give us a certain potion 'to help matters considerably', so he assured David. Come hell or high water, every morning Chris had cornflakes, so my part of the plan was to creep into Chris's caravan next morning, with the lark, and pop the white powder into his cornflakes milk. Looking back at that ghastly episode I wonder how I summoned up the nerve to go through with it. But we were all desperate; without this scene there was no film, so at the time I felt more like Florence Nightingale. Having done the dirty deed, I crept back out again and into David's caravan which was parked next door.

'Well done, Sarah,' said a tired David. 'We can do nothing now but wait.'

I watched David meticulously clean out all the tar from his filter with a paper hankie, while the time dragged on.

'I only hope the chemist knows what he was up to,' he said doubtfully.

A quarter of an hour later, as David and I peeped from behind David's caravan curtain like a couple of school-children, Chris came stumbling towards his caravan looking half out of his mind already. He was flanked as usual by his two managers: Stuart, and Rudy who had recently returned from his Charles Manson murder mansion.

'Such a bizarre lot. If I was to make a film about them no one would believe it.' Satisfied at last that his filter was clean, David lit up his fourth cigarette of the day.

Both Rudy and Stuart left the caravan, just as they did every morning. I think it was because Chris liked to eat his breakfast alone. Once David had given him sufficient time to digest his cornflakes, he sent in an assistant to tell Chris to be in the barn within five minutes. I went to get into my clothes, and on my return I saw David talking to the two managers, so I knocked on Christopher's door. 'Chris, may I come in?'

'Why not?'

Such a shame his two bodyguards never allowed any of

the actors near Chris's caravan. It was an error because it alienated him even more from the rest of us. He was sitting there staring at his mug of coffee.

'Come on, Chris, I'm just as nervous, so let's get it over with.'

He gave me a faraway look and rose on to his wobbly pins. I do hope the chemist knew what quantity of whatever it was to give him, because by the look of him he'd been given too much of the tranquilliser and not enough *oomph!* Still, he was at least following me out of the caravan, which was a miracle.

Once the first mission impossible had been accomplished and he was kneeling in the bluebell barn I could tell he was about to keel over, so I got up and suggested to David we'd better shoot immediately. David came over and gently told Chris to unbutton my shirt, slowly, seductively, on 'action'. Chris's pupils were dilating, and I was feeling more vulnerable than I'd ever felt before. Playing this kind of scene was bad enough, but under these stressful circumstances, with the whole crew finding the episode incomprehensible and David wanting to strangle him, I found it hardly conducive to performing the kind of love scene required. No one asked if I was all right, after all I was merely the FO – and the writer's wife.

'Concentrate now, the pair of you. *Action!*' Chris did nothing. He looked exactly as if he'd come from a living-dead horror movie. Nothing was happening, so David said, 'Cut!' The barn was thick with atmosphere.

Things suddenly took a turn for the better when Chris spoke for the first time.

'Why can't she undo *my* buttons?'

I could hear sniggering from certain members of the crew. David, who had a twig of hazel in his hand, was thwacking it against his thigh.

'Because heroes seduce the maidens. OK?'

Chris was quick, so there was hope still. 'You've been in the ark too long.'

David chose to ignore this. 'Right, let's go again. *'Action!'*

Because I felt so desperately sorry for the pair of us and he wasn't getting on with the job, I began unbuttoning his shirt. The whole point of the scene was two people starving for each other. Oh, where was my Heathcliff?

'Cut!' David grew so agitated I thought he might use the twig.

After about an hour of this fiasco David said he had sufficient unbuttoning to edit together, and for the pair of us to remove our clothes and lie down on the mossy earth. 'Are you warm enough, the pair of you?'

'Yes, thank you.' Was Chris too far gone to reply? So sad it was to have to play my most important love scene with someone asleep. Our clothes now removed, Chris was lying on top of me as vibrantly alive as suet pudding. I was almost past caring. All I wanted was to get home to the arms of Robert and those divine bats. Making love to a bat would have been infinitely preferable.

'Action!' Chris apparently didn't hear, so I wiggled about under him, pretending to be in seventh heaven. There were certainly no wineberry wagtails on the barn ceiling that day. Come to think of it, I'd probably never see a wineberry wagtail again. I pretended he was Robert, I pretended he was Heathcliff, Hamlet, Othello, Mr de Winter, Mr Adam Allthings – a bat, even – all to no avail. He was fast asleep on top of me and I wanted to go and strangle the chemist for getting the dosage so wrong. Still, I was an actress, wasn't I? I began some heavy breathing, thrashing about, panting, heaving, cooing, oohing and aahing. I kissed him on his open mouth, kissed his closed eyelids, his nose, ears, on and on I went, trying with all I had to make it look erotic. Olivier once told me to watch out because I have the knack of raising people's spirits and they know it, so like vampires they suck

at my light. Is that what Chris was doing – lying there, a great lump of dead, unraised spirits – sucking at my light?

'Cut!'

I raised my head to find David beckoning to me – he must be joking, I thought. 'You come to me, I'm stuck!' I shouted. There was no need to whisper, Chris was out of it.

David finally realized and came over. He bent down and whispered, 'I know we're on his back, but it looks dead. Can't you do anything to liven him up?'

'Perhaps, David, you'd like to swap places?'

He let that one go. 'Just try something, Sarah – anything, please, for my sake!' I wasn't sure what else I could do, I'd already tried everything.

'Right – *Action!*' It was totally useless. The more I tried to awaken him, the more idiotically unbecoming, unfeminine and certainly unsexy I became. Why, oh, why did these catastrophes follow me around? So angry was I that desperation crept in. Past all caring, I moved my hand up his back away from the camera, slid it inside his underpants, and poked my index finger up towards his bumhole. Reaction at last! He went from a dead fish to a live fish wiggling about on a hook. I kept saying to myself that it was all in the name of art, because I found the whole experience perfectly repellent. Furthermore I had to look into camera and make as if it was the most sensational, earth-shattering orgasm of my whole life. Bats and vampires! God forgive me!

The next day (too late for my performance, the butterflies, dragonfly, bluebells – and my Oscar!) Chris became a veritable Don Juan. (The chemist's potion, obviously, had a delayed effect – just my luck!). He got really keen, couldn't get enough of me, so we shot his close-ups again.

P.S. All you Chris Jones fans, who write asking me what happened to him, will be relieved to know that he isn't, as believed, dead, but alive and well. I bumped into him recently in LA where he paints quietly in the valley, has a lovely wife and babies, and decided to confide in me as to why his behaviour on *Ryan's Daughter* (his last film) was so bizarre.

While pulling his chair closer he whispered, 'Just previous to shooting in Ireland, I was having the kind of relationship in Rome that only dreams are made of.'

'So?' There was nothing he could tell me that could possibly excuse his behaviour.

'I fell so deeply in love that I just couldn't see straight.'

'So?'

'We were going to meet up after filming was over and live happily ever after.'

'So?' I still wasn't impressed.

'Her name was Sharon Tate.' And then he added, nervously perusing the room with a potent paranoia, 'It *is* true that Polanski can't return to these shores, isn't it? If he can, I'm a dead man.' Make of it what you will. He gave me permission to use it in the book. (I only hope I don't end up a dead woman!)

CHAPTER FORTY-SEVEN

MITCHUM'S BIRTHDAY PARTY, in August 1969, had strict door control, the lesson of my own gate-crashed party and the Irish bush telegraph having been taken to heart. Dorothy Mitchum flew over from LA, and my brother Chuzzer was invited along, too. Chuzzer had come over to visit bits of Ireland that had already stolen his heart for he had previously spent a year in Cork, working for Daddy's company, and had fond memories of the surrounding area. On this trip he met a new friend of mine, a wonderfully colourful six-foot blonde artist, Maria Simmons Gooding, who lived in a romantic stone cottage in Dunquin, across from the Blaskets. A fine angular thoroughbred was Maria if ever there was one and she and Chuzz became good friends (still are). Many years later when Fungie the dolphin arrived in the bay, with a commercial pulling power that swiftly put Dingle back on the map, Maria (whose paintings fetched thousands of pounds by this time) laid down her tools, put on her wet suit and for two years swam with Fungie. Their love made them inseparable until one day in she plunged to be with that same love and he elbowed her. Yes. Fungie told her to get lost, for a harem of lady dolphins had miraculously swum into town. Poor Maria is still pining.

It was the one party I remember Chuzzer attending, and I think he only came because Robert and I gave him such a hard time. Dorothy met the three of us at the door.

I had grown fond of Dorothy: she had a knowingness in her great brown eyes, which I suspected held the secret to taming Mitchum.

Mary Hayley Bell was there too, cuddling an inflatable man-size Playboy doll. Its tactile squashiness was so alien that, like Mary, I could have spent all night fingering it too. Alas, I never got the chance because the last time I saw Mary she was hauling the great doll upstairs. The mind boggles!

Most guests became more and more *non compos mentis*, as the evening wore on, but Chuzzer was sober, standing in the hallway with his asthma inhaler, breathing with difficulty. I was concerned that we should leave, as soon as Robert had finished his game of darts in the back room with Trevor and Johnnie. They were firmly stuck into a serious needle match.

'Can you hang in a little longer?'

'Don't worry about me, I'm fine.' Chuzzer was always fine – he never complained. The odd thing I'd noticed as we arrived was that he towered almost two inches above Mitchum, yet it was Mitchum who gave the impression of being the giant.

While dancing with Mitchum in the front room we heard shouting from the darts room so we went to investigate.

'Go home, then! Take the fucking plane home, you bitch!'

Whenever Trevor was smashed and Helen threatened to leave, he made every wrong effort to prevent her.

'You'd better stay here, you old cow, or—'

It was always the same story with the same ending, Helen going home alone. Patiently she put her beloved black poodle, Matthew, on the leash, said goodbye and left. What a saint-like woman she was! She never held any of his bad behaviour against him, she just didn't want to be part of it, and who could blame her?

With the temperature in the darts room going down a little, Mitchum and I went back to dance. I loved to dance more than anything, and hadn't really done so since my early days with Willy Fox at the Royal Court Theatre Club. Mitchum wasn't half bad at it either. After a few minutes I noticed Chuzzer trying to get my attention but since I didn't think it was anything urgent I kept on dancing. Gradually, though, he became more persistent.

'E-E-Excuse m-me, S-Sarah,' said Chuzzer, with the family's stammer, as well as its manners.

'What is it, Chuzzer?'

'Help yourself to anything you want,' said Mitchum, still dancing and singing to Roger Miller's 'In the Summer Time'. I defy any woman not to feel good dancing with Mitch.

'E-E-Excuse m-me S-S-Sarah,' said Chuzzer patiently for the third time, taking an almighty swig from his inhaler.

'What is that weird contraption?' asked Mitchum, somewhat pissed off at being forced to stop dancing. Chuzzer's large inhaler had a black handle and a glass bulbous top with a funnel, giving it a rather exotic flavour, similar to a hubble-bubble. 'Does it get you high?'

Chuzzer ignored this question; he wasn't in the mood for small talk, obviously. 'A lady has f-f-fallen th-through th-th-the door.'

We pushed past into the hallway, and there was Helen Cherry lying flat on her face, unconscious, with blood oozing from her skull. Not a palatable sight.

'Why didn't you say something?'

That didn't go down too well with Chuzzer. None the less it did seem terribly odd.

'How could she possibly just fall in through the door?'

'I heard a fumbling with the latch so I opened it and she simply f-f-fell in, f-f-f-flat.'

As I turned her over, she awoke and said in a strange drawl, 'Where's Matthew?'

I ran to get a cold cloth from the kitchen.

'Don't worry about Matthew right now, honey, you're badly hurt,' said a perturbed Mitch.

'I want Matthew! I want my Matthew!'

As I blotted the blood on her matted hair, she flinched and tried to get up but a pain in her lower back prevented her.

'I want Matthew! I want my Matthew!'

'What happened?' asked Robert.

'I forgot your hotel was so close to the cliff top.'

'You fell off the top of the cliff?' We all knew about the danger of Mitchum's hotel being so close to the edge. There was a plunge of about twenty feet to the jagged rocks below. Helen, obviously being a bit miffed with Trevor, had grabbed Matthew and in the darkness lost all sense of direction, walking straight ahead without thinking.

'Call the ambulance immediately,' ordered Robert.

'I'll go and find Matthew.' Two hours later I did and I took him along to the hospital.

It turned out that Helen was badly hurt. Not only from a cracked skull but a broken coccyx as well. Only those who have damaged their spine in this way can know the pain poor Helen had to endure.

One morning early in the slippery rain Christopher Jones asked his stand-in to go for a spin with him in his Ferrari. His stand-in was a little hung over and declined, so Chris went alone. On one of the hairpin bends outside Dingle he didn't attempt to make the turn and went straight on over a stone wall, tumbling over and over three times, and coming to rest a few feet from the cliff top. The Ferrari was a write-off. Its top was crushed inwards, and all four sides were so hideously buckled that had his stand-in, being of normal height, accepted the offer of a spin, he would have been killed outright. Chris, being a midget, came out alive, but I don't think he was too happy about that. We all know that to become a legend you have to be either killed or kill yourself, but poor doomed Christopher hadn't counted on being so small.

So proud was he of the accident that he inveigled the stills man into coming out immediately afterwards and taking pictures of the accident. He had them blown up and stuck around the walls of his caravan. One day when he wasn't called to work, I crept in to have a peek. The macabre quality of the display reminded me of *Blow-Up*, with signs of mad recklessness – if not attempted suicide – apparent in many of the photos. Because of the rain the skidmarks were still clearly visible, and his failure even to attempt the hairpin bend puzzled me. I believe the episode was a grotesque plea for help that went unheeded. His performance in the final film had an extraordinary quality to it, a rarity which deserved nurturing. But had David taken the time to talk through Chris's troubles with him, he would probably never have got him to perform at all. The bluebell woods were proof of that. Like the Ferrari's skidmarks, Chris and David's attitude to one another showed no sign of them having tried to straighten it out. We actors could see the skidmarks, but were powerless to help, being forbidden past the guards at the caravan – until Mother arrived.

Mother being Mother wanted to have a natter with all the actors, and because she was so queenly by nature, everyone enjoyed her company enormously. When she put herself out to enchant, it was as if the Irish sun had suddenly burst forth. That first day she spent about an hour in each actor's caravan, giving them moral support (which, incidentally, we all craved by now). She returned to my caravan, having been with Trevor.

'He hasn't changed since Celia Johnson and *Brief Encounter*. He's a real rascal, that one.' Helen was back in London having treatment on her coccyx.

When Mother began advancing towards Chris's caravan, I intervened. 'Not in there, Ma.'

'Why ever not?'

'It's forbidden territory.'

'What nonsense!' She made her way directly towards his caravan with her head held high and stubborn.

I became nervous, not wanting any conflict with those two managers. I pulled her away. 'Mother, it's strictly out of bounds, is that clear?'

Lady Caroline dressed up as
a topless blackamoor in order
to win back Byron.

Above: Lady Caroline Lamb.

Left: Robert, the director, asking Lionel if he has enough props.

Lionel playing the Iron Duke. How good it was to have his grey chest hairs sprouting back once more. I missed them when he shaved them off for *Othello*.

Right: Shortly after Tomcat asked Lionel, 'Why are you wearing a wooden nose?'

Below: The only shot I can find of Lionel being himself.

Reunion.

Robert and me trying to make a go
of it again, but because of public pressure
it became impossible.

Saying goodbye to the Old Mill House, this idyllic fairyland on its own Fairy Island,
was hard – very hard – but it Served me Right.

She brushed me aside like the little girl I still was and knocked on the door. As it opened I saw both Rudy and Stuart eyeing her up and down. Mother's naturally gracious demeanour stopped these two LA bruisers dead in their tracks. 'Hello,' she said politely. 'I've come to have a word with Christopher Jones.' She delivered this line in the dignified knowledge that her wish would be granted.

'Leave us please, guys. I'll be fine,' I heard Chris say to Rudy and Stuart. We all filed out as Mother achieved the unthinkable; to be all alone with Christopher Jones in his caravan. Would she reappear in one piece?

Roughly three-quarters of an hour later from my caravan window I saw her emerge with Christopher. He was holding her firmly by the hand and together they marched into David's caravan. As usual we weren't shooting because of the rain. No one dared to imagine what would happen if it kept up much longer. Without a miracle another year in Dingle was a certainty. Also, the film needed a storm sequence and the main reason we chose that location was because of the sure-fire regularity of the storms. Yet that year had been a freak. The first for a century in which there had been no storm, so the Dublin Meteorological Office had told us, and we all knew how reliable they were!

Once Mother and Chris had returned to Chris's caravan clasping one another like long-lost lovers, I ventured in to talk to David, intrigued to find out what the hell was going on. David looked up, giving me his usual disgruntled glare. 'Chris says I'm bullying him, so he won't work unless Mrs Miles is there at all times.'

I laughed. It was a funny situation; my mother playing nanny to Christopher Jones – not exactly type-casting! But Chris got his way for the whole week until Mother began visibly to dwindle, having bitten off more than she could chew, what with filming being as tedious as watching paint dry.

Finally she plucked up courage to say to Chris, 'I'm afraid

I have to return to England, my husband needs me, too.'
Chris wasn't too happy, but Mother held firm. Once she had
left, Chris deteriorated once again, back to refusing to allow
any member of the company to enter his caravan. What a
nightmare it was, on top of which autumn would soon be
winter again, and I wasn't growing any wiser.

CHAPTER FORTY-EIGHT

OVER AT MITCHUM'S one evening, with him as usual all aproned up ready to cook dinner, I found myself alone in the kitchen. Never before had I seen live lobsters in water. They were both staring at me from their glass containers. Have you ever looked a lobster straight in the eye? Don't, if you intend to eat it the same night. It was so clear, the good-humoured curiosity shining out from their don-like pupils, that I had no choice but to return them to the sea. My strenuous journey across a quarter of a mile of slippery rocks took me only part of the way, for once in the sea I waded out another two hundred yards. The lobsters were bloody heavy and because of the tides I had to put them far enough out to sea, otherwise they'd get washed up and die a much worse death than Mitch had in store for them. They gave each other a smug little sideways glance as I released them as if to say, 'Our plan worked out perfectly.' Watching them fumbling their way to freedom downward towards the sea-bed felt good. So good that it stirred in me the strength to meet the punishment that I knew would be in store.

What I hadn't bargained for was the enormity of Mitchum's rage. I knew we were friends and that a couple of lobsters couldn't break the bond that had grown between us. None the less I certainly wasn't expecting the tirade I received.

'What the fuck am I going to give everyone tonight?'

'I'll go to the butcher and see if he'll open up for me.' I was willing to do anything to make amends.

Mitchum came up, looking me straight in the eyes just like I had, so fatally, with the lobsters. His eyes were cold, so cold that shivers of dread went through me. 'I'll get you for this one day, Miles. Yes, one day you'll pay for this. So beware.'

I know it was both wrong and stupid to do what I did that evening. I'd been so left-footed by the lobsters' unexpectedly hip brown eyes that I'd failed to look ahead to the consequences. Yet the question I often ask myself is this, Did I deserve the punishment I received seven years later? For Mitchum told a bunch of press guys that I drank my own pee. The story ran in enough British newspapers for journalists to contact me to hear it from the horse's mouth. I didn't think to deny it. Yet again, I failed to look ahead to the consequences. How could I deny it and spend the rest of my life living out a daily lie? Drinking your own pee is one of the most harmless, and some would say beneficial of daily activities. I don't drink alcohol (it doesn't make me feel good), I don't take drugs, I don't eat red meat, neither do I drink anything much other than water, so my pee is pretty pure. How could such a private, innocent act bring such judgemental alienation upon my head?

'Sarah Miles/actress/urine drinker.' On and on it goes, never ceasing long enough for the media to look at *why* I drink it. I don't judge others for deteriorating intellectually in a sea of alcohol. Get wise and learn *why* science has finally proven why one's own urine is so beneficial. Find out *why* those who drank their urine survived in Auschwitz. Start learning about ancient medicines, and *why* the yogis of India have been drinking it for centuries, Gandhi and Nehru too. Get hip and find out *why* it immunizes you against your own allergies. Discover *why* it's so beneficial in the treating of cancer. Start pointing the finger inwards, to ask *why* your own pee repulses you so profoundly. But did my crime with Mitchum's lobsters merit the punishment? Sixteen years of alienation and bad press, and I still have to suffer for those two lobsters. The strange part is, I'd probably go and save them all over again.

*

A local table-tennis tournament was advertised at the front of the Dingle village hall. I was passionate about table tennis, and having played all my life I felt sufficiently competent to give any pro, let alone a few keen amateurs, a good run for their money. I put my name down, as did the rest of the actors, the crew and most of Dingle.

During my stay in Dingle I'd become acquainted with a little chap with a club foot who was an exact replica of Johnnie Mills's character, Michael, in the film, and when I was asked who I'd fancy taking on in the first round, I decided on him, guaranteeing, I thought, my place in the second. Stephen Potter, author of the book *Oneupmanship and Gamesmanship*, wasn't a family friend for nothing.

Entering the hall I was startled by the turn-out. The little chap and I shook hands and said hello before he hobbled over to his side of the net. The umpire said, 'Are you both ready?'

'Yes,' we replied in unison, and off we went.

He was a real sweetheart, so brave, I thought during the knock-up. He kept hobbling and smiling benignly all through. I noticed during the match itself that his game went up a few notches when he realized my standard wasn't too low. In no time I found myself well up on my toes. Finally it became necessary to do a few dirty shots, forcing him to leap from side to side on his club foot. But the more I humiliated him, the more he rose to the occasion. If I fooled him with a sneaky net shot he was on to it like a bleedin' vampire bat!

Strike a light and shiver me timbers! The little chap slaughtered me – annihilated me with no effort whatsoever. I left the hall with my tail well between my legs, not because I'd lost but because I'd been publicly humiliated, having foolishly chosen what I thought was a pushover. I can't explain the relief I felt when he finally won the tournament, turning out to be the two to one favourite *and* Southern

Counties' ex-champion. Outward appearances are no way to judge anyone or anything.

At the Skelleg hotel one afternoon, David Lean was giving me some bad news. Because there had been such relentless rain all year, yet still no storm, I was going to have to spend Christmas out there in Dingle all alone with the second unit. Under ordinary circumstances I might have had some compassion for his predicament, but I felt both used and abused. I had been called six days a week for a whole year, come rain or shine, hanging about the production office or my caravan waiting for David to show up. (He was rarely seen before eleven a.m.) On *Ryan's Daughter* I probably ended up earning less money than the Irish extras, all of whom were on a daily rate, as well as the rest of the actors, who were well into overage. I'd accepted a paltry lump sum for what I'd thought would be three months' work. Normally I would have stuck in my heels and fought for a better deal, but this time I'd felt disinclined, being the writer's wife. Ruining my Christmas, not seeing my horses, and sitting all alone with the second unit on a sodden Irish hillside was too hard to come to terms with.

'No, I won't,' I said firmly.

David, walking towards the stairs to go down to the lobby, responded with his usual challenging secret smirk, the one he always gave when I dug in my heels. 'You do what I say.'

'Why should I when you rarely show up for work till the day's nearly done?'

'You will stay out here with the second unit.' He was standing proud and ruthless, right at the top of the landing, so I pushed him straight down the stairs. I couldn't have killed him, even if I'd wanted to, because the stairs ended in another landing – and, besides, I still had a soft spot for the fellah. As he hauled himself up from the shock of it and brushed himself down he gave me a funny look as if to say, well done, old thing, before walking down the rest of the stairs with his head held high. The next thing I knew was that the whole film unit was going to South Africa, to Cape Town, after Christmas for six weeks, to finish off the beach scenes. I was pleased as punch. We had to return to Ireland for the storm sequence, but at least Christmas was secure. South Africa turned out to be a stroke of genius. Eddie Fowley came up trumps again, and miraculously not a seam can be seen between the beaches of Ireland and those of South Africa. Of course, the real miracle was throwing David down that staircase. Without that we'd never have gone to South Africa and therefore probably never finished the film.

While we were in Cape Town, a black photographer helped me across a sand dune. A police officer approached us and told me I had to go down to the police station, because holding hands with blacks was illegal. I insisted he first came over to meet the famous director David Lean. Fortunately he'd heard of David, who somehow managed to swing it for me.

Altogether poor David wasn't too pleased with me. Within three weeks I'd had my car blow up on my driver and me, and been almost caught in a secret meeting with the black sympathizer Big Ben Decker. I had got lost in the famous District Six, ending up with severe sunstroke. David thought I was exaggerating when I explained that I always puff up like a balloon in extreme heat. 'Just get out there and shoot the scene please,' he said. Next day, 'What the hell's the matter with your face?' It couldn't be shot for three days. I think David and I ended up testing each other something chronic.

CHAPTER FORTY-NINE

B ACK HOME I was in seventh heaven. My stud farm was mushrooming like Mitchum's pot plant, with welcoming signs of its rampant blossoming scattered throughout the meadows. I could hardly boast of it being a money spinner. It was more a standing-under-a-cold-shower-tearing-up-fifty-pound-notes affair. Nevertheless, my dream of breeding heavyweight palomino hunters, rarely seen in England, was at last a reality. I had a beautiful girl called Jacky to work with me, and her husband helped with the cars and garden. We had quite a number of brood mares at livery for servicing, and Roundhills Golden Cavalier was proving a worthy stallion. I preferred doing most of the covering with the mare in hand, because I could keep an eye on which mares hadn't been serviced yet.

One afternoon a visiting mare came into season. It was essential to get her serviced as soon as possible because, like humans, each mare's seasons are a different length. That day, there was no one to help me so with great trepidation I went and knocked on Robert's study door. 'Come in,' he grunted. He listened to my plea while puffing nervously on his pipe. 'What do I have to do, then?'

'Just stand in the stableyard with the mare's halter rope in your hand while I bring out Cavalier and cover her.'

'What d'you mean?'

'Hold the mare's rope while he mounts her.'

'What if she doesn't fancy him and makes a run for it?'

'She's in season, and horny as hell.'

He looked most doubtful, but reluctantly followed me, pipe in hand, to the stableyard.

He stood there nervously, holding the mare as far away

from his body as he could. She was rubbing her upper thighs together, making all as it should be, creamy and moist, ready for entry.

'Bring him out and let's get on with it.'

I opened his stall and Cavalier came snorting out from his loose box, head held high, muscles flexed, pawing the stable-yard with excitement. What a fine sight he was, flouncing and pouncing, head wild and wired for a baser hunger as he reared up whinnying into the fresh spring leaves of the chestnut tree. At once his gaze became businesslike as it fixed on the mare. At that moment Robert turned round, so shocked at the sight of this monster rearing up behind him that he dropped his pipe. As he was reaching over to pick it up, the mare danced sideways. Cavalier took his eye off her for a split second and came down all over Robert.

The sight of Robert Bolt, the distinguished and erudite schoolmaster/playwright, submerged in the lust of my stallion was a sight to cherish for the rest of my days. 'Get this fucking stallion off my back!' he cried from underneath Cavalier's belly.

I hauled him off as carefully as I could. Miraculously Robert wasn't hurt, in fact he took it like he took everything – in his stride with great humour.

'My bloody pipe's gone out.'

When he had sufficiently recovered, he suggested we go again and this time all four of us were successful.

Driving to London airport with all five dogs to meet a friend, I parked the Land-rover right outside Terminal One for the few seconds it took me to race in and get my passenger. On returning to the Land-rover I counted only four dogs. Gulliver had obviously jumped out of the small slit I'd left in the window for air.

I hunted for that wretched dog day and night all over five

square miles of soul-destroyingly bleak airport property. Eventually every policeman over a twenty-mile radius knew Gulliver's precise colouring, even to his birthmark on his left ear. Police everywhere began running when they saw me coming, for I was boring them to death with my repeated description of this stupid little Yorkshire terrier.

'He'll be shot if he goes on to the landing apron,' warned the airport police. 'Call it a day, Sarah, he's a goner.' The more they all tried to get rid of me the more I hung in there. If he was dead, surely he'd be reported dead. No, I knew he wasn't dead, but where was he? Coming home weeping each evening, I'd stop off at every police station along the way.

'Please, Miss Miles, if your Yorkie is handed in, we'll notify you immediately.'

One night ten days later, while beginning to think someone had taken him and kept him, as we were entering Staines police station yet again, Addo and Betty heard something and began to yelp. Addo and Gulliver were best friends, the Laurel and Hardy of the dog world, and on this particular night Addo was in a state. I stopped the car and went into the police station. The regular copper was at the desk. He looked up, and gave a sigh. 'Yes, Miss Miles, we know all about your missing Yorkie.' He was most patronizing as he flipped through some paperwork and pulled out the full details. 'If he turns up, you'll be the first to hear.'

On the way out, Addo went wild. I let him pull me round to the back of the police station and there was a whining Gulliver, skinny as a rat, tied to a post. We both ran towards him. Poor Gulliver was too much in a state of shock to be fully aware of what was going on. As I untied him, 'Is that your dog, ma'am?' Another policeman was standing there.

'Yes. How long has he been here?'

'Three days. You can count yourself lucky. He was off to

356

Battersea Dogs' Home in the morning.' It's a shame the police are so overworked.

We had other mating problems. Betty, the miniature Staffordshire bull terrier, had come into season. This was a frustrating business, for Gulliver was too small to do any damage and Addo was too large. None the less I allowed them both a turn at trying. Betty loved the attention and flirted outrageously. The only thing to be careful of was that Addo be kept well away when it was Gulliver's go. Gulliver, although recovered sufficiently from the airport trauma to go in and bat with Betty, was still a little delicate. When it was his turn to attempt the ultimate pleasure, I locked them in the house, and asked everyone not to let Addo in under any circumstances. Besides, having them both enclosed in the house might give Gulliver the necessary height to do it from the sofa. We all agreed that if he made it, the cross-bred puppies would be a delight.

While I was grooming Cavalier in the stableyard, however, I looked up to find Addo making a bee-line for the open front door. I rushed after him into the sitting room, and saw him career over to Gulliver snarling and growling. Gulliver, upon realizing that he was about to be eaten by a massive, devilish dragon, promptly died of a heart attack. Addo hadn't had any intention of killing him. He hadn't even touched him, for they were, after all, best buddies. It was one of the saddest animal moments I have witnessed, to see Addo pawing Gulliver's limp body so gently, whining and sniffing as it dawned on him that Gulliver, his partner in crime, had gone to pastures new. Meanwhile Betty, still hot with yearning, was right there beside him. Had Addo's grief overcome and dispersed his lust? The two of them were still wanting it, still smelling it, yet too overwhelmed to give it a thought. That's not mere animal instinct – that's love.

The boat that Robert was making with so much care in the bottom part of the mill was coming on in leaps and bounds. I was astounded that he knew so much about boat building. Whenever I asked him where he'd learnt the knack of moulding and honing such a streamlined professional shape, he shrugged it off as if anyone could do it. When the boat was just about completed, Tomcat, who was now three and a half, came plodding into the mill, eyeing the boat thoughtfully before turning to look at the door. 'Daddy, how you get in on to de river?'

'Through that door, Tomcat,' pointing in a businesslike fashion.

Tomcat, equally businesslike, shook his head sadly, like some old sage. 'No good, Daddy.' Both Robert and I had failed to notice over the past two years that the boat had expanded beyond the size of the exit. The mill being a listed building prevented us from extending the aperture, so Robert's lovingly constructed boat was doomed never to see the light. Eventually he sold the house with it still denied its maiden voyage. Perhaps it's still there inside the mill's dark depths. If only we'd checked with Tomcat earlier.

Tomcat's first little white pony, Yorick, had turned out such a bundle of wilfulness that I found Thunder, a buxom little grey, for him instead – alas, poor Yorick. Tina, his nanny, thought it would be fun to enter him for his first show, in the leading-rein class. It would be only for fun, since Tomcat's little legs had difficulty encompassing much of Thunder's massive belly. But the effect on the day was enchanting. About twelve tiny toddlers, all looking like real professionals, entered the event, so we stood not a chance in hell of a rosette.

'I want a rosette, Mummy,' demanded Tomcat from beneath his new black velvet riding hat. 'I want a red one, *please.*' (His new word, making it, 'Gun, *please*, gun, *please*, gun, *please.*')

'Don't think about rosettes, Tomcat, just enjoy the event.'

'No way,' accompanied by an arm gesture going straight across his body, slowly, just like Mitch. 'I want a red rosette.' As luck would have it we were pulled in eleventh rather than twelfth and stood there in line waiting for our turn. Tomcat checked up and down the line with a wary look on his face. Although only three years old, I think Tomcat knew the difference between first and last, but I wasn't about to draw attention to it.

'You're sitting up very straight today, Tomcat, well done.'

He wasn't wearing it.

'No way! I want a red rosette.'

'All's not lost, yet. Just concentrate and do your best when it's your turn.' It was true, for we might be brought up a few places if Tomcat managed Thunder well in the individual display. I noticed Tomcat sizing up the judge, a benevolent grey-haired lady, talking to the little girl next to us.

'What do I say?'

'Whatever you like, darling.' At that moment the judge came over.

'Your pony likes his grass!' she said, patting Thunder's enormous belly.

Tomcat ignored this, and responded with deft sincerity. 'You've got beautiful blue eyes.' This sentence came out quite naturally – so it should, having been thrown at Tomcat enough times. Luckily her eyes *were* blue.

'Well, well, well. No one has ever commented on my eyes before.'

Tomcat went on, 'My Daddy's got blue ones, but yours are more bluer.' After doing a passable trotting and cantering display he threw her his ultimate winning smile, which promptly put him up to fourth place and a yellow rosette.

Had Tomcat been corrupted already? I don't think I have consciously flattered anyone to get what I wanted – my problem had always been the opposite. I always managed to say the wrong thing at the wrong time. Tomcat taught me a few lessons that day.

Johnnie Windeatt had been living in Hasker Street for well over a year. One weekend in the sunny spring of 1971 he came down to visit us in a Rolls-Royce. Even Fellini would have elbowed the apparition that swung up our drive that Sunday as being too ostentatiously incongruous to suspend disbelief. Johnnie was driving, but it could have been Beethoven at the wheel as we could see only their two heads. Beside this white two-headed monster sat a little silver-haired lady with a bun. She was wearing a floral cotton dress and looked as if she had recently stepped out of an old-English-style country cream commercial. In the back seat were three degenerate-looking young dandies with hair dyed all the colours of the rainbow. Had you seen them in a Soho hairdressing salon you might have wondered which planet they were from, but here in the countryside one simply marvelled.

'Hello,' said a dazzlingly healthy and streamlined Johnnie, who was growing more like Cary Grant by the week. Addo and Beethoven greeted each other as long-lost lovers.

'This is my mother.' I was drawn to her open sweetness, and that she seemed oblivious of being surrounded by these exceptionally colourful pansies.

After the introductions were completed the young bucks draped themselves over the purple Rolls, passing Tomcat to and fro so caringly, as if he were made of eggshell. During this bizarre spectacle, Johnnie's mother stepped forward suddenly and stole Tomcat, skipping away with him down towards the swing within the cedar trees. The rest of us went into the conservatory for tea and crumpets. Johnnie was pleased with his landscape-gardening commission on Mount Etna, which had apparently matured beautifully, like Johnnie himself. How emphatically mysterious he was; never a dark thought, as though blessed, like my brother Chuzzer, with an ability to replace the sun itself. Like Chuzzer again, Johnnie never volunteered a speck of information on his private life. I wasn't sure whether he was still working for his millionaire, so when we were alone in the conservatory, I jokingly inquired how the pimping was going.

He flashed me a dirty look. 'I told you I gave all that up before I went to Mount Etna.' He came over to me. I was watching Addo chase Johnnie's mother's feet as she sat on the swing with Tomcat. The cedar's great canopy encapsulated the timelessness of the moment to perfection.

'I love you, Sarah. But then you know that.'

I wasn't sure what kind of love this was, so I kept silent.

'I feel uncontaminated around you somehow.'

'I hope it's a love that I'm able to reciprocate, Johnnie, because I'm a happily married woman,' piped I a trifle pompously.

He was such a one, was Johnnie. Impossible to know how he would respond if I allowed him to demonstrate this love of his.

'My mother is my whole world now.' What was it about Johnnie? Why did everyone want to mother him, when he looked so strong and healthy? Saying goodbye on the door-step, later that spring afternoon, I had to stop myself from sliding my fingers through his thick dark brown hair and brushing it away from his eyes. It was a shame, because if it hadn't been for his previous declaration of love I would have finished the gesture. Such were the feelings that Johnnie brought out in one.

'You always manage to look so spruce,' I said limply, deciding to clear the hair from his eyes anyway.

'Don't tease me, it's too cruel,' he replied, backing away into his three rainbowed musketeers.

'I'd like to see him a little plumper,' said his proud pigeon-plump Cornish mum.

Waving goodbye to the purple Rolls as it floated down the drive, Robert said, 'Has he ever paid you any rent?'

'Not yet. Why?'

'I think it's been long enough to warrant an explanation, don't you?' As usual Robert was right. Johnnie hadn't mentioned money for well over a year and the agreement was on a monthly basis.

'Is that his Rolls?' Robert asked as we were walking down the drive in their wake, for a needle match on the croquet lawn.

'He said it was.'

'So he can't be short of a few bob.'

Nevertheless, I didn't want to be the one to ask for the money; money and I had a problem. 'Will you ask him for it, Robert?'

'No, you must. It's your house. I did your dirty work last time in asking Nona to leave.' That was true. And look what happened to Nona.

'I'll go to London and ask him next week.' And that was that.

Johnnie was so generous and caring in Hasker Street the following Wednesday, and even better, the house was gleaming, as, indeed, was Johnnie himself. He'd bought new curtains, and an antique circular pine dining-room table, with four beautifully carved pine armchairs, transforming Nona's quarters into a man-about-town's sophisticated den. 'I needed a dining room to equal my gourmet food.' He was renowned for his French cuisine, was Johnnie.

'Why don't you become a chef?'

'I easily might, if all else fails.'

'What is "all else", Johnnie?'

He hesitated. 'Just to be with you sometimes.'

Lionel's warnings pealed within. 'Beware they don't vampire your light.'

Being cowardly I refrained from puncturing Johnnie's need to be with me. Why couldn't we remain as we were? I thought I'd hold back asking him for rent until later in Hyde Park.

'I miss our walks together, Smiles, more than you could imagine.'

'I miss you and Beethoven, too.' I found myself meaning it. 'You should open a restaurant in Byfleet.' In the park we walked under the Serpentine bridge, then on to where we first met, in the Kensington Garden fountains, before I blurted out, 'Johnnie, could I have some rent, it's been over a year?'

He jumped in, cool as a cucumber. 'Say no more. I'll bring it all down this coming weekend.'

'You don't have to bring it *all* down, just some of it to keep the peace.'

'I never like having debts hanging over me and it isn't as though I'm broke.'

'Thanks, Johnnie, we would appreciate it.' We had a nostalgic walk round Hyde Park, touching on various trees and landmarks that were familiar. Saying goodbye to Johnnie I couldn't help wondering how I'd ever managed to live in London for such a long while.

'Think about chef-ing in the country, Johnnie. Imagine how overjoyed your mother, Addo, Beethoven – we all would be.'

'I'll think about it, I promise,' he said, waving to Addo in the back of the Land-rover.

Two mornings later, I received a phone call from the Chelsea police station.

'Is that Sarah Miles of 18 Hasker Street?'

'Yes, speaking.'

'Do you know a Mr John Windeatt?'

'Yes, I do know him. He's living in my house.'

'Last night he committed suicide in your house by placing his head in your gas oven.'

I wasn't sure whether I was being had or not. 'I beg your pardon?'

'I'm afraid he's dead, has been for twelve hours.' I immediately thought of that millionaire, those strange boys. His dark secrets had surfaced, all right.

'You say it was suicide?'

'No doubt, I'm afraid.'

I slumped on to my bed as familiar globules of hysteria welled up from my gut. I was being forced to look at why two people very close to me had chosen death rather than life. Lionel's warnings shrouded over me, 'Beware they don't vampire your light,' piercing me with inklings that there was no light in me at all, only darkness that drew death towards it like Mitchum drew violence. I was indeed bad news. Again, you see, I was using guilt to block out the reality of death – lust, too, is convenient for the same purpose. I saw death then as something quite unthinkable and, thank God, it was never going to happen to me. I chose not to enter into the darker side of my Johnnie, to find out what, in that foul underworld of his, had forced him to such an end. All I was aware of was that I had lost a genuinely unique and mysterious friend. If I hadn't gone to London asking him for rent money, would he still be here now?

A few months later a friend of my brother Chris from Paris stayed in Hasker Street for a while. This chap, who put up some of the financing for *The Virgin and the Gypsy*, knew nothing of the history of the house, yet later Chris told me a story that made my hair stand on end. This fellow didn't feel at all comfortable staying there, but couldn't put his finger on why. Night after night he tossed and turned in bed, thinking he was hearing clocks ticking and banging noises coming from the kitchen. One night the banging noises were so real that he took courage in both hand and went down to investigate. In the kitchen all the pipes and the main flue had been neatly dismantled from the walls and placed in a pile in the middle of the room. On hearing this story I was filled with a great sadness, which was strange because at that time I hadn't experienced any supernatural goings-on myself and didn't believe the incident took place. Yet I wondered . . .

I thought it was perhaps time to sell Hasker Street, but Robert said, 'Wait a while, because you may have a long West End run on your hands.'

CHAPTER FIFTY

ROBERT HAD WRITTEN a new play during our stint in Ireland. It was a Tudor piece, *Vivat! Vivat Regina!*, a play about Elizabeth I and Mary, Queen of Scots. He came galloping into the drawing room one afternoon, well out of his mind as he surrendered to triumphal oblivion.

'I've finished it! I've finished it! Listen!' He sat me down, put on the tape machine and for three hours I listened to a most enlightening experience. I'd often heard David Lean swearing that on *Lawrence of Arabia* he could never have got those performances out of the actors in the desert if it hadn't been for Robert's tape of the whole script, with Robert playing all the characters himself.

Peter O'Toole told me once, 'David wasn't good at getting performances out of the actors, but I felt safe knowing I could always nip into David's caravan and find out what Robert meant when he originally conceived it. His interpretation was continually helpful because it made complete sense.'

Sitting there listening to his instinctive acting ability – a side of him I'd never known he possessed – was disconcerting. 'You should go round England, just you alone, playing all the characters.' I put my nose rather far in the air as I uttered this remark. Was I jealous of his amazing talent for acting? It wasn't *that* so much as a nagging feeling that anyone could act. Acting to my mind was not an art but a craft. That's why Olivier was so tremendous at it, having craftily honed it. He also felt the same way. 'Acting is a minor art form, if indeed it's an art form at all,' he once told me. Robert's tape that day was living proof of this.

'I'm a terrible actor, but I write lines to be said in a certain way. If the inflection is wrong the sense is meaningless.'

I listened to the tape over and over again.

What fascinated Robert about these two formidable women was that they remained obsessed with one another, each keeping a miniature of the other's image hidden around her neck, while they never actually met. Binkie Beaumont decided to put *Vivat! Vivat Regina!* into the Chichester Festival for the summer and, if it was a success there, transfer it to the West End. I knew from day one that Mary, Queen of Scots, even in Robert's talented hands, would remain the mysterious, shadowy, romantic figure that we stubbornly perceive throughout the history books – and the director was no help to me either. At that time Antonia Fraser had just published her fat biography of Mary. I read it enthusiastically, trying to find something the least bit revealing about the woman I was playing; something I could use to my advantage rather than the hopeless Catholic victim that I was tired of reading about. Antonia Fraser's account threw up no such revelation, alas. Nowhere was I going to get true insight, nowhere was I to find the real 'other side' of this brilliantly astute, true-grit-tough, uncompromisingly ambitious and profoundly feminine Mary, Queen of Scots. Our director had not the slightest comprehension of womanliness, or the powers that lay therein so if I was in need of enlightenment into the darks, lights and shades of what made up the magical Mary, I could whistle for it. On top of which I was the writer's wife and therefore, like Mary, doomed.

During the stint at Chichester I found myself so distressed that I wanted to jack the whole thing in. I could find no footholes into my character, whereas the playwright's Elizabeth was a different matter altogether. I dreaded going into the West End with this unromantic, pedestrian production. Robert got an obvious kick from seeing the woman he loved interpreting his work. (He's been a faithful fan.) But I believe he wrote the play for love of *me* rather than from admiration, or indeed respect, for Mary. He was in love with the character of Elizabeth. Who could blame him? She was, after all, one of the greatest characters, man or woman, of all time. It was Elizabeth who got his creative juices flowing and therefore she who got the best scenes and the wittiest lines.

'Was it sour grapes on my part?' I asked Robert.

'I wrote Elizabeth as a witty, intelligent man.'

'And me? Mary?'

'Oh, Mary represents the heart of womanhood.' Perhaps that was the problem. I hadn't yet experienced womanhood. It had nothing to do with his interpretation of Mary, it was solely to do with some lack in me. I began to have wrestling matches with my conscience as I tossed and turned on my pillow at night. It wasn't as if I'd asked Robert to write any of these parts for me. I hadn't. I was still merely the FO in everyone's eyes and this strayed over into how I thought of myself, which was very little. I suppose I saw myself as a fairly OK actress, ex-mistress, faithful wife, fairly OK mother, and horse breeder, aimlessly blundering down a path that perhaps didn't lead where I needed to go. Was this all part of dreams coming true? Was I in that dangerous place of limbo where some of us find ourselves prior to our first little glimmer of self-knowledge? Would I learn the lessons therein to help me reach my next step of evolution or would I fall into the eternal compromise of a lesser self?

Going into the Chichester Theatre every day and seeing huge blow-ups of Lionel didn't help my loneliness. How often I wanted to discuss the playing of Mary with him. I longed to have the input of his intuitive yet crafted wisdom. With Lionel I alway felt free of archetypal role-playing, probably because he himself didn't fit into any category, and made me aware of the abundant possibilities to be grasped within that freedom. How often he would speak of us being such free spirits, and at the time, in the safety of his quietest smile, we knew that no one could ever know us as a pair or, indeed, our secret. That face of Olivier's! Even though the blow-ups showed him as Astrov in *Uncle Vanya* and not in *Wuthering Heights*, I could still recognize the pulling power –

both public and at my soul-strings. I never dreamt of contacting him, I knew my place. Ex-mistresses have to, it's part of the job. Just as playing faithful wife is a job. I was never going to damage my marriage. Never.

Two good things happened at the Chichester Theatre, both to do with dressers. I met a great big ray of sunshine called Sarah Gough – Goffie. Her sweet fresh innocence blazed forth backstage upon everyone who bumped into it, highlighting their own state of well-being. Her sunshine even warmed up little bits of my own neglected self, all a trifle frozen, and we became good friends. My own personal dresser, Frannie, suffered from a terrible illness. Hiccups. Only those who suffer from serious hiccups will understand just how life-threatening it can be. She came into my dressing room one evening weighed down as usual with the hefty costumes that Carl Thomas had designed for the production – and with even heftier hiccups. So heavy were they (the costumes, not the hiccups), the neck and wrist ruffs, huge headdress, boned corset, boned petticoat, boned bodice, three more layers of petticoat followed by dresses and jewels of such lavish accuracy, that I felt a growing admiration – and indeed compassion – for those medieval knights going to war in their cumbersome armour. Frannie was hiccuping for the third day on the trot.

'When it gets to a month of it non-stop I'll have to give in my notice, because last time I got into a state of complete exhaustion,' she said. Her hiccuping went on for days and days. Nothing would budge it. I tried her with all the old wives' remedies, being quite a hiccuper myself at one time, but to no avail; Frannie's hiccups were there to stay.

About a week later I watched her, staring out of the window towards the car park trying not to hiccup. I was afraid that she was teetering on the edge of leaving, and I didn't want that because we got on so well.

'Laurence Harvey used to come to work by helicopter. Now, that's posher than you in your chauffeur-driven Rolls,' she said, with only two hiccups that time. I was so embarrassed coming to work in Robert's Rolls (even though it was one of my dreams and the smallest, maroon soft-top sports model), but he had forbidden me to drive myself. I'd been caught speeding too often, so we sadly had to sell the Lamborghini.

As I watched poor old Frannie standing there at the window, hiccuping away with her back to me, I suddenly had a brainwave. I crept over to her and with phenomenal dexterity, slid my hands up her skirt and pulled her knickers right down to the floor. The look of shock on her face was perfect. What an unforgettable matinée that turned out for the pair of us, for it was the day her hiccups left her completely, apparently never to return. I wonder? She wrote twice, thanking me. I thanked her too in my heart because for me it was the only positive thing that happened in Chichester that summer. Thanks to Mary.

Our season at Chichester came to an end and, since we had been a success, our transfer to the West End was secured. As soon as I could, I went to talk through my unhappiness with Binkie Beaumont, whose offices were above the Globe Theatre. When I suggested that for the good of the play I should be replaced, he didn't like it. Why should he? He wasn't trying to play Mary.

'I'm not up to it. Please find someone else.' I made a note for him to work a little on his astonishment. I thought it too rehearsed.

'Your husband has written such a gift and you intend to throw it back in his face?'

'No, Binkie, I intend it to be given to some other actress better equipped to play it. There must be a cluster of well-known and equally worthy actresses, since the part is so wonderful Why not start at the top and work down?' Binkie looked me up and down, daggers gleaming, taking in my black stocking-seams.

'I've never seen you wearing black before.' It was true, I never wore black, but since playing Mary, I'd found it comforting. 'Why *are* you all dressed in black?' he asked impertinently.

How dare he? I lowered my eyes in fury. 'My mother's just died.' That stopped him in his tracks. As silence reigned I remembered lying once before about my mother being ill in hospital, when I was caught speeding, so I quickly told him the truth. 'She's not dead, but I will be if I open in the West End. Mary's killing me!'

'Robert will have to be made aware of what's going on.'

'He already is.'

'What if I can find no one to replace you?'

'Then perhaps that might mean the part needs attending to.'

Before I left he gave me a kiss. 'How's Robin Fox?' he asked sadly.

Robin had just found out he had cancer. I went to visit him at the nursing home. My arrival coincided with him receiving some X-ray results. He looked his usual impeccable self, so brave as he told me the bad news. The manner in which he did so was similar to when he asked me if I'd like to go backstage and meet Edith Piaf. I wondered how I'd react in the same situation. Little did we know then the pain that lay ahead of him. Later Edward, his eldest son, who was with Eileen Atkins at the time, took Robin over to Dr Issels' clinic in Germany. Dr Issels was accepting guinea pigs for his new treatment, the beginnings of chemotherapy. Although Robin fought like a mogul while being fried alive, his cancer was too far gone, as he'd known in the nursing home. Edward said he remained immaculate in dress and manner right up to the last – but then he would, wouldn't he?

That day Robin reminded me of Lionel – the same silk dressing gown coupled with as much grace. As I sat talking to him in the empty drawing room of an austere upper-crust nursing home, memories of Lionel's 'phone-ins' as Robin came to me. Lionel didn't half give a brilliant imitation of Robin Fox – how it had improved over the years, too, just like his tickling. No wonder *that* was so special: he put such energy and time into perfecting it. That's what I missed even more: his dedication to self-discipline. If he found he wasn't his best at something, he'd practise, practise, practise, practise until he had inspired himself upward doggedly to meet what he considered *was* his best. We all have that same 'best' within us; the difference lies in the daily application of stretching upwards. Robert reached for it, too, of that there was oodles of proof (but, alas, not in his tickling)!

Robin Fox, having done all his reaching, was finally sitting comfortably in his 'best'. Not the slightest self-pity was to be seen; his familiar elegance remained, right down to the polished lustre of his hand-made shoes. What's more, I believe the lump of ice that was forever lodged under his hand-made shirt collars had finally dissolved. The warmth of coming to know his real persona, his true self (the key to all our 'bests') had started a thaw. We knew as we kissed goodbye that it would be the last – but would it be the last I'd ever see of Lionel's superb Robin imitation? After the fare-wells, Robin tossed over to me, 'I'm still sorry you never married my Willy. But you chose an excellent second best.'

They don't make men like Robin any more, and certainly not agents. Neither do they make Binkie Beaumonts. I loved his camp cunning.

'Well, darling, I've been from Glenda and Vanessa right down the list and they all want to play Elizabeth.'

'Naturally.'

'A couple said they'd be happy to alternate, but Eileen doesn't want to, nor, I may add, does her contract state that she should.'

'Can we not do a bit of rewriting with a change of director?'

'Too late, everyone's got run-of-the-play contracts.' Binkie sat me down with all the *Spotlight* books under 'leading actresses'.

'Come on, let's go through them.'

Binkie had won, I couldn't be held responsible for just any old body playing the part of Mary – the part my husband had written from his heart with love. I was in dire need of clarification.

'Binkie, am I right about Mary? Is she unplayable?'

'Ophelia's patchily written too.'

'That wasn't my question.'

He looked a trifle uncomfortable. 'Quite frankly I hadn't realized quite how patchy until I began offering it elsewhere.'

'Our director still hasn't realized.'

CHAPTER FIFTY-ONE

W<small>E OPENED AT</small> the Piccadilly Theatre in the West End to good reviews, but not raves. Robert never got raves, hardly even 'good' for *A Man For All Seasons* when it first opened with Paul Scofield. So patronizing were they that Binkie, dismayed by the lack of attendance in that first crucial week, explained to Robert, 'I'm sorry, Bob, but I can't keep the play on with half-empty houses.' Robert was so sure that the word of mouth, which was excellent, would build sufficiently to turn the tables that he paid another two weeks' running costs out of his own pocket, thus giving the critics' puddles of piss time to dry out. Funny business, fashion. Robert Bolt was never fashionable like Pinter, Wesker or Osborne, but I'm happy to make a bet that when this century is well tucked up in bed, let's say in 2010, *A Man For All Seasons* will be up there joining the main beam of great twentieth-century writing – but then I'm merely the playwright's biased wife.

On the first night of *Vivat! Vivat Regina!* we gave a little party in my dressing room, just for a few people – family mostly. I think my parents enjoyed the first night, but what astounded me was that my brother Chuzzer tipped up. I was delighted to see him, standing in the corner, so tall, wheezing away as usual. 'Well done,' he said, butting me, just like Daddy did, with the crown of his head against my crown.

'Thanks for making the effort.'

At which point Peter O'Toole came up to me and pulled me to one side, whispering in my ear, 'You have grounds for divorce.' And just before vanishing back into his underworld, he added, 'The part is unplayable.' I'd only met Peter twice before, once when he floated around his Roman hotel suite convinced he was Jesus and once down in Dingle when he materialized drunk as a lord in an old Irish van in the high street. 'Move that vehicle immediately!' David had bellowed down his megaphone. No one had taken any notice, forcing him down to see for himself what was going on. Out jumped Peter, frightening David out of his wits for two seconds before he chose to take Peter to his breast like a long-lost buddy.

I caught sight of Eileen Atkins standing very still, staring across the dressing room. Who was she staring at? I made my way over to her.

'Who is that wonderful man standing over there?'

I looked and couldn't see anyone. 'Over where?'

She pointed across the room impatiently. Over there was only Chuzzer. 'I can see no one.'

Eileen gave me a look. 'That fuzzy, romantic-looking wizard.'

It *was* Chuzzer. Well, I'll be blowed!

'That's my brother Chuzzer, with his hubble-bubbling asthma machine.'

'Bugger the asthma – introduce me, for God's sake!'

'Where's Eddie?'

'Working, we're meeting later.'

I introduced them and Eileen played her role to perfection, the 'thinking man's crumpet', while Chuzzer took quite a number of puffs on his hubble-bubble. He said a few words to her, being a well-mannered Miles, then bowed politely to Eileen, explaining that there wasn't sufficient air and he must be off home. Eileen fawned after him like a soaked spaniel who was forbidden to cross the river to retrieve its delicious bone. The odd part was that Eileen went on about Chuzzer as relentlessly as Tom did over that wretched gun. Our West End run ran on and on but Eileen never ran out of her romantic dreams of Chuzzer. Robert had written a great line for Mary when she was told to choose between Bothwell and going to prison. In the courtoom Mary responded thus, 'For prison I will quit it, and then woe to you and woe to this country. As for Lord Bothwell, my lords, I would follow him to the edge of the earth – in my shift!' Great line, great writer, great lady, great stuff. As the weeks passed into months, Chuzzer's name regularly popped up.

'It's no use, Eileen, Chuzzer lives in Chania, Crete.'

She looked straight at herself in her dressing-room mirror, transforming herself into Mary, Queen of Scots. '"My Lords, I would follow him to the edge of the earth – in my shift!"' Obviously Eileen was not to be budged. 'When the play is over I will go to Crete and seek him out.'

When our year was up and the time came for Eileen and me to be released from bondage, true to her word and finding herself on holiday with a friend in the Greek islands, she took a trip to Chania. I'll let Chuzzer take over the story. 'There I was, having put the kettle on for a nice cuppa tea, dreaming out the window while washing up a few odds and ends in the kitchen when, lo and behold! Queen Elizabeth the First comes strutting up the cobbles! I take a closer look just to make quite sure my eyes are not deceiving me. Realizing they certainly were not, I left everything as it was, and leapt out the back exit which led on to the quay,' clasping his hubble-bubble, no doubt. Chuzzer's scarpering had nothing to do with Eileen Atkins, the woman, or indeed Queen Elizabeth the First. No, Chuzzer would have scarpered from anyone, even Elizabeth II at that time of the morning.

Eileen takes over. She had come down to visit us at the Old Mill. 'It was strange, Sarah, because the door was ajar and the kettle was boiling. It was all quite odd, actually, because there was not a soul in the house. I have to confess I poked my nose around the place, well I had to, didn't I? I mean, why was the kettle on? Why was the washing-up half finished? Why was the back door to the harbour also ajar?'

'So what did you do then, Eileen?'

'I wasn't sure what to do. I went on to the quay and asked

a few locals if they'd seen a Mr Martin Miles recently, but most of them didn't speak English.'

'And the others?'

'Three Greek ladies dressed in black robes, and referring to him as The Fair One, said, "He is in hospital in the mountains with an asthma attack." What could I do but wait? I booked myself into a sweet little pension overlooking the fishing boats and did just that – I waited.'

'Did he return?'

'No. After a few days I packed it in.'

One night Eileen came into my dressing room just before the half. I took my opportunity to smooth over the Julian Glover episode, for although nothing had been said, I felt I needed to clear my name. 'Do you remember phoning me up and accusing me of being a slut and a tart?'

Silence.

'Julian made it plainer than plain that your marriage was over. Had I known you were still trying to mend the pieces, Julian wouldn't have seen my arse for dust.' There sank another silence. It wouldn't have been correct for me to have needled her into an unnecessary guilt trip, so all was over from that moment. Besides I had grown to admire Eileen as well as her performance. Both as actress and woman, she was, and is, sexy, talented and intelligent.

CHAPTER FIFTY-TWO

THE PLAY WAS such a success in the West End that Hal Wallis approached Robert, offering him a fortune for the film rights. This was a great coup for Robert and, of course, we were delighted. The casting would remain the same. So for Eileen, playing a by now magnificent Elizabeth, and for me, giving my best stab at Mary, the hard grind of a long West End run now seemed well worth the effort. However, we hit upon a problem that couldn't be overcome: Hal Wallis wanted to cheat in the film and have Elizabeth and Mary meeting. Robert thought the essence of the drama lay in that they *didn't* meet. This conflict went on for months, but Robert wouldn't budge and, since it wasn't historically correct, why should he? Besides, what mind-blowing revelation could happen in this invented meeting between the two women that would justify the falsification of history? Fuck all, is the answer to that. It all ended sadly because Hal Wallis went ahead anyway, with Vanessa Redgrave, Glenda Jackson and a rotten script. At their encounter nothing of interest took place – how could it? The film was instantly forgettable.

It's always a miracle to me that any film of substance, let alone integrity, gets off the ground at all. Just as it's an enigma to me how those great heads of studios get voted into office. One afternoon in 1971 the head of one of the famous American film studios (for his sake we'll keep him nameless) phoned Robert with his great idea for a new movie. I listened in.

'Hi, Robert. Are you sitting comfortably?'

'Yes, I'm at my desk, why?'

'I have one hell of a great idea for a movie.'

'Yes?'

I knew Robert well enough to understand that this movie mogul, however gigantic, was interrupting his train of thought.

'This is sensational, it's going to make a fortune.'

'I'm glad to hear that. What is it?'

'Are you ready for this?'

'Yes, I'm ready.'

The studio boss gave his idea great importance by delivering a hefty silence beforehand. 'William the Conqueror.'

Silence.

'Hello, Robert, are you there?'

'Yes, yes. I'm still here.'

'Well, what do you think?'

'William the Conquerer . . . yes . . . yes.' Robert's voice faded way, as if lost for words.

'Robert, he was without a doubt one hell of a guy – one of the greatest in history!'

'He most certainly was.'

After some more silly talk and awkward silences, the Head of Studio sighed a great Head-of-Studio sigh. 'There's only one problem, Robert.'

'Oh? And what is that?'

'There was no battle,' he said regretfully.

'No battle?' replied Robert. Was he being had on, or what? I mean what kind of a moron was this man? Even *I* knew William the Conqueror conquered *something*.

'I'm afraid not, Robert. No battle.' His voice deflated.

'But there was a battle, you know,' replied Robert as gently as possible.

'There *was* a battle?' His voice rose with enthusiasm again.

'Oh, yes. Quite famous it was, too.'

'It was?' Really excited he was now.

'Yes. The Battle of Hastings, 1066.'

The studio boss, hardly able to contain himself, said with enormous satisfaction as if the deal had already been struck, 'Well, there you are, then!' That was the call almost verbatim.

He wasn't having Robert on, as it turned out. But eventually, after a little more homework, he came to the sad conclusion that the battle scenes might be too expensive.

At the end of the curtain call each evening, Eileen and I, having bowed to the audience, would then turn to acknowledge each other. It was always a good moment because the applause rose to a crescendo. One night as we turned to bow to each other Eileen whispered to me, quick as a flash in my upstage ear, 'Queen's in tonight.'

Why was I always the last to hear the gossip? Had I known she was coming I might have baked a better performance. From then on many royals from many countries came to see the show. It was, I suppose, the nearest they could ever get to revelling in the familiarity of their very own *Coronation Street*.

We were invited to Buckingham Palace one night after the performance. I was never sure what this was in aid of, but Eileen and I were told it was perfectly in order for the pair of us to arrive late, since the Queen knew we were performing our own queens. Robert, however, would be there on time. We were told to dress up smart and to curtsy if any of the royals approached us, and if they did approach us never to be the first to leave, always wait until they left us.

On the night it was a nerve-racking rush. I wore soaped black eyebrows for Mary, and heavy make-up, so I had a lot of work ahead of me if I wasn't to look ghoulish for the Palace. Finally there we were, Eileen and I, looking as posh as poss while we sat silent with trepidation on our way through the Palace gates.

'When do we curtsy?' asked an uncharacteristically nervous Eileen.

'Whenever they approach, I think.' But I wasn't sure. Once inside I caught a fleeting glimpse of Eileen, who had

obviously decided to cover her bets and bob up and down
furiously to butlers, guards, maids, old Uncle Tom Cobleigh
and all.

The royals were then hitting the headlines, with their lack
of funds for royal duties. Having to play host to endless
foreign dignitaries forced them into a lifestyle not their own;
therefore they believed it was only fair for the Government to
foot some of these enormous bills. The Government was
playing Mr Tight Arse. As I stepped inside, sniffin' an' sussin'
out the glory of grandeur for the first time, it took my breath
away.

Because we were late we had missed the introductions, so
we were escorted into an awesome room which I was astonished to find almost empty of theatricals. Not a single Lionel
to be seen. I couldn't even spot Johnnie Mills and he *had* to
be there, surely? The room melted into a massive chunk of
magnificence, and behind every pillar I swore a shadowy
Heathcliff lay lurking. Finally I spotted someone I knew, so I
felt safe in saying what was on my mind. 'I thought this lot
were meant to be hard up?'

My friend gave me a withering look, much worse than
backing away. I wasn't sure what I'd said that perturbed him,
until I saw the Queen standing right beside me. I quickly
gave one of my well-practised deeper curtsies.

'Your Majesty.' I lowered my eyes to the floor. When I
raised them again she was wiping her nose with a hanky, just
like Mummy always did. Same gesture, same white lace
hanky. She looked tired, but so kindly, with her slightly
swollen nose. Had she heard my remark to Paul?

'Forgive me. I'm recovering from flu.' She then blew her
nose as only queens can blow – mothers, too, of course! I
longed to pluck up courage to ask if she and Mummy were
really cousins. My grandfather, Francis (Frank) Remnant
(means a piece of old cloth off the main roll), was the son of
the late Queen Mary's brother, also Francis. This Francis,
apparently known as Sexy Frank, used to come and stay at

the White Lodge at Richmond where little spurts of hanky-panky with the seamstress (my great-grandmother) resulted in Grandad, Francis Remnant. As I watched Queen Elizabeth blowing her nose I wondered if she ever thought what it might be like for some of her subjects not to have proof of their existence? Was she aware of the havoc wrought by lack of such knowledge? Is it self-indulgent of me to need to know why Grandad Frank had never been registered at Somerset House? How would she feel if she went to her grave without her birthright being acknowledged? I must talk to her about Grandpa. I must. (Since writing my autobiography, I have received a letter giving me the proof my mother so desperately needed.)

'Your Majesty . . .' Something gagged me. Wench! Ungag thyself! Here is your only opportunity to give Mother some peace. Besides, if not now, when? Yet I didn't dare. Cowardy, cowardy custard: unacknowledged Ma met her grave still a bastard.

I stood there, watching her move her mouth, mesmerized (just like Mummy's). Having tucked away the white lace hanky, she told me all about Windsor Castle. I had no idea they played host to so many foreign officials so regularly. Retrieving her hanky again, she took me over to the centre of the room where, doing their duty on display, were many precious letters and memorabilia belonging to ancient kings, queens and a host of other history-makers. My gagging was swiftly followed by that familiar silver screen with the black edges, as if I were being blinded from perusing too much splendour. I looked round, for where was the Queen? Watching her profile, while she was deep in conversation with Robert, something became clear. I liked her. I liked her no-nonsense approach. Definitely someone to trust. With my eyesight fully returned I tried reading some of the letters on display. Fascinating to see the original handwriting of the greats. What's happened to ours, that it lacks so much flourish? Any style that takes patience went out of fashion yonks ago.

The room wasn't full. Those present were the Duke of Edinburgh, Princess Anne, Prince Charles, the Queen Mother, Princess Alexandra, Princess Margaret and Lord Snowdon – but *where* was Johnnie Mills? There was only Eileen, still to be seen bobbing up and down to a footman or two.

Just as I was beginning to feel nervous that perhaps we should be departing, Prince Charles approached me. While I gave him one of my better curtsies I wondered whether I had guts enough to ask him about Grandad Francis Remnant's origins, having failed to do so with his mum? Looking up at him his resemblance to my brother Chris was so uncanny that all desire to trace our family tree was washed clean away. Remember, all this took place when Charles was a young man of twentyish, and I was twenty-six . . . ish. And with my penchant being for gentlemen old enough to be my father, grandfather, even, I wasn't about to be tossed over, pancake-like into toyboys. The reason I found him so impressive was something more startling than mere family likeness or sexual attraction. Albeit that he was the Prince of Wales, I wasn't sufficiently thrilled by that, surely, to be quite so bowled over. He had charm enough to talk on any subject with ease, dexterity and grace, nimbly highlighting every subject matter with an impressive knowledge of history – but if not the Prince of Wales, then who? No. It was much more than all the outer shows that he unquestionably possessed. It was more a solid, quiet integrity simmering among the plush, pomp and privilege that intrigued me.

Robert appeared just as I was about to ask Charles if he had any of the dope on Mary Stuart. Perhaps he knew something that might help me unravel my Mary mystery, even if the origin of my own ancestors was to remain as frustratingly mysterious as ever. He seemed modest yet *au fait* with every play and film of mine plus all those Robert had written (*A Man For All Seasons* being his favourite). It made me wonder if he did homework on all his guests. I suppose he must, poor chap. While wondering if we were overstaying our welcome, Charles said, 'Please come over here. I'll show you a letter written in Mary's own hand.' She had strong yet soft feminine writing, full of contradiction, just like her nature.

Later that night as Robert and I drove home, we couldn't help unpeeling memories of the evening's larkier moments.

'They seemed a merry lot tonight, don't you agree?' We had recently been to a dinner at Number 10 Downing Street with Edward Heath, the then Prime Minister. It was a dour, false, stiffly pompous evening until the end when, in the hall, he conducted the St Paul's School Choir. As he stooped forward whispering little words of encouragement before proceeding, I noticed how pliable and sincere his back was, conflicting hugely with his previous stiffness at dinner. His conducting was surprisingly sensitive, showing such a quiet consideration for the boys that it made a most touching display. This epitome of the unintegrated Englishman saved himself at the eleventh hour.

Prince Charles seemed his antithesis, and, for a twenty-year-old, pretty free-flowing. But that was before the enemy well and truly got their teeth stuck in, tearing at his confidence like a pack of wolves, devouring all true sense of self. Over the past twenty-five years since that first meeting, the poor man has had mockery flung at him, envy dripping off him, his brief privacy violated at every corner. It's a miracle to me he's intact at all, still very much his own man. Charles is in need of a bit of England's heart.

'Prince Charles was a surprise,' said Robert thoughtfully.

'Why?'

'He wasn't at all as I imagined.'

'Better or worse?'

'Odd, finding myself impressed with a member of the

Royal Family – he's witty, too.' Praise indeed, for Robert: though having drifted slightly to the right of Communism he remained a serious 'leftie'.

Five years later (twenty years ago), I had a burst of vision (sounds too New Age) . . . 'Nebulous fancies'? 'Phantasmagoria'? Most of them recently have come true – not this one though. Yet it won't go away either. 'You'll get mauled to death by the media if you put that in,' warned Bolt. So be it.

A human hand with the royal signet fills the frame. As we track back we see the hand sweeping a great golden crown aside, disclosing Prince Charles. As he renounces the throne so we start renouncing too. Charles sits at a plain round wooden table surrounded by the finest brains in the land, chosen for integrity, courage and devotion to their country. A corny, clichéd, King Arthur romantic fancy maybe, but it still lingers twenty years later stronger than ever. Wasn't it Aristotle who said that Democracy was the best form of government, failing a wise and just king? (Since I can't see renouncement ever becoming a fad, I'll have to elbow my Phantasmagoria.)

Ryan's Daughter opened in London to a gala première. I couldn't go because I was still in *Vivat!*. Unfortunately the lights in the Empire Cinema, Leicester Square, chose to black out right in the middle of the first-night showing, but then they would, wouldn't they, for the film was jinxed. On that dark freezing-cold night my parents, celebrities, hoi polloi, VIPs and, what was worse, the critics gave up waiting to witness the end of the tale. The critics fell upon it with bloodthirsty relish, using butcher's knives to mutilate our three years of toil, sweat and strain. David Lean, Robert and the writer's wife came out worst. I never expected good reviews, because the theme was unfashionably romantic for the times, but this carving up took the biscuit. I had no notion of how much the critics detested David Lean, and because of his twice successful partnership with Robert Bolt they decided to go to town. The effect it had on David was destructive, for he was unable to gather up sufficient courage to work again for another ten years, whereas Robert's gift of rallying finally ended in a stroke. Is it the critic's job to annihilate greatness? If their response is that greatness can never be destroyed, I disagree. What makes someone great is the ability to fight off demons daily, and the greater the genius the more vulnerable he is to the dark forces around him. Critics don't comprehend the 'dark versus light' tussle, because they live in an area of perpetual grey. I believe David was one of the greatest directors of all time. So when the critics decided to crucify him with their *Ryan's Daughter* reviews, they denied the public perhaps three more great films.

One night, sitting at my dressing-room table during that sad, unable-to-leave-for-home time, because of nasty gunk still sticking to my face, Olivier entered while knocking. 'Oh! I thought you were Noëlie.'

He gave me a brief look while his lips brushed the top of my head. Oh! That briefness is etched in eternity. He reminded me of someone on the run. Seedy almost, unloved and a trifle tortured.

'Keep away from her hot spots.' He was focused and businesslike.

'What are her hot spots?'

'The trouble is, she has so many.' He paced up and down, looking at his dusty shoes. Hot spots are claimed places on stage where other actors have had some great moment. (I wouldn't have a clue about Eileen's since I'd never watched her. How could I? While she was claiming hot spots I was forever doing my bleedin' quick changes.)

I riposted, pouting, 'The whole stage is just one great big fat Elizabeth the First hot spot!'

'Why didn't you deliver some better pillow talk?' slyly

sliding his tongue over his lips. I didn't know what he was on about. 'If he wouldn't give you Elizabeth, then at least he should allow you to alternate.'

'Eileen wouldn't.'

'I bet she wouldn't.'

'Help me to play Mary, rather than plot against poor Mary to get me Elizabeth.'

'What would poor Mary think?' He acknowledged her with a fey camp gesture up there somewhere before brushing the top of my head again, too briefly. Little did he understand, as I watched him blowing me a kiss from the door, that I knew what Mary was thinking. I should play her more like Elizabeth.

I wish Lionel hadn't trespassed back into my life that evening. The healing process was considerably put back. The shock of seeing him again, for only a few cruel minutes, was hard, very hard. In those early days I was unable to reach upward and see my life from a less constrained viewpoint. All I did was hurt inside, night after night. Not because I didn't love Robert. I did. I loved Robert with a fine, enduring respectful love, but . . .

Being unable to veer clear of Eileen's hot spot on stage made me more and more uneasy. I wasn't cut out to be an actor. Other people's hot spots wouldn't have crossed my mind; all I was interested in was finding the truth within my own character. Somehow Olivier had introduced a competitive cunning that just wasn't me, so I became less confident. The gowns began to weigh me down, heavy as my heart. Because the costume changes were longer and more arduous than performing the scenes themselves, I was unable to eat and went down to six stone in weight. My doctor had to come to the theatre twice a week to give me injections in an attempt to prevent me from disintegrating altogether. Getting up in the morning and going to bed at night had both become a nightmare.

I had been convinced since Chichester that the real Mary

was hanging over me – fearfully sad she was, too. The more I pushed her away the more she came on, bullying me at night so I couldn't sleep. How her nocturnal naggings shook my consciousness: she used me as her puppet, pulling at my merely mortal strings, forcing me to play her this way and then that. On and on she went, until her relentless *triste* became unbearable. The time I felt her presence most power-fully was at the end when I threw off my black gown to reveal my scarlet dress underneath as I faced the executioner's axe. (That really happened.) But Mary was screaming at me to play it differently. I wasn't sure whether it was my perform-ance or Robert's writing that displeased her so, but displeased she most certainly was. Was I letting her down? Or was she trying to pull back that moment of her life so she could relive it with a different outcome? Is that what Johnnie Windeatt was doing with the chimney flue in the kitchen? Both scream-ing through time to change the outcome of events? How often my heart went out to Mary. I tried and tried to ignore her – after all, she was only in my imagination.

'We'll see about that,' Mary interrupted again. No wonder they chopped off her head.

I believe one of my more serious errors was telling Robert, after I'd caught up on his work, that fine writer though he undoubtedly was, as yet he was no great writer of women's roles. This wasn't a direct challenge to his capabilities, but rather in the context of why there were no women writers of any merit. For surely man cannot write for woman as pro-foundly as woman would write for herself? But because at the time this was purely an observation, I didn't think it would be a red rag to a bull, spurring him to write two fine roles for me on the trot. I'd never bemoaned the lack of such parts, because right back to Shakespeare's day that's the way it always had been. Women's roles have been mostly sketchy, sometimes misconceived, oft-times a diabolical insult.

This wasn't helped, however, by my lack of intellectual self-worth. I hadn't had the guts to talk through with Robert at the very beginning any fears or criticisms I might have had regarding the development, or lack of it, in Mary's character. Neither was he able to share his creative process, not even so far as confiding in me the subject matter before it was ready. But why should he? His road to far distant lands wasn't via 'me'. We had already cast ourselves in our 'real-life' roles.

Neither of us was sufficiently mature to identify the mass of ego, doubt, and ambition, hurtling us forward, but to where? My appetite for loving was always robust (to put it mildly!) and learning to curb it was a new departure. The rot set in with the doubt. That great slithering reptile slid its way in, nibbling at confidence, sexuality, womanhood, and my ability to give a whole-hearted Mary, Queen of Scots. How I wish we could do the play again, now that we are back together having grown into our truer (though still far from perfect), better selves.

Robert was a lark and I was an owl. Robert liked the room cold, I liked it warm. Robert liked the curtains open, I liked them closed because I awoke with the first dawn light. Perhaps it would have been wiser to work out answers to these differing idiosyncrasies before tying the knot, because afterwards they grow into marriage-threatening afflictions. Because of working nights, and returning home too full of adrenalin and Mary to embrace sleep, I'd stay up late so as not to wake him with my tossing and turning. Thus began the sad time of passing Robert often on the stairs. 'I'm off to work. Goodnight, darling.' Off he'd march to his study with that familiar spring to his gait . . . perhaps owls and larks should never marry?

My need for Robert's comradeship was hurting so much that one morning, yearning to find out what went on behind that implacably sturdy green study door of his, I humped the fire ladder (with the help of Bob, my stable boy) round the side of the mill, placed it in the shallow part of the river to one side of the sluice gates and gingerly climbed up. I knew never to look down, even while descending. No, I have to keep my eyes up to heaven. The ladder just reached his study window. Guess what I saw as I peeped through? Robert typing! He'd type for a bit, pause, and take a drag on his fag; pull out the piece of paper from the typewriter, scrumple it up, then throw it in the bin à la Bertie Russell and the faulty cucumber sandwiches. He'd take a swig from the whisky bottle, type for a bit, pause, take a drag on his fag, scrumple up the piece of paper from the machine and throw it in the bin. Take a mouthful of chip butty, type for a bit, pause, take a drag on his fag before stubbing it out, take a sip of coffee, type for a bit, scrumple up the piece of paper and throw it into the bin, take another swig of whisky, type for a bit, light up his pipe, type for a bit, scrumple up the piece of paper and throw it into the bin. Another great bite of chip butty, type for a bit, puff on his pipe, another swig of whisky, type for a bit . . . No wonder I nearly fell into the mill race – no wonder he was to end up with a massive great heart attack!

Tom wasn't sleeping well and would come into my bed as soon as he heard his father go down to the study at 5.30 a.m. Sam's sleeping habits had been angelic by comparison. It wasn't Tom's fault: it was that confounded asthma which came between us so suddenly, brutally severing our joy. I don't know where it surfaced from, or why, but it entered our lives like a curse. It was hard to bear the look on his face as I left him behind to go for a ride on the common. Riding to the pub with him on the leading rein had become a weekly treat. What a gas it was, trying to cross the A3 with Tom, such a mindful little rider, looking both left and right as we hurried across, with all the dogs. Tom loved the pub and tethering Thunder to the rail, just like he'd seen them do in cowboy films.

Tom never cared to connect his asthma with horses, riding and hay, even though the moment he mounted his breathing caved in and his eyes swelled up red with their familiar puffiness. It was the same when he entered the stableyard – the smell started him off immediately. To hear him at it broke my heart. It remains such a mysterious ailment because I never understood why Tom didn't have asthma around horses from the beginning. Why did he start wheezing at three and a half years old?

On top of Tom's asthma he was already in trouble at his first kindergarten school, outside Cobham, and I was asked to take him away. What could he possibly be up to? I went to see the headmistress.

'I'm afraid, Mrs Bolt, your son is an inciter.' I wasn't sure what an inciter was, so I hedged my bets.

'What form does this inciting take?'

'Removing the children's attention away from the teacher, on to himself.'

'But since he's not yet four, that's the teacher's problem, surely?'

The headmistress remained firm. 'His strong will contributes nothing to the overall harmony. I'm so sorry.'

'I'll talk to him, and then perhaps you could give him another chance?'

She was a sensible, sweet woman, so I was confident Tom would get a reprieve. Tom and I had a little chat, and gently tried to discover what his motives were for being so disruptive in class, but he was far from forthcoming. I found it tricky explaining to him why school was so important. Though he was too young to know about my various expulsions, listening to my own voice banging on made me shudder at its falsehood echoing through great halls of hypocrisy – no doubt he got a good whiff of it, too! Still, we got him reinstated and given one last chance to become part of the 'classroom harmony'. He was asked to leave the following month instead.

Little did I know, then, that he was showing us the pattern of what lay ahead. For Tom, bless his cotton socks, was either asked to leave or got himself expelled from ten schools. Because my parents weren't keen to listen to my schoolday grievances – 'Just get on with it and behave yourself' – I tried to listen to Tom more carefully. But still being unaware of dyslexia I never quite saw his reasoning. Now I understand that he had no choice but to remain on the defensive because he knew, like I knew, too, that we weren't just stupid. Why didn't I connect my schooldays with his? Why didn't I read the warning signs when, just like me, he repeatedly insisted that all those in authority were a bunch of morons? Tom, like me, always thought he knew best. For better or for worse he was always to be his own man. Only now, with hindsight enabling me to see the mistakes and catastrophes in my wake, do I realize how essential it is to find at least one teacher to respect, as well as discipline for finding one's better self. Thank God I found Robert Bolt. But, alas, my hindsight clicked in too late. Now Tom is grown up and I won't have a say in the bringing up of my grand-children. How hard it's going to be for me as I observe them being spoilt to bits. 'Discipline alone will win and boredom is the ultimate sin.'

Ryan's Daughter opened in LA in time for the Oscar nomina-tions and, although we were slated again, the Academy decided to give nominations to me, Johnnie Mills and Freddie Young, the lighting cameraman. It was exciting to be nomi-nated but I believe Robert, David, Trevor – even Mitchum – deserved a nomination more.

One night during a performance of *Vivat!* before going on stage for the death of Rizzio I received a telegram from LA. It was from William Morris, my agents at the time, and I was busily opening it while walking towards my entrance. Goffie, the chesty ray of Chichester sunshine, was now one of my dressers, being the only blind dresser in town.

'What does it say?' she asked, peering down my front to check if she'd buttoned up the millionth button. I read it out loud.

'You are becoming a cult out here in LA.'

'Here, give it to me.' As I handed it over, she called after me just before I made my entrance. 'That's not an "L" that's an "N".' It wasn't until the murder of Rizzio, who gets stabbed in the back forty times as he falls down the steps of our secret rendezvous, that, 'That's not an "L" that's an "N",' rang in my brain with the slow peal of dawning. I got it! 'You are becoming a *cunt* out here in LA.' So impressed was I by Goffie's quick-wittedness that she went from my dresser to aide-de-camp, to my partner in crime to a very dear friend.

My West End run with *Vivat! Vivat Regina!* was almost up – I'd made it through! Yet why did I suppose that when the run of *Vivat!* was over, Mary would stop pestering me? Maybe it wasn't Mary, but if not Mary then what was this sense of hopelessness? I was unable to share it even with Robert. Yet I loved my husband dearly. Admittedly, my dream list was finally ticked off, but the feeling of, 'Is this all there is?' was nothing compared to this new sense of unfathomable despair. Now I can say: What a spoilt, privileged bitch! But at the time, nothing could help take away that hopeless feeling of doom. Now I know better, for only those who know the darkness understand its ruthless dependence on earthly things. If only I hadn't been so ignorant I would have simply tapped into my inner resources, for only within me is the unpicking ground for those tangles of despair.

I started fox-hunting again, to try and chase away my own demons. In a chocolate-brown riding habit, I rode sidesaddle on Cavalier, my palomino stallion. Daisy, who adored a day's hunting, pummelled furiously at her stall door as the trailer left without her. But out on the field I couldn't keep control of her lust for leadership. She persisted in surpassing the Master and that doesn't go down well in hunting circles. The meet is the best part of hunting for me; like lovemaking when everything rises up in a nectar of tasty anticipation. Struggling through Guildford today amid the endless traffic jams called progress, it's impossible to imagine that we once met with the hounds and hunting horns echoing on those high street cobblestones. Alas, hunting never drove away my demons, so I soon packed it in for good, and haven't hunted for over twenty years.

I'm not sure of my motives for packing it in. What I am sure of is having experienced a day in a slaughterhouse and a day out foxhunting, I bags be in the fox's shoes.

Was I an animal lover when I hunted? Certainly. Foxes need to be culled. Living in the countryside I sometimes see them slowly dying in traps, even on occasion badly wounded by a mis-shot. Killing foxes humanely is a huge problem because they are mighty fast but killing them is a necessity as they begin to multiply like rabbits. Chairman Mao demanded the killing of all sparrows among other things because he thought they were a threat to the crops. With his orders obeyed and all sparrows eliminated, the crops, without their sparrow protection, were completely devastated by insects. This brought mayhem upon Mao's head, together with ten million Chinese dying of starvation. Preserving the balance of nature (and we humans are only one part of that) is my most coveted dream.

CHAPTER FIFTY-THREE

I'D NEVER BEEN to LA; indeed I'd only visited America once before, when I went to New York for a week to publicize *The Servant*. My publicist this time was a beautiful ex-girlfriend of Robert, Carolyn Pfeiffer, who ran her own publicity agency in London and had a client list that read like *Who's Who*. She met Robert on *Doctor Zhivago* when she was Omar Sharif's secretary. Carolyn was one of the blessed, cherishing all those in her care, for she was strong yet not tough, honest, efficient – a beautifully sleek North Carolina dame.

She had set out for me a gruelling two-week publicity tour, a week in LA and a week in New York. I hadn't been looking forward to leaving Robert and Tom behind; so far I'd never left Tom for more than ten days. Some actors I know don't mind the limelight, others live for it, and I envy them. Nevertheless Robert told me it was my duty, for selling one's wares is all part of the job.

How I yearned to make enough money at my stud farm – no limelighting needed for that.

'Never mind, honey,' crooned Carolyn. 'It'll fly by.'

We arrived at Bungalow 14 at the Beverly Hills Hotel. It was a pleasant enough bungalow, all very suitably decorated, with a kitchen, two bedrooms and bathrooms *en suite* and an ostentatiously large drawing room.

'It has to be this way, honey, because the journalists bring their own photographers.' It reminded me of a posh dentist's waiting room. Four long sofas and four armchairs made me wonder how many photographers were coming along. 'You and Glenda are the favourites.' I knew that and I also knew Glenda was bound to win. She'd received reviews for *Women*

395

in Love that hailed her as the second coming. It must give one an almighty high to receive notices like that.

Walking round all the bungalows, the swimming pool and the hotel gardens, I was reminded of a story Lionel once told me. He was staying here in the fifties when he found himself being hounded by a famous, glamorous movie star. (Giving her name would better the tale, but not her reputation.) This lusciously well-endowed beauty had a helluva lot of hots for Lionel. Now I cannot think of any man who wouldn't go weak at the knees knowing that this particular dame was after him, but not Lionel.

'I just wanted to be alone,' camped Lionel, imitating Garbo. 'Having politely kissed her goodnight on the cheek, I locked my door. Once in bed I heard a strange rustling outside my window. Thinking it was my imagination I turned over to try and sleep. The rustling continued, however, so I went to my window, and there she was, having climbed halfway up the ivy. She would have done herself damage had I not helped her up the rest of the way.'

'Of course.'

'Once in the room she sort of flung herself at me. And without you there to protect me, what could I do?'

'And did you?'

'No, I couldn't, so I got her well and truly pissed before sending her on her way.' In a whisper Lionel made his confession. 'I've only had as many women as fingers on one hand.' Quite a few thumbs as well, I warrant!

The day before Oscar night, after three days of solid interviews, Carolyn said, 'There's a young man coming to interview you this afternoon from *Time* magazine.'

'Will he be bringing a photographer?' I didn't want to be photographed because I'd come up in an enormous boil on my cheek. David Lean always used to say, 'You can bet your bottom dollar the leading lady will appear with an enormous boil on her face for her most important close-up.' I suppose

Oscar night was an enormous close-up with the whole world out there watching your boil.

The young man who arrived threw me completely for, though blond, he was a cross between Johnnie Windeatt and Robin Fox. He was dressed in a Savile Row suit, hand-made shirt and shoes, with a battered brown briefcase. His thick straight golden hair framed a pair of finely made tortoiseshell specs. He exuded frighteningly zestful energy, forcing his anglophile speech patterns into a jerky lilt. After Carolyn had done the introductions she asked him if she should stay.

'I'd feel more at ease if you didn't.'

Carolyn turned to me to find out how I felt about this, but because of his direct tone, I thought it best not to quarrel with him.

Once Carolyn had closed her bedroom door he immediately said, 'That's some boil you have on your cheek.'

'Your skin's no baby's bottom.'

'Tomorrow night's too close to take my ointment alone, but if I dash home and fetch my boil pills, your boil will have vanished by Oscar time tomorrow.'

'Impossible! I know how long boils take – unless I squeeze it.'

He came over to scrutinize it further. Though it's hard to believe, I never once got the feeling that he was trying to flirt with me, seeming too intent on the boil problem.

'Don't do that, it'll leave a scar – look at these motherfuckers!' He pointed out two pockmarks on his neck. 'I've learnt my lesson now. No squeezing. I'll fetch the pills.'

'Where's he gone?' asked a bewildered Carolyn, who had come in to order us some tea.

'He went to get some boil pills.'

'What?'

I told her all and she couldn't believe any of it.

'But he's the main West Coast Showbiz *Time* Correspondent!'

'Apparently a mere youth with pimples of his own.'

Within an hour, true to his word, David Whiting returned with both ointment and pills. I followed his instructions, although while downing the pills I did fleetingly wonder what I was swallowing. Towards the end of the interview he said, 'I think I could get you a cover story out of this.'

'Why? I haven't done anything.'

'Trust me.' I wasn't sure what a cover story meant, for I never read *Time* magazine, but I had seen many powerful leaders and suchlike on the cover.

'I'm not a complete fool, you know.' As I laughed off the idea my cheek seemed to set itself on fire. 'Ouch!'

'That means the pills are taking effect.' There was something endearing about this quaint English-American.

Oscar night and over half an hour late the limousine drew up at the back entrance of the Beverly Hills Hotel. It was without a doubt the biggest, longest, blackest, most serious limo I'd ever clapped eyes on. Carolyn climbed in, plus an elderly queen, old friend of hers, who was my escort for the night.

The traffic was appalling. Because of interviews all day in the bungalow, I'd only been let loose in LA once. That was yesterday, to go for an 'Oscar practice' and then on to visit Mitchum and Dorothy in their mansion in Bel Air. It seemed completely foreign for Mitchum to be prissed up like some poodle, surrounded in absurd trinkets of splendour. He belonged earthed on a ranch with horses and wide open spaces. Dorothy greeted me with her usual all-knowing wicked warmth. I found myself admiring her more and more. All through her life with Mitch – and they were, after all, childhood sweethearts – all women have been panting, aching, dying to get into his pants. His voice alone sends us weak at the knees. Once he and Dorothy attended a huge showbiz party with Rex Harrison and Rachel Roberts. Rachel got a little tiddly and ended up crawling across the floor in front of everyone (including Rex), roaring like a bitch tiger on heat and coming to rest on her knees in front of Mitchum, who was quietly minding his own business with one elbow on the mantelpiece. Without even a 'may I?' she unzipped him with her teeth and attempted to remove his trousers. Utterly exhausting it must have been for Mitch, continually fighting for his virtue. Presumably Dorothy smiled on benignly as she has done for nigh on fifty years. That to me is real love and I salute it. Do people respect Dorothy less for behaving well? No, they admire her hugely. She still has her man without ever seeming to be a downtrodden wife and is as far removed from the word 'victim' as it's possible to be.

'When you find yourself backstage tomorrow night, seek out the company of Greg Peck, he'll really entertain you,' said Mitch with a knowing wink.

At Roedean I'd fallen for Peck briefly in *The Purple Plain*. If it hadn't been for my allegiance to Lionel, and his photo stuffed under my pillow at night, I might have stuffed Gregory under too. But two men at once didn't seem right to me at the time – I only began to be in love with Laurence Olivier after King George VI died.

Later, after a swim in their pool followed by a delicious tea, Dorothy put on her red Bette Davis lipstick, donned an elegant pair of slip-ons, and drove me through the palace gates, back to the Beverly Hills Hotel. Kissing me firmly on the cheek, she said, 'Come by again before you leave town.'

Was I being fooled, looking into her eyes?

'I do believe you mean it.'

She smiled a secret gentle smile. 'Robert will never leave me.' It was a fact. He wouldn't. She held the secret, whatever that was, and she had the confidence to know that she held it. What's more, Mitchum knew she held it . . .

What an extraordinary woman. Although I had to practise unconditional love throughout my time with Lionel, would I have the 'Dorothy strength' to keep it up year after year in the same house with my husband? Yes – if my love was strong enough to overcome mere possessiveness.

In the limousine Carolyn looked at her watch. 'Perhaps we should walk it.' We all sat in maddening silence, wondering if Cinderella would ever get to the ball on time. The nerves in the pit of my stomach didn't bear thinking about. I was in a black nightmare. Carolyn asked the driver if we were OK for time.

'Maybe, maybe not,' I heard him grunt.

'What is your name, driver?' I asked, trying to remain quiet-spoken while throwing my voice across what seemed acres of limo.

'Sam, ma'am.'

I'd been in a few limousines before, so why was this driver almost a football pitch away?'

'You seem an awful long way away, Sam. Are LA limousines always this long?'

'No, ma'am, limousines are never this long.'

'So why are we being honoured with such a long one, then?'

'This is no limo, ma'am, this is a hearse.'

'A hearse?!' There's no doubt we were all taken aback. Carolyn obviously didn't want me to get paranoid on my big night so, light as a feather, she said, 'Sweetheart, your boil has completely vanished.' It was true, it had disappeared by teatime, just like David Whiting said it would.

'Why are we being honoured with a hearse, Sam?'

'Because MGM ran out of limousines.' Seemed a fair enough answer, though it confirmed my suspicions that MGM didn't much reckon my chances of winning. But that came as no shock. I'd spent an hour practising my losing-well smile, convinced that Glenda was simultaneously practising her thank-you speech. Besides, how could I have driven off clasping my Oscar victoriously to my bosom in a ruddy hearse?

As luck would have it, our by now precious hearse conked out, roughly a hundred and fifty yards from the entrance to the Chandler Pavilion.

After a minute or three Sam straightened, as he reappeared from the hearse's gigantic engine room. 'Now you do have to walk it. Sorry, folks.'

It felt surreal, like a Buñuel film, walking along the road as Mary, Queen of Scots, with all the famous sliding elegantly past in their limos. (Not one other hearse did I see.) My long black and gold velvet gown, with its flamboyant train dragging along the dusty street, was boned to the hilt; with my tightly nipped in eighteen-inch waist (couldn't make seventeen like Vivien – bitch!) pinching me into the cruellest of cramps. Lifting mind over matter, however, it seemed a perfect moment to have a little chat with Mary herself. 'Am I jinxed? Am I the jinx? Or is it because I'm wearing *your* dress?'

The Oscar practice the day before had been horrific. I was having to present an award jointly with George Segal. Nothing wrong with George, but a great deal wrong with the patter that had been dished out for us to read from cue cards (no telly prompter in those days). I said I wasn't prepared to read off such rubbish, but I was told I had to. It included garbage such as: 'My husband keeps his two Oscars in the toilet.' So I informed the chap in charge that I thought the line had a whiff of bragging about it, and I didn't use the word 'toilet'.

'What word do you use, honey, or don't you use them at all?' He must have thought this a real hoot because he looked around the theatre's scattered celebrities for acknowledgement of same.

'It would perhaps remove the sense of boasting if George were to say the line instead.'

George made it clear he didn't like the line either, and why should he? But the old boss-pot dug in his heels and said I had to say it. I wasn't prepared to go into battle surrounded by famous Oscar nominees all waiting like me to get back out of there quickly, so I let it go. I was determined though to say whatever I liked on the night.

But now it was the night, and here I was waiting backstage, staring into Gregory Peck's great handsome face, haunted by that damn line. I sat there, watching Peck's mouth move. He spoke so slowly, with such a profound significance, that the thought of 'My husband keeps his two Oscars in the toilet' blotted out his words with ease. Greg was nice as anything to me, but while he was refilling his lungs I snatched an opportunity to say, 'I'm just going to find George Segal and practise our patter.' As I searched for George through the mass of showbiz élite, I wondered if Mitch had been having me on about 'good old Greg'. Surely not. It must have been me. I was in no state of mind to appreciate the finer points of Greg's wit.

'Quick, Sarah Miles, you're on!'

I was thrust forward to the wings and pushed on stage, where I saw George Segal entering from the other corner. All I ever wanted to do was act. Not this pompous, self-promotional pantomime.

My silver screen with serrated edges plopped into view, closing off the rest of the world. It was cruel having it happen that night of all nights. I could see nothing, not the audience, not George Segal, not a damn thing – let alone the cue cards. George began with his first line of our pathetic patter. I replied with something vaguely appropriate, and so on until the cue line for 'My husband keeps his two Oscars in the toilet.' I want to make it clear that I wasn't trying to be bolshie for the sake of it; I felt strongly that the line was unnecessarily boastful. Proud as I am of Robert's Oscars (for *Lawrence of Arabia* and *Doctor Zhivago*), I didn't think the whole world needed me to tell them. I had to do something.

'I'm afraid I haven't brought my specs, so I can't read the cue card.' I didn't expect the hushed silence that followed. Only later was I told that the viewers had no idea we used cue cards. Apparently until that moment the whole world had been convinced that Oscar night was a free-flowing, gay, impromptu celebration.

'What utter nonsense!' I said afterwards. 'We can all see

402

them peering hazily into the far distance – the viewer wasn't born yeterday!'

'That may be so,' said a patient Carolyn. 'Nevertheless, honey, no one, as yet, has come straight out and said it.'

'It needed to be said, in that case.'

I was called back on stage to collect Freddie Young's Oscar in his stead. This delighted me hugely because Freddie Young is the magician of lights. It's staggering to think that he was lighting in the days of the silent movies. Talking of which, I had the great honour of meeting Lilian Gish at the party afterwards. I heaved a great sigh of relief to find no bullshit issuing from a single orifice. Her quiet sincerity and an almost translucent openness gave me a necessary breath of spring that evening. I also met Edward G. Robinson and so stunned was I at seeing him standing right before me that I found myself saying, 'Good Lord, I thought you were dead!'

He laughed, and replied, 'So did I!' He turned out another rare jewel. Perhaps the bullshit drops away as one grows older, though something, alas, tells me different.

Walter Matthau read out the best actress award. I had already met him backstage where he told me I was two to one favourite, but I got a feeling he said that to all the girls. On stage he looked me straight in the eye while undoing the envelope. '. . . and the winner is – Glenda Jackson.'

I gave my extensively rehearsed smile. And that, I thought, was that. But it wasn't.

CHAPTER FIFTY-FOUR

NEXT DAY PEOPLE telephoned to congratulate me on winning the Oscar – because most newspapers had my photograph on the front page holding Freddie Young's. This was all that was needed apparently for most people not to read the copy that went with it. And I'd hit the headlines by openly blabbing the secret of Oscar cue cards, causing a mini furore, which hadn't abated a week later in New York. I was forced there to see a dentist because David's boil pills had driven the pain into my wisdom tooth. The dentist peered into my mouth while congratulating me on my Oscar. As did many a taxi driver, strangers in the lobby at the Sherry Netherlands Hotel, some of the room-service waiters, and quite a few journalists, who should have known better. Carolyn and I thought it was an absolute hoot!

David Whiting, however, never went away. He stuck to us both like cuckoo spit. Carolyn was at her wits' end as to how to lose him – if indeed she should, because David persisted in the idea that I was cover-story material. When Carolyn and I both sat him down, still in LA, and asked him from what angle he saw this potential story, he replied, 'Just put all your films together and see.'

'See what? That I'm married to Robert Bolt?' I said defensively.

'That's a small part of it, yes. But you're the only one with the ability to take on a completely different persona. My angle would be, "The Little Chameleon".'

I found this most extraordinary and I felt flattered as a surge of the warmest gratitude swept over me. It was the first time any journalist had ever taken me seriously, believed in me, or indeed taken the time to see all my movies. Robert,

David Lean and Olivier believed in me, too, but David
Whiting was prepared to go out there on a limb for me.
How could I not be flattered? And that was my downfall.
Vanity.

Carolyn and I waved him off at LA airport. We were
relieved that there was no place for him on the flight to New
York, because he would most certainly have come along.
'Thank God the Sherry Netherlands is completely booked
out,' sighed an exhausted Carolyn. David drained everyone
around him in minutes, so high was his energy level.

Although I found it deeply flattering, doubt hovered.
'Carolyn, let's check out his credentials when we get to New
York.'

'How do you mean? I know he's genuine,' she replied
grudgingly.

'Yes, but let's check out if he has sufficient clout for a
cover story.'

'OK.'

And that's exactly what we did. Well, not *exactly*. Carolyn
and I had a shock, coming out of our suite at the Sherry
Netherlands that same evening, because we bumped straight
into David Whiting. He was coming out of the next-door
suite.

'Good God!' I jumped.

'This hotel was completely full,' exclaimed an astonished
Carolyn.

'They always have a few rooms left for *Time* magazine,'
said David with a businesslike smile. He and Carolyn had a
little chat, and two days later David arranged a luncheon for
me and the top guy at *Time*, the editor, Mr de Grunwald.

'I don't ever have lunch with movie stars, so this makes a
nice change,' he said.

'Why *are* you having lunch with me?'

'It's hard for me to resist a David Whiting request, because
he's my golden boy. He's the youngest journalist that *Time*
has ever recruited, and he gets things done. He's a light

mover, I like his style.' I liked Mr de Grunwald, too, he reminded me a bit of Sam Spiegel. Warm, round and dreadfully sentimental. 'David was a child prodigy – quite brilliant, even at the age of four. When he came of age I immediately took him on. Why, has he been molesting you?'

'No . . . not quite.' Mr de Grunwald laughed. 'He thinks I'm possible cover story material, and I think he's bullshitting me.'

'If that's what David thinks, then I would give him a free rein to go for it.'

What else was there to say? Yet as I thanked Mr de Grunwald for lunch, something didn't feel quite right.

That whole week in New York, David never left us. Wherever we went he was always there, taking notes. Even when going to the loo we had difficulty shaking him off. Carolyn became increasingly agitated by his proximity, even though it never seemed flirtatious.

'Maybe he really does believe in you, and wants to observe every detail.'

'You sound as doubtful as I feel.'

Carolyn shrugged thoughtfully. 'I think he's a bit crazed, but maybe he's just too brilliant for his own good.'

'I don't know what to do.'

David had asked me to stay an extra two days because he wanted me to see Greenwich Village. He had said, 'My story'll need shots of you in New York as well as England.'

I asked Carolyn if I should stay. 'Sure, honey, but I have to leave tomorrow as planned.'

I was still not comfortable. I even found myself telephoning *Time* magazine to thank Mr de Grunwald in person for lunch rather than writing because I wanted to know for certain that he *was* the editor. David could easily have set me up – he was capable of anything and therein lay the nub of my doubt. Mr de Grunwald turned out to be real, all right. But as for David Whiting . . . He was the kind of mysterious young man you might read about in a Scott Fitzgerald novel.

He kept *The Great Gatsby* with him at all times. He had a great selection of brand-new hand-made suits, shirts, shoes, and colognes, and a fresh rose in his buttonhole, but always the same ancient copy of *The Great Gatsby* in his briefcase.

'You like Scott Fitzgerald a lot then?'

'It's more than "like". *The Great Gatsby* is my bible,' he said, caressing the book. It had masses of scribbling inside, with hundreds of underlinings. 'Read it yourself, and then you'll understand me better,' he said, guiding me gently into the cupboard of my suite at the Sherry Netherlands Hotel, whereupon he took out a cigarette case of marijuana. We shared a joint. 'Acapulco gold, there's nothing like it.'

'Why in the cupboard?' I asked.

'Because you get stoned quicker in a confined space.' This was pretty new to me. Except with Mitchum in Ireland, I'd never smoked the stuff, so ridiculously early on my mind was completely blown. Yet we had two more joints after that.

I'm not blaming the marijuana for what happened in the cupboard that night; I blame only myself. In those days I was in great need, but being out of touch with my real self, I wasn't sure what I was in need of. All I knew was that I had an aching void to be filled, but no notion of what to fill it up with except lovemaking. (I didn't know then the love to be found in silence.) My ego, my vanity, my pathetic need to be admired as an actress of merit by even *one* member of the media took precedence over everything that really mattered to me, such as Robert, the marriage vows and my son. I didn't want to lose David's admiration, or blow my chances of that cover story. I can't remember enjoying making love with him. I never reached the ceiling, let alone saw any wineberry wagtails fluttering by with their turquoise wings dipped in gold. I did, however, get a fleeting glimpse of a snow goose sinking towards the horizon, wings flapping with profound regret at the great loss of fidelity.

I couldn't wait to get out of New York. Those high buildings added another paranoid dimension to my already guilt-ridden heart. I yearned to be back at home in Robert's hopefully forgiving arms. Would he forgive me, though? It seems infidelity had been the final nail in his first marriage's coffin. What the silly night in the cupboard had also done was allow me to get a few things into perspective. I realized I didn't give a tinker's fart any more for the stupid cover story. I decided that when I saw David again I'd make damn sure he wasn't thinking of getting me in any more cupbords.

He was there, naturally, to see me off at Kennedy airport the next day. 'If I'm to complete this cover story I'll have to hang around your life for at least a month or two.'

Now was my opportunity. I cleared my throat. 'David, I don't want a cover story. Everything has become very obvious to me. I made love with you for a cover story, not because I fancied you.' I thought this was cruel but necessary. (It was more the marijuana than the cover story, but he needn't know that.)

'Stupid to throw away a *Time* cover story for half a night's cupboard's worth of guilt.' He smiled, secretly twirling his rose. 'Unforgettable though it was for me.' He smelt it.

'Maybe, but that's how it is.' I was businesslike as I waved farewell from my first-class 'surrey with a fringe on top' that whizzes you and your baggage to the flight. How relieved I was to see his rather strange shape (beautifully masked in a finely cut suit) slowly fade from view. I was devastated by the strain of the past two weeks, and, with the shame simply too heavy to bear, I began to cry quietly out of the window.

There was a baggage strike at Heathrow, so I had three hours to sit quietly and contemplate the shamefully dirty incompleteness of infidelity. To some, I know, it isn't a big deal, and indeed I was unfaithful to each of my four lovers with Olivier, but I hadn't been married then. Those vows for which I had separated from Olivier, I had broken with half a one-night stand in a small dark cupboard with someone I hardly knew. Such a tawdry, common, grey little tale. Geese, hawks, eagles, penguins can remain true to one mate all their lives, but not tacky Sarah Miles. I was now swirling downward, flailing out of control within that same doom that I had foreseen months before.

After my luggage finally came bumbling through and I was in my limousine, homeward bound, I decided it would be best to tell Robert as soon as possible. Not because I wanted to dump my guilt on to him, but if David ever continued with his project for a cover story, and he might, being the terrier he was, it was somehow cleaner if Robert had all the facts before him.

Turning into Mill Lane would normally have filled me with the sweetest joys of homecoming, but approaching the house up the long straight drive all I could see was that abysmally dark cupboard seeping guilt. Then two men arrived at the front steps to greet me. I recognized Robert's bonny shape, but who was the other? As we drew closer, the nightmare began to unfold. How could that familiar pear-shaped body cleverly encased in its Savile Row suit – that I had waved goodbye to at Kennedy airport this morning – be standing there next to my husband? I longed at that moment for my limousine to metamorphose into my Oscar hearse and shoot me off to the mortuary. Anything would be better than what was to follow.

As the limousine came to its final crunch on the gravel, I sat there, unable to think of what to do next. Robert came down the steps and opened my door. He took me in his arms, and I bit my lip to prevent the rising panic from taking charge.

'You've already met David from *Time* magazine?'

'Of course, but—' I couldn't finish my sentence.

'I nipped across and caught a Pan Am flight. I find Pan Am most reliable.'

Robert looked delighted. 'David got the go-ahead for his cover story, which means he'll be staying with us for—'

'As long as it takes,' butted in a triumphant David.

'I'll be in presently, I can't wait to hear all your news.

Tomcat's having his rest.' Robert strode back towards his study. How I cherished, needed that formidable Staffordshire bull terrier bounce of his! But watching him disappear, a shiver came over me, for I had no right to that walk any more. So lost was I in regret I failed to notice my dogs leaping to greet me, with Addo himself standing upright pawing at me.

'Would you kindly show me to my quarters? I need a wash,' said David suavely as he scrutinized his overly clean hands.

CHAPTER FIFTY-FIVE

I N NO TIME at all David became firmly ensconced, inte-
grated, one of the family firm. It didn't seem strange
that he and Tom became good friends pretty well
immediately. After all, Tom was still a baby and therefore
unaware of the calculation behind David's considerable
charm. What did seem odd was the way my mother didn't
see through him. She took a real shine to him, finding him
hugely entertaining, cultured, smart and clever.

Nothing got any easier. David still hadn't finished his
cover story, yet he kept what he had written so far an almost
coy secret. I asked Robert to hint heavily that he should hurry
up and finish the piece, but as David had only been around
for six weeks, Robert couldn't see what there was to worry
about. It was only me who was being sent potty. Was he
going to follow me around for ever, my shadow of guilt,
taking ridiculous notes? I turned desperately to Carolyn. She
came down for weekends occasionally with her new little
daughter, Lola. She had decided to have a baby out of
wedlock, never telling a soul who the father was. That
takes great strength. As for Lola, she turned out a perfect
charmer.

'Can't you tell David to take his ruddy *Time*-bomb piece
and screw it up his—?'

'You've made your bed, honey. Now you must lie on it.'

'What's that meant to mean?' I had never told Carolyn
about David and the cupboard. The more I thought about it
the more I realized Carolyn was to blame. 'It was you who
brought him into my life.'

'Exactly. But it's you who must get him out.'

'Can you find out if the cover story is legit?' I asked feebly.

'We already did all that in New York.' She was right. I knew the cover story was for real because David would await the mail for his pay cheque, yet I still smelt something rotten.

'How do I get him out?'

'He'll leave once he has his story, believe me. *Time* will order him back soon enough.'

I tried to get on with my life as best I could, but I was unable to breathe easy. Robert, on the other hand, was well into his next project, and found nothing too tiresome – to start with anyway – in David's suffocating presence. Where David was canniest was in his subtle talent for ego-boosting. I had, too late, alas, seen through it, but Robert was now the centre of David's formidable interest.

Another incident only added to my uneasiness. I was clearing out some papers in the drawing-room desk, when I noticed that something was missing. My heart skipped beat after wretched beat as I went frantically through every drawer in the house, searching, searching, searching, unusually thoroughly for me. I could find nothing. Where was my modest little bunch of Lionel's love letters tied up with a rather dirty, frayed piece of pink ribbon? I knew I should have thrown them away after reading them. Although he never instructed me to do so, it was surely the correct action for a loyal mistress? However impossible I might have found the thought of throwing away or burning such beautifully scripted declarations of love, my slackness was that of someone putting their own need to possess before discretion. Nevertheless I went on searching. Had I finally failed as a mistress as well as a wife?

All lost. Who would have removed them? Trina and José wouldn't even know who Lionel was. Were they all signed 'Lionel' or were some signed 'Larry'? Tina the nanny wouldn't do such a thing in a million years. What bothered me was a niggling feeling that a couple of them referred to Joanie, and another to the National and Noëlie. It wouldn't take anyone with any nous to put two and two together, added to which they were all written in his own beautiful hand. I was well and truly drawn and quartered. With no amount of imagination could I see Robert capable of such a scruffy deed, so it didn't take much detective work to arrive at the obvious conclusion. I had to face the fact that David Whiting was in possession of those letters.

One day, having become sufficiently convinced, I went through all David's things while he was up in London. I'd never in my life read anyone's mail before, even if it lay open before me. Yet here I was riffling through David's private belongings in *his* bedroom. There was nothing there. No little bundle tied up with a dirty frayed pink ribbon. As I left his room I swore I'd never spy again and I never have. Meanwhile guilt, like the cuckoo, had flown in, making room for herself by conveniently pushing the eggs of truth to one side. Little eggs like, 'When will I muster the courage to confess the cursed cupboard night?'

If only I hadn't gone to LA for those stupid Oscars I would never have met the man. Now here I was in much the same situation as I had been with Nona. I had to start looking at the faults within my own nature that brought all this crap upon my head. For obvious reasons I couldn't face David head on with stealing my love letters. So by degrees our cat and mouse existence developed.

'*Time* have asked me to cover the Cannes film festival, so I've hired a beautiful villa right on the sea. It would be wonderful if you, Robert and Tom would come out there for a bit of a holiday. You could all do with a break,' David preened cheerfully.

'But how can you be covering two stories at once?' I asked, suspicious.

'This story needs a change of scene. By coming to Cannes

I can finish both my assignments and kill two birds with one stone – plus get a bit of sun into the bargain.' David was a sun-worshipper, very much aware of his golden appearance.

'How can you afford such a holiday?'

'I can't, but believe you me, *Time* can.'

I asked Robert what he thought of a holiday in Cannes.

'Yes. You go on ahead and I'll follow after Thursday's meeting.' He looked tired.

'Please come, darling. Promise?'

His study phone rang. Watching him talking deals I realized how much he would benefit from the break. He had been working so hard on getting his next project off the ground, his own original screenplay of the romantic story of the doomed Lady Caroline Lamb.

So it was that Tomcat, David and I arrived in Cannes, with Robert following next day. David hadn't been giving us any tall stories regarding the generosity of *Time*, for the rented villa was most impressive. Late eighteenth century, one road back from the beach, the rooms cool, almost palatial with their massive high ceilings and great wooden shutters, protecting you from the midday glare, and beyond the shaded, elegantly laid out gardens, a secluded swimming pool.

Robert called the next day to say he was sorry but an important meeting had cropped up preventing him from coming, after all. My joyous mood plummeted back into my gummed-up cuckoo-nest of lowered standards and guilt. I didn't want to spend every evening running away from David's advances, yet now he held a key card. What had he done with Lionel's letters?

It turned out, astonishingly, to be a well-needed ten days of rest. David conveniently left early to cover the buying-and-selling jamboree on the seafront, leaving Tomcat and me to our own devices. I kept myself clear of the carnival. It's easy not to be recognized, even in Cannes during festival week, if you so desire. Mind you, I was no Robert Mitchum.

I slept with Tomcat, finding in him an effective guard for my honour. He had never been the same chap since we sold the Lamborghini, and desperately needed his daily fix of speed to keep him at peace with the world. I remember vividly his eye-popping euphoria when motorbikes zoomed by, and when David suggested we should go to watch the Monte Carlo Rally up the road I thought it an excellent idea. What I didn't know was that everyone in the South of France had had the same idea. Approaching Monte Carlo it was plain that we hadn't a hope in hell of being able to park the car anywhere near. The whole area for a two-mile radius was awash with vehicles.

'Doesn't matter, Mummy, we'll walk.' He was right. We parked, then walked a good mile and a half. It was more of a run, actually, because we were already late. I had on a strange outfit, with rollers visible in my hair, and a headscarf over the top. This prevented anyone from recognizing me (not that they would have anyway, but it's better to be safe than sorry).

It was impossible to get close enough to the action. Too many thousands of people all pushing forward to get a peek at the track. Not being one for crowds, to put it mildly, I wasn't prepared to submit to the glares and aggro you have to face as you push your way up to the front of anything. 'Sorry, Tomcat, but I think we didn't organize this outing too well. It's hopeless.'

'No!' screamed Tomcat. 'I want to see! I want to see!' As I have already explained, when Tomcat wanted something, come hell or high water, he ended up getting it.

I looked up to my left and saw many people watching from the balcony of a delectably old-fashioned hotel. How lucky they were, leaning out from their perfectly situated bird's-eye view, sipping champagne cocktails, while their smug smiles skimmed over us plebs below. 'Come on, Tomcat, we'll go in and watch from that hotel.' This turned out differently from what I anticipated. Not only was it as tricky to get to the hotel entrance as it would have been to stuff two sardines still alive into the tin, but as we climbed the steps to go in a man dressed in authoritarian stripes stepped forward to block our way, and blurted out something in French.

'Je suis anglaise,' I said as sweetly as I knew how.

'Ah! *Oui?* Where is your pass?'

'What pass?'

'All residents 'ave a pass.'

I quickly conjured up a new ploy which I immediately shot across his bows. I raised Tomcat's arm to the striped authority. 'This is the son of Jackie Stewart.' It was a real shot in the dark, for I didn't even know if Jackie Stewart was in the race, though I presumed he might be since his was the only name other than Stirling Moss that I knew in the racing world – apart from that of my childhood sweetheart, Piers Courage, of course. He wasn't sure whether to believe us or not and went into the hotel to produce another set of stripes. As they spoke together in French I thought it timely to produce some of my own.

'Ce garçon est le fils de Jackie Stewart.' They both gawped at Tomcat.

'Le fils de Jackie Stewart?' the first pair of stripes' eyes almost popped out of his head. I went onwards.

'Oui. Jackie Stewart demande moi escort le fils à l'hôtel parce que le "boum boum" de le racing cars est terrible pour l'enfant.' I put my hands to my ears demonstrating the agony of noise. They both just stood there as if my French was incomprehensible. Silly twats, I thought, not knowing their own language. So I tried again in English.

'Are you the mother?'

'Non, je suis la nanny.' As he looked up into my rollered hair under the headscarf, I had my first inkling of victory, so I pressed home. 'Surely he has a right to watch his own father's participation?' While they discussed this between themselves I quickly bent down, ordering Tomcat to cry, 'Daddy'.

'I want my daddy! I want my daddy!' What a thespian he was already!

'*Oui, oui*, I know it, I know it,' exclaimed my original set of stripes, picking up Tomcat. 'Follow me.' I had no idea how popular Jackie Stewart was. Both sets of authority, however briefly striped, expanded with every breath of the magic name.

'Le fils de Jackie Stewart! Excusez-moi. Le fils de Jackie Stewart!' he continued to shout as he held Tomcat high above the seething mass. I followed in their wake. What power there was to be found merely in a name! How exhilarating it was to climb the beautifully carved main staircase and float through the vast expanse of peopled terraces – I felt like Moses parting the Red Sea.

We arrived at the balcony I had noticed from the trackside. What a view we had! The only problem was that by now most of the people on the terrace were aware of this 'fils de Jackie Stewart'. The name Jackie Stewart was not only to be heard roaring over the Tannoy, but echoing endlessly around the hotel. From what I could gather he seemed to be the only person in the race. This was my first race meeting ever, so I knew nothing about the form, or anything else. From the general gist I gathered Jackie Stewart was not only favourite but way in the lead, making our situation even more dodgy. Tomcat had been lifted on to some tall German's shoulders so he could get a better view of Daddy as he came swooshing past us.

'Look at Daddy!' shouted the masses. 'Look at Daddy!'

To think that I was the cause of Tomcat's confusion. He'd never realized before what a real goer he had for a dad. He kept checking with me before getting hooked back into his trance of adrenalined hysteria as the cars zoomed by, again and again, accompanied by—

'Look! Daddy! Look! Daddy!'

'Jackie Stewart is winning! Hooray for Jackie Stewart!' Everyone round us had obviously put their money on Jackie Stewart. How in God's name was I going to get myself out of this one? What if Jackie Stewart was to win? All I could do was to stand and wait, while Tomcat grew more and more flushed by the minute, his face veritably bulging with speed, triumph and power. Mainly, of course, the power he found himself able to wield as the son of Jackie Stewart.

Out of the corner of my eye I saw an old friend of Robert, Nancy Holmes. She immediately recognized me. She was bound to be there, on a professional basis, being both a first-class photographer and a journalist. Nancy had been down to the mill the previous year, taking some excellent shots of the family, dogs and horses. I had to think on my feet, which were killing me. I'm useless at standing on my pins for very long.

'Tomcat, hang on up there, I'll be back in a jiffy.' Tomcat gave me one of his reprimanding looks before turning back to the action. I made my way over to Nancy.

'Hello, Sarah. What are you doing here?'

'Oh, we just popped in to watch the race.' I looked at my watch. 'We have to leave in a moment.'

'My goodness, your son has grown.' As luck would have it, just as Nancy was about to make her way over to get a better look at Tomcat, Jackie Stewart won the Monte Carlo Rally. The place went into an uproar. Bottles of champagne were poured, and Tomcat became a mass of bubbles as everything seemed to go berserk. All Tomcat knew was that Daddy had won. I had to get him out of there while the euphoric screaming was at its peak.

'Take him down for the lap of honour,' said the big German on whose shoulders Tomcat had been for the last ten minutes.

'Yes!' cried another. 'Come, I'll show you the way!'

This seemed the perfect opportunity to get lost. I waved

418

quickly to Nancy Holmes who hadn't a clue what was going on. 'Cheerio, Nancy. Come down to the mill soon, Robert would love to see you!'

With that Tomcat and I were manhandled by a group of men down the stairs towards the exit. 'Come, it's this way!' shouted the German, obviously wanting to use Tomcat for his own needs, which were to get into the pits.

'On second thoughts I don't think Mr Stewart would like his son to return to the pits, having sent us away earlier.'

The German couldn't believe his rotten luck, so I added, 'Would you go down and congratulate Monsieur Stewart on our behalf?' As he went to leave, Tomcat began to scream, well aware that I was keeping him from his daddy.

'I want my daddy! I want my daddy!'

The German turned back to us. I wanted to strangle Tomcat. 'Tell Jackie we'll see him at the house later, OK?' I didn't wait for a response, I just took Tomcat from him and ran. I was positive Tomcat and I were being followed. Carrying Tomcat high above me, pushing my way through the sea of people with no power of Moses to part the waves, I wondered at the amazing energy that can be mustered up when the need arises.

It just so happened that having found our car (about an hour and a half later because I'd forgotten to make a mental note of where I left it) I heard the noise of a siren. As soon as we had jumped into the car, the siren almost burst our eardrums and an ambulance went blasting past. Since the roads were blocked solid with traffic in each direction, I simply followed the ambulance. I'd always longed to do that, and I'd never had such an ideal opportunity. For the next quarter of an hour the power of Moses returned to me as once more I parted the Red Sea. It was certainly a most exhilarating day.

'Daddy won! Daddy won!' Tomcat couldn't wait to relay the whole experience to David, who in turn wished he'd been with us.

'What a story! I was the wrong end of town.'

'Yeah,' I said. 'Too busy killing two birds with one stone.'

Robert rang me next morning. 'Come on to Rome with me, and have a little rest before we begin.' If we were ever to get *Lady Caroline Lamb* up and running it would be through turning it into a joint venture with the Italian producer Franco Cristaldi (next to Carlo Ponti, the most powerful), husband of Claudia Cardinale. They had kindly invited us to stay at their villa for a few days prior to shooting, so we could check out the Italian locations. This was the first time I had had an opportunity to study a famous movie star at close quarters. It really opened my eyes, and left my mouth watering.

Claudia came into my room one evening before a night out in Rome. 'Would you like me to dress you up for dinner?' She seemed so keen that I hadn't the heart to let her down.

'All right, Claudia, if you think it's worthwhile.'

'What do you mean, "worthwhile"? You don't do the best for yourself, not at all.' She led me through their glorious modernized ancient villa, which sat in the countryside half an hour's ride out of Rome. Why is it that famous people's homes are so much more glamorous than one's own? My house resembled a large messy dog-kennel, whereas their villa was fit for a king. She led me through marbled corridors until we came to her private quarters. The lighting, textures and colours of her bedroom and four-poster bed forced me to pause, transfixed.

'Come through here into my dressing room,' said the Queen, gently.

It being still only the early seventies, remember, was it any wonder that her dressing table made me feel like an alien entering a foreign spaceship? I didn't possess a dressing table, always preferring to sit on the floor to make up – but this! I'd never seen the like before, complete with radio, cassette machine, record player, television, mirrors every which way, scripts, script holders and telephone. Special constructions to embrace a prodigious amount of different

make-up, lipsticks, scents, and even more for creams. Everything fitting in just so, with its overall order functioning
immaculately. Above us I noticed hundreds of little cubby-
holes all along the walls. She noticed my interest and opened
a few. Each contained a wig. Hundreds of wigs of all shapes,
colours and sizes. Mind-boggling.

'Sit down and make yourself comfortable.' The phone
rang, which enabled me to catch my breath and sit there,
watching her perfect mouth encompass the magnificent music
of the Italian language.

'Ciao.' She replaced the white receiver and smiled at me
apologetically.

'Would you like to choose one for tonight?'

I wouldn't, actually. I wanted to run away and hide, to
find a place where I could come to terms with the compari-
sons I was bound to make.

Claudia was a fine, exotic creature, moving through her
domain like a tigress in full control. Anybody who has
glimpsed her in the flesh could not fail to be moved by her
black eyes and her thick tawny hair, Delilah-like, framing her
provocative smile. Later I got a glimpse of Sophia Loren and
felt the same awe. Monica Vitti was Italian, too. So what was
it with these Italian women that made them so many streets
ahead of the rest of us?

'Come on, Sarah,' said Claudia, reaching up to a higher
cubbyhole. 'There must be one little wig that you like.'

'I think I'm best left alone, Claudia. I'm simply not the
type.'

'I won't hear of such nonsense.'

If I hadn't been feeling so defensive it would have been
enchanting to watch Claudia doing what she obviously did
best – apart from acting, that is. She put the whole of her
concentration into making me the belle of the ball (secure in
the knowledge that I would never succeed!). I found myself
musing what an Italian mama she was at heart, busily
tweaking the red wig she'd chosen for me this way and that.

Half-way through I was ashamed to find a little sour-grape pip lurking between my teeth. I couldn't help it, I just didn't want to be seen competing on the same playing field. (I trust I've grown up a little since then!)

'Claudia, I was never cut out to be a redhead.'

'Then let's try this one.'

I have to admit I did suit silky ash-blonde hair. Why, oh, why had God been so harsh with my fuzzy straightened brown brush?

I'd been feeling belligerent ever since I arrived, although at least I was free of David for a while. Was Claudia so serene *all* the time?

I asked her straight out, with no frills: 'Claudia, are you faithful to Franco?'

She caught the comb, having almost dropped it, looked at it, then decided to exchange it for another, all the while thinking how to play her answer. 'Of course.' She continued with her favourite sport, backcombing. 'We haven't been married that long.'

'Will you stay faithful, however long?'

She fruitlessly fussed with my wig. 'The woman doesn't stray, surely? Isn't it only when her man strays that she's finally left no choice?'

I loathe having my hair backcombed and a wig is no better. How could I say so to sweet Claudia? The time to leave was drawing nigh, so I rose. 'My, my! You've certainly transformed Cinderella!' I said, lying through my teeth. I stood for a moment watching her pouting at her reflection, then touching up her lipstick. She ended up looking the very best of Claudia, which wasn't half bad, believe me. I, on the other hand, resembled Vivien Leigh's second eleven in a rep version of *A Streetcar Named Desire*, at the end of an empty matinée. Much as I didn't want to be seen in Rome looking thus, I didn't want to make a scene either. So I thanked her, kissed her on both cheeks and retired to my room to fend off a most fearful attack from those two insatiable monsters, guilt and envy. 'See you downstairs in ten minutes. We mustn't keep the men waiting.'

As I walked down the regal marble staircase I caught sight of Claudia at the bottom, all alone in the main receiving room, checking herself in the mirror again. She was not aware of my presence so I was able to examine the private moment I had stepped into. I felt like I did when I crept into Mummy's bedroom at ten years old and found her naked, for that is how I caught Claudia – fully clothed yet totally naked. I knew I should make myself known, but felt a more urgent need to digest all before me. The secret look she gave her reflection that evening has stubbornly haunted me ever since. It was a look that only a great beauty would give, privately regarding her own perfect image. It stemmed from the solid confidence of knowing, without a doubt, that you *are* the most beautiful being on earth, yet with no arrogance, vanity or self-delusion whatsoever attached to that self-regard. She was returning the reality of her beauty, its blessedness, back to herself, and in return revelling childlike in its perfection. Beauty that simply *is*. Yes, that was it. Beauty simply *being* was what I found so compelling.

CHAPTER FIFTY-SIX

MIRACLES NEVER CEASE! *Lady Caroline Lamb* had finally got the green light. Robert's trepidation melted beautifully once Franco Cristaldi said, 'Full steam ahead!'

Robert had a great team around him. I was particularly pleased that Ossie Morris was lighting cameraman, because he was an old mate from both *Term of Trial* and *The Ceremony*. David Lean's editor, Norman Savage (doing a job I wouldn't like!), was not only first-rate and a saint but also a good friend of ours. It was thanks to Norman that Robert took that final leap of faith.

This film mattered more to Robert than anything in his whole life so far. This time he wasn't merely the writer, but was also producing and directing. I think all creative talents reach a stage in their career when they need to see their initial vision up there on the screen, without the inevitable distortion that occurs once it's handed over to someone else, not so much the need to go on a power trip as a deep desire to witness the original vision becoming *your* reality. It's also taking a stand against producers ripping off the artist as they cream off all profit to line their own pockets. *Lady Caroline Lamb* was to be a shit or bust gamble for the Bolt family – and why not? You're a long time dead.

I found the casting sessions thrilling, as we flipped through *Spotlight* looking for the right face. Margaret Leighton, someone I'd admired all my life but had never met, was to play Lady Melbourne (my mother-in-law). Jon Finch was Robert's final choice for William Lamb, and Richard Chamberlain had been keen to give us his Byron. Ralph Richardson had accepted to play the Prince Regent. This was specially good news because Ralphie had been a great old friend of Robert ever since he'd starred in Robert's first West End hit, *The Flowering Cherry*, with Celia Johnson.

'Who do you see as the Duke of Wellington?' asked Robert.

I couldn't think of anyone who was sufficiently aristocratic, with a long beak of a nose. 'John Gielgud?'

'No!' retorted Robert. 'Not enough balls.'

Rang a bit true. Besides, the script stated that Caroline Lamb went to bed with the Iron Duke one night in Paris. Once bitten, twice shy, perhaps, as far as Sir John and my lovemaking attempts were concerned.

'What about Larry?' asked Robert, straight in my eyes.

I hadn't thought of Lionel lately. All memories had been temporarily blotted out with the sadness of lost love letters. Needing to gather my senses, I settled for, 'He hasn't got enough of a beak, surely?'

'No. But ask the old bugger if he'd mind wearing a false nose and you've hooked him.'

He had a point there.

I wobbled into bed a few nights later, my thoughts whirring. Sir Laurence Olivier had accepted to play the Iron Duke (wig, false nose and all!). The plot of the film was mirroring life a little too closely for comfort.

Lady Caroline Ponsonby, daughter of the Duke and Duchess of Devonshire, was a mysterious creature, unlike anyone else. A free spirit whose head may have become bloody but never bowed in her quest for truth. She chained herself to life's edge, that dangerous spot where truth is most tangible. That's why I salute her, for she never wavered in her quest, even though it ultimately destroyed her.

This exotic butterfly married William Lamb, the shrewd, sensitive, considerate, nineteenth-century politician. Caroline was soon unfaithful to him with Lord Byron. Their affair shook the very cobblestones of Regency London's high society. He was flattered by her attention for a while, but eventually grew tired of her. Once she realized his love was on the wane she went to extremes to excite him, to lure him and, through her own demonstrative excesses, to fling herself back into his favour.

On one occasion she appeared as a topless blackamoor page at a fancy-dress ball just to be near him; another time she slit her wrists at a public dinner party in a desperately cocked-up attempt to draw attention to her aching heart. Her yearnings for Byron knew no bounds. On and on she went, continually making a public exhibition of herself, until Lamb's political career was in jeopardy. Caroline, still loving William, yet knowing she had foolishly compromised him as well as putting herself socially beyond the pale, went to Paris to pay court to the Duke of Wellington in one last bid to regain her position. With one snap of that great man's fingers, Caroline could indeed be accepted back in London's high society.

Alas, Wellington saw her arrival in Paris as merely an opportunity for some overnight poking. Once he had used her in his infamous 'hidyhole' (cupboard!), he threw her out with the early-morning curfew. Caroline returned to England, where she found herself with nothing, not even a smidgen's-worth of self-respect to keep her sane.

In the meantime 'Prinnie' (the Prince Regent) warned William of the consequences of his wife's actions, strongly advising him to take on the job of Secretary of State for Ireland. This advice didn't sit too well with William, for he was still deeply in love with Caroline, and left him with a cruel decision. Feeling rightly that his destiny lay in politics (he eventually became a distinguished Prime Minister to Queen Victoria), he finally sailed for Ireland, distancing himself from the stench of scandal and leaving poor Caroline all alone. She died soon afterwards of a broken heart.

This film's plot made me even more nervous than the plot of *Madame Bovary* or indeed *Ryan's Daughter*. I was secretly as proud of myself for keeping my dignity over being Lionel's mistress as I was ashamed at having succumbed to David

Whiting's night in the cupboard. I still hadn't found the guts to tell Robert. Besides, having David still in the house made my confession a wholly different basket of gooseberries. The truth was that Robert and I were still happy together, my love for him stronger than ever, so why destroy all that? My ears rang with that question, yet my heart yearned to come clean. I went over it all till I was dizzy. To which I now had to add Olivier! A twist to the plot in which I'd played no part. Was it coincidence? Fate? Luck? Doom? Or just showbiz? (Mind you, at this stage of my life I wasn't concerned about never being accepted back into society. That happened afterwards, in Hela Bend, Arizona.)

Two weeks later the whole film circus made its way north to Derbyshire. We had been given permission to shoot in Caroline's real home, Chatsworth, still inhabited by the Duke and Duchess of Devonshire. I had managed to persuade Robert to let me use Daisy as Caroline's own steed in the film. Unfortunately none of the stunt boys and gals would ride Daisy in the film, having all had a test run and politely declined. They offered me horse after horse, but I shook my head, determined that Daisy had every right to be immortalized with the rest of us. Besides, it was perfect casting. Both Daisy and Caroline relentlessly clung to life's edge.

The first shot was an interior. I used my Skye terrier, Gladys, as Caroline's dog in the film. 'Action!' shouted Robert.

I ran up the corridor past the third assistant, who was hidden in an alcove holding Gladys. He had to wait for his cue to release her, and in the preceding three seconds Gladys panicked. Thinking I had forgotten her, she tried to escape the third assistant's clutches. Poor sweet Gladys was left no alternative but to bite him viciously on the hand, forcing him into hospital, never to return. I took it as an omen, or had Mary, Queen of Scots, followed me to Chatsworth? Mary herself went everywhere with two Skye terriers hidden under her great skirts. When her head was finally sliced from her neck the terriers didn't know which end to mourn and both died soon after from broken hearts. That's how the story goes, anyway. I didn't wholly blame Gladys since I had warned every crew member not to go near her. On this occasion, though, the poor chap had no choice.

Once outside in the glorious gardens of Chatsworth, things improved greatly. The Duke and Duchess swanned down to the main lawn to fulfil their promise of moral support. How splendidly ostentatious Chatsworth was, a backdrop to end all backdrops with the foreground flaunting its fountains, beside which the Duke was elegantly uncorking a bottle of bubbly. The Duke and Duchess didn't leave, so I was forced to do the first outdoor shot in their presence. This made me doubly nervous since both were renowned horse-men and I had to gallop across the moorland and into the gates of Chatsworth at full speed. It was a long shot because we were going to use it for the front titles. Normally the film company would insist on a double doing such a reckless piece of riding. In the event I was glad all the stunt crew had declined. Robert promised me the camera would be close enough at the finish for the audience to know it was me and not a stunt girl doing the riding. (What vanity!) Fortunately my prayers were answered, and Daisy was as good as gold. So with the Duke and Duchess duly impressed, Robert and I were invited in for tea.

Walking through Chatsworth was as impressive as I knew it would be, but I wasn't expecting the Duchess to end her mini-tour by leading us up a narrow back-staircase. She checked her watch. 'Come on up. Let's have a drink, it's gone six.'

I wanted to hug her, once I'd taken in 'the private quarters'. Lucky things! They lived as snug as a bug in a rug.

'The dogs have taken over.'

I noted no inkling of apology, nor should there have been. It was a perfectly adorable patchwork quilt of a dog-kennel! Dirty blankets screwed up or hanging forlornly across ancient chewed dog-baskets, which in turn were scattered among precious antiques. The four-poster bed was littered with various breeds of spaniel and the like. Shoes had been tossed hither and thither; there were even a few cobwebs à la Miss Havisham. Hooray! A total lack of pretension – it smelt almost as doggy as the Old Mill to boot. So perhaps there *was* another way of living, after all. Claudia's villa was not the only route to good taste.

CHAPTER FIFTY-SEVEN

BEING THE CAPTAIN of a ship, especially the circus attached to a showbiz ocean liner, with millions of pounds riding on your back, wasn't in any way eating at Robert's good nature. He was astonishingly easy, bright and courteous under all the daily pressure.

In bed one night he said, 'Since that boy is still mooning around the place, I'll hire him in the publicity department. He'll be useful when dealing with the Americans. What d'you think?'

I buried myself in the pillow against his upper arm. Robert and I were under the impression that David was going to cover the making of *Lady C* for the eventual *Time* piece. Therefore *Time* magazine's timing was doubly unfortunate, for just as David had been hired by Robert Bolt, so he was fired by *Time*. They had decided not to pay any of his expenses during the 'Killing-Two-Birds-With-One-Stone-Cannes-Villa-Saga', or even the Sarah Miles/Bolt cover story. In firing David, *Time* magazine proved not to be the schmucks we had both taken them to be. No, the Bolts were now the schmucks!

We had a stiff two-week schedule in Italy with most scenes requiring a mass of extras, so we decided to leave Tom behind for the first week. He could rejoin us when the pressure was less hectic. It wouldn't have been much fun for him in a foreign country with neither of us around till ten at night.

Robert was turning into a fine director – except for one charming aspect which would give Ossie Morris (the lighting cameraman) the heebie-jeebies. During the shooting of a

complicated garden-party sequence, in a sumptuous villa
outside Rome, I noticed Ossie all pent up and went over to
him. It was probably going to turn out Robert's most challenging sequence so far, with almost a thousand extras and only
two days to shoot a three-day schedule. Ossie repeatedly
alternated a look at his watch with a quick gander at the sky
through his lens.

'What's up, Ossie?'

'His Nibs is driving me potty. Look at the time, it'll soon
be lunch.'

He was quite upset – for Ossie, that is. Robert was leaning
towards Jon Finch, orchestrating with his arms, obviously
wanting Jon to say the line in a certain way. Robert could
spend all day trying out different word emphases with the
actors, and completely forget about the camera.

'Watch this,' said Ossie, going up to tap Robert on the
back. Robert turned, and by the look of horror on his face,
Ossie could have been an intern come to take him away for a
serious operation without his pre-med. I laughed.

'Excuse me,' said the new third assistant. 'I have a phone
message for you.'

Tom had been taken to Great Ormond Street hospital and
was in an oxygen tent. I read it over and over again. I had to
go home, but how *could* I? We hadn't been away more than
five days. He had had no asthma when we left. Not wanting
to disturb Robert before the lunch break, I went to the
production office to phone home. David Whiting answered.
'He's OK. I just thought it was better to be safe than sorry.'

It transpired that David had taken it upon himself to
organize Tom's stay at Great Ormond Street.

'It's hard for either of us to come back today, unless he's
in danger.'

'I'm just about to leave now. I'll call you when I've seen
him for myself.'

I was grateful for David going up to see him, but why did

he send Tom there in the first place? I rang the hospital. They thought he was in no immediate danger, but said to ring again at lunchtime.

A strange feeling suddenly overwhelmed me. What if Tom were to die and I wasn't there for him? I had to go home at once. I didn't see myself as one of those 'showbiz' parents who were unable to be by their child's side because they were too busy filming out in sunny Rome. I would tell Robert at lunchtime that I was going home willy-nilly.

'But, darling, we can't stop filming now.' Robert was marching up and down, hardly able to contain himself. 'Bloody typical!' I caught the gist of 'Wouldn't he just!' It was true, though. While the mother in me wanted to run to my child's bedside, something else told me it was one of Tom's canny timings.

'Let me go, Robert. Just for twenty-four hours.'

'How can I?'

'Please!'

He marched up and down, up and down. 'What about it, Fernando?' he asked Cristaldi's second in command. Fernando weighed the balance manually, Italian style. 'Out of the question. All these extras have to be paid and tomorrow they get paid elsewhere.' He pouted apologetically.

Fortunately David Whiting called back to say he would stay at the hospital, and that he and Tom were getting on like a house on fire. Tom recovered rapidly after David's appearance at the hospital. He often talks about the time he was dying in an oxygen tent and neither Mummy nor Daddy came to see him. He talks of David Whiting, too, and of his kindness at the time. What a cocktail of confusion. Nothing is ever as it seems.

Such a titanic terror met me when I awoke a few mornings after that I ducked under the sheets to escape reality. Today was the big day. I was about to start the sequence in the great Palace of Caserta with the Duke of Wellington (Paris had come to Italy). I hadn't seen Olivier since Hasker Street when he walked around my bedroom auditioning for Gandhi with a sheet over his head. Oh, and that brief time in my dressing room after *Vivat!*. It was going to be tricky, especially since Tomcat and David were arriving the same afternoon. Hardly tricky, though, more the excruciatingly tender merging into downright unbearable.

In my dressing room next morning I was quaking all over, wondering if the flame would still be burning just as bright. It mustn't be, I thought. I knew for sure that whatever else happened we were not to risk rekindling it. While these emotions persisted in playing havoc with my insides, he tiptoed quietly into my dressing room, unannounced. He saw me through my mirror and smiled his wonderful affectionate smile. Christ! My heart sang!

'I haven't put my nose on yet. Thought it best to say hello first.'

I can't for the life of me remember a nose coming between us before. He kissed me thoughtfully before bending the top of his head at me. 'Going bald on top. See?'

'You always were.' I kissed his bald patch, which hadn't got any bigger.

'When you've finished making up come with me—'

'While they fix your nose.' He gave me a knowing look before exiting. I knew his habits, I knew the regime, I knew his ways. It was quite simple, nothing whatsoever had changed. I just knew him, that's all.

I wore a short blonde wig for *Lady C*. What joy it was having the extra two hours in bed rather than stuck in make-up trying to get my hair to do nothing more than *look* like hair. Lady Caroline was famous for wearing strange eye make-up, which was rather complicated for me. I realize now how wrong I was in choosing to wear it, because people thought it wasn't the character but Sarah Miles being vain. There we are, you can't win 'em all.

Once make-up and wig were shipshape, there was no time to go to Olivier while they 'did' his nose. I was called on to the set for rehearsals. I'd much rather have had a few moments more with him somewhere private; after all, it had been almost four years. The set – the main ballroom of the Caserta Palace (we're not talking small here) – was not the ideal place for a pair of long-lost lovers to hold their reunion.

How regal, spiffing, and splendid he looked, standing by the immense fireplace, all white, scarlet and gold with his immaculate posture unyielding. He *was* the Iron Duke. Iron-grey hair, great beak of a nose, white breeches and a silver sword glittering as only the Iron Duke's would dare. My heart came pitter-pattering back from my dressing room, so I smacked it hard and sent it packing. He did a double take, for he didn't recognize me immediately now that I was fully made up and ready to shoot. Slowly we closed the distance between us – that is, the Iron Duke was making his way over to Lady Caroline Lamb. I noted a few scattered traces of Laurence Olivier here and there in his walk, but Lionel Kerr was nowhere to be seen.

'You look a lot like Vivien in that gear.' He looked neither left nor right, simply kissed me on the tip of my nose. 'I love you still.'

'Don't play with me. It's hard enough without—'

'Without what?'

I looked downward, embarrassed.

'Where's Tom?'

I was intrigued that he knew his name. 'He's arriving with nanny this afternoon.'

'Bring him on to the set. Eh?'

'I don't usually because he's so obstreperous.'

'I want to meet him.'

Although his tone was brimming over with Wellingtonian command, I didn't bring Tomcat on to the set that day, simply because I couldn't cope with it all. David came in later, buzzing around us like a demented dragonfly, never leaving us alone for a moment. I knew he knew something . . . perhaps he *had* guessed who the love letters had come from.

'Who's that chap over there?'

'Publicity. Shall I bring him over?'

'No. I don't want publicity and I don't like the look of him.'

'Why not?'

'I watched him with you earlier. There's something manic about him.'

I remained silent as we watched the shooting in progress.

'Robert's working his balls off, I see.'

That was for sure.

Because of Lionel's badgering that Tom be brought on to the set, I found myself wondering if perhaps Lionel thought Tomcat was his.

'He couldn't possibly be yours,' I said next day while we hung around either waiting to shoot or for Tomcat's arrival.

'I know that,' he replied with a double wink. 'Look, here he comes.'

How did he know that the little fellow making his way along the great expanse of marble was Tomcat? I rushed over to say hello. Considering he'd recently been in an oxygen tent he looked ravishingly rosy. He threw himself into my arms as he always did.

'See? I've brought him back safe and sound,' said David who was suddenly, as always, at my side.

'Yes. Thank you, David.' I meant it. 'Tomcat, come over and meet a friend of mine.'

I took him by the hand and crossed the ballroom to Lionel, who had taken up his favourite stance beside the great fireplace. He was looking more regal today than ever before – positively aglow with fearsome authority. Boots shimmering, sword gleaming, brass buttons brighter. 'Tomcat, this is Laurence Olivier. Larry, this is Tomcat.'

Tomcat looked him up and down. 'Hello, cunt face.'

The Iron Duke was aghast – as indeed was I. 'Haha! I haven't been called that for quite a while,' quipped the Duke with a debonair toss of his cuffs.

Tomcat immediately pointed at him. 'Why are you wearing a wooden nose?'

The Iron Duke clutched his nose like a captive maiden
might her private parts before being raped. Then he stood
straight as a giant and bellowed, 'Make-up!' before departing.

Tomcat eyed me.

'How did you know he was wearing a wooden nose?'

'Because it was coming off.'

Seemed a fair enough assumption to me. 'But don't let me
hear you ever saying cunt face again, it's very rude. Where
did you pick that one up?'

'From you and Daddy.'

That, too, seemed fair enough.

Next day David Whiting was doing his rounds and Robert
was, as usual, going over and over other actors' lines,
orchestrating them to within an inch of their lives. Lionel and
I were in bed together. Under the bedclothes Lionel was
being sweetly wicked, or was it the Duke of Wellington? I
was too nervous to feel the difference.

Suddenly Olivier laughed. 'Vivien was the last one to call
me cunt face. And she only did so in jest. But your little
blighter meant it.' He bit my finger, hard. 'Your language is
almost as blue as hers.'

'Which in turn is not so purple as yours.'

He nipped my bottom. God almighty! How desperately
tender it turned out to be as he began playing his toe against
mine; yes, deep down in bedclothes, beneath endless woolly
nighties, things were shaping up.

'Did you fancy Robert Mitchum?'

'Yes. Very much.'

A long silence followed.

'Did you go to bed with him?'

'Yes.'

Another long silence. I think an Othello jealousy was
creeping in.

'Was it fun?'

He was fumbling around beneath blankets and nighties.

'Hardly. We had too much nightie to negotiate.'

He looked at me oddly, fighting his way through nightie tangles, so I told him about our love scene in *Ryan's Daughter*.

He laughed. 'I'm glad nighties are in.'

It was touching to feel him relax so, after clarification. He really had been jealous of Mitchum.

'Tom's too skinny. Needs fattening up.'

'He blows his food straight out again.'

'Nonsense. I'll come down this evening and show you how to feed him. I have a knack with kids.'

Lionel was certainly going to need one with Tomcat's determined eating habits. He had no idea what he was in for.

'OK. You're certainly welcome to have a go.'

He gave me a strange look as we went back to snuggling under the blankets. 'I've never stopped loving you.'

My heart came pittering back disobediently from my dressing room. Fortunately David Whiting, barging his way into our private hidyhole with a couple of photographers, stopped it in its tracks.

'Could you both tear yourselves out of that bed a moment?'

'Why?' snapped Olivier.

'These two guys have come to photograph you both for *Paris Match*.'

'Tell them to fuck off!'

That did it. David vanished, dumbfounded. Watching his Savile Row suit disappearing I yearned to share all my sins with Lionel, because I knew he of all people would understand.

Out of the blue he said, 'Where do you collect them?'

'What do you mean?'

'He's obsessed with you. Another schizophrenic, manic-depressive nymphomaniac.' He was off again, tumbling his tongue-twister back and forth.

'Bullshit! Not everyone can be a schizophrenic, manic . . . whatsit.'

'Maybe not, but he is. I'll bet my life on it.'

With the warmth of the bedclothes giving me confidence, very slowly I thawed sufficiently to relate to him most of David's history (leaving out the cupboard – for the moment anyway). Lionel's toes twitched under the bedclothes as I shared my love-letter fears. He put his head on his arm, deep in thought. 'Did I sign them all Lionel?'

'If I remember rightly. With no address.'

'When you get them back, destroy them.'

'He may not have taken them.'

'Course he has, little fucker. I'll twist his balls off if he comes near me again.'

When my tale was over, he took my skull in his hands precisely in the same fashion as he'd done all those years ago over Nona, high up on Chanctonbury Ring.

'You must have slept with him, for him to behave thus,' curling his tongue across his ever thinner bottom lip.

'I never slept with Nona, or Johnnie Windeatt.'

'Perhaps. But you've slept with him.' He chinned in David's direction. 'Don't fool your old Lionel. Get back my love letters, destroy them, then get *him* out – hear me?'

'Easier said than done.'

'Of course. He likes the way you raise his spirits—'

'While he vampires my light, I know.'

'Then learn.' Still holding my head in a vice, his hands firmly drew my face into close-up. 'Before it's too late.' That wicked, wicked chameleon tongue of his slithered briefly across lizard lips before glossing my forehead. Then, after a regal swirl of the bedclothes, he galloped off to Lionel Castle (his dressing room).

The next evening, our last night on that location, there was a knock on the door of my suite, I opened it and there he was. 'Aren't you going to invite me in?'

Lionel was correct in his claim to have a knack with kids. He did indeed. Most patient he was as he piled up the spoonfuls and gently placed them an inch before Tom's mouth. I watched Lionel opening his mouth, just like I remembered my mother doing with me when I was little. How odd it all is. Humans nursing, eating, teaching, living, coupling, breeding and then dying with no real change along the rocky way. Pity, that. Just at that pitiful moment Tom blew his dinner, which Lionel had kindly placed most diligently into his mouth, straight back into his face.

'Now I *am* a cunt face!' said Olivier, wiping the nasty substance from his front.

Tom thought this an absolute hoot, splashing his fork into his dinner. 'I'm not going to eat – no way!'

Lionel couldn't fail to catch Tom's excellent Mitchum impersonation. He twirled round and looked straight into my eyes. It was a haunting glare out of which sprang: 'Has Ralphie played his scenes yet?'

'Yes.'

'Was he good?'

'I have no scene with him.'

'Rushes?' He looked right into me, dying for the answer.

'Brilliant.'

Silence. The great rival Ralphie had got him going.

'Can I have a brandy?'

I had been too busy thinking about Tom's mess everywhere.

'Since when a brandy?' He had always been a whisky or a champagne man.

He bellowed softly, 'Twenty-two years'll soon be up and then I can crack open the coconut.'

I gave him a brandy. His nostrils twirled around the rim. 'Not Napoleon, I'm afraid.'

'The Duke of Wellington can't get a Napoleon?'

' 'Fraid not, sire. Where did you plant your coconut?'

He kissed my hair. 'Right here.'

Robert came in soon after that. I was, for some reason, most relieved to see him. We talked about the film for a while.

'Have dinner with us, why not? Just Dicky and me?'

Dicky was not much more than a month old when I first met Olivier. Watching him sitting there, a confident eleven-year-old cracking creaking jokes beside my Heathcliff, I realized for probably the first time how old his Cathy had got. During my years with Lionel I had been living in the land that time forgot. Yet how it had galloped since then. That evening time didn't pass for a while, it simply was. In that moment of time not passing I realized most clearly that the ache within me for Lionel wasn't one of wishing, but wishting. How can one waste one's life on a wishting love? Lionel wasn't part of my world any more. He never really had been. Different worlds spinning within different timings. How often have the mistimings of fate abandoned lovers to fumble through different worlds? Our two worlds had intertwined once more, thanks to Robert. It felt good that both Olivier and I had chosen to enter Robert's world together for a while. It had been a sparkling affair.

'Thank you, Larry, your Iron Duke surpassed the character written,' said Robert sincerely.

'My pleasure, old boy.'

Having allowed the correct time to elapse, Lionel and a charming little old man called Dicky bade us farewell. He kissed me briefly on the cheek and that was the last I was to see of him for quite some time.

CHAPTER FIFTY-EIGHT

B ACK IN ENGLAND we had to return to Chatsworth for some of the more dangerous riding shots to put over the titles. (These had been purposely saved for the end of the film in case I killed myself.) Daisy was feeling a touch overly perky that day. We had to gallop beside the Land-rover for about quarter of a mile and then turn off to streak down across the moorland with Chatsworth looming in the distance. Robert had the Land-rover rigged up with two cameras. He turned to the driver and warned him, 'This horse is fast, so be prepared.'

The driver gave Robert a don't-teach-your-grandmother-to-suck-eggs look.

'Action!' yelled Robert.

Daisy was away like a rocket. The Land-rover had enormous difficulty keeping abreast of us. 'Christmas! Forty mile an hour!' shouted the astonished driver.

'OK. Veer off now, Sarah!' commanded Robert through a megaphone. I turned Daisy towards Chatsworth way down beneath us. She was going a bit too fast for the sharp angle, so I tried slowing her up, but she was well past paying any heed. I felt her whole being shiver with the ecstasy of power, speed and freedom. As she showed her gratitude by doing her oh-so-familiar buck-and-a-rear, my hands slipped a fraction on the reins. Daisy recognized her moment and wasted no time in whisking them from me. Ludicrously at her mercy, I caught a glimpse of my future – Daisy and I galloping out of control all through the fountains and over those immaculate lawns. The prospect of the Duke and Duchess's disdain was more than the snob in me could endure. No, it didn't bear thinking about. I knew I had no choice but to bail out. The ground was rough and stony, and in the valley below Chatsworth loomed closer every second. Memories from all my childhood experience of bailing out (I practised balancing on my pony's rump at the canter when I was little) rushed to the fore, bolstering the fear. Then, out I bailed.

What was it that followed next? Imagination? Illusion? Out-of-body experience? Make-believe or the near-death experience? Whatever name we settle on – it happened.

My neck was first to make contact. Sadly it met with a rock. A great deal of pain followed, but fortunately my own bodily anaesthetic came into play and put me out. But was I really out? I could still feel the pain, but gradually it dispersed as I began to lift, then float upwards, seeing everything from above. I saw myself clearly lying there on the ground, as a few people from Chatsworth came running out to catch Daisy. The Land-rover came trundling up, and figures jumped out hurrying to check if I was hurt.

But I wasn't hurt, I was high above them, safe within my bird's-eye view. As more people came running, I zoomed back even further to see figures arriving and leaning over my still body on the ground. The end result was a very long shot of a circle of onlookers on the moors beside Chatsworth. That was the last image I can recall before waking up in hospital.

'Lucky your neck wasn't broken.' Robert was leaning over me. How I loved him. 'Lucky for me, anyway, since it was my fault for letting you do it.'

He knew that was rubbish.

'Did we get it in the can?'

It transpired we hadn't.

'We need a linking shot of Caroline and Chatsworth together,' said the editor, Norman Savage. Unfortunately we had to wait, for I was forced to wear a brace round my neck for eight weeks. A bloody bore it was too.

The crux of the film, the centrepiece of Robert's theme – the Romantic versus the Classic – was a dinner-party scene shot at Chatsworth over two days. It was brilliantly written,

Robert's best, and superbly acted. The main players were all seated waiting for Lady Caroline's entrance. She had been in Paris visiting Napoleon and Josephine and while there she'd danced the wicked new waltz which had been raging through the nation like a bush fire. (No one before then held their dancing partner in their arms.) She made her entrance that evening in another fashion sweeping Parisian high society: freshly dampened transparent gauze was laid across heavily rouged nipples protruding above the exotically feminine Empire line. So all in all the screenwriter gave his wife some entrance.

Norman was explaining the sad state of affairs in the editing room. 'If you want to keep the scene we'll have to accept an X certificate.' (Financial suicide.)

'But that scene's what the whole damn film's about!'

Robert's toes started twitching.

'To be honest Robert,' – Norman was never anything else – 'will anyone digest the brilliant patter of your theme with those breasts cocked high in every shot?'

'But that's the whole point. Those nipples are part of the whole Romantic versus Classic argument!'

Norman took Robert's shoulder in an attempt to keep his lid on. 'But, Robert, no audience will be listening to your argument with juicy nipple hovering.'

'You mean the whole scene has to go unless we accept an X certificate?'

Norman nodded sagely, knowing we would never get our money back if we were released as an X. 'You can keep the scene up till Sarah's entrance.'

Just my luck. Everyone else's too. Shimmering performances mangled on the cutting-room floor because of Josephine's blasted tit fashion.

Robert clasped Norman by the shoulder in a friendly fashion, but Norman flinched, quite badly. 'I hardly touched you, man.'

Next day, Norman pulled up his sleeve and there they

were, two purple marks where Robert had barely touched him. Robert took him to our London doctor immediately.

It turned out that Norman was far gone down leukaemia's pathway, and in the early seventies there was little hope of a reverse. His last weeks were spent in the cancer ward of St Bartholomew's Hospital with all his editing toys around him. While he finished editing *Lady Caroline*, not a single fellow-patient died. But after he completed 'The End' titles, many of those in the ward fell dead in agreement, including dear, saintlike Norman.

I went over to talk with Robert in his study one day. It was hard to console him after Norman's death: theirs had been a rare friendship. And because Robert wouldn't hear of another editor taking over, I believe that same loyalty strangled *Lady Caroline Lamb*. However good an editor Norman was, how could he possibly function from an inner place of balance while dying of leukaemia? Although I know in Robert's place I would have done the same, I would still love to get hold of the film today and re-edit it, adding the scene that was removed. But staring out of his study window that day, without the wisdom of hindsight, I only knew that the film's brightest, wittiest, cleverest scene lay dead on the cutting-room floor.

The mill race, like my whole life, was pounding onward regardless, and the river was awash with flotsam, jetsam and pollution. 'It's becoming whiter and whiter by the week.'

As Robert looked out on the sorry sight, he suddenly stretched his head upwards. 'That's not detergent, that's Addo!'

Indeed he was right. A pair of black shiny eyes struggled among the raging white bubbles. We both ran like crazy.

Robert plunged in, with me close on his tail. We grabbed Addo's and together managed to bring him ashore. I dried him out completely with the hair-dryer and we snuggled up on the sofa, warm and cosy together. At about ten that night, as I kissed him gently, he gave me such a contented smile. I crept out of the room. Next morning he was in exactly the same position with exactly the same smile on his lips, but all was frozen in time. Two years previously the vet had warned me to keep Addo out of the river. But why should I ban Addo from his river when it was his life, his castle's moat, his home? I had no right to take it from him, for *my* sake. No, I did right to let him die as he did, living his life to the full – of that I am sure. The Addo era was my best time. He had brought me ten years of good luck. Bad luck, I believe, like good, comes in cycles, usually a decade at a time. I'd had more than my share of ten years' good luck, give or take a pain or two. Now my sixth sense began quivering as, surreptitiously, the first whiff of bad luck bowled itself in.

David Whiting, still hanging around the Old Mill, drove us beyond the point of no return. I hadn't been nearly so compassionate of late, probably due to my neck brace, which rattled at his presence. Since returning from Italy I didn't know how to deal with him. Lionel's warnings didn't help, neither did they solve the mystery of the lost love letters. I *had* to get rid of him.

Oddly enough, as David grew impossible, Mother still wouldn't hear a bad word against him. I often wondered what he had done to her to make her loyalty towards him so unshakeable? Perhaps she had ordered him to steal Lionel's letters? See how easy it is to become paranoid and untrusting of everyone? Let this be a lesson to all who are in the midst of deceiving those they love.

'Robert, I can't get him to leave. He says he's still working for you.'

'Let's put him in Hasker Street for a while.'

Finally he was persuaded that living in Hasker Street

445

would be beneficial; after all, there's a limit to what journalism you can do stuck out in the English countryside. He reluctantly packed his bags and I drove him up.

'Can I come down to see you all soon?' He looked soulful at that moment and I kissed him politely on the cheek. He was OK when he put on the charm and sparkled, whatever Lionel said. 'Of course you can.'

I showed him how Hasker Street functioned. He liked it a lot, he said. I wasn't too keen on him being there, but at least it got him out of the Old Mill and one step nearer to New York.

A few weeks later I received a message to ring him urgently. I found this rather foreboding. Even more so when I couldn't get him on the phone, for it was continually engaged. I kept ringing and ringing, I'm not sure why. Late that same evening, 'Go up and check that he's OK,' advised Robert. I did just that.

As soon as I entered the house I could smell something rotten. There was David on the drawing room floor. His arm had fallen on top of the telephone, forcing it out of its socket. I couldn't move him, he weighed a ton. It brought back memories of Nona and her overdoses. Was this an overdose or was he dead? I called an ambulance, then went to fetch a mirror to check if he was still breathing. I couldn't tell too well. Besides, I was numb inside my neck brace. I sat, feeling nothing, in the ambulance while it squealed its way to oh-so-familiar St George's Hospital.

'You'll have to wait here, miss,' said a young woman dressed in some kind of uniform.

'Will he be all right?

'Hard to tell. He took a massive overdose.'

I was past caring as I sat waiting to hear if David would pull through. What was his life or death to do with me? His life wasn't my life, we were merely connected, momentarily, via a cupboard. My desire to solve the riddle of the missing love letters made it hard to think rationally. Finally all became clear. Love letters or not, if he lived he must leave England immediately.

Should I let him depart with the letters in his briefcase? Should I challenge him with stealing them? Should I hint at him taking them? I began to realize that my need to get rid of him once and for all was far more urgent than any missing love letters. If the truth be known, everything had been numb since Lionel gave me that final brief kiss on my cheek. I hadn't known how much I had been longing to see him once more. I could feel only one thing: Lionel's fingers pressing my skull. 'Get rid of him. Before it's too late.'

It became just that: too late. I was about to reach my lowest point. The excuse I gave myself for my coming actions was that the role of mistress was the only part of my life that I hadn't (yet) fallen short in. We were in Hasker Street, and David, once again, was looking his manic best. Polished, witty, swooping here and there. (Thank God there were no fax machines in his day. Who knows what the bills would have been otherwise!) Out of nowhere he turned to me with the devil dancing in his eyes. 'Lionel's the Duke of Wellington. I knew long ago but we won't split hairs.'

Silence. Lionel's demands echoed in my ears. 'Get my love letters back, destroy them, then see him out.'

'I'll return your love letters, if you'll sleep with me.' He went all coy, the bastard.

CHAPTER FIFTY-NINE

IN 1973 I PLAYED opposite Robert Shaw in a film of L. P. Hartley's *The Hireling*. Ironically it was a project that for many years my brother Chris and I had been desperate to make. All it required were two actors and a car, but we couldn't get the rights. I would have loved to have done the script for this sad twenties' tale of a chauffeur falling in love with his boss, a lady, but I couldn't write.

With Alan Bridges directing, there was a happy, professional atmosphere on set. My dream of real team spirit came true, despite the dreaded Whiting waiting in the wings. My home in the film was the elegant Sutton Place near Guildford, owned at the time by Paul Getty. His flirtation was drier than Bertie's, if one could call it a flirtation at all. More a leisurely confrontation. Until the moment he tapped his lap for me to go and sit (while keeping his beady eye on every crew member) I'd heard nothing but derogatory things about the poor fellow: meanest, stingiest, grumpiest man on earth, and so on. Since I was passing time before the next shot, humouring him didn't seem a bad idea. Besides, the way he tapped his lap at me as he sat on the window-seat reminded me of Lionel. I had been snooping around the stately home in search of the infamous public phone booth that the press was forever mentioning. I plucked up courage to ask him outright. 'I can't find your payphone. Where is it?'

He shrugged. 'How the hell would I know?' He bade me follow him around Sutton Place. He gestured left and right, authorizing me to look anywhere I wanted for the phone. We finally ended up in an elegant corridor leading to his bedroom. Sitting on the edge of the bed, he reached under to retrieve a pair of ancient leather slippers. Even empty he seemed to remain in them, for they had moulded lovingly to his foot shape. While he slipped his stockinged feet into them, I noticed how like a monk's cell the room was – one wooden chair, bare walls. OK, there was a Picasso above his bed, but that was all. Once he was comfily beslippered we returned to our ringside view on the window-seat in the front hall. As he tapped me back on to his lap, we watched the crew setting up the gear before us.

'How many weeks is the shoot?' he inquired.

'Ten.'

'I've been watching them and their workload. I've counted sixteen out of twenty-eight redundant. I'd cut the crew in half and sack the *Sun* readers.' He had a point.

'But no one would be left.' It was the same on every film when we had the unions. Hundreds of fat bellies sitting around reading the *Sun*.

Tom struck up an affiliation with Robert Shaw from day one and quite rightly so – the man was a wizard with little ones, being a packhorse of energy with an invincible sparkle. While we were filming in the Royal Crescent, Bath, he knocked on the door of my room. The hotel was ancient, its suites named after historical figures. Looking at my four-poster bed he smiled wryly. 'I should have brought Mary with me. She'd rest most suitably in the Mary Stuart room.' (Robert Shaw was still married to the beautiful but doomed Mary Ure.)

'It's odd they put me in here.'

'Why? You played her, didn't you?' I was amazed he knew, let alone the hotel management. That evening Robert Shaw and I weren't too comfortable with the silence – we hardly knew each other.

'Could you bear it if I read a bit of my next book to you?'

'Please do.' I was unexpectedly moved by the tale that Robert read to me that evening. It was the swan-song of two old-timers falling in love in an old people's home, and it was fascinating listening to an actor performing his own written work so colourfully. To be honest, I'd never thought about two eighty-year-olds doing it. Shaw opened my eyes to the fact that we're all capable of romancing till we drop, and some of us do.

Shaw came down for the weekend with a pale and listless Mary Ure. I immediately took a shine to her mysterious, poignant femininity. I brought her breakfast up on a tray and she remained in bed while Robert and I played table tennis. Some men don't like women beating them. Robert Shaw wasn't one of those. No, he hated *anyone* beating him. He was a ferocious competitor, though I didn't quite ascertain the depths of his feverish desire to triumph until we were playing table tennis that evening.

We had left my Robert and Mary in charge of the kitchen activities (I'd just put the chicken in the Aga) while we went up into the mill to have a couple of games. In the third game out of three, I won with some to spare.

'I'd better get back to the chicken.'

Shaw went ashen, barring my way. 'Go back and play.' I could tell he meant it by the continuous jaw-clenching rippling across his handsomely carved features. Attempting to remain the calm hostess with the mostest, I returned to the table for another best of three. I decided to beat him again in the final game, and again he didn't like it one little bit. I became more than a little perturbed. Was this his usual behaviour, or was it me again? What did I do to bring out the worst in everyone?

'I must go and see to the chicken—'

'Oh, no, you don't! You stay here until you're well and truly beaten.' Should I quickly play him again and let him win? Why should I? Why did I always have either to pretend to lose or to ingratiate myself into the favours of those I was beating? Tired of men and their egos, I played him again and decided to slaughter him. I'm not a brilliantly talented sportswoman, but then we are only as good as the hours we put in; as the dunce of the classroom I compensated elsewhere. As I went to the door, again he blocked my way. Observing him standing there, simply ravenous for revenge, was a pretty lethal sight. It was as if all humour had bled from his face, draining him of his usual buoyant chirpy benevolence. Every smidgen of the lighter side of Robert Shaw had gone walkies.

'We'll swap bats this time. Come on, the best of three.'

My Knight of Shining Wisdom appeared, perfectly on cue. I was hugely relieved to see him. 'What's going on? We're waiting for dinner.'

Later that night I told Robert of my experience. He hooted. 'I know how he feels. It's infuriating being beaten by a younger woman.'

'It shouldn't be,' I replied grudgingly. Mind you, I was no better, having recently felt like bashing Robert over the head with my croquet mallet . . .

CHAPTER SIXTY

ROBERT WILL, I think, back me up when I say that any woman who relies totally on her husband for her own well-being is going to need more from him than he is capable of giving. A brilliant mind such as Robert's needs space and aloneness to function. As I never saw him in the daytime, my whole life revolved around our nights together. I had no enriching inner life to fall back on. I had my stud farm and Tom, but I was still ludicrously primitive both intellectually and spiritually. I relied on Robert to satisfy my yearnings. As life food, saviour of my soul *and* Don Juan he didn't stand much chance. So like two over-sensitive snails we retreated backwards into our individual shells, mine being thickly encrusted with shame and lacking the lustre of self-respect.

At around this time, Mitchum came into town – which had the potential to be pretty darn dangerous, especially for someone in my vulnerable position. No sooner had he rung to tell me his Dorchester suite number, than David Whiting stole it from my address book and went knocking on his door. I'll let Mitchum take over the story.

'I opened my door to a juicy carrot [a joint] dangling in front of my nose. Jaundiced and jet-lagged, I gently sniffed the air. Smelt real sweet. Just about to thank him and pay up when this weirdo pushes past me, slamming my door. I caught his eye and there was death perching right in the corner of it. Man, that was plenty enough for me. I went down on all fours on the floor like a wounded animal. It was the only time in my life I chose not to fight back. No way, man! Never fight when you see death in the eye.'

Apparently, so Mitchum says, David just kept kicking

452

him on the floor, over and over again. Once exhausted, he took the stash and ran. Mitch rang soon after.

'Come on up, lady, I wanna see you.' I've never been able to share my fears with anyone, not with my mother, father, brothers, sister or friend. It was a long time since I had indulged in public tears and I hadn't realized until I found myself confessing my Mills and Boon necrology to Mitch just how frail I had become.

'You gotta get him out, honey. He's lethal.' Everyone was giving me such sound advice and I, like most who knew him, was frightened of David Whiting.

'Even if he kills himself?'

'Sure, honey, do him a favour. Guys like that don't need to hang around.'

Whiting did the same with Robert Shaw on set one day. Like a bull elephant in musk, David charged his way through an upstairs door of a pub. It was a room we were using for make-up. I wasn't there at the time, but I heard terrible fighting going on. By the time I got there David had scarpered, leaving Shaw lying on the floor in a heap of stunned humiliation. David thought we were having an affair. We weren't. David thought I was having an affair with everyone, even my stable boy. What a power there is in obsessive jealousy! What neither Olivier nor Mitchum understood was that while under normal circumstances it would be easy when someone says, 'If you don't sleep with me, I'll kill myself,' to tell them to get lost, when it is your third potential suicide – and at the same time a few intimate love letters are still unaccounted for – you think again. When I let it be known, as kindly as possible, that David's time was up (though, I have to confess, it hadn't been *that* horrendous), he began to get frighteningly violent.

'I still have one letter,' he snarled triumphantly.

'Publish and be damned,' I retorted, or something equally unoriginal. But what followed was just as unoriginal, for it seems to be happening all round the country behind closed doors: educated grown-ups slamming into each other with insults and muscle power – mindless brutality – over and over again. It was the only time (except my attempted rape when I was fifteen) that anyone has ever beaten me up. Something hardened like ice within me and I knew that all compassion and all blackmail fears had gone.

David, realizing this, became frantic. He was in the habit of borrowing my Deux Chevaux, which I'd recently bought from my brother Chris (who was going from strength to strength as a film director, having got great recognition for his film *The Virgin and the Gypsy*. (I wasn't pretty enough or, indeed, sufficiently virginal to play his virgin. Pig!) The police rang one day to say they had found a completely flattened, written-off Deux Chevaux on the hard shoulder of the A3. No driver was to be seen. I wondered which hospital he had been taken to. Was he dead? I remember having to stamp on the tiniest pinprick of hope that was eager to spread its way through my worn-out veins. All this mayhem for half a night in a cupboard. *Serves me right*.

David – dash my wig 'n' Beez (as Daddy always said) – was already safe and sound in Hasker Street, having thrown himself clear of the car. It was a strange accident and he let it be known that he had been about to kill himself again but had had second thoughts at the final minute. Only David Whiting would have had the audacity to come out of that one alive. Yet even this shave with death wasn't sufficient for Whiting's morbid sensibility. Now that our affair (if one can call it that) was most definitely over, and desperate that I had cut myself loose from his stranglehold, he attempted another overdose. Because he knew I was coming up that day to Hasker Street (he was still being paid for publicity on *Lady Caroline Lamb*) he arranged for me to find him in a coma. I almost let him get on with it. What must Hasker Street have been thinking with all these attempted suicides going on? I rang Robert before driving off in the ambulance to good old faithful St George's. As I sat there waiting for David to come round after being pumped out, a beautiful extravagant bouquet of roses arrived from Robert. Seeing himself as the instigator of Nona's and Johnnie's end, and after David's three suicide attempts, Robert felt enough guilt pangs to return David to the bosom of the Bolt family to recuperate once more.

More and more black marks began to pile up against David Whiting as he put himself way beyond the pale. One day when he was snooping in secret places he came across information that I apparently hadn't been given my contractual just deserts regarding my third of the *Lady Caroline Lamb* profits. I wasn't sure what he was on about, never having been too clever with figures, but so serious an error was it that David arranged for all lawyers to be present while Robert, Fernando Ghia (Franco Cristaldi's second-in-command), David and I sat around a big table at Pinewood Studios while minutes were taken of the two-hour meeting. Robert didn't seem to know anything either. It was as mysterious then as it is now except that there was suddenly more money in my bank account than I had previously thought.

'That's because *I'm* taking care of you now,' said David, proudly. 'I'll be your business manager and make you as rich as Croesus.' I wasn't taken in for a second.

'I'd prefer it, David, if you would leave both Robert and me in peace and return to New York, like you promised.'

'Nonsense. Your career is much more important than anything I could be doing in America.'

Robert knew we had been having an affair but I hadn't told him the reason. Why not? Because all I had left was my role as perfect mistress and, besides, Robert also knew it was over. Finally, when Robert noticed that certain documents within his private filing system had gone missing, things came to a monumental head. Robert, quite rightly, ordered David out of his house. Robert was the only one to take him head on, man to man. My blessed Knight of Wisdom came to the rescue of his faithless, unworthy, soiled, elderly (so it seemed to me by now) maiden by taking on the madman. Watching Robert lose his temper properly for the first time was so hideous that I was forced to find José to break it up. Robert showed great courage because Mitchum had observed the truth. There *was* death lurking in David's eyes and it was creeping nearer and nearer to the surface. What was creeping nearer and nearer to my surface was a great love for my husband. How could I ever make up for the wrongs I had done?

CHAPTER SIXTY-ONE

O H! THE TWISTS and turns of fate. Another dream was about to come true. (Not even on my dream list because it seemed too impossibly far-fetched.) I was off to star in a cowboy film! Think of it. A little girl from Essex about to enact her childhood dream. Here I was on a TWA flight to Hollywood. David Whiting had pulled off a real coup. He had somehow managed to land for me one of the most coveted parts of the year. MGM was making the screen version of the popular American novel *The Man Who Loved Cat Dancing*. Every eligible American star was after this role opposite Burt Reynolds, who was now the hottest property in Hollywood, and had proved himself in John Boorman's *Deliverance*.

Both Robert Shaw and I had received Hollywood scripts on the same day. Add to his childish need to compete the big Hollywood break he had been waiting for and Robert was swapping scripts in no time. 'There's no contest,' he bragged with challenge in his eyes as he handed back my script. His was called *The Sting*. Need I say more? His script was to pave the way to immense popularity, international stardom, heady power and wealth whereas mine led me to hell and damnation.

David Whiting had insisted (since he was entirely responsible for getting me the role) that he come along too, and no amount of arguments or pleadings would stop him. Because he hadn't attempted intimacy since he beat me up, I presumed that if I took along his girlfriend to be nanny to Tom I would be safe. To give him his due he had been behaving better lately. The fight with Robert had shaken him up considerably: he genuinely respected, admired and –

strangely enough – loved Robert. With the air cleared, David had returned to Hasker Street where he lived a much calmer, more mature existence. My sister Vanessa was also staying there because her marriage to Ceredig Davies had bitten the dust, although not before Ceredig had written and produced a West End musical starring both himself and Vanessa, called *Lay Down I Think I Love You*. They were both enchanting in it. Although unfortunately it didn't run, the late Harold Hobson gave it a rave in *The Times*. Vanessa went on to join the Royal Shakespeare Company and did some excellent work before falling in love with the actor Michael Osborne, and packing it all in to start a family.

Cat Dancing boasted some fine American talent. Lee J. Cobb, George Hamilton, Beau Hopkins and Jack Warden, all of whom made me feel right at home immediately. Dick Sarafian, the director, was a fat sloppy puppy-dog of a cigar-smoking cowboy-villain type. I liked him a lot. Martin Poll was the producer and we were to shoot the whole film on location in Arizona and Utah. We all met up first at the Beverly Hills Hotel. I had flu on arrival (probably due to the thought of three months with David Whiting – nanny or not!), so wasn't at my best to meet my leading man. When Burt first came into my suite I felt that he was already lugging around that serious-big-Hollywood-star status. Neither was he slow in letting me know how many film deals he had signed in the past few months. Burt Reynolds was on his way, all right, and nothing was going to stand in his path. He had a great deal of cowboy charm, coupled with a quick, typically American-media humour.

Arriving in Arizona was enthralling, although it wasn't the vastness of the sandy open spaces spiked with cactus that thrilled me so much as learning to ride Western style, doing my own stunts and the experience of working with genuine wranglers (cowboys) and genuine Red Indians. On one of the first days of shooting, Burt had a complicated action-packed fight scene with Jack Warden. Both being athletic and fit, they wanted to do the sequence themselves rather than use stunt doubles. The shot involved both characters tumbling down the stairs, punching each other about across the bar top of this uninhabited old saloon, then a twist across the floor, smashing through the glass window as they flung themselves outside. Without a cut in the action they both returned through the door of the saloon to continue fighting. Real man's stuff. And so it was.

It was a complicated three-minute shot, so it took time to rehearse but finally they were ready for action. Tom came to hold my hand in the front row, so to speak, for by now he was completely gun mad and needed his daily fix. Burt was particularly sweet and patient with Tomcat because Burt, unlike the Duke of Wellington, was no cunt face in Tom's eyes. Far, far from it, for Burt wore the magic gun 'n' holster rather than a dangling sword. He had to put up with Tomcat forever trailing after him like a star-struck groupie.

'Action!' shouts Sarafian. Off they went. Burt and Jack tumbled down the stairs, punching each other like fury. They really needed to get it in one take if they could because extra window glass had been overlooked. How professional they were. No doubt they both knew their stuff – each thump looked so real! Everything was going according to plan, and they flew back through the special glass, splattering it magnificently. Just as they were tumbling into the saloon door for the home stretch a voice cried: 'Cut!'

It wasn't the director's voice. It was Tomcat's. A very nasty silence fell. I felt as embarrassed as I had that time on *Term of Trial* when I laughed at Olivier.

Burt came right up to Tomcat, towering above him in his lifts, volcanic with fury. 'What the hell's going on?' All eyes were on Tomcat.

'Look at his gun. It's all bent!' And so it was. We were all so engrossed in the action that we had failed to notice that Burt's gun barrel (they use rubber guns for stunts) was completely bent over. Thanks to Tomcat's passion for guns, he went from sinner to saviour in a very few seconds. It felt good.

I had one shot where I had to fall off, and since the film company had witnessed my dexterity on the horse, they allowed me to do my own stunts and even my own falling off. They gave me my own masseuse (a Japanese girl called Letsgo). It was perfectly wonderful having Letsgo to come home to. There she'd be, waiting for me in my bedroom all ready and eager to walk over my back after a hard day at the office. Another stunt was where I had to hang off the saddle, head down, as if I was almost being dragged. It was great fun pulling that one off. If I wasn't an actress (and I still had my doubts on that score), I would have got a buzz from earning my pennies as a stunt girl.

One evening after shooting I was on the phone to Robert. I wanted some comfort because I had been shooting a horrific fighting scene with Burt Reynolds's gang (in the movie I was kidnapped because I ran away from my husband, George Hamilton). During this fight sequence I fell on a pointed rock, which dug so deep into my knee that I could clearly see the bone. That made me realize how frail, vulnerable and temporary we all are, with our skeleton being so thinly protected. I was immediately rushed off to hospital to have it stitched up. Unfortunately we had to shoot the same sequence again two days later even though the doctor had warned the producer that my knee might split open again. It did. I was taken to that blessed hospital to have my wretched knee sewn up three times. It was a complete mess, but finally I only had myself to blame. 'The only way to survive in movies is to behave badly,' warned Fay Dunaway later when I was working with her. If that is true, it's a sad state of affairs.

So there I was on the phone to Robert, with the whole team now holed up in a motel in Gila Bend. Tomcat and the nanny were in the suite next to mine and although David Whiting's suite was opposite (motels are often L-shaped, with

460

a courtyard in the middle), he was usually to be found next door with the nanny. These suites were open plan. You had your bedroom, living and dressing areas all in one with the bathroom off – a most unattractive way of living.

I kept the adjoining door open because of Tomcat. David, on hearing the name Robert (the red rag to his bull), charged through into my suite and began throwing things at me. I quickly rang off while ducking the main vase as it went flying out of the window landing right at the spurred heels of a wrangler who came in to inquire if all was well. David had vanished. 'What the hell's going on?' I said nothing. 'What are you going to do with that guy?' I didn't want to talk about it. 'Tell him to fuck off,' he said incredulously. I wasn't about to explain how that was easier said than done, not then anyway. No one would understand and besides it was no one's business but my own.

As the temperature rose so did the heat of David's madness. The desert was very hot, yet every day Whiting would show up on set exceedingly bossy and exceedingly out of place in his immaculate pin-striped Savile Row suits with everyone else wearing jeans and sweat shirts. I recognized that a diabolic manic phase was approaching by the dreaded sign of his comforter, *The Great Gatsby*, which he would fish out of his briefcase and promptly home in on certain pages, scribbling notes in its already overly pencilled margin. I warrant no Bible ever received the cherishing of Whiting's copy of *The Great Gatsby*. It was as if it alone held the key to the mystery of his oncoming madness. Neither Debbie nor I could do anything to prevent the overpowering energy of the man erupting into its fearful volcano of chaos. This frightened me as well as being an embarrassing liability on set.

'Couldn't you tell him to cool off?' George Hamilton braved one day.

'Not a hope in hell.'

'Jeans and T-shirt may help a little.'

'You tell him, perhaps he'll listen to you.' To my astonishment George Hamilton told him that same day. Yet I was convinced that David Whiting would never in a million years go for jeans and a T-shirt, never having once got out of his three-piece suits over the past two years. I'd never managed to persuade him to relax so why on earth would he listen to George Hamilton?

The next day was Burt's birthday and *The Merv Griffin Show* came down to film the celebrations and do a good piece of promotion for the film itself. What better publicity than Burt's birthday (the great new Hollywood superstar) could any film possibly hope for? *The Merv Griffin Show*'s main focus was to be a rather extravagant birthday party the next evening. Burt asked me to be his date for the evening. It was said in a tone that meant I had better accept. I had nothing against Burt Reynolds except for being astonished at his temper one day. He was screaming at Dick Sarafian over some triviality and punched his fist right through the wall of his caravan. Apart from that incident which made me a trifle wary, I think we got on well.

David arrived on set wearing a pair of jeans and a T-shirt. The difference was amazing. He was shrewd to have remained encased in his Savile Row for so long, desert or no desert. Thank God no one teased him about his new look – his reaction might have been catastrophic. George Hamilton actually said, 'You look cool, David.' But I could see David's hips were over-burdened with doubt, among other things.

'As I'm your business manager, I'm taking you to Burt's do tonight.'

'I've already accepted to go with Burt. I'll see you there.'

'No way will I go without you.'

I found myself cursing for accepting Burt's invitation. Whatever lack of constancy was apparent in my marriage, I had remained flawlessly constant in my feelings of awkwardness at parties. All I wanted to do was dance, but since Burt was too busy quipping for the cameras there was no dancing.

During the festivities Lee J. Cobb asked me if I was having a good time. I wasn't. I often wonder what would have happened if Lee J. Cobb hadn't whispered in my ear, 'Come on, I'll drive you back in my new Maserati.' During the filming of *Ryan's Daughter*, I had often attempted to pluck up the courage to ask Christopher Jones if I could go out for a spin, so Lee J. Cobb's invitation tickled my rather bored fancy.

'I'm not sure if I should leave Burt. Merv Griffin is still filming and I'm meant to be his date.' Lee J. Cobb tossed all doubt aside.

'Nonsense! You've done your bit. Besides, he's a big boy now. Just tell him you're tired and that I've offered to take you home.' And that's what I did, though I was slightly floored by the absolute daggers of a look that Burt threw at me while I was making my request. Beau Hopkins saw it too – he never missed a trick.

It was no let-down, spinning across the Arizona desert in Lee's new toy. It brought back nostalgic memories of the dear old Lamborghini. I missed speed, but not as much as Tom did. When we arrived back at the Gila Bend ranch motel quite a bit later, sounds of music and dancing were coming from it.

'Come, let's have a dance before turning in.' Not able to resist a bit of a knees-up with the wranglers (the *crème de la crème* on any cowboy film) I accepted. But, alas, like everyone else, within no time Lee J. Cobb was blotto with booze.

'I'm off to bed now.' He waved me off, weaving and reeling his way towards his motel suite.

Beau Hopkins came across to me. I liked him, he was fresh, keen and had a good heart. 'Care to dance?' We danced awhile. 'You know, you shouldn't have deserted Burt on his birthday like that.' This alarmed me. Beau went on to tell me of American ways and how if someone asks you out on a date it's terribly rude to stand them up like that. I had almost a whole movie to shoot with Burt and he was not someone who would be pleasant company if you happened to get on his wrong side. And that's where I was now, apparently. This unnerved me somewhat.

'Well, it's too late now, Beau, the damage is done.'

'Oh, no, it isn't. He's back in his room, so just pop in and apologize. It won't take a second and I'm sure it's worth it.' Beau pointed me in the direction of Burt's room and off I reluctantly went.

I knocked on his door. 'I've come to apologize for standing you up.' He preened as if it really mattered to him. I'd done the right thing obviously.

'Letsgo is coming to give me a massage. Sit down for a while.' I wanted to go but one has to be so careful of these Hollywood idols and their egos. No sooner had I sat down in the corner, like the good girl I was trying to be, than I heard the familiar knock of Letsgo. Within no time at all she was getting down to work on Burt's back. He moaned and grunted with the familiar pain and pleasure he was receiving from my Letsgo. He turned his attention back to me.

'That's OK. But don't do it again. OK?' he quipped. I went to leave. 'Your Letsgo is a real gem.' He reached over to get an orange. 'Here, relax. Have an orange, hon.' Not knowing the American way and also not wanting to snub him a second time, I sat down and ate my orange while Letsgo continued trampling back and forth over Burt's impressively muscular torso. It was as if he wanted me to watch, but it was one o'clock and I was totally pooped. 'Sleep tight,' he grunted, half keeling over with pain and ecstasy. After a while, with the orange still in my hand, I dozed off. When I awoke Letsgo was leaving. It seemed a perfect opportunity to make my exit.

I think Burt wanted me to stay longer, but I jumped up. 'Sorry to be a party pooper.' I kissed him on the cheek, hoping it would make up for any misunderstandings, and left.

I entered my suite through Tom's room because I wanted to check that all was well. Both he and the nanny were sleeping peacefully so I gave Tom a quick kiss on the forehead before entering my own room through the adjoining door. As I began to undress I thought I saw my clothes moving in the open-plan closet. Content that it was merely imagination I continued undressing. When I was down to my bra and pants David came looming out of the closet like an Arizonan vulture on heat. He was dribbling with mad uncontrollable jealousy. It was so foul I honestly thought he was having a fit and – who knows – perhaps he was. It made Olivier's Othello pale by comparison. How the death in his eyes gleamed as he towered over me, punching me repeatedly. He chanted over and over again, like some hideous Satanic ritual, 'It's late, where have you been? Look at the time! It's late, where have you been? Look at the time!'

'It's none of your business!' I regretted saying that because his fury quadrupled. What business was it of his where I'd been? He had a girlfriend, for heaven's sake. I knew I couldn't argue with him, so I took Mitchum's advice and I went down on all fours like a wounded animal. He simply picked me up and started punching me all over again. I must have gone through the fear barrier because everything went into familiar slow motion. I remember seeing my blood spurting out. Scheduled the day after tomorrow was my rape scene with Jack Warden and all I can remember thinking was I must protect my face for work – and, of course, I thought of Tomcat waking to find his mother being mashed to a pulp. It dawned on me then that I wasn't going to be able to protect my face much longer. I do remember realizing it wasn't fear or even vanity – it was a total obsession for remaining professional, which meant a face ready to shoot. But when he turned me over I knew David had reached face-mashing time. I screamed. 'Help! Help!' The nanny was a hell of a long time coming. As soon as her head appeared, I screamed.

'Get him off! Get him off!' The nanny was so taken aback by the violence she stood gawping in the doorway as if in a trance. Burt! He must be still awake.

'Get Burt! *Please* get Burt!' The moment he heard the name, David stopped pummelling me and flew out into the night.

I couldn't be certain how much time passed before Burt came in. Maybe two minutes. Once he saw the state I was in he said, 'Get some ice and bathe your face, I'll be back in a minute.' He went out. Again, because I was in shock, I couldn't be certain how long he was gone from my room. A few minutes, anyway. I remember going to the fridge and reaching for some ice. I remember looking at my face and being absolutely certain that they'd have to recast, though most of the blood seemed to be spurting from my nose. Although my stomach hurt badly my face could have been worse. I started cleaning my nosebleed off the wall, thinking it wouldn't wash off so easily when dry. I sat down to begin icing the throbbing heat. Burt soon returned and said to the nanny, 'I'm taking her back to my room to bathe her face.' The miracle of miracles was that through all that mayhem Tomcat didn't wake.

'Gotta keep bathing the bruises else they take hold.' Burt reached into the fridge for the ice. I was shivering, unable to stop. 'Easy, easy, it's OK, hon. He won't be getting you again, I promise.' How grateful I was that Burt should be so caring. He laid me down gently on his bed and painstakingly bathed my face. While I was still shivering and in shock, two white pills appeared before me.

'No, thanks.' I very rarely took sleeping pills. I hadn't smoked marijuana since the cupboard, yet some of the media accused me of being on drugs.

'Do as you're told. You gotta relax, honey.' I was past arguing, though I wish I hadn't been. As I was not used to pills, they put me out like a light.

I awoke to a head bulging with raw tenderness, completely at odds with the brightness of the day. Burt was at his mirror fixing his toupee, unaware that I had awoken. I'd been riveted the night before at how his toupee had remained so firmly fixed with all the pillow-bashing Letsgo had been giving him – it must be nailed on, I had mused. How strange to wear one all the time, how difficult for stunts, wind, love-making, swimming. It must make life a living hell. He had quite a few toupees. Having settled for one he then got down to the mammoth task of fixing it on his head. At last he climbed gingerly into his high-booted lifts. A toupee and lifts – the man's an impostor, I thought. Will the real Burt Reynolds please stand up. He saw me.

'Good morning, let's take a look at you.' He seemed quite chuffed with his handiwork of the previous night.

'Take a look and see for yourself.' I did. I wished I hadn't, though it wasn't as bad as a few hours before. His ice had certainly done some good.

'Thank you.' I meant it. I sighed with relief.

'You'll be able to film in a few days if you keep bathing it. Promise me?'

'I promise.' As I went towards the door, Burt charged in front of me. Staggering towards me in those high lifts and that toupee, he was transformed before my puffy swollen eyes into a veritable werewolf.

'Keep away from there!'

'But I want to go back to my son.' The werewolf had completely blocked my path, snarling as I tried to pass.

'You damn well do as I say! You stay here until I come back and give you the all-clear.'

'But what if David has got hold of Tomcat?'

'You do as I say!' He moved to the window, and some-what tentatively lifted the curtains. Merv Griffin and some of his crew were standing in the open courtyard drinking coffee. 'You see?' I saw all right. But my heartstrings were being pulled. I had to get back to Tomcat, quickly.

How logic is blinded when motherly love comes into play! What if David had bashed up Tomcat? I made a beeline for the door, hoping that if I moved fast enough no one would recognize me. Within no time I was back in Tomcat's room. Debbie was in her bathroom making up and sweet Tomcat was crawling over the floor with his cowboy gun. I lifted him up and gave him a hug. Oh, how wonderful it was that we were both alive! Putting him down, I went through into my bedroom. He followed.

'Can I come to the set today?'

I told him we had the day off. He looked crestfallen. Tomcat would be hell on earth with a whole day of no guns firing, no cowboys and no Indians. Perhaps we could sneak off to the Indian reservation and have a chat with Big Chief Sitting Bear in his tepee while he smoked his pipe of peace decked out in all his feathers. I found the contrast ticklingly funny, to be inside the tepee with the Big Chief while his grandchildren went flashing past on their Lambrettas, transistor radios blaring. But how could I go anywhere with my battered face? People would ask questions. I stepped into the bathroom to check the damage in private. I nearly tripped over David, for there he was on my bathroom floor. He was dead. I quickly turned, picked Tomcat up in my arms and walked away in a daze to find the producer. I wish I'd stayed longer and studied his corpse because perhaps then I might have unravelled part of the mystery that still haunts me today. The producer's wife took me into her room where I mumbled something about David being dead. She immediately called Burt. With hindsight I might have queried why she didn't immediately call the producer, but I was too shocked to question anything. Burt arrived. He knelt before me.

'He *is* dead, hon, he *is* dead.' He then handed me an empty pill bottle. 'I found this in his hand.' He took the pill bottle back from me. Subsequently it disappeared, not to be used in evidence at the inquest. Burt then described how David had pills scattered all over his body and the floor. I remember thinking how powerful shock is because I didn't recall any pills at the time of discovering David's body.

CHAPTER SIXTY-TWO

W HAT YOU HAVE read above is the whole truth and nothing but the truth. As fate would have it, Robert was staying in Los Angeles with Carolyn Pfeiffer at the time of David's death – at the very Bungalow 14 where Carolyn and I had first met David Whiting. Robert was in LA doing a publicity tour for the American opening of *Lady Caroline Lamb*. He came straight over to Arizona to be with me. It was wonderful to see him, even though he couldn't stay because of his schedule. It transpired that Robert was advised by MGM to make certain I took on a lawyer for the inquest.

'I don't want one, Robert. I've done nothing wrong.'

'Nevertheless, darling, do so. You're going to need one. I promise.' Before he left, and believe me I would have paid any price for him to have stayed, I recounted to Robert the whole of my side of the story.

'Serves you right!' he said, kissing me with forgiveness.

Apparently you have to have a lawyer in America whether you're innocent or guilty. I still refused. I didn't want one and that was final. I never needed one when Nona committed suicide, or indeed Johnnie Windeatt. So why should I want one now? On hearing my refusal to be budged on this score, the head of MGM himself, John Aubrey flew down to Arizona to force me to get a lawyer. His considerable charm caused fear to slither through my very bones. With so many people insisting I finally gave in. The lawyer assigned to me was one recommended by Dinah Shore, Burt's girlfriend. A redneck, brash, southern type, I didn't trust him further than I could throw him. What was more, he seemed hell bent on clearing Burt's name rather than mine.

As the inquest unfolded I realized that there were many details that I hadn't been aware of. I never knew, for example, that there had been three autopsies. Suicide. Murder. Suicide. I hadn't been informed that there was blood all over David's room. Apparently a deep spur-shaped gash was found at the back of his skull. So why had he ended up on *my* bathroom floor? Though I wasn't aware at the time, all the men who wore spurs had been taken to the local police station to be fingerprinted. Poor Beau Hopkins was kept in jail overnight and Lee J. Cobb downright refused to be fingerprinted at all. Perhaps it was because I was so numb with shock that none of this sank in at the time. The media had a field day. But it was Her Nibs here who was the scapegoat. No wonder Robert was convinced I should take on a lawyer. The evidence reeked of foul play. Why did I have to find out in the cruellest of ways with headlines like, 'Femme Fatale', 'Man Eater', 'Whore', 'Witch', 'Scarlet Woman', 'Murderess'?

I cannot speak for Burt, or any of the other players in this death, only for myself, and I chose to keep silent throughout the whole of those months of media circus, because I didn't want to brand Robert as a cuckold – I'd done him enough harm already. Also, it was my third death and I in no state to talk to anyone.If my silence was interpreted as guilt, then so be it. I was innocent, so why should I give a damn? I was guilty only of infidelity with Whiting and that was a private matter between myself and Robert.

Will the horror of it ever go away? No. Unsolved mysteries never do, they haunt you. I would dearly like the mystery to be solved, so my name could be cleared once and for all. Not one of the family called me at the time. Only Mitchum, Shaw and, oddly enough, Trevor Howard. 'You couldn't hurt a fly,' he shouted cheerily down the phone. How true that was and how good it was to hear a familiar voice. I cried.

'There, there, don't cry. Tell you what, I'll come out and cheer you up.'

'Oh, Trevor, would you?'

'Where are you again?'

'Utah.' There was a long pause.

'Utah?' Trevor echoed. Another long pause. 'Utah . . . If I'm not mistaken, Utah is a dry state. Tell you what, old gal, I'll see you when you get home, eh?' I laughed. Fortunately my brother Chris arrived. He was kind enough to take a trip out from LA where he was setting up his next film project. I was set to play Shaw's St Joan in LA the following season, but after the scandal, I got a call to say that I'd been cancelled.

'Why?' I asked, bewildered. Apparently the board of directors, which included Katharine Hepburn, remained adamant. 'We can't have a whore playing a saint,' she'd apparently said. That was my first inkling of the pattern that was to follow. I was being black-listed.

It was tough comprehending the devastation that David had left in his wake. My parents were forced to leave Barn Mead because of the lack of ease they felt in the village of Ingatestone where they had been living for forty years. In the beginning Father chose to believe what he read in the papers, whispering conspiratorally, 'C'mon, Pusscat, you can confide in me. *Did* you murder the fellah?' I am hearing him as I write, for the echo still vibrates through unhealed, tender places. Robert and I couldn't stick our marriage back together again, thanks to the slime of public innuendo and my shame. Every trip to the village was accompanied by a chorus of moving curtains and culled whispers. Hovering vultures picking at private pain, tearing the meat from the bones of the marriage remain.

Finally I had no choice but to leave England and my marriage behind me. Robert deserved some peace and quiet too. Apart from the media giving us no opportunity for privacy, I was yearning for the necessary anonymity to return me some of my lost sanity. I would have to revert to being seventeen years old to regain a glimmer of self. I didn't choose to be a movie star with a gun to my head, but I knew the time had come to be one of the crowd, so I plumped finally for LA. On a mountaintop in the Himalayas I would still be *Ryan's Daughter*, but in LA I would merely be a tiddler in an ocean of sharks. Yes. That was the answer – to be in a place where movie stars were two a penny and fame grew on every palm tree. My dream list had finally been ticked off. Yes. All my dreams had come true at the price of three dead friends, a broken marriage and a very fishy tale hanging over me. Beware of dreaming silly, shallow dreams. Look where it got me. Serve me right.

In his biography of Olivier Donald Spoto claimed that Olivier and I had a brief fling while making *Term of Trial*. The *Sunday Times* followed this up, forcing me to stall a third attempt from different sources wanting to write my biography. I thanked each one kindly, explaining that I was in the process of writing my own. I wasn't writing my own, but the curse of having the blue print of some stranger's fingerprints pressing around my larynx for ever and a day was more than I could bear. Not feeling good about lying, or about a love being described as a brief fling, plus the prodding memory of Lionel's words 'write about us when I'm dead', I felt the time had come to sit down and do just that. Write my own.

Only through silence was I able to start comprehending the more enduring qualities that lay beneath my shamefully shallow dreams. Only through silence was I able to find a completely new territory where I could start building on a different quality of dreams. Slowly, step by step, on a daily basis, I try out my new dreams not linked to fame, wealth, lust and ego, but to that better, more enduring part of my nature that I'll be taking with me when I pop off to get myself recycled.

Silence also pointed out the need to let Bolt know that my love for him had always been of the enduring kind. How lucky I was to be given that second chance and return to Bolt after his stroke seven years later. I didn't return out of guilt, shame, compassion or pity. No, I returned to him because all the way along my love for Robert had remained perfectly intact and solid as a rock. I think we're succeeding because as I sit here tapping away we are utterly content in our almost lost-forever precious continuity. We've been back now for thirteen years and, with Tomcat being close too, why – the family is finally back in order.

May the power of silence devour our violence.